Graduate Admissions Essays

Graduate Admissions Essays

WRITE YOUR WAY INTO THE GRADUATE SCHOOL OF YOUR CHOICE

FIFTH EDITION

DONALD ASHER, PhD

TEN SPEED PRESS
California | New York

Published in the United States by Ten Speed Press, an imprint of the Crown Publishing Group,
a division of Penguin Random House LLC, New York.
TenSpeed.com
Ten Speed Press and the Ten Speed Press colophon are registered trademarks of Penguin Random House LLC.

Typeface(s): Commercial Type's Styrene and Graphik, and Adobe Font's Kandal

Library of Congress Cataloging-in-Publication Data
Names: Asher, Donald, author.
Title: Graduate admissions essays : write your way into the graduate school of your choice / Donald Asher, PhD.
Description: Fifth edition. | Emeryville : Ten Speed Press, 2024. | Includes index.
Identifiers: LCCN 2023039909 (print) | LCCN 2023039910 (ebook) | ISBN 9781984863546 (trade paperback) | ISBN 9781984863553 (ebook)
Subjects: LCSH: College applications--United States. | Universities and colleges--United States--Graduate work--Admission. | Exposition (Rhetoric) | Essay--Authorship.
Classification: LCC LB2351.52.U6 A74 2024 (print) | LCC LB2351.52.U6 (ebook) | DDC 378.1/6160973--dc23/eng/20230927
LC record available at https://lccn.loc.gov/2023039909
LC ebook record available at https://lccn.loc.gov/2023039910

Trade Paperback ISBN: 978-1-9848-6354-6
eBook ISBN: 978-1-9848-6355-3

Printed in the United States of America

Editor: Zoey Brandt | Production editor: Serena Wang
Designer: Annie Marino | Production designers: Mari Gill and Faith Hague
Production manager: Dan Myers | Copyeditor: Tom Pitoniak | Proofreader: Hope Clark
Indexer: Ken DellaPenta
Publicist: | Marketer: Allison Renzulli

10 9 8 7 6 5 4 3 2 1

Fifth Edition

CONTENTS

A great professor of history can make the French Revolution come alive so that you can see the barricades in the streets of Paris and hear the swish of the guillotine's blade as it descends. Likewise, a Shakespearean scholar can help you feel the anguish of the protagonists in the tragedies and can show you the contemporary nature of the humor in the Bard's comedies. But how do you excite and entertain an audience when talking about getting into graduate school? Well, Dr. Donald Asher does exactly that . . . you'll find you not only enjoy yourself, but you'll also learn a great deal about tactics and strategies that will help you increase the odds of getting into the graduate or professional program of your choice. Donald is uniquely qualified to present this program. He's met with admissions officers all across the country and spoken at hundreds of colleges and universities. His book *Graduate Admissions Essays* has been a huge seller, and he's written a variety of other books and articles. I'm proud to introduce . . . Donald Asher.

—**DR. ROBERT GREENBERG, NACE** fellow and host of the National Teleconference on Graduate Admissions

ACKNOWLEDGMENTS

I owe special thanks to: Debra Freeman; Dr. Lillian Khristina Hendrick; Michael Hunt, Ariel & Michael Hunt Consulting; Dr. Julie Rojewski, Director of PhD Career Development, Michigan State University; Fred Pierce lll, Dean of Admissions & Marketing, Lake Superior State University; Molly Kinard, Director, Professional MBA, University of Tennessee; Long Nguyen; Dakota Kim Keblbeck; Trey Wineglass; Kathleen (Kat) Rivers, McNair Scholars Program, Sul Ross State University; Dr. Joseph Brown, Graduate Diversity Recruitment Officer, Stanford University; David Chernew; Irma (Gaby) Gomez-Dominguez and Tigress Briggs-Wroten, CSU-DH; Brandon "Spot" Mayers; Jacey De La Torre; Roma Tarquinia Rogers, Career Services, Hillsdale College; Shania Siron; Alice Harra, Associate Dean, Center for Life Beyond Reed; Dr. Carolyn Herman, Associate Dean, PreHealth Advising, Washington University in St. Louis; Dr. Molly Minus, St. Edwards; Dr. Mary McCall, Fielding Graduate University; Maureen Walz, Special Programs, Lafayette College; Dr. Wilmetta Toliver-Diallo, Assistant Dean of Strategic Initiatives, Washington University in St. Louis; Dr. Raymond Herrera, Washington State University; Dr. John Mateja, Goldwater Foundation; Dra. Maria Elena Cruz, San Jose State University; Nanette Cooley, Center for Career Development, Washington College; Dr. Zen Perry; Nishit Sahay; Cheryl Woehr; Dr. Bob Belle and Dr. Ansley Abraham, SREB; Dr. Jason Morris, ACU; Pier He; Dr. Samantha Aaron and Ms. Chantal E. Fleming, NCA&T; Fatemma D. Soto-Herrera and Cindy Neal, University of Arizona; Kim Heitzenrater, Sewanee; Dr. Johnson-Winters and Robin Melton, UT-A; everyone at WAEOPP; Munichia McCalla, Spelman; Dr. Joe Green, Earlham; Michael Aldarondo-Jeffries, UCF; Carl S. McNair; Angelica A. Benitez, Rider University; Dr. Ronnie Hendrix, Wesleyan University; Courtney Simpson, NCSU; Marsha Sawyer, Director CSTEP & McNair, St. Lawrence University; Deborah Shipp, Student Success Center, Clarkson University; Dr. Jacqueline S. Moore, Educational Opportunity, Rutgers University; Darrell C. Balderrama, UTSA; Dr. Charlesene McNeill-Blue, UNC-FSU; Wendy Alvarado, Kean; Dr. S. Ernest Lee Jr., John Jay College of Criminal Justice; Dr. Marcus L. Arrington, Marquette; Dr. LaTrina Parker Hall, TCU; Ashia Hall Muhammad, UALR; Steven Fernandez, SOAR, Baylor; Zara Williams, NJIT; Monique Posadas, UC-R; Terri Bernstein, UNLV; Dr. Orlando Taylor, President, Washington, DC, Campus of the Chicago School of Professional Psychology; Dr. Judith L. Kuipers, President, Fielding Graduate University; Dr. David Payne, Executive Director, GRE; Charles Johnson, Director, Master's & Executive Programs, Krannert School of Management, Purdue University; Roger C. Stewart, Director, Graduate Career Services, Krannert School of Management, Purdue University; Geri Weilacher, Director, Penn State TRiO Training Institute; Dr. Thomas Rochon, President, Ithaca College; Mary L. Gonzalez, Assistant Vice President, Division of Special Programs, Texas A&M University–Kingsville; Cherryl Arnold, Director, Educational Opportunity & TRiO Programs, Georgia State University; Michael L. Jeffries, Associate Dean and Director of Minority Student Affairs, University of Illinois at Urbana-Champaign, and Founder, McNair Scholars National Conference; Dr. Priscilla J. Fortier, Assistant Dean of Students, University of Illinois at Urbana-Champaign; Colin Diver, President, Reed College; Dr. Ruby Ausbrooks, Educational Consultant, Gerlach, Nevada; Dr. Jennifer Vega La Serna, Dean of Arts and Letters, College of the Sequoias; Julie Kern Smith, Career Services–Experiential Learning, Reed College; Dr. George B. Robbins, Associate Director of Graduate Academic & Enrollment Services, Rensselaer Polytechnic Institute; Samuel T. Lindquist, Director of Admissions, The Amos Tuck School of Business Administration; Dr. Gerald Foster, Director of Admissions, Harvard Medical School; Richard Badger, Dean of Admissions, University of Chicago Law School; Kathleen Plessas, Director of Admissions, School of Medicine, University of California, San Francisco; Louise Goldsmith, Graduate Assistant Admissions Coordinator, UCLA Architecture; Judy Colwell, Assistant Director of Admissions, Stanford University School of Medicine; Russ Coughenour, Director, Career Services, University of Tennessee, Knoxville; Dr. Cathi L. Eagan, Assistant Dean, Research and the University Graduate School, Director, McNair Scholars Program, Associate Director, MEDIC-B Program, Indiana University; Dr. Barbara A. Herman Center, University of Wisconsin–Madison Medical School; Dr. Linda Arbuckle,

Graduate Coordinator, University of Florida, Gainesville; Dr. Judy Jones, Executive Director, Pond Mountain Lodge & Retreat–Eureka Springs; Dr. Manuel Febres, Programa McNair, Universidad de Puerto Rico–San Juan; Dr. Michelle Sparacino, Director of Recruitment & Admissions, School of Public Health and Health Services, George Washington University; Dr. Kay Reed, Graduate School of the University of Tennessee, Knoxville; Bertha Thomas, Director, McNair Scholars Program, Truman State University; Dr. Vicki M. Curby, Director, McNair Scholars Program, University of Missouri–Columbia; Dr. Steven M. Ehrlich, Assistant Dean, College of Arts & Sciences, Washington University; Jeffrey Johnson, NAGAP Membership Director and Director of Admissions, Tulane School of Public Health and Tropical Medicine; Dr. Janet Goebel, Rhodes Advisor and Director of the Robert E. Cook Honors College, Indiana University of Pennsylvania; Nick Ewold, Director, McNair Scholars Program, Beloit College; DeVon Wilson, Assistant Dean, University of Wisconsin–Madison; Linda Vivian, Coordinator of Special Projects for the Graduate School of the University of Florida; Dr. Larry Duffy, Chair, Pre-Medical Advising Committee, University of Alaska, Fairbanks; John Garic, Esq., Pre-Law & Graduate School Advising, Franklin & Marshall College; Dr. Mary E. Kirtley, Office for Graduate and Professional Studies, Dickinson College; James A. Marino, Director, Career Center, Rutgers University–Camden; Katherine K. Nobles, Director, Career Services, Oglethorpe University; Dr. Thomas Q. Reefe, Director, Career Development Center, University of California, Santa Cruz; Tom Francis, Director (Ret.), Career Services, Swarthmore College; Dr. Robert C. Pebworth Jr., Director, Career Planning & Placement, Wabash College; Saul Reyes, Director, Career Center, Jacksonville University; Dr. Edward Zovinka, Chemistry Department, St. Francis College–Loretto; John Adams, Director, Career Services, Davidson College; Tony Butchello, Associate Director, Career Services, Davidson College; Gar Cropser, Associate Director, Career Services, University of California, Irvine; Tom R. Cath, Director, Career Center, DePauw University; Carla Mollins Rinde, Director, Career Center, Ursinus College; Lisa B. Dickter, Associate Director, Career Services, Carnegie Mellon University; Judy L. Fisher, Director, Career Center, Harvey Mudd College; Pamela S. Backes, Associate Director, Career Services, Keene State College; Patricia M. Campbell, Director, Career Services, Keene State College; Dr. Rebecca A. Emery, Director, Career Services, Salisbury State University; Stephanie Paramore, Assistant Director, Priscilla A. Scotlan Career Services Center, University of San Francisco; Amy Wilms, Director, Career Services, University of Redlands; Dr. Tariq Shakoor, Director, Career Center, Emory University; Yolanda M. Manora, Associate Director, Pre-Professional Advising, Emory University; Katherine Harper, Director, Career Center, Western Oregon University; Patrick D. Mullane, Director, Career Development Services, Dickinson College; Rob Felton, Public Affairs Officer, George Fox University; Seth L. Smythe, Willamette University; Nancy Norton, Director, Career Center, Willamette University; Anne Hardin Ballard, Director, Career Development Services, Linfield College; Peter S. Van Houten and Mary Blakeslee, Pre-Professional/Pre-Graduate Advising, University of California, Berkeley; Dr. Dandré Desandies, Associate Director, Career Development, Stanford University; Toinette Menashe, Director, Master of Arts in Liberal Studies Program, Reed College; Dr. Walter Englert, Chair, Classics Department, Reed College; Lisa Garb, Director of Public Relations, Peterson's Guides; Ricky L. Parham, Applicant Relations, American Association of Medical Colleges; Brian P. O'Driscoll, Director, Career Services, Pacific University; Dr. Jason Morris, Director, Master's Program in Higher Education, Abilene Christian University; Jennifer Tucker, Associate Director, Field and Career Office, Beloit College; Nancy B. Karpinski, Director, Career Development Services, Wells College; Maureen Daly Pascoe, Kilian Kerwin, Mohamed Yunus Rafiq, Michelle Levy, Fang-Yuan Chang, Rob Saldin, Gerrad Jones, Damian Madan, Brian T. Powers, Rachel Elizabeth Anderson, Erin E. Bonuso, Yung-Hsiang Hsu, Jonathan Doti, Manny Mora, Juana Gatson, Senetta Bancroft, Catherine Glew Hylands, Todd Hobler, Adam N. Green, Flay Rogers, Margie Lariviere, Andrea J. Morgan, Brad Wurtz, Meyer M. Speary, H. Glickman, Bob Muldoon, Victor F. Simonyi, Kevin Kelleher, Gennine Zinner, RD, Jennifer Ferenstein, Lisa Kemmerer, Linda C. Saremi, Gretchen Craft, Wendy Richardson, Tod Cochran, Molly Stenzel, Deborah E. Gallant, Brian Boyl, Sabrina Gee, Dr. Anastasia Pinoris, David Lawrence Conlin, David Coleman, Dr. Bruce Johnson, Kevan Shokat, Dr. John

R. Vasquez, Debbie Redd, Shane Whittington, Rebecca Weller, Dr. Majid Tavakkolijou, Dr. Arturo F. Muñoz, Robert Fallon, Paul F. Laubscher, Ranessa L. Cooper, Jeffrey P. Henkle, Jennifer Drayton Sohn, Jennifer Nagy, Charles Kosan, and of course, anonymous.

I owe special thanks also to Aaron Wehner, Julie Bennett, and the late Phil Wood of Ten Speed Press for their continued support of this book. Special thanks also to my in-house editor Zoey Brandt, production editor Serena Wang, designer Annie Marino, and production manager Dan Myers for their work on the fifth edition. And continuing debt to George Young, Mariah Bear, and Becky Lemov for their guidance on the first edition. The errors are all mine, but many, many people have contributed to the success of this book. Thank you all.

Many of the names, dates, schools, firm names, and other specific details in these essays were changed at the request of the contributors, and others were changed at the discretion of the editors. No particular individual named in these essays should be presumed to be any particular actual individual, and any such assumption would be unwarranted.

Some of the colleges and universities sponsoring talks and workshops by Dr. Donald Asher

INTERNATIONAL: Hong Kong: HK-UST (Hong Kong University of Science & Technology, "Top Ten in the World"); India: India Institute of Foreign Trade, Birla Institute of Management Technology (BIM-Tech), Visvesvaraya Technological Institute (VTU, one of the largest in the world, 410,000 students), Rai Institute, Rayat-Bahra Technology Centre of Excellence–Chandigarh, IESC, IIMT, Sheshgiri College of Engineering & Technology, SDM College of Engineering & Technology, RV College of Engineering, Chitkara University, Delhi Public School (which is not public at all); Ireland: Limerick Institute of Technology (LIT)-Moylish, LIT-Tipperary, Limerick School of Art & Design, National Franchise Centre, Limerick Chamber of Commerce Enterprise Acceleration Centre, Institute of Technology–Tralee; Morocco: Al Akhawayn University; Canada: University of Victoria (BC); Mexico: Universidad Tecnológica de Nuevo Laredo Tamaulipas, Universidad Autonóma de Tamaulipas, Facultad de Comercio, Administración y Ciencias Sociales; China: Beijing Foreign Studies University, China Agricultural University, Global IELTS School, Shanghai University, Zhejiang University; Germany: Christian-Albrechts-Universität zu Kiel; South Korea: Hallym University, *and more.*

EAST: EducationUSA (US Department of State), Morehouse, MIT, Brown, Columbia, University of Pennsylvania, Cornell, Wellesley, Boston College, Penn State, NYU, Suffolk, University of Connecticut, Georgetown, Oberlin, Babson, Carnegie Mellon, Swarthmore, Case Western Reserve, Clarkson, Xavier, University of Maryland, UMBC, Middlebury, Colby, University of New Hampshire, Wesleyan, Haverford, Bryn Mawr, University of Pittsburgh, Indiana University of Pennsylvania, University of Massachusetts Boston, Hillsdale, Grove City College, Villanova, Arcadia, Ithaca, Keene State, New England College, Wells, Cedar Crest, Muhlenberg, Dickinson, Rutgers–New Brunswick, Rutgers–Camden, New Jersey Institute of Technology, Gettysburg, Franklin & Marshall, Washington & Jefferson, Washington College, Westminster (Penn.), Stevenson, John Jay College of Criminal Justice, SUNY Institute of Technology, SUNY Geneseo, SUNY Fredonia, SUNY Stony Brook, SUNY Potsdam, SUNY Purchase, Post, Kean, Kean–Ocean Campus, Rider, Providence College, Cayuga Community College, Buffalo State, University at Buffalo, University at Binghamton, University of Rochester, CUNY–Hunter College, Mercy College (New York), Daemen, Niagara, St. Lawrence University, Ursinus, Skidmore, Lafayette, Moravian, Elizabethtown, Baldwin-Wallace, Ohio University, University of Dayton, Cleveland State, St. John's (Annapolis), Northern Michigan University, Lake Superior State University, Michigan State, WVU, Fairmont, Pierpont Community and Technical College, University of Tennessee–Knoxville, University of Tennessee–Chattanooga, Tennessee Tech, Davidson, University of North Carolina at Chapel Hill, NCSU, Mary Baldwin, Marywood, Mary Washington, Christopher Newport University, Piedmont Virginia Community College, Embry-Riddle Aeronautical University, Castleton University, Rhode Island College, Goucher College, Hood College, Notre Dame of Maryland, St. Mary's College, McDaniel College, University of Puerto Rico–San Juan, *and more.*

WEST: Reed, Stanford, Caltech, Harvey Mudd, Scripps, UC Berkeley, UC Los Angeles, UC Santa Barbara, UC Irvine, UC

San Diego, UC Santa Cruz, UC Merced, Cal State–Dominguez Hills, Cal State–San Bernardino, Cal State–Northridge, Cal Poly–Pomona, Cal State–Fullerton, Cal State–Monterey Bay, San Jose State, Hult International Business School, Lewis & Clark, University of Santa Clara, Claremont Graduate University, Fielding Graduate University, Academy of Art (San Francisco), College of the Sequoias, Azusa Pacific, University of Arizona, University of New Mexico, Portland State, University of Portland, University of Redlands, Occidental, George Fox, University of Colorado, CU Denver, University of Denver, University of Northern Colorado, Colorado School of Mines, University of Washington–Seattle, EWU, CWU, WSU, Westminster (Utah), University of Alaska–Fairbanks, University of Alaska–Anchorage, University of Texas–Austin, University of Texas–Arlington, University of Texas–Dallas, UNT, Texas A&M, Texas A&M–Kingsville, University of Texas–San Antonio, TAMIU, TAMU–Commerce, TAMU–Texarkana, Texas Tech, Baylor, TCU, Abilene Christian University, Our Lady of the Lake, St. Edward's, Incarnate Word, Houston Baptist University, Southern Nazarene, Trinity, Texas Women's University, St. Mary's University, Lamar University, University of San Francisco, San Francisco State, Mills, University of Oregon, Oregon State University, Willamette, Whitman, University of Nevada, UNLV, Brigham Young University–Hawaii, Heritage University, *and more.*

MIDWEST/SOUTH: University of Chicago, Roosevelt University, Northwestern (Kellogg), Northeastern Illinois University, Tulane, Purdue, Indiana University, Kent State, Washington University in St. Louis, Virginia Tech, Rose-Hulman Institute of Technology, Marquette, University of Wisconsin–Madison, UW–River Falls, UW–Platteville, UW–LaCrosse, UW–Whitewater, UW–Milwaukee, UW–Stout, UW–Oshkosh, UW–Superior, Beloit, Creighton, University of Nebraska–Lincoln, IUPUI, Concordia (Minn.), North Dakota State, Minn. State–Moorhead, Minn. State–Mankato, University of Missouri (Mizzou), University of South Carolina, Babcock, Rhodes, Hendrix, University of Arkansas–Fayetteville, University of Arkansas–Little Rock, Henderson State, Oglethorpe, Earlham, DePauw, DePaul, Wabash, Truman State, Kansas State, Wichita State, Principia, Knox, Albion, Hanover, University of Oklahoma, Concord State, Harding, Emory, SMU, Montevallo, Troy, University of Georgia, Georgia State, Southern Regional Education Board/Compact for Faculty Diversity, Centre, Transylvania, Murray State, Berea, University of Indianapolis, University of South Carolina–Upstate, New College, Florida International University, University of Central Florida, University of South Florida, Rockford, Franklin, East Central University (Oklahoma), Jacksonville University, University of Alabama, University of the South (Sewanee), Coastal Bend College, Mercer University, *and more.*

To arrange speaking engagements on graduate admissions or career development issues, at graduate or undergraduate levels, contact Asher Associates, 415-710-4289; email info@donaldasher.com.

INTRODUCTION

How to Use This Book

The best way to use this book is to read it in its entirety, even the sections that do not apply to you directly. Then start over, completing each assignment before you go on to the next. Plan on rewriting your essay several times. Whatever you do, do not write a word until you have done the personal assessments in chapter 5, Getting Ready to Write.

If you have procrastinated until the last minute, the first thing you need to do is *relax*. You can still finish a good essay by tomorrow morning. Just read chapters 5, 7, and 8 in order and follow the assignments as you come across them. Do not read ahead. If any sections do not apply to your particular case, just skip them.

This book makes only one assumption about you, the reader. Readers in general tend to be much smarter than the average human; given this book's topic, it is probably safe to assume that you are much smarter than the average reader. Incidentally, after years of having college professors focus on your errors and shortcomings, you are probably a lot smarter than *you* think. It is a luxury for an author to be able to write for such an audience.

This book presents a variety of techniques that students use to gain admission to highly competitive graduate programs. Some are so competitive that only 2 percent of applicants are accepted; for every fifty students who apply, only one will be entering the program. Even if your targeted schools are relatively easy to get into, these techniques should be of interest to you in winning scholarships, assistantships, and other valuable considerations. Pay particular attention to the strategies for contacting professors and overcoming liabilities in your background, and you'll be able to gain admission to more competitive programs than you otherwise might.

One of the unique features of this book is its inclusion of a full chapter on letters of recommendation (chapter 10). Letters of recommendation are a critical component of your application process, and they deserve full and separate consideration. In addition to providing a plan for selecting and motivating writers of these letters, the chapter provides a handout you can give them—"Better Letters of Recommendation"—to guide them through the process. See pages 234–235.

Another unique feature is the inclusion of diversity and adversity, scholarship, residency, fellowship, postgraduate, and postdoctoral essays. This information was available in no other book at the time this edition went to press. As one proceeds up the ivory tower, essays become more precise, more specific, and less personal, in a seamless continuum. Reading these samples will help you see your own in the larger context of academic essay and proposal writing.

This book's goal is to take all of the mystery and most of the stress out of the graduate applications process and guide you through drafting a compelling graduate admissions essay. This is also a resource book, with recommendations for supplementary reading, websites, and other materials throughout the text. I have included information on financial aid, graduate admissions testing, and other aspects of the graduate admissions process to give you a clearer picture of the graduate essay as an integral part of the entire application process. You should also seek the advice of other guides that focus exclusively on these topics.

This book is not intended to replace the advice of professors, college career counselors, and undergraduate advising officers. On the contrary, this guide is meant to encourage you to *visit them as early as possible*, and with more knowledge than you would otherwise have possessed, so that you can be a more intelligent user of their services. Spend time learning the mechanics from this book, and you can devote more of your time with advisors to true counseling.

Over the years students have made two complaints about the early editions of this book: too many of the examples are from people with unusual backgrounds, and I advocate that the student do too much work to apply to graduate school (surely, they plead, there must be an easier way). For example, one grad applicant wrote:

> *The purpose of your book should be to help the graduate student who isn't from Russia and taking theoretical physics, hasn't set up an educational program at Yale, hasn't overcome severe hardships because he's a refugee, etc. If I had something like this, I probably wouldn't need your book. Please keep in mind, for your next edition, the essays of the more ordinary students like me. We can't all run away with the carnival.*

In response, I have included more essay samples from regular students; that is, students of traditional graduate school age, with traditional academic experience. Nevertheless, you will note that these too are unusual students: they are unusually well prepared, unusually thoughtful, unusually well directed, unusually well-read in their chosen fields. Further, it is my contention that all students are unusual in one way or another; the prewriting exercises in chapter 5 will help you discover how you differ from the background noise of common applicants.

As to the amount of work involved, it is important to remember that this is a book about gaining admission to *highly competitive graduate programs*. It has been my goal to find out what the students who are admitted to these programs do differently from the students who are not admitted. This book is the answer.

As you read, remember that this is, to some extent, a study of the ideal way to apply. You needn't do all this if you are not applying to highly competitive programs, or you have some safety schools on your list, or you have a backup plan, or you are just too darn busy. Take the tips and pointers that you can, that make sense to you, and do not worry about the rest. This is a guide, not a recipe that you must slavishly follow. Adjust it to suit your particular needs, and let it improve the job you do in applying to graduate school.

While you cannot change who you are and what you have done with your life so far, you *can* make a good graduate application. Students are not always able to accurately estimate their academic value. The number of students fully qualified for graduate study far exceeds the number who actually apply. To the extent that this book facilitates your application and contributes to the realization of your potential, so let it be judged.

1

Should You Go to Grad School, and How Are You Going to Pay for This?

Before launching the application process, it seems prudent to consider whether you should go to graduate school at all.

Good reasons to go to grad school

1. You have a passionate interest in a narrow topic or an unusual combination of topics.
2. You have a vocational interest that carries a graduate degree credential as an entrance requirement.
3. You want to earn more money than you otherwise would have.
4. You want to ensure continued career advancement.
5. You seek a richer and more satisfying life.
6. You like to do research.
7. You want to stay competitive in an increasingly credentials-driven job market.
8. School is easy for you and you like it.

The single best reason to go to graduate school is because you have a passionate interest in a subject area. There is some molecular process that just fascinates you, or some nineteenth-century French feminist poet whose words wake you in the night with a start. Graduate school offers a chance to advance your understanding of those topics that have fascinated you as an undergraduate. Graduate school is often also a place where you can combine disciplines that are not combinable in undergraduate studies, such as chemistry and art history, or acoustics and marine biology. You could be the one to discover a fail-safe method for dating and authenticating oil paintings, or you could discover once and for all how to communicate with dolphins. These interdisciplinary inquiries offer some of the most exciting opportunities for study at the graduate level.

Many students are motivated not only by the study itself but also by the desire to pursue a profession that requires a graduate degree as a credential. To become an attorney, doctor, dentist, scientist, veterinarian, architect, psychologist, or college professor, you must successfully complete one *or several* graduate degree programs. There may be some rare exceptions, but certainly the overwhelming majority of practitioners in these fields will possess the normal academic credentials.

If you are interested in becoming a college professor, you need to know that the competition is fierce at this time, with many more highly qualified candidates completing their preparation each year than there are available slots. For more on this, follow the ongoing debate in the *Chronicle of Higher Education* and the newsletter for the Modern Language Association. Being willing to move anywhere increases your chances, but a prudent person will also have a parallel career goal.

Perhaps you are interested in earning more money over the span of your career. The Bureau of Labor Statistics has studied high-income individuals for decades and found that high-income people have more education than lower-income people. As a matter of fact, there is a lockstep relationship between education and income (see table).

As you can see, after completing your bachelor's degree, you are making a million-dollar decision whether to get the doctorate. These are not decisions to make without considering the lifetime income implications. Even a master's degree will give you a $300,000 boost in lifetime earnings, which will certainly allow you to pay back any loans you take out along the way. In the top earning category, a recent study found that primary-care medical doctors average $265,000 in annual income; specialists earn even more. In addition to the strong positive impact on income, higher education has a strong negative impact on unemployment. For example, the unemployment rate for PhDs runs around 1 percent or 2 percent. (There is a myth that PhDs are unemployed and underpaid; the exact opposite is true.) Further, those PhDs who don't find academic jobs earn even more outside of academic life.

Median Lifetime Earnings for Workers

Ranked by Education

Professional degree*	$3,802,000
Doctorate	$3,772,000
Master's degree	$3,274,000
Bachelor's degree	$2,983,000
High school graduate	$1,977,000

***MD, DDS, DVM, JD**

Source: Synthetic analysis of Bureau of Labor Statistics data

Graduate school is probably the second-best investment you will ever make in your life, after your bachelor's degree. And remember, the beautiful thing about investing in education is that it cannot be repossessed.

Also, if you're interested in continued career advancement throughout your working life, plan on graduate school sooner or later. We are in an era that touts and believes in continuous learning. It is becoming hard to find a senior executive *without* a graduate degree—whether in business, nonprofit, or government. The trend toward higher education for all senior managers is compounded by the trend to work for more and more employers over the span of a career. The latest business school data suggest that current graduates will work for *six to fifteen employers* between graduate school and retirement. This means that even if you are an outstanding performer, you will need to prove yourself to others who are not personally acquainted with you. Credentials are essential for smooth and continuous career advancement.

Money and career advancement aside, graduate education contributes to a rich and full quality of life. If you are an engineer and you drive under a bridge, you see more than a bridge; you see stress dynamics. Everything you see, do, touch, or think about will be influenced by your graduate education. At least one longitudinal study of college-educated workers found a lockstep relationship between education and reports of satisfaction with life (not just work life, but all aspects of life: work, family, social, financial, and so on). Plato's dialogue, *Philebus,* amounts to an elaborate argument in favor of the intellectual life. Don't trust me; trust Socrates as quoted by Plato.

If you like to do research, then graduate school is an opportunity to pursue that passion without regard to any immediate industrial or economic benefit. If you enjoy designing research methods that can support or disprove hypotheses and you can live with the results either way, then you're truly a candidate for graduate school. Even if you eventually pursue a career in industrial research, you may forever think back fondly to the intellectual freedom of your academic years.

If you just enjoy going to school and you're naturally good at it, going to grad school is certainly a better use of your time than whiling away a few years in an entry-level job. For those who find the academic life easier than, say, learning how to sell insurance by phone, pursuing graduate education is a logical endeavor.

Finally, it has been proved that with each year of graduate study your IQ will go up, and that people with higher IQs have more sex than people with lower IQs. (There's another study that says graduate students have a below-average frequency of sex, so this may be a delayed benefit.)

So if you are going to have more satisfaction, more money, and more sex, why *wouldn't* you go to grad school?

Reasons *not* to go to grad school right now

Three warning signs concerning your graduate school plans:

1. You're going to grad school to please someone else.
2. You're clueless about a subject to study.
3. You're secretly trying to avoid the job market.

If your primary motivation for going to graduate school is to please someone outside yourself, then you had better rethink the whole endeavor. If your father thinks you *have* to be an attorney or your mother thinks you *have* to be a doctor, and that's your main motivation for pursuing these goals, then you're in trouble. One study of unhappy attorneys showed that a significant proportion of them went to law school in the first place to please a close family member. You need strong *internal* motivation to thrive in graduate school. If you and your mother agree on your academic plans, fine, but if you disagree, better think twice before making a move not in alignment with your own interests.

If you're not at all sure what you want to pursue at the graduate level, that is a milder warning sign. You may need to seek more academic and career counseling; discuss your plans with mentors, parents, and other people you admire; take some career aptitude tests; take a few more classes in the subjects that interest you; and otherwise explore your options. Some schools will admit you as an unspecified-major graduate student and allow you to take graduate courses in one or more disciplines for a year or two while you decide. Even some outstanding students find themselves unsure of their next academic step.

Finally, some students seek to avoid a bad job market by hiding out in graduate school. This is okay as a general rule, as long as hiding out in graduate school does not take the place of prudent career planning. In other words, if you choose a graduate degree program that will enhance your career goals later, then fine, but if you're just passing time and running up loans—that is, if you are just *delaying* confronting your career problem—then you'd be a lot better off facing your career issues now. Interestingly enough, the skills required to get into a highly competitive graduate program are the same ones that would allow you to seek and obtain desirable, career-launching employment right now.

If you're unsure of your academic and career plans, answer these questions: When were you the most excited about your studies as an undergraduate, and what were you doing that caused all that excitement? What would you do for a living if money were no object—or, taking this to the logical limit, what career would you be willing to pay someone else to let you do? What have you fantasized about doing for a living? Think of several people you deeply admire. What do *they* do for a living?

Many, if not most, graduate applicants are somewhat vague about their career plans, but you certainly should have some plan for utilizing your education in a career, no matter how tenuous that plan may be and how many times you change that plan later.

One of the worst reasons *not* to go to grad school is that you do not know how you are going to pay for it. If you want to go, you can find a way to pay for it.

Getting financing for grad school

There may be no more confusing and illogical thing in the world than graduate school financing:

1. You cannot tell how much it will cost until you apply *and are admitted.*
2. It's often cheaper to go to an expensive school.
3. It's often cheaper to pursue the PhD than the master's.
4. It's often cheaper to borrow the money and go full-time than to work your way through part-time.
5. Even if you're wealthy, you should apply for financial aid.

Suppose you wanted to buy a car, and you went down to the car lot and asked the salesperson, "How much for this beautiful red convertible?" Further suppose that the salesperson then said, "Well, I dunno. You need to apply for the car, and if we decide to sell it to you at all, it's either going to cost you $60,000 *or we'll pay you to drive it home.* First, you have to fill out all this paperwork, pay a nonrefundable deposit, give us three references, and wait for months."

That's a nutty way to do business, you might think, but that is exactly how graduate financial aid works. You simply cannot tell how much it will cost until you apply and are admitted. The sticker price on that car and the sticker price on graduate education are often meaningless.

It's often cheaper to go to an expensive school because those schools have deeper resources for aid. At some schools, in some departments, no one has paid a dime to attend the program in decades. The tuition is offset by grants, foundation monies, and various endowed funding mechanisms; the schools continue to publish tuition rates because other departments may be actually collecting tuition (for example, the chemistry department is well funded and nobody ever pays, while the theater department collects tuition).

Sometimes students are forced to make a decision on which graduate school to attend *before* they receive a financial award. A close friend of mine received a letter from a Harvard graduate program that started out like this:

> *We are happy to extend an offer of admission to you for the fall incoming class. It is absolutely imperative that you respond by April 15th or your seat will be offered to another . . .*

The letter was dated April 17th. It didn't say one word about a financial award. So he crafted a quick and clever response:

"I am honored to be offered a position in the fall incoming class. I am slightly confused by the fact that I have not received a financial aid package. However, since I know as esteemed an institution as Harvard would not make such an offer in jest and, as you know all my financial particulars in my application, I assume the award, when it does eventually come, will be sufficient to allow me to participate in this wonderful opportunity. So, I am delighted to accept." (To be clear, this weird practice is hardly unique to Harvard.)

It's often cheaper to pursue the PhD because PhD candidates are better funded than master's candidates. Even while they are taking the same classes and sitting side by side, PhD candidates may be paid to attend class, while master's candidates pay for the privilege. Do not let financial fears keep you from pursuing the degree you want. It does in fact make sense to borrow your way through certain graduate programs, like medical school, in large part because the earnings potential of the degree is so high. Be attentive to career outcomes, obviously. Do not borrow a fortune to go to a program with a modest return on investment. For more on these issues, visit the website for the Council of Graduate Schools, www.cgsnet.org, and the National Center for Education Statistics, www.nces.ed.gov.

By the way, never pursue the PhD unless you want the terminal degree; in other words, don't apply for a PhD when you really want a master's just because the PhD funding is better. The "bailout master's" is not counted the same in industry or academe as the master's you intentionally obtain; you will be seen as someone who "dropped out of a PhD program." If you're unsure, pursue the master's degree first. Many people have a master's in one topic and a career in another field, or have two master's degrees in unrelated topics, but getting a PhD is like getting married in a Catholic church in a Latin American country. It's a real commitment.

In general, it is cheaper to go to school full-time rather than part-time for two reasons. First, the money you borrow to go full-time is repaid after you graduate, when you should have a much higher rate of earnings. Even considering the accrued interest on the loans, it will probably cost you less overall. Second, students who go to school part-time frequently do not get the career boost that comes from completing a full-time degree program. The big reward for those students who go to school part-time is frequently a card of congratulations from their employer. So what? If you end up having to change jobs to achieve the market rate for your education, what have you gained by working your way through?

Many college graduates seek an employer who will pay for their graduate education. Is this smart? Sometimes absolutely yes, and sometimes not. Employers place many restrictions on these programs, including a period of time after completion during which, if you leave your employer, you must repay their investment in your education. This is called a "clawback" clause. If the employer

Pro Tip: Programs Never Publish All Their Funding

Dear [Admissions Coordinator by Name],

I have been thoroughly reviewing the website, and I still have some questions about funding. Can you help me understand all the forms of funding and support available to students in the program? For example, when and how do you choose your TAs, RAs, and GAs? Are there fellowships, grants, and assistantships that I might be qualified for, that I might not know of? I think a brief call or video connection could clear all this up for me. Would you have a chance to speak with me next Wednesday at any time of your choosing, Thursday before noon EST, or on Saturday at any time?

Respectfully,
Your Name
REU Scholar

you already have and are happy with is willing to pay your education expenses, fine. However, you should not choose an employer based solely on this factor. Whether you are choosing an employer who may fund your education or considering whether to take advantage of your current employer's funding, be sure to run the numbers yourself before you think you are getting something for nothing. Usually your greatest boost in salary will come from going to school full-time, with the goal of aggressively seeking a full-time career position *that requires your new education.*

Even if you have the means to pay for your entire graduate education, it is often advisable to apply for financial aid. Much financial aid at the graduate level is merit based, and failing to pursue these awards will leave you without the necessary credentials to obtain postgraduate employment and other appointments. In particular, if you eventually want to be a college professor or a university-based research scientist, you almost have to be a teaching or research assistant while in graduate school. Although these assignments are most often run as aid programs, you should consider their other benefits.

Here are the most typical aid sources:

+ Teaching assistantships
+ Research assistantships
+ Fellowships
+ Grants
+ Tuition waivers
+ Loans

Teaching assistantships require you to teach undergraduate courses or labs. You will probably have your tuition waived, and usually receive a stipend (which varies widely from school to school). Having a teaching assistantship is very prestigious; if you plan to become a college professor, it's an impressive addition to your credentials. However, the workload can be severe, with all your preparation and grading effort in addition to your class time each week. Whatever your estimate of the time commitment, you should expect it to be almost double during your first semester.

You get teaching assistantships by applying to the department you will be in as a graduate student. You need grades good enough to impress everyone in the department. It also helps to have done some teaching, tutoring, or proctoring as an undergraduate. Sometimes students get assistantships in other departments to offset their educational expenses. For example, I interviewed one student, a native speaker of French, who got an assistantship teaching first-year French even though he was studying something else at graduate school. You can also supplement your income with less well-known, assistantship-like assignments elsewhere in the university system; for example, you could serve as a residence hall advisor or a career counselor, especially if you're studying any kind of psychology, counseling, business, or higher education administration.

You get research assistantships by applying to a specific professor or laboratory at the graduate school. These are much easier to get, in that you don't have to impress a whole department to win an assignment. The best way to earn an assignment like this is to learn as much as you can about the research going on in the lab, then let the laboratory chief know of your desire to participate in that research. It's a big plus if you have a great respect for the concept of integrity in original research, have conducted original research as an undergraduate, or have already been published. You do not need perfect grades to earn these jobs; I spoke with one dean who funded a research assistant whose overall GPA was 2.85 (but it is important to note that his GPA in math, physics, and fluid dynamics was 3.85, and this was a fluid dynamics lab).

If you are admitted to a program and then invited to visit, this is not really optional *even if they say it is optional.* If you decline, you may be giving away your assistantship. We'll have more to say about this in a later chapter. When you are invited to a tour or a meet-and-greet with departmental faculty, it is a very serious error in protocol not to appear. Assistantships are often assigned, formally or informally, at these types of tours. If you cannot afford the ticket, ask them to pay for it. In many cases, they will.

If you cannot get a research or teaching assistantship with your department, look for other part-time jobs with the department that could gain you both exposure to professors and savvy in how the department operates. This can cut down on your time to complete the degree program and help solve any problems you may run into as a graduate student. It's important to note that scholarships and fellowships are not taxed, but the IRS considers income from assistantships to be wage income. This has become a political football of late,

Testimonial

Dear Dr. Asher,

Three summers ago I had the opportunity to attend one of your workshops. You spoke of ways of not only getting into graduate school but also how to fund it. You told a story about a woman raising children getting accepted into graduate school and how she stayed persistent about obtaining more funding for her doctoral education. She paid for her entire degree by just asking. I remember thinking there's no way that can happen, so I decided to test it. The worst they can say is no. Unable to bring in significant income over the summer between the first and second year of my master's program, I used your strategy and emailed my program chair and the director of graduate studies. I said this: "I'm very fortunate to receive some scholarships from the university. I am grateful for that. With money becoming tighter, and with the cost of living going up, I was hoping to receive a little bit more in scholarships this year. With the goal of finishing my master's degree academically strong, I was wondering if there are any further opportunities to receive more financial support to help fund my education so I can fully focus on my studies?" They rewarded an additional $1,400 to my account with guidance to check back in the spring. Ain't that something! Following up in the spring, something amazing happened. Lo and behold! There were unclaimed grants available. They awarded an additional two grants totaling $2,313. Your comment of schools having more money to give than what they say is correct. Being in a bind, I was forced to ask for help. Now I wish I had asked sooner. I learned not to be afraid to ask for help and that there's money available until someone takes it. It might as well be me. Writing just two emails put $3,713 towards my education. I'm on track to finish my program, thanks to this additional funding.

Take care,
Diligent Scholar

so check with the IRS and your university for the latest guidance.

Warning

Assistantship applications may have very early deadlines—sometimes months before the deadline to apply to the graduate program—and often require another essay and a different set of letters of recommendation. Visiting the department can greatly increase your chances of being selected for an assistantship.

Fellowships are large awards that come with no strings attached; that is, the student doesn't have to perform any work to earn the award. They are reserved for those students whose academic promise is so great that they shouldn't be distracted at all from their studies—or, more rarely, for underrepresented students the program has a great desire to recruit. Fellowships come in two flavors: internal and external. You learn about internal fellowships from the graduate school or department to which you're applying. You learn about external fellowships (the same as a scholarship, really) by researching them yourself. At the end of this chapter are some great online resources, free and open to all.

A good primer on scholarships and fellowships is *The Best Scholarships for the Best Students* by Asher, Morris, and Fazio-Veigel; this is a book of scholarship portals, more than random specific awards. Your academic or career development advisor can point you to more specific guides, such as ones on paying for medical school. It is your job to do the research. For example, the Environmental Protection Agency (EPA) offers a generous fellowship including research-related expenses for graduate students in environmentally related fields of study. The Gertrude Fogelson Cultural and Creative Arts Award was created to encourage and honor mothers who demonstrate talent in visual arts, creative writing, or vocal music. The Paul and Daisy Soros Fellowships provide stipends and tuition for "new Americans" who hold green cards or are naturalized citizens, or who are the children of two parents who are both naturalized citizens. Just to give you an idea of how obscure some scholarships can be, there is a scholarship for fans of Klingon, the language spoken by a warrior class of aliens in the *Star Trek* science fiction franchise, offered by something calling itself the Klingon Language Institute. You don't actually have to speak Klingon to apply, but it helps. You can get graduate scholarships and fellowships for everything from world peace (Rotary World Peace Fellowship) to world conservation (Doris Duke Conservation Program), for going to medical school while being Scottish (Dr. Edward May Magruder Medical Scholarship Clan Gregor Society), and for being a woman (Woodrow Wilson Doctoral Dissertation Fellowship). Interested in veterinary science? The American Kennel Club gives millions to vet students. You don't even actually have to own a dog.

All joking aside, if you are in the sciences, you are expected to apply for four or five third-party fellowships when you apply to graduate school. You don't actually have to win the scholarships, but you are supposed to have been savvy enough to know you were supposed to apply. (This is one of those unwritten rules that ought to come from your advisor.) Now you know. The National Science Foundation (NSF) and National Institutes of Health (NIH) offer, literally, thousands of appropriate awards. A little research on your part should uncover funding that matches your background and interests.

Grants are just smaller fellowships, ranging from a few hundred to a few thousand dollars, and they work exactly the same way; you can find them by using your fellowship research resources. With a little effort and experimentation, you may find extra money available to you because you graduated from high school in Iowa, or your father works for a telephone company, or you're left-handed, or have been convicted of a felony. No kidding. The money's out there. You just have to go seek it.

You should not pay for a scholarship search service. My review of them is that none provides anything you cannot get for free online or from books. Do your own research.

Tuition waivers are extremely common for PhD candidates and for all candidates in the laboratory sciences. They are less common for master's degree candidates in the humanities and for most students in preprofessional programs such as business, law, medicine, architecture, and so on. As mentioned above, many programs list tuition in their bulletins and literature, even though no one has paid that tuition in years.

When all else fails, you can fund the gap between what you need and what you can get granted or waived with education loans. If you have a pulse, are a United States citizen, and have not ruined your credit rating entirely, you can borrow $20,500 each and every year you are in graduate school. Federally guaranteed student loans have been simplified, and a great place to start is on the Department of Education's own website: studentaid.gov. Plan on preparing a FAFSA (Free Application for Federal Student Aid). Coordinate with the financial aid office of the graduate programs to which you are applying, but be mindful that financial aid offices at the grad level administer loans; they do not broker fellowships, scholarships, assistantships, and tuition waivers. Those go through each department. Complex, right? The "financial aid office" is about loans, and the term "financial aid" means loans at the graduate level; the term for the whole spectrum of financial assistance is "funding and support." Use the wrong term and you'll miss all the free money.

By the way, family money and borrowing are generally the primary ways to finance graduate study in professional schools (business, law, medicine, especially). There are hidden assistantships at some professional schools (business, law, public policy, architecture, social work, and similar), such as working for the career placement office, which helps place graduate students in summer training and internship assignments, or serving the admissions function as a program admissions coordinator. Inquire about how to apply for these coveted slots before you attend. Otherwise, plan on borrowing a lot. You will get the payback if you complete the program in a timely manner and launch a career with average success.

A student did ask me once if she should borrow $90,000 to study dance in Manhattan. I asked her to explain to me her plan for ever being able to repay this money. She decided not to borrow the money. Though the program very strongly encouraged her to take on this large debt, even they couldn't tell her how she would be able to earn enough as a dancer to pay it back.

Be careful about interpreting average income for professionals as a form of guarantee as it may take years to hit the top of the earning curve. Starting wages for college professors and lawyers and so on may be rather modest. Also, be careful about projecting your income from tables like the example on page 2. In the highest earning category—doctors, lawyers, dentists, and veterinarians—the big money goes to the doctors and the top lawyers. Many veterinarians and lawyers have trouble repaying large education loans.

Student debt is not to be taken lightly. Even though it is almost always a good investment, you need to watch your total indebtedness. There's an old saying in law school: "Live like an attorney while you're in law school and you'll live like a law student when you're an attorney."

Remember, your first source for financial aid information of all types is the program to which you are applying, but *you may not find out how much it will cost until you've applied and been accepted.* Even after you've gotten a financial offer, however, there may be room to play. Some schools are responsive to appeals based on need (married with children, long distance to relocate, medical needs, and so on); others have responded to appeals based on competing offers. I know one student who was offered admission to Harvard and Stanford, but only got a support offer from Harvard. He took Harvard's written support offer to Stanford and said, "I have this offer from Harvard. I think your program is better, but of course I'd be foolish to turn down this stipend." Stanford came up with a slightly higher award. Some deans have told me that they try not to do this—adjust an offer on request or match another school's offer—but students tell me it happens all the time. Especially when the difference is small, say $5,000 or less, going back to a program to ask again may result in a matching offer. It can't hurt to ask, especially if you explain that you are only asking because you think their program would be a better match for you. There is more on this, including sample appeal letters, in chapter 4, What Happens to Your Application.

Finally, on the whole topic of paying for your grad school education by assistantships and fellowships, you need to know about *Getting What You Came For* by Robert L. Peters. This outstanding book goes into greater depth on different funding sources, the benefits of assistantships, selecting an advisor, departmental politics, and other important matters. I could not recommend this book more strongly for anyone pursuing an academic master's or PhD. Two books that explicate academic culture are *What They Didn't Teach You in Graduate School* by Paul Gray, David Drew, Matthew Henry Hall, and Laurie Richlin, and *The PhDictionary: A Glossary of Things You Don't Know (but Should) about Doctoral and Faculty Life* by Herb Childress. These are excellent guides to understanding the sometimes bizarre world of graduate academic programs, and are must-reads for new graduate scholars.

In addition to these books and *The Best Scholarships for the Best Students,* check out these resources:

Funding the Humanities PhD: The Grad Student's Guide to Grants & Fellowships by J. Martin, PhD (highly recommended)

Underrepresented Students: lendedu.com/blog/financial-aid-for-minorities/

Undocumented? See these resources:

+ https://immigrantsrising.org/resources/
+ scholarshipsaz.org

Cornell's grad school funding instructional pages: gradschool.cornell.edu/fellowships

COS (Community of Science): 15,000 grant sources, now accessible only through each of 700 member institutions, see your reference librarian

Cost of Living Calculator: money.cnn.com/calculator/pf/cost-of-living/index.html (You can compare two cities.)

FAFSA: studentaid.gov/h/apply-for-aid/fafsa

FASTWEB: fastweb.com

FINAID: finaid.org

Foundation Directory: fconline.foundationcenter.org, subscription (Do not pay! Visit your library reference desk to see if you have access through an institutional subscription.)

GEM: gemfellowship.org/gem-fellowship-program

MIT living wage calculator: livingwage.mit.edu (Please note that frugal students can live cheaper than this tool indicates.)

NASA: nasa.gov/learning-resources/internship-programs/nasa-fellowships

NIH: grants.nih.gov

NSF: new.nsf.gov/funding/opportunities

UC Santa Cruz portal for external funding: graddiv.ucsc.edu/financial-aid/fellowships and graddiv.ucsc.edu/financial-aid/minority-fellowships.html

The following pages list some of the most prestigious scholarships in the world. To win these, undergraduates typically work with the scholarship committee on their undergraduate campus, and *early planning is absolutely critical.* The application processes typically require essays, recommendations, and personal interviews. Some applications are regional, which may give an advantage to those applying from less competitive regions.

Be sure to apply to regular graduate programs at the same time. No one should be so confident as to assume they will win one of these elite scholarships. In any case, any graduate program will grant you a deferral if you are selected for one of these scholarships. Ask your academic advisor or scholarship committee chair for more information.

Top Scholarships

RHODES Two- or three-year graduate scholarships, with generous living allowance, to attend the University of Oxford, England. Funded by Cecil Rhodes, an Oxford alumnus and South African colonialist; he was the first to consolidate the De Beers mines (at one time in control of 90 percent of the world's known diamond reserves), and eventually had a country named after him: Rhodesia, now Zimbabwe. The applicant must be an unmarried United States citizen between eighteen and twenty-four, and have a commitment to public service and athletics (physical vigor is an explicit requirement, even though Rhodes was a sickly child). This is arguably the most prestigious scholarship in the world. You will forever be a Rhodes Scholar. Most successful candidates work closely with advisors toward this goal from the sophomore year.

FULBRIGHT One-year grants for postgraduate study abroad, with extensions possible. Host country language skills are required. Emphasis on promoting better understanding among differing cultures. Highly prestigious. Most Fulbright scholars return to complete their graduate programs at top-ranked US universities.

MARSHALL Similar to the Rhodes. Applicants must be under twenty-six at the time they apply, but there is no athletics requirement. According to the scholarship's own material, "In short, the programme looks for tomorrow's leader: for high intelligence and academic achievement; for social commitment and responsibility; for leadership potential; and for originality and flair." Go for it.

ROTARY This program is similar to the Fulbright: a full-ride year abroad to advance cross-cultural human understanding; in fact, Rotarians will call you a Rotary Ambassador. The odd thing about the Rotary International Fellowship for US Graduate Study Abroad is that if you have any close relationship to a Rotarian, you're ineligible. Contact your local Rotary Club to learn how to apply. One candidate I interviewed read thirty years of the *Rotarian Magazine.* "I may not have been the best candidate that year, but I knew more about the Rotary Club than anybody, including the selection committee," he told me. He was selected.

WATSON The Watson favors travelers and adventurers, with "an initial postgraduate year of independent study and travel abroad." The foundation "hopes to provide Fellows an opportunity for a focused and disciplined Wanderjahr of their own devising." A good independent study plan is de rigueur, but prior experience abroad is not required.

MELLON For seniors or recent graduates interested in pursuing the PhD in the humanities at an institution in the United States or Canada, who have *not yet applied nor been admitted to* a program of graduate study. Apply directly to the Woodrow Wilson National Fellowship Foundation, Mellon Fellowships, Humanities, Princeton, New Jersey.

NSF GRFP The National Science Foundation Graduate Research Fellowship Program provides significant support to STEM scholars. You can apply from your senior year in college through the first year of your graduate program. The award is very prestigious and includes a $37,000 stipend for three years. Any US citizen is welcome to apply, and "GRFP seeks to broaden participation in science and engineering of underrepresented groups, including women, minorities, persons with disabilities, and veterans." You will need a sponsoring faculty mentor. You write a statement of research intent, as well as other application essays. For more on statements of research intent, see page 88.

Also consider:

+ Winston Churchill Foundation Scholarship to Churchill College, Cambridge University
+ Keasbey Fellowships to United Kingdom universities
+ St. Andrews Society of New York Scholarship for graduate study in Scotland
+ OAS Academic Scholarship Program
+ Luce Scholars Program (Asia)
+ Abraham Lincoln Institute Scholarship Award
+ France Excellence Graduate Scholars
+ American-Scandinavian Foundation Award for Study in Scandinavia
+ Wallenberg Foundation Scholarships
+ Roothbert Fund Scholarships
+ Carnegie Endowment for International Peace Junior Fellows Program
+ Ford Foundation Fellowships
+ Jacob K. Javits Fellowship for Doctoral Studies
+ National Defense Science and Engineering Graduate Fellowship Program
+ Howard Hughes Predoctoral Fellowship in Biological Sciences

There is a Fulbright essay beginning on page 166, and NSF GRFP research proposals beginning on page 190 and page 210; your college or university scholarship committee can provide you with more examples.

Note: Do not even think about modeling your essay too closely on someone else's example; essays in this book are provided so that you may learn how to write the best statement for your own unique background.

2

Choosing a School or Program

The biggest mistake you can make in selecting a graduate program is to just choose "the best program I can get into." Annual magazine rankings notwithstanding, there is no one criterion, no single hierarchy of good-better-best on which to base such a decision. You must consider several criteria and develop your own standards for evaluation.

If your choice is good, there will be a good fit between you and the program; you will enjoy your studies, you will find friends among faculty and fellow students, and your education will further your career goals both directly and indirectly. If your choice is poor, the opposite will be true.

This chapter will guide you through the process of compiling and ranking a list of the good-better-best programs *for you,* and the following chapters will tell you how to get in.

Build a list of possible schools

First, you need to build a list of possible schools. What is a reasonable number of schools to target? Many aspiring graduate students really do apply only to one program. If you have strong grades and scores and you are pretty sure you can get into that program—and the program suits your needs—that strategy may even make sense. But if you are going to have a well-planned application season leading to a high likelihood of success, most advisors would recommend applying to four to six master's programs, about ten law or MBA programs, about fifteen medical schools, and for doctorates, a carefully chosen six to ten programs, and sometimes even more. I interviewed one college professor who applied to fifteen doctoral programs, and was admitted to only one. He succeeded in becoming a college professor, so those fourteen schools rejected a winner. I recommend that you find a minimum of twenty schools to look at, before deciding where to apply.

Be sure to search nationally, for two good reasons. First, the market for students in higher education is national, so if you don't look nationally, you're putting yourself at a competitive disadvantage. Second, graduate programs are concerned with a concept called "reach," as evidenced by statements in their viewbooks, such as this one: "Our program draws students from twenty-one states and three Canadian provinces." If your application represents a twenty-second state, and you are genuinely interested in the program, you have an advantage. Most students err in looking for a graduate program only within a four-hour drive of their current home. What if a school on the other side of the country would *pay you* or *pay you more* to pursue graduate study? Consider expanding your horizons, especially if you are looking for funding.

Tap these resources to find out about graduate programs:

+ Professors
+ Internet searches
+ Alumni
+ Specialty guides, such as *Graduate Study in Psychology, MSAR,* or *AIP Directory of Physics and Astronomy Graduate Programs*
+ Your parents, your friends' parents, your parents' friends
+ Practicing professionals
+ Academic journals, including citations
+ Annual business magazines' rankings

Your first stop for all your grad school planning should be a visit to your faculty mentor or academic advisor's office. They know graduate schools from coast to coast in their own area of expertise, although they may be a little weak outside that specialty. Next, identify faculty in other departments who may know about your chosen field. It doesn't matter whether you have ever taken classes from them; just send them an email, introduce yourself, and ask for advice. Even if you graduated from college ten years ago, or even twenty, professors at your alma mater will help you learn about graduate programs. Faculty can help you with way more than a list of possible schools. They can help you refine your plans for graduate study. Their wide-ranging advice and counsel can be invaluable. See the sample letter on page 16 asking for a discussion on all things grad school with a faculty member.

One of the fastest ways to find graduate programs is to do an advanced Internet search on obscure terminology that will be unique to your area of interest. Restrict the search to .edu domains, and then search for "Ancient Egyptian mathematics," or "pollen morphologies," or "Bas van Fraassen," or whatever subject you're interested in, and you will find faculty members with the same interests as you. This technique is quick and easy and produces very high-quality contacts.

You can also identify alumni of your alma mater who are currently enrolled in graduate programs in your subject area. Faculty, your career planning center, and the alumni office can guide you to graduates currently in graduate school in any given topic, or you can use LinkedIn or alumni databases to find them yourself. Currently enrolled graduate students can often give you long discourses on the differences between graduate programs: which is hot, which is overrated, which has this emphasis or that approach, which one lost its superstar faculty, and so on.

Don't be shy. Poll *all* your personal contacts for recommendations of good graduate programs in your area of interest.

All the resources just described will give you the bulk of the twenty-plus list of schools that are appropriate for you, with heavy emphasis on the types of programs in which prior alumni, with backgrounds similar to yours, have had success. There are several grad school search engines that purport to help you find appropriate graduate programs, but I cannot recommend any of them (except the specialty ones and Peterson's—more on those in a moment). The commercial search engines are geographically restrictive, mix elite programs with completely undistinguished options, and do not always reveal that they feature "sponsored results" such as online programs that pay a fee to appear at the top of your searches. They work okay for getting ideas, but don't rely on them to build your list.

Peterson's is a site that tracks every accredited graduate program in the United States, and for that reason it can be invaluable, especially for filling your mandate to look for graduate programs nationally and for discovering programs that match obscure interests. See www.petersons.com and click on "college and scholarship search."

I used to love Peterson's search engine more than I do now. It is the unchallenged best source for learning about all available accredited graduate programs, but it's also difficult to use and bland, making every program sound the same. Students also complain that they do not get results that match their needs.

There are hundreds of specialized guides for programs in fine arts, geography, marine sciences, neurosciences, film, environmental engineering, dance, teaching English as a second language, art therapy, religion, business, women's studies, and so on, ad infinitum. No field is too obscure to have its own guide; here's a typical example: the American College of Sports Medicine's *Directory of Graduate Programs in Sports Medicine and Exercise Science*. There are also affinity guides, such as *National Science Foundation Alliance: Graduate School Opportunities*, to assist you in discovering elite programs. Some of these guides are books and some are now online.

There are many ways to find out about these guides. Your academic advisors can make sure you don't miss any major ones; for example, you'd be nuts to even think about applying to medical school without using the Association of American Medical Colleges' *MSAR* (full real name: *Medical School Admission Requirements Annual: The Most Authoritative Guide to U. S. and Canadian Medical Schools—Medical School Admission Requirements, United States and Canada*. No wonder they just call it the *MSAR*). Similarly, no one should apply to psychology programs without consulting the American Psychological Association's *Graduate Study in Psychology*, an online database, especially useful for those interested in focusing on clinical psychology. It is easier to get into Harvard Medical School, statistically, than to get into many of the clinical psych programs, so no student should head in that direction without this specialized guide.

Sample Letter to Faculty Mentor

Dear Dr. Gonzalez,

I wonder if you would have some time to help me with my graduate school plans. I need help narrowing down my focus. I know there is more than one right answer, but if you could help me just by talking about this with me that would be great. I don't necessarily expect this meeting to lead to a letter of recommendation, although I am sure letters of rec will be part of our discussions. I need help with planning how to build a list, understanding how to think about rankings, considering starting with a master's vs. going straight for the doctorate, understanding career options (including Alt-Ac), and just getting a feel for grad school culture. Any advice you can share would be appreciated. I can be available by phone or on the video platform of your choosing at any time of your convenience on Wednesday, Thursday any time before noon, or Friday any time after 10 a.m. What works for you? Would you be willing to help me?*

Grace Dennis

Psychology major

*Alt-Ac stands for "alternate to academic," that is, all the jobs *outside of the academy* for people with advanced degrees

Students interested in philosophy programs can check out the Philosophical Gourmet, a site dedicated to ranking the top philosophy programs in the English-speaking world. That's available at www.philosophicalgourmet.com. Their methodology gets challenged from time to time, but it is a place to start.

Students interested in law school should try the Law School Admission Council's Law School Finder, at https://www.lsac.org/choosing-law-school/find-law-school/jd-programs. This tool allows you to enter your LSAT score and weighted GPA and matches you to law schools to which you have a good chance of gaining admission. This will not tell you anything about the vibe at the law schools, however. There are always entities compiling lists with different focuses and of varying quality. Just run a search and see what you can find. "MBA programs with a focus on entrepreneurial studies," or "law schools with emphasis on social justice and equity." These can give you a better idea of the focus of curriculum or the social world of grad programs. Just be smart and realize that the compilers of these lists and "rankings" may have biases that are not immediately evident. Some are no more than musings of some bored graduate student or faculty member, posted online for all to see.

If you are long out of college, or your undergraduate advising center is nonexistent or parochial, then, unfortunately, the full burden of research falls upon you. The *Encyclopedia of Associations* can lead you to obscure guides. For example, you may discover that there is an American Speech-Language Hearing Association, visit their website, and discover that they publish a *Guide to Graduate Education in Speech-Language Pathology & Audiology.*

In addition to seeking out guides, remember to pursue word-of-mouth advice. Poll your parents, your parents' friends, and your friends' parents for recommendations. Survey your entire network of acquaintances. Visit the alumni database to identify practicing professionals in your chosen field. Email them and ask for a moment of their time to seek advice on getting into the field, as well as grad program recommendations. Here are some suggested questions:

1. How did you get into this field?
2. What education or credentials are required for *continued* advancement in this field?
3. What was different than what you expected? Any myths you want to shatter for me?
4. What advice would you have for a young person interested in this field?
5. Should I go to grad school right away or work for a year or two first? If work,
6. What kind of experiences would be best?
7. Which grad schools do you think are best in this field? Why?
8. Do you know any professors that I should contact?

If you are shy, just keep this to an email exchange.

Savvy students, with the drive and preparation to get into the most highly competitive graduate programs, get their grad school leads straight from the academic journals for their fields. This is doubly smart because not only are the programs generating the most recent articles on the cutting edge in their fields, but the articles also give the student a good idea of the type of work coming out of those programs. Seek out articles in popular and specialty academic journals, find out where the authors teach and do research, and you'll have an "A" list of graduate programs in your field. Read the citations, too—they can lead you to brilliant professors who might not write a lot, but are highly respected. If you want help with identifying appropriate journals and learning how to track down professors based on articles about their research, see your academic advisor.

Business and news magazines have gotten into the practice of writing annual graduate school guides. They are a decent source for learning about graduate programs, but you should not give much credence to their ranking systems. They are most useful when focusing on a narrow, unusual topic, such as "Best business schools for future consultants," and not so useful when ranking programs in which they have no editorial expertise.

As you build lists of schools, be careful not to put too much weight on rankings, and never confuse "rankings" with "fit." Fit is much more important than rankings.

Rankings are always a blunt instrument, at best. They lump large areas together; for example, psych rankings are going to lump programs that are strong in clinical psychology with programs emphasizing social psych, developmental psych, ed psych, or neurosciences. So, knowing that one program is ranked higher than another in psychology is not going to be that useful a datum to a prospective student who is going to spend the bulk of their time in a specific concentration.

To really drive this home, one ranking system named as the top school of architecture a program that didn't even offer structural architecture in any form—it was in fact a landscape architecture program. As a spoof on rankings, one faculty member asked faculty at other programs to rank law schools from a list of universities. One of the universities on the list didn't even have a law school. It had closed in 1852. It still did well in these "rankings," however. Similarly, a foreign student wrote to me for help to get into a specific Ivy League university in engineering. He had heard that Ivy League universities were the best in America. The specific university he had chosen, a fine place in general, did not have an engineering department that would appear on any top ten list except, possibly, "closest to the ocean."

Be smart about rankings and use them as just one piece of information about a school, and possibly a very suspect piece at that. We'll have more to say about that in the next section, but for now, just use rankings as one point of introduction to information about schools that you might find interesting. Build a robust initial list, with a variety of programs on it.

With all these resources available to you, you should have no problem identifying twenty programs that have what you want. Basically, if you have a heartbeat and a bachelor's degree, there's a grad school out there for you. There are more options for graduate education than you can imagine. You can go full-time, part-time, nights, Saturdays only, or one weekend a month to study anything from engineering to nuclear medicine to recreation to general liberal studies. At the low end of the scale in terms of time commitment, there are more one-year master's programs than ever before. At the high end, there are more part-time doctoral programs and more postdoctoral research fellowships than ever before, extending your educational options into the multiple decades. There are many online and hybrid options that allow you to gain advanced degrees while working full-time and raising six kids. If you want to go to school, whatever your motivations and whatever your goals, there is a grad school out there for you. Go find it.

How to explore your options

The process of selecting a graduate program involves balancing at least six main components:

+ The academics
+ The people (faculty, students, administration)

+ The locale
+ The cost
+ Admissibility
+ "The Love"

The academics

The academics can be thought of as the intellectual feast. What are you going to learn? It should certainly be something you want to learn. Read the journals in your field. Read the writings of the faculty at targeted programs. Ask your professors to evaluate the schools on your short list, and be sure to ask them to suggest particular professors, writers, and researchers who could further your academic interests. Professors are your number-one source of really useful information about graduate programs—talk to them often.

As mentioned in the handout on the next two pages, you should write to prospective programs for more specific information on what they teach, what they research, and how they operate their programs. Ask questions that you genuinely want the answer to. Here is a sample:

Dear [Admissions Officer by Name]:

I intend to pursue the DBA starting with, of course, the MBA, and I am attracted to your program. I have been told that sometimes MBA programs have invisible doctoral programs with very few students in them. Does your graduate business school have doctoral students? If you could let me know more about that, that would be very useful. Also, in addition to a strong foundational business education, I am interested in specializing in the quantitative side of marketing, market segmentation, analytics and metrics associated with designing and evaluating marketing research, and statistics and finance related to marketing. Since these areas are quantitative, I would like to pursue the MBA and the DBA as a straight-through. I have a strong academic background, clear intentions, and clarity of purpose. I will of course pursue internships and co-ops focusing on my area of interest, quantitative areas of marketing, all the way through to the DBA. Is my plan sound? My eventual goal is to be a professor of business, and to operate my own consultancy focusing on marketing analytics. I am eager to read your advice, or if you would prefer, we can connect by Zoom. I am truly grateful for any advice you can share with me!

Respectfully,
Arunda Kotabi
Wesleyan University

Here is another email to consider as a model:

Dear Dr. Russell:

I am a senior biology major at Truman State University. Because I have taken almost every biology course offered at Truman, I will graduate in May with an unusual double degree: a bachelor of arts in biology and a bachelor of science in biology. I also pursued two years of Latin, which helps with nomenclature.

Since the beginning of my sophomore year, I have been conducting research under the guidance of Dr. J. M. Osborn. For the past two years, I have been studying pollen and anther morphology in the Callitrichaceae, a family of aquatic flowering plants. During the course of this project, I have learned a variety of laboratory techniques, written research proposals, and delivered oral presentations of my findings. I have attached a copy of my curriculum vitae to give you an indication of my research experience and educational background to date.

For the past two summers, I have been funded to do full-time research. I very much enjoyed the opportunity to participate in these programs without the added responsibilities of coursework. I am looking forward to focusing more on research at the graduate level.

Due to my interest in pursuing the doctoral degree in structural/developmental botany, I have discovered your laboratory and read some of your more recent articles. Can you also let me know if you will be accepting a graduate student next fall for your laboratory? I have had a Zoom meeting with Dr. P. Johnson, the graduate studies chair of your department, for general information about your department and graduate study at the University of Oklahoma, so there's no need to cover basic information. If you could please just share with me information about your own projects and your laboratory, and what you look for in an academic mentee, I would be most appreciative.

Thank you for your assistance, and I look forward to hearing from you via email at your earliest convenience.

Sincerely,
Hannah R. Watson

(There are more sample letters to faculty and admissions officers on pages 25, 77, and 79.)

If you are evaluating preprofessional schools—business, law, medicine, public health, architecture, and so on—it is somewhat more difficult to discern the differences between programs. Nevertheless, these schools are each quite distinct, and understanding this not only increases your chances of finding the right one for you, it also increases your chances of developing a compelling application and gaining admission to your first-choice schools.

For example, some medical schools have an emphasis on public health built into the regular medical school curriculum, others offer a special combined MD/MPH program, and some have both. Some teaching medical centers are located in the heart of underserved urban centers, taking pride in serving these patient populations, while others are famous for their cardiology units or their pediatric hospitals. Some architecture schools are known worldwide for their concern with accessibility and social issues, while others remain devotees of the International Style of Mies van der Rohe. Failing to research such differences between programs is akin to going to the lake and diving headfirst into unknown waters. Obviously, if you are applying to thirty medical schools you cannot take a year off and research every one of them, but you should have a very well-defined impression of your top three to five choices.

Be careful of confusing reputation with academics. A school's reputation is certainly a consideration, but what you are going to learn is far more important. If reputation is highly important to you, you need to evaluate this factor carefully. Since reputations lag behind current conditions by three to five years, a school's current reputation may reflect circumstances that have passed. A school's reputation five to ten years in the future will be more important to your career than its reputation at the moment you matriculate. So you should analyze and project long-term trends and not fixate on any one year's rankings. Is the school investing in infrastructure, faculty salaries, and new programs that would indicate it has a commitment to continued excellence? Or has it not implemented a new idea in ten years?

Rankings really annoy most academics. They are mostly invalid, if not downright iniquitous. Recent scandals in law school rankings revealed wholesale fabrication of data by elite institutions. Undergraduate rankings have perverted institutional priorities to the detriment of the undergraduate experience. One of the better ranking systems for grad programs ever invented, the Faculty Scholarly Productivity Index, has gone defunct, along with another honorable attempt by the National Research Council. Nevertheless, their data appear online as if current and valid. *U.S. News & World Report* publishes one of the most common rankings, but their methods have been debunked repeatedly. For just one example, see Malcolm Gladwell's *New Yorker* article "The Order of Things: What College Rankings Really Tell Us." Also check out the "data and rankings" sidebar at archive.sciencewatch.com/dr/.

Warning

At the graduate level, schools as a whole do not have reputations—only programs do. There are outstanding programs nestled in otherwise undistinguished institutions, and there are we-don't-care-we-got-tenure-twenty-years-ago graduate departments ensconced in some of the most elite universities on the continent. You want information on the reputation of specific departments, not institutions as a whole.

It may also be helpful to look into various "academic family tree" and "scholar genealogy" charts, which show who mentored whom going back for decades. This is a form of academic gossip, maybe, but still considered important in science. There are many of these charts; one place to start is academictree.org.

Gossip may actually be the best way to rank graduate programs. Faculty and currently enrolled graduate students have the latest and best information about whether program A is better than program B, or whether program X is improving or waning. So seek and consume gossip. A student can design their own ranking system by looking at the per-capita number of peer-reviewed articles produced by faculty at any given school and by seeing if authors from school A are citing authors from school B, *or are cited by* authors from school B. To get really sophisticated, you can use Eigenfactor .org to rank journals and see if a faculty member is publishing in the most reputable journals. This is not easy, but then again, neither is graduate school.

My personal recommendation is to downplay reputation and concentrate on what the program can offer you. Learning nothing of use to you and being miserable at the Number-One School of Business is probably not as good for your career as being really excited about the entrepreneurial program at the Number-Thirty School of Business. Think about it.

Accreditation, on the other hand, does matter. Peterson's does not list unaccredited programs on its search engine, but many of the other sources you might use may sneak in unaccredited graduate programs. Your investment in your graduate education—your money, sweat, and tears—could be wasted if you inadvertently attend a program that is not accredited. Many governments and employers will not honor a degree from an unaccredited program. There are many diploma mills out there, some appearing very legitimate. As some are shut down, more are constantly being created by domestic and international criminals. You don't want to get involved with them.

The Council for Higher Education Accreditation publishes a searchable database of accredited institutions. If the institution is not on CHEA's site, it's not accredited. It's that simple. Agree to abide by CHEA's terms of usage at www.chea.org and the service is free. Also, be aware that some disciplines, such as nursing, psychology, business, and others, may have further accreditation issues. In addition to *institutional* accreditation, these programs are recognized for *departmental* credentials. For example, the Association to Advance Collegiate Schools of Business (AACSB) accredits graduate programs in business—see www.aacsb.edu—and the American Psychological Association (APA)

Warning

The reputation of your graduate program is important for one reason. If you want to be a college professor, you need to know about the Law of Descending Prestige. According to this law, in general, you will teach at an institution with less prestige than the one that granted your highest degree. There will be exceptions, but an investigation of any random group of higher education hiring decisions will support that the law is in effect for the overwhelming majority of cases. Also, be aware of the strong competition for academic positions in general. For example, as this book goes to press, the number of PhDs being granted in some disciplines is ten times the number of all announced teaching positions. So, nine out of ten of those degree recipients will need some other career option, like it or not.

Pro Tip

Do not reveal to a graduate program where else you are applying. This never serves the applicant. It is a proven psychological phenomenon that if a program finds out you are applying to ten programs, they will be less interested in you. Think about dating. Who do you want to date? Someone interested in you alone, or someone interested in you and nine other people of all genders? So, if you come across an open slot in the application that asks, "Where else are you applying?" it is my counsel to leave that blank. If a professor or admissions officer asks you live in an interview, "Where else are you applying?" give them two or three schools off your list, but not the whole list. Or you can be noncommittal and say something like, "I'm still deciding where to apply. I'm absolutely going to apply here. This program matches my interests really well. I'm also thinking about maybe Northwestern and MIT, but I haven't decided yet. Definitely here, though."

approves graduate programs in psychology—see accreditation.apa.org. Faculty can warn you whether you need to worry about more than simple accreditation of a university as a whole.

The people

All other things being equal, people are the most important component of your graduate education. This means the faculty and fellow students with whom you will live and work closely for the next two to six years, or more. You want to be sure that you can work with them and that they can work with you. If you've attended a large university, you may not have spent more than twenty hours in your entire undergraduate career in the presence of a full professor; now you will work hand in glove with them on research they will monitor closely. If the best place in the world to study fractals is a program dominated by tyrannical gargoyles, you might want to take a look at the other schools on your list.

Similarly, if you have just spent four years fighting every day for the creation of a major in feminist political theory, do yourself a favor and find a graduate program with that established focus. Graduate school is not a good place to pioneer a new topic or to study without guidance. Although forging a new path is not impossible, studying in a program that aligns with your interests will probably be more gratifying and productive. When you choose a school whose program closely matches your interests, and your application essay explains this clearly, your essay can vault you further than your grades and test scores ever could.

The locale

The school's physical locale will be important to some applicants and totally irrelevant to others. If you are committed to your studies, you will not be too concerned with the weather or the proximity of ocean beaches. However, if you truly believe that you will be miserable in New York City, or Iowa City for that matter, then that has to be a factor in your decision. Wherever you attend graduate school, you are likely to make many friends and contacts you will wish to keep for a lifetime—this will prolong your relationship with the location of your school.

You should also consider the benefits of studying in a city where you would like to be employed after graduation. Be mindful, too, of the "spouse factor." If you fail to consider the needs of your spouse, you may find yourself in need of a new one.

The cost

The cost of living in the area around the school will have a direct bearing on the cost of your graduate education, but students are usually quite creative at controlling overhead. Even if you have been living the good life between college and graduate school, you can return to a frugal lifestyle more easily than you might think. Cost of living is considered in all financial aid arrangements. If you get admitted to Columbia in Manhattan, *figure it out.* Do not avoid an expensive location if it makes you avoid a great opportunity. In general, cost of living by itself should not be a determining factor in your selection.

On the other hand, the cost of the programs themselves can be quite daunting. As related in the prior chapter, that cost is often difficult or impossible to estimate before you apply and are accepted.

Warning

Be wary of choosing a graduate program because of just one professor. Professors move, go on sabbatical, fail to win tenure, serve as guest lecturers and scholars in residence at other institutions, die, lose favor in their departments, and change their beliefs. In each program you consider, try to identify two or three professors who have something to offer you.

Admissibility

Here is a formula for selecting schools to apply to. First, rank all the graduate programs you have been investigating in order of interest to you, from most attractive overall to least attractive overall.

Then, *in a completely separate list,* divide your schools into three categories:

1. Those schools to which you are pretty sure you can get admitted, namely, safety schools.
2. Those schools to which you probably, *maybe* can get admitted.
3. Those schools to which it would be a reach for you to be admitted, perhaps even a miracle.

You can assign these categories based on what you have learned of the schools to date, combined with hard data, such as the percentage of applicants admitted, available from the Peterson's guides, or the schools' own websites. Most professors can handicap your chances with particular schools in their own field.

Next, going back to your ranking of schools from most desirable to least desirable, choose the *first two* "reach" schools, the *first two* "probably/maybe" schools, and the *first two* "safety" schools. This leaves you with a list of six schools—a reasonable number of graduate programs to apply to—and with a statistically high probability of getting admitted overall. If you are a borderline student or need maximum funding, or if you are applying for med schools, law schools, or a PhD, you'll need to apply to more schools. However, and this is a very important point: You must customize every application. If you do not customize your applications, your "safe" schools are no longer safe. Failure to customize is the biggest mistake that graduate applicants make, and this is true across the board, from medicine to exobiology.

How to Approach a Graduate School (ideally)

Using the Internet, go from

The University Home Page

The Department Home Page

Specific Labs or Subdepartmental Specialty Areas

Individual Faculty Home Pages

Picture (why not take a look)
Research interests
Grants and awards
Publication record (bibliography)
Work in development
CV
Almae matres
Coauthors on papers of interest
Advisees, i.e., currently enrolled grad students

For the doctorate, in particular, identify one to four faculty members who have the potential to be future mentors to you. Look for faculty who publish, who have ongoing research projects directly related to your interests, and who win grants, honors, and awards. You can usually read writings by that faculty member by linking directly from faculty home pages to research summaries, abstracts, or academic journals.

Write to faculty by email

1. **Ask for some clarification of the program.** Keep your query as specific as possible: "I noticed on the departmental home page that you are the expert in microdynamics. Does your lab have any plans to pursue projects in nanomachinery?" Or, "I am interested in cultural anthropology of Native Americans in urban settings post-1945. Who would be the most appropriate faculty member to contact about this interest?" Read some of a professor's publications and consider offering some thoughtful comments. Don't be afraid to state your own views, but exercise caution when it comes to outright

disagreement. If you point out, "On page 3 of your proof in the most recent edition of *Mathmatica,* I noticed a fatal error in logic . . .", you'd better be sure you are right.

2. **Propose a study topic, if it is directly related to their research specialty.** Be sure to follow Asher's Law (see page 44). Here is an example of such an email:

Dear Dr. Herrick:

I am interested in continuing my graduate work in history at SUNY Binghamton. I recently completed my master's project at NYU under the direction of Dr. T. L. I. Fitzsimons (see attached CV), and I will be receiving my degree this February. After a brief hiatus, I hope to return to my studies next fall with the intent of pursuing a program of study culminating in the doctoral degree.

My area of interest within the Binghamton History Department is US social history. I am particularly intrigued by the history of the New Left in the United States and did my research project on student movements of the late 1960s and early 1970s. In the course of my research, I came across your name often. I would appreciate the opportunity to further explore and analyze this topic, as I believe that we all have much more to learn about the American New Left and its shifting place in history.

My current interest is an analysis of the schism between . . .

If a professor does not write back, *do not be discouraged.* Professors get tons of unsolicited email. They are used to skimming and delaying response to a lot of it. In workshops, it seems students get about a 20 percent response rate to queries like this. If you really want to reach them, email them and wait a day or two at most; if there is no response, email them again, with this added to the top: "I'm not sure you received my recent email. Here's what I emailed before." If there is still no response, print it out and snail-mail it to them, with this added at the top: "Perhaps I don't have an accurate email address for you. Here's my query printed out. I hope to hear from you by email or regular mail at your convenience. Thank you so much." If they *still* do not respond, it's probably just as well to leave them alone. Even if they never respond, it does not mean they are not with a good graduate program. They may be under deadline on a book project, or out of the country, or have another perfectly good rationale for not being able to get back to you.

Write to others who can help you decide if this program is a good match. Do not hesitate to make contact with a school at multiple levels: the graduate school office, the departmental office, key faculty members, student associations you would like to join after admission, and perhaps even friends of your family who are prominent alumni.

If you're really interested in a program, go ahead and email currently enrolled graduate students. Ask: Is this a good program? Which professors would you recommend? How long do you think it will take you to complete the degree program? Any hot tips for a prospective student? Then be sure to ask them about their studies and research projects.

What is the gold standard for customization? Readers should not find it evident that you are applying to any other program. Where will you find the time for all this? If you are working or going to school full-time, you need to carve out the equivalent of a half-time job to prepare your applications properly. This will only last a few weeks, but it is a big set of tasks. You need to research the schools, differentiate each one, scour their websites for application guidance and instructions, and for the PhD, research possible faculty mentors. You need to fill out applications that are frustrating, arbitrary, and sometimes require following paradoxical instructions: "submitting test scores is optional," "submit test scores if your GPA is less than 3.2," "do not reveal your test scores to the department even if you know what they are." "You must submit a supplemental essay for each department," but the department has zero instructions on fulfilling this commandment. "Stand on one leg and repeat this phrase three times, 'I want to be a Wildcat! I want to be a Wildcat . . .'" You get the idea. All this will take some time, so plan on finding that time. Stop working three jobs. Drop a time-sucking activity. Break up with that high-maintenance romantic partner. Prioritize. You are trying to change your life, and this is important.

The best students often overestimate their admissibility and omit safety schools, while students with less-than-perfect portfolios often self-select out of graduate programs that would have been happy to have them. Don't fear rejection. If you do this correctly, you'll be rejected by about half the places you apply. You may choose another method for selecting schools if you wish, but this formula is prudent for all applicants.

I once interviewed a student who applied to thirty-four medical schools. A little strategy on his part could have saved him considerably on application fees. I have interviewed hundreds of students who applied only to top schools and were rejected by all of them. One student provided the most interesting probability analysis I have ever heard: "I applied to Harvard, Princeton, Yale, and Stanford. I figured I had a 25 percent chance, since that's four schools." Deconstruct that logic if you can. I know of one student who graduated with a 4.0 and won a $24,000 fellowship applicable at any accredited graduate program, yet she was rejected by every one of the top ten programs in her field. Unfortunately, those were the only ten programs she applied to.

The dean of enrollment at a graduate school of business told me about rejecting a student with a perfect GMAT score. "He was arrogant," the dean said. "We didn't think he'd be a welcome addition to our student body." On the other hand, I've interviewed numerous students in medical school with an

Applying to a European Graduate School?

If you're applying overseas, you might want to reconsider the tone of your documents. United States citizens are notorious for bragging, whereas in Europe the norm would be to be a little more circumspect. Thus, in the US we might say, "I conducted an experiment . . ."; in Europe, one would more likely say, "I was fortunate enough to be selected as the junior member of a team doing some rather exciting work . . ."

Second, I know from interviews and information from my correspondents that European schools almost always read all of every portfolio, even the students they summarily reject. This changes the dynamic. You can trust the readers a bit more than in the US, where you sometimes have to speak up—shout, if you will—in order to be sure that readers notice your best parts.

Third, European educators in particular find vague, generic letters of recommendation to be insulting, both to themselves and to the student being recommended. Although they are an accepted part of the process in the US, be sure your recommenders write individualized letters for each program outside the US.

Finally, European faculty and admissions officers tend to respond to inquiries promptly and personally, whereas in the US it is common for even very good schools to ignore student queries unless and until the applicant is actually admitted.

undergraduate GPA right around 3.0. I interviewed a dean who gave full funding to a student with a 2.85 when the school's target minimum GPA was 3.5. Another student told me that when she first contacted her graduate program they actually told her she'd never get in, yet she did.

Why would you need two safety schools if a safety school is, by definition, safe? There are two good reasons. First, things go wrong; second, one might give you generous funding while the other offers none. Applicants want to believe that the graduate admissions process is fair and scientific, but in practice it's a mixture of science, art, and accident. Graduate admissions professionals work very hard to choose an incoming class and, believe me, they agonize over the borderline applicants. Nevertheless, the outcome is not always as it should be. Here are some actual cases:

+ A student had a wonderful exchange of letters with a department chair, some of which included such statements as "We're so delighted that you will be joining us next year." Nevertheless, she was rejected by the graduate school office, which had more authority than the department.
+ A student failed to send original transcripts from a community college she had attended while in high school. The transfer grades from the community college appeared on her regular college transcript but, through a bizarre chain of events, an overzealous student employee and a 50-cent library fine from six years prior conspired to keep her out of graduate school.
+ Another professor was not granted tenure and stopped performing all duties whatsoever that were not contractually required. This included writing letters of recommendation *that he had already agreed to write.* At least one of his advisees was not admitted to a graduate program because of this. The student never knew what happened.
+ One professor forgot to upload and post a wonderful letter of recommendation he had written for his favorite advisee, and she was rejected.
+ One student was rejected because her portfolio was "accidentally placed on the wrong pile." The graduate school discovered its mistake later in the season, but had already sent the

Rankings for Grad Schools Abroad

One problem when you leave the United States and Canada to study is finding good schools. While a "study-abroad experience" can be pursued pretty much anywhere, an advanced degree is a much bigger investment. You don't want to get one from a poorly ranked, unranked, or unknown institution.

To protect your investment of time and tuition from an undistinguished institution, you'll want a reliable ranking system. The problem is that there isn't one. International rankings are plagued by cross-cultural limitations, poor methodology, and disputed data reporting. So, my advice is to find a faculty member from the country in question, and ask them to tell you the top schools and programs in their country. This type of faculty "gossip" is the best way to learn which schools are excellent, and which are not as well regarded.

But, despite their uneven reputation, here are commonly used rankings:

U.S. News & World Report—United States

Maclean's—Canada

Times Higher Education World University Rankings—Global (that's the *London Times*)

Academic Ranking of World Universities (ARWU), aka *ShanghaiRankings*—Global

QSIU (Quacquarelli Symonds Ltd. Intelligence Unit), *QS World University Rankings*—Global

American Universities in a Global Market, National Bureau of Economic Research

For more on this, see "What Global Rankings Ignore," by Indira Samarasekera, on www.insidehighered.com.

student a rejection letter. Rather than admit what had happened, they let the decision stand. (This is the kind of thing you hear at national conferences, when no students are around . . .)

+ A student applying for a PhD in philosophy received notice from a major university rejecting his application for a PhD in Germanic languages.
+ A student was rejected by an internationally acclaimed architecture program after his portfolio was reviewed by Prof. X. When he called to inquire about the status of his application, Prof. Y picked up his portfolio, glanced through it while the student was on hold, and reversed the decision of Prof X. Thus was he admitted.

Applying to Oxford?

Oxford offers one- and two-year master's degrees, where one studies a field in depth (MSt or master of studies, MSc or master of science, MPhil or master of philosophy). Then one can attempt the doctorate, which they call a DPhil.

Oxford requires a level of specialization that is somewhat out of sync with the American educational process. Even undergraduates focus on narrow fields, and graduate students are expected to come in the door with both broad understanding of their field and advanced understanding of and interest in a particular topic. It's as if to get into graduate school, you had to be halfway through already.

Oxford may be one of the last meritocracies on Earth. You have to have stellar marks. No exceptions and no bending the rules for the rich or famous. You have to have clarity of purpose. No exploring the field of options for a couple of years before settling onto a research idea.

Finally, Oxford values something that other schools have abandoned as an ideal: dialectic. You have to be able to state, explicate, and defend your ideas in scholarly discourse. Suppose someone handed you a model of a novel complex molecule and inquired, "What's missing here?" Suppose someone handed you a bit of writing and inquired, "When was this written?" At Oxford that type of thing happens every day.

On the other hand, everyone I've ever met at Oxford has been extraordinarily nice.

As you narrow down your choices, resist the temptation to apply for two different programs at the same institution. Applying to multiple programs (at different schools) is expected; applying to multiple *different* programs is a warning flag to faculty about the depth of your commitment. If you truly have divergent interests and decide to apply for graduate programs in history and mathematics, for example, apply to mathematics programs at some institutions and history programs at others.

On the other hand, applying to combined degree programs, such as the MD/PhD or JD/MBA, has no negative implications. Processes vary from institution to institution, so inquire at the targeted programs for more information.

Finally, as a strategic hedge, some PhD-bound students will apply to a mix of PhD and master's degree programs (of course, not at the same institution). This way, if they don't get into a PhD program of their choice, they can continue their studies uninterrupted and apply again when they are near to completing the intermediate degree. By the way, you do not need a master's degree to go for the PhD in most fields. The master's degree is just a step designed into the doctoral degree process. There are some exceptions: in business, public policy, public administration, public health, nursing, education, international relations, and social work, the tradition is to get the master's before entering a PhD program, but policies will vary even among these programs.

"The Love"

Some schools are welcoming, and some are not. Some schools ignore your questions, send out automated communications that do not have anything to do with your application, and act like they are doing you a huge favor even letting you apply to their program. Then they underfund you, with no explanation. Other schools answer all your questions, hook you up with appointments with famous professors, assign a graduate student to be your admissions correspondent, and find generous aid and support for you. They may even send you relocation money, so that you can get to their city without having to hitchhike. I call that "The Love."

Unfortunately, some of the best schools in the nation have an abrasive and arrogant way of engaging with the world outside their gates. They disdain to admit you at all. And some schools kind of treat you like dirt until you are admitted, and then they turn on the charm. Suddenly they like you, late in the game. I gave a lecture at NAGAP (National Association of Graduate Admissions Professionals) in which I argued that the most elite programs, say those rejecting 90 percent of applicants, are making a mistake by doing this. If they admit 10 percent and expect to enroll 5 percent (50 percent yield), they are likely getting the bottom half of the students they admitted. If they had been a little nicer in the process, they could have been harvesting the top half. They are not exhibiting "The Love."

"The Love" matters. You want to feel wanted. You want to feel welcome. You want to feel that your personhood is acknowledged, not just your GPA and your work and your credentials. So, as you choose a program, consider whether they treated you with respect during the process. Let that be one of your criteria for selection.

Pro Tip

As soon as application portals go live, open an account and fill in all the contact information, and at least specify what program you are applying for. Do this even if the deadline is months and months away. This will alert the school to your existence. They may send you announcements, encouragement, tips, invitations to preview days and open houses, assign you an admissions ambassador correspondent, and so on.

First-choice school?

It is perhaps human nature to have a first-choice school on your list, but smart students avoid locking in on any one school or program. Select a wide range of schools, make your best application to each of the schools on your list, and let the process take its course. Besides, you learn constantly about programs by the very act of preparing to apply, applying, talking to faculty and friends, and watching how the schools treat you as the process unfolds. You may discover that your first-choice school has gargoyles for faculty, has zero funding for you, is famous for the work of several key professors who are about to retire, and so on, while a school you thought was not really a match turns up to have "hot" professors doing cutting-edge research, or is about to launch a new lab or research initiative focusing on your favorite topic. Or maybe they're just super nice and convince you you'd thrive there. Or you can always use the selection criterion of a student I interviewed at Oxford: "It's really quite easy to select programs. I apply for a lot of funding and awards, and I consistently find that the opportunities that come through with the most money attached are in fact the most interesting." (It sounds very logical in a British accent.)

• • •

In subsequent chapters, I assume that you have selected and ranked a group of viable graduate programs; from this point on, the focus of the material is entirely on how to get in. There is no one formula that all successful applicants have followed, but applicants who are consistently successful, who win scholarships and grants and admission to several of their top-ranked schools, tend to use most of the strategies and follow most of the guidelines presented to you in the following chapters.

Again, this book's main focus is to present the *ideal* way to apply to *highly competitive* programs. If you've already selected a program that you're pretty sure you can get into and just want help writing a good essay, feel free to skip ahead to chapter 5, Getting Ready to Write.

3

Planning and Managing Your Application Process

Applying to a graduate program requires more than writing an interesting essay. You must successfully orchestrate a number of independent assignments in order to complete them all ahead of the application deadline. Some of the major steps of your application process are:

1. opening and managing online application accounts with each school;
2. obtaining multiple letters of recommendation from faculty members and other busy people, a multistep process;
3. drafting, rewriting, and polishing compelling and fully customized essays, statements of purpose, diversity and adversity statements, and/or autobiographies;
4. taking the appropriate standardized graduate admissions test(s);
5. getting the test scores forwarded to your schools of interest;
6. obtaining official transcripts from all your schools of record;
7. converting your writing or research sample, if required, into the desired format;
8. entering data on forms, writing peculiar mini-essays that may appear on application forms, hitting "submit"; and
9. verifying that your application is complete.

Throughout the process, you must be sure to double-check every step that depends on other people's actions.

Not only do you need to worry about the final deadline to apply, you need to worry about a whole series of deadlines. You'll have deadlines to register for exams, deadlines for filing for financial aid, and deadlines to apply, at the very least. You'll need to program them all into whatever calendar system you use.

Oddly enough, if students are given four years to apply to graduate school, 50 percent of them will apply in the last ten days anyway. Whatever you do, strive to apply at least two weeks early! (If you are a premedical student, you need to know that most premed advisors are now trying to get all their students to complete their applications at the beginning of the summer between the junior and senior year, that is, months before any "deadlines.")

Deadline

1: a clearly marked line around prisoner-of-war camps at which an escaping prisoner would be shot to death, orig. US Civil War

2 a: a date or time after which a story cannot be accepted for publication or broadcast

2 b: the worst possible time to turn in your application to graduate school

There are two good reasons to turn in your materials early. First, it gives you more time to make a mistake. You can send another request for documents lost in the mail, motivate any slow-moving recommendation writers, and fix any disasters. It is always the student's responsibility to make sure that every document requested by the admissions committee is in their file before the deadline. This is reason enough to plan on submitting your application months ahead of schedule.

The second reason to apply early has to do with the other end of the admissions process and what happens to your application when it arrives. Almost all admissions officers use some form of three-tiered ranking system for applicants: (1) those students they definitely want to admit, (2) those they are not sure about, the "maybes," and (3) those they will reject. If the school uses a rolling admissions process, admissions staff read and evaluate applications as they arrive. Most of the hard work in admissions is done in the "maybe" pile. The closer you get to the deadline, the greater the number of candidates already selected for admission and the longer the internal wait list will be.

If the school uses a fixed-date system instead of rolling admissions, the essays may or may not be read all at one time. In any case, the earlier your application arrives, the greater its chances of being favorably reviewed by an alert, intelligent, compassionate admissions representative. The later it arrives, the more likely it is to receive a cursory examination by an overworked admissions representative who has already reviewed a large number of outstanding candidates.

I once asked the dean of an elite graduate school what she did with the applications that came in late. "Confidentially?" she asked. "Strictly background," I assured her. "We keep their fees," she replied.

All of this should be taken with a grain of salt, however. I have interviewed students who applied late, whose applications were incomplete, and so on, who were admitted to graduate programs. If you are applying to an obscure program that is not swamped with applicants, if you are an outstanding or unusual candidate, or if you have made several contacts with the program and they are expecting your application, then you need not worry overmuch about turning in your application several weeks ahead of the deadline. If you are applying to a highly competitive program, however, timing is simply too important a factor to ignore. For the most competitive programs in the nation, my recommendation is to apply more than a month early. If you are unsure of the best time to apply for the type of programs you have targeted, be sure to discuss it with your advisor.

• • •

Take time to really read online program information, faculty home pages, and the application forms. Then prepare your activity log and timeline. Start with your first-choice school. Reread the materials with a magnifying glass in one hand and fine-tooth comb in the other. Break down the application process into a series of smaller assignments, like the list that starts this chapter. Then, arrange these assignments in the order in which you plan to complete them. Put a target date next to each assignment, and check off each one when it is finished. Most students use calendar apps or spreadsheets to manage this process. See the next page for an example of how one student managed her deadlines in a spreadsheet.

After you have prepared a detailed activity log and timeline for your first-choice school, make activity logs and timelines for all the other schools you plan to apply to, but keep your first-choice schools first in mind. If you miss an interim deadline for your first-choice school because you were chasing down an obscure community college transcript for your last-choice school, you are not prioritizing your tasks wisely.

Most schools do not start an applicant file on you until you actually push "submit" on your application and pay your application fee. So anything that comes into the program earlier has a greater chance of being lost or misdirected. Be sure that transcripts, for example, get matched to your application if they arrive before you push "submit." If at all possible, try to submit e-versions of your transcripts. By the way, I checked with several graduate offices and they *can* look at your applications in progress, before you finalize them. They're probably too busy to do this very often, but don't put anything embarrassing or damaging anywhere on these forms, even as a note to yourself, before you settle on your final wording.

It is your responsibility to discover each graduate school's preferred procedures and to comply. It is also your job to make sure the application is, eventually, complete, that is, that all transcripts, letters of recommendation, or especially anything sent in the mail are properly logged in. These processes are overwhelmingly online now, and anything mailed has a high chance of not getting scanned and matched to your application account. For example, try to submit writing samples and transcripts through the application portal, if at all possible. Most schools' application portals have excellent "check-off" features so you can see that materials are properly posted. Schools will sometimes wait for a straggling letter or late-arriving test scores but, unfortunately, most will not begin to review your application until it is complete. If anything is late, the whole application is late.

I hate to add to your stress level, but I must warn you that I have interviewed several students who were assured by the online process software that their application had been completed, that there were no missing items, and then they were later rejected because something was in fact missing. The only way to guard against this is to check with each recommender, for example, to be sure they submitted the letter successfully, and to apply to a reasonable number of schools.

A word about fees: Application fees usually run from $45 to $150 per school, which can get expensive for your typical poverty-stricken undergraduate. *Do not scrimp on application fees.* Remember, whether you get in and whether you get any funding are determined by applying to a reasonable, strategically chosen number of schools. This is a very large financial decision you are making, ultimately worth hundreds of thousands of dollars to you. Do not make this decision based on an application fee of a few tens of dollars. Some schools

Warning

Approach your letter-of-recommendation writers at the earliest possible moment. Be sure to read the instructions on page 40 and in chapter 10, Letters of Recommendation.

Target List for Madison Allbrecht

Program	Mega U.	Northern U.	Wassamatta U.	Outback U.	Close to U.
size of department	23	4	16	8	6
# of faculty with my interest	3	1	?	2	1.5
ranking, if known	tops	very good	so so	very good, but mostly for bioinformatics	so so
PhD or master's	PhD	PhD	PhD	PhD	start w/ master's
deadline to apply	Jan 1	Dec 1	Feb 1	Feb 15	Mar 15
deadline for support	Nov 15	Dec 1	Jan 15	Feb 1	Mar 1
date application verified as complete					
waiver of app. fees	yes	never	yes	yes	yes
app fee	75	80	early only 45	45	90
fellowship or assistantship	all admitted students get first-year fellowship	minority fellowship teaching and research assistantships	"We select students for fellowship and assistantship funding in March or April. Not all admitted students receive these types of funding."	all admitted are funded one way or another	no
GRE requirements	yes, plus subject test	yes, but "not very important"	optional for students with 3.5+ subject test is also optional	yes, plus subject test subject test "recommended"	yes, but "there is no minimum score, we look at each candidate as a whole"
Are they nice to me?	not really	yes, very	so far	yes	yes
minimum or target GPA	no	3.0 minimum	website says "students with less than 3.5 are not usually successful, but are not discouraged from applying" whatever that means . . .	3.0	no
faculty connections	Dr. S. Smithers Dr. L. Joss Dr. R. Massey	Dr. J. Watkins have very encouraging letter from Dr. Watkins	need to find	Dr. W. Moss Dr. V. Martin Also, spoke with the chair of the dept. at national meeting in Chicago last year, Dr. Stossen	Dr. Wilson
admissions contacts, the "official" contact	Melissa Martel (202) 555-0117 mmadmin@mega.edu	admis@noru.edu no other contact provided	dir@adm.wassa.edu also: "each department directly"	Lynda Granger (412) 555-0191 apply@obu.edu	Grad office: Lawrence Millhouse A&S@closeto.edu Department: Maria Menendez mm@bio.closeto.edu (513) 555-0128 (she's very nice)
Notes	19% admit rate submitting a research sample is "recommended"	separate applications for research and teaching assistantships!	need to do further research re: mentors Dr. Wilson knows somebody at this school; email her soon re: this	need to read some abstracts of Dr. Martin to be sure of fit	admit is only to the master's program, can go directly on to their PhD if they like you NO FUNDING first two years
Accepted? Rejected? Wait listed?					
Deadline to respond?					

will waive fees if you apply early and submit a letter from your undergraduate financial aid officer (or in some cases, your advisor) explaining your financial need. Your financial aid officer is accustomed to writing these letters and knows exactly what to say. Letters from students, no matter the circumstances described, are usually ineffective. Some schools will not waive application fees under any circumstances. Finally, just to confuse the matter totally, some schools that claim they never waive fees have been known to do so when the student is an outstanding applicant and has made a personal and direct appeal to the right administrator. Most schools still accept checks by mail, and sometimes your aunt Chrissie wants to help out by paying your fees by check, but using a credit or debit card reduces the chances of error. When you get a waiver, the school will give you a code to use in place of a credit card on your application form, or they will provide other instructions for submitting your application. Be aware that asking for a waiver can add considerable time to the process, two weeks or more, and may require you to pester them for a response, so plan ahead.

Testing

Proper preparation for the graduate admissions exams requires extensive lead time. The summer before your senior year is a good time to take the exams, as is fall break. Students often pick one of the worst times—the end of the fall semester. Students don't mean to take the exams then; they just fail to take them sooner, and then that's what time it is.

Here are some of the more common exams.

Graduate Record Examination (GRE)
Main test and subject tests

Graduate Management Admission Test (GMAT)
For B schools; many B schools also accept the GRE

Law School Admission Test (LSAT)
Many law schools also accept the GRE

Medical College Admission Test (MCAT)
Some medical schools accept the GRE (however, this will cause them to look very closely at your grades in prerequisite science classes and labs)

Dental Admission Test (DAT)
Pro tip: Dental schools do not like it if you submit GRE or MCAT

Physician Assistant College Admission Test (PA-CAT)
Most PA programs also accept GRE or MCAT

Pharmacy College Admission Test (PCAT)

Applying to Medical School?

Washington University in St. Louis did a five-year study of medical school applicants and found that, all other factors being equal, applying early had a significant influence on whether an applicant was admitted.

Warning

Some poets want to believe that their math scores don't matter (and some English departments might agree with them), but in spite of the information on page 37 from *GRE: Guide to the Use of Scores*, the graduate schools often have minimum scores that students must exceed before their folios can be forwarded to the department for final consideration. No one can afford to totally bomb any part of the GRE. If you want to avoid mathematical testing, see if your graduate school will accept the MAT in place of the GRE. Some will.

Optometry Admission Test (OAT)
Most optometry programs also accept GRE or MCAT

Veterinary Schools accept GRE or MCAT

Miller Analogies Test (MAT)
Used by nursing programs and some education programs

Test of English as a Foreign Language (TOEFL)

Most academic graduate programs expect you to take the GRE, or Graduate Record Exam. This test has three sections: verbal, analytical writing, and quantitative. This test is very much like the tests you took to get into college, but how long has it been, really, since you saw a question like this: "Six young people are standing on the edge of a river. They have two large sea kayaks, one of which is freshly painted a bright blue. They have no life vests, and two can't swim. It is four o'clock in the afternoon, and the sun is 15 degrees above the horizon, obscured by clouds. Where are these people, what are they doing, and which one is pregnant?" Think you need some practice? Yes, you do. Good news: the math on the GRE is high school math, but how long has it been since you reviewed that? Even STEM majors may have forgotten some geometry or how to manipulate fractions. A good solid review is in order. (The GRE actually specifies the topical areas covered in the exam; you can see for yourself if you think you are up-to-date, gre.org.) One of my correspondents who coaches students on testing has identified that today's students do not know their multiplication tables, thus making it difficult for them to do quick estimates in their head. If you have been using calculators your whole life, and you do not know in your head what 4 × 7 is or 8 × 9, then practicing your multiplication tables can improve your quantitative reasoning score.

Warning

There is a rumor floating around university campuses that you can take the GRE and see if you like the score before accepting the test as official. This is absolutely false. Once you push the button to compute the final score, your record is *automatically and immediately official*. That score is tied to your Social Security number and stays on record for five years. Never take an official test for practice.

Much has been made of abandoning the GRE. Many schools have tried out making it optional and they discovered that they could still identify and recruit good students. If programs make it optional for you to tell them your test scores, then you can report them if they are high and withhold them if they are not. Some programs forbid you to reveal test scores even if you know them. I do have a warning for students, however: many of the programs that stopped using the scores invisibly increased their requirements for other pieces of your application to make sure that you possess the skills the test is designed to measure. So you need to have even more evidence that your quant skills are strong, your academic writing is up to par, and your research skills are robust. Undergraduate research projects, particularly impressive write-ups of labs, other writing samples, particularly strong and detailed letters of recommendation, and such demonstrations of potential as presentations at academic meetings and undergraduate publications are more important than ever.

These are called "shadow requirements" and, unfortunately, we may have traded one dimension of bias—the GRE and the way the GRE is sometimes used—for another, elevating the types of undergraduate experiences that elite institutions provide to their students. I generally tell students this: Standardized exams are a rite of passage. Prepare properly for them. Take them. Integrate that experience into your overall strategy, even if it means never telling anyone at all what your score was. Meanwhile, think deeply about what evidence you can present that will prove quant skills (high marks in math and quantitative classes, experience designing and conducting quantitative research), and academic verbal skills (strong writing samples, articles submitted for publication, presentations, table posters, high marks in English comp or specialized courses like "scientific writing" or "business writing").

Top students sometimes make the mistake of going in to take these tests cold, without any preparation at all. Let there be no doubt: You should study for any graduate admissions test; studying *will* result in a better score. Take a test preparation class or buy test preparation booklets. Study in those areas in which you have forgotten basic material. Brush up on your math. Play logic games. Specific questions will vary, but the types of questions and the material covered stay the same year to year. Remember, these tests cover a set of basic knowledge and concepts, so you need not worry about truly in-depth or obscure knowledge (although the GRE subject tests can be exhaustive, their focus is on sophomore-level survey course content). Be sure to take as many practice tests as you can get your hands on. Most study books and prep apps have at least one full-length sample test. GRE gives free access to five sample full-length practice tests on their website, gre.org.

If you need accommodations it will take (a) time, (b) an official diagnosis, and (c) confirmation by your disabilities services office or medical professional. By the way, if you are interested in taking the GRE on paper, you can. You have to coordinate with GRE, and it can take some time to set up. Paper tests are administered only three times per year, and GRE is thinking about reducing even that availability.

For descriptions of the other tests, see their official websites. Almost all provide free study guides. There are also study prep companies that offer classes in all manner of formats (live, online, synchronous, asynchronous), study guides and websites, and individual tutors.

Studying a couple of hours a day for thirty days before the test is more than sufficient. The study preparation courses are expensive, but they are (usually) effective. Some regional test preparation companies are significantly less expensive. Search for "cheap test prep" or similar to discover options.

Here are some interesting observations from *GRE: Guide to the Use of Scores,* a publication available from the Graduate Record Examinations Board of the Educational Testing Service (published at www.ets.org/gre):

> **GRE scores should not be used in isolation. Use of multiple criteria is particularly important when using GRE scores to assess the abilities of educationally disadvantaged students, students whose primary language is not English, and students who are returning to school after an extended absence. . . .**
>
> **GRE scores, like those on similar standardized tests, cannot completely represent the potential of any person, nor can they alone reflect an individual's chances of long-term success in an academic environment. . . .**
>
> **Special care is required in interpreting the GRE scores of students who may have had an educational and cultural experience somewhat different from that of the traditional majority. . . .**
>
> **A cutoff score below which every applicant is categorically rejected without consideration of any other information should not be used. . . .**
>
> **A low score may be the result of a lack of exposure to an area rather than a lack of mastery.**

You may wish to review this booklet yourself, and perhaps even quote some of these observations in your essay.

Again, you must read the application requirements carefully, and read the test manuals carefully as well. Do not rely on the advice of others. Talented faculty, deans, and even the test preparation companies have, occasionally, gotten basic facts wrong about the tests. The test protocols and even test offerings change surprisingly often, as do schools' published requirements. *It is your job to read the official bulletins!*

Long-term preparation to be an outstanding candidate

As you may have realized by now, time is one of the most important factors in your application process. Some of the best techniques require extensive lead time. For example, it is much easier to get into a summer program at a top-tier school than it is to get admitted to a regular degree program at the same school. Some medical and dental schools even offer auxiliary summer premedical classes open to undergraduates. You must plan to attend such a program as much as a full year before you intend to apply to a graduate program, but the advantages are immense. If you study hard and make high grades, you will have demonstrated that you can perform at the level the school demands. Besides, the experience looks great on your transcript wherever you go.

If you get into *any* summer program at a highly selective institution, you can walk over to the department you are interested in for graduate studies and make friends. This should not be difficult. Just walk over and say, "Hi, I'm Andrea Tipton and I'm interested in graduate studies in cultural anthropology. Could we discuss your program?" Be friendly. This edge, and the names you can weave into your essay later, can cinch your admittance. I met one American student who got admitted to Oxford by taking a summer enrichment program and impressing the professor. I'll let you in on a little-known secret: At some of the most elite universities on the continent, there are no admissions requirements for summer school. If your credit card is good, you are in.

Similarly, you can take internships or gain employment in your field of interest. This demonstrates commitment to your career goal and reassures admissions counselors that your interest is not a passing fancy. If you intend to study law or medicine, it is a real plus to show that you know what the daily life of an attorney or a physician is really like. Applications for summer internships are typically accepted the winter before, and by March most programs will be full. You can obtain a summer job later, but it is a good idea to start making contacts months before summer break.

Here are some specific tips to up your chances with law, medical, or business schools. Anyone planning to attend law school should read *Double Billing: A Young Lawyer's Tale of Greed, Sex, Lies, and the Pursuit of a Swivel Chair* by Cameron Stracher; *Full Disclosure: Do You* Really *Want to Be a Lawyer?* compiled by Susan J. Bell for the Young Lawyers Division of the American Bar Association; and *Running from the Law: Why Good Lawyers Are Getting Out of the Legal Profession* by Deborah L. Arron. Extra points for reading the novel *The Paper Chase,* which was likely published long before you were born. What law schools love to see: exposure to real lawyers doing real lawyering in place of idealistic fantasies about the law (or, even worse, anything you might have picked up from watching glamorous and powerful lawyers on television and in the movies). For example, litigators are only in court about 5 percent of the time.

Did you know that? Well, every single attorney in North America does know that. Attorneys spend very little time doing what most people imagine they do. To be fair, law school admissions officers tell me they do not care whether you have exposure to lawyers and law. But I think you really should. There are too many unhappy lawyers, and you want to be sure you will be one of the happy ones.

Anyone planning to attend medical school should read books like *The Intern Blues* by Robert Marion, *The Emperor of All Maladies* by Siddhartha Mukherjee, *Mountains Beyond Mountains* by Tracy Kidder, *Black Man in a White Coat* by Damon Tweedy, *Rough Sleepers* by Tracy Kidder, and an old favorite, *Kill as Few Patients as Possible* by Oscar London. What medical schools love to see: exposure to medical procedures, especially those involving bodily fluids, rather than the more common "feel-good" internships in nonclinical medical settings. Extra points for blood, fewer points for reading to kids with cancer. A solid 3.5 GPA student with extensive exposure to medical procedures is more desirable than a 4.0 student who has never been outside the confines of a chemistry lab and has little evidence of people skills. Work closely with your institution's premedical advisors; they know how this works and can offer sound advice. And there is a robust online community organized around premed and medical school application issues, with more essay tips and the latest advice and information on interview questions, how to deal with a bad grade, and so on.

What business schools love to see: two to four years of experience with a large organization or a famous and successful startup *with rapid advancement* and a high salary for your age. More experience than that is not really necessary. If you have several significant internships, high grades, proven drive and ambition, and a clear vision of what you want to do after you graduate, you shouldn't hesitate to apply right out of college. Be sure to read these MBA guides: *Case in Point, The Wharton MBA Case Interview Study Guide*, vols. I and II, *Ace Your Case!*, and *15 Questions: More Practice to Help Ace Your Consulting Case.*

Volunteer to gain related experience. Volunteering in public service areas demonstrates social commitment, in addition to whatever skills and maturity you may gain from the experience itself. Volunteering is also a way of creating your own business internships. Students have volunteered at such venues as television stations and architectural studios to gain experience and explore their interest in a particular field of graduate study.

If you are applying to competitive programs, your activities and honors can sometimes be a deciding factor between admission and rejection. However, students tend to overestimate the value of activities. As a rough guess, activities are worth one-quarter of a grade point; maybe a half point in truly extraordinary cases. It is better to devote yourself to your studies than to explain your weak grade-point average with a fistful of activities. In general, quality counts over quantity. It is preferable to be an officer of one organization than a member of five or six.

Warning

Do not ever make up even the smallest item on your application. It is patently immoral, and ultimately it may ruin your life. Schools routinely request supporting material whenever they get an application that seems unlikely, and they all subscribe to the same Listserv to alert one another to fraudulent applicants. News item:

> **A federal judge in Hartford, Conn., threw out the defamation lawsuit against Princeton University filed by disgruntled, would-be medical student Rommel Nobay, who claimed that Princeton's having bad-mouthed him for lying on his application discouraged other schools from accepting him. Nobay admitted to fudging his class standing, SAT score, and other things that applicants sometimes exaggerate; however, attracting more attention were his personal statements, in which Nobay wrote that a family of lepers in Kenya had so much faith in him that they had donated "half their beggings" to help him with his education. (News of the Weird)**

Getting Fantastic Letters of Recommendation

You shouldn't just suddenly appear in a professor's doorway and ask for a letter of recommendation. Instead, visit your professors often during your undergraduate years. Show them your list of targeted schools, and discuss your motivations. Usually, the professors will bring up the question of letters of recommendation themselves.

Take these materials to the meeting:

+ your printed transcript (which is available online) or a list of your most important classes with grades for each class
+ a paper or a lab showing some of your best work
+ a resume or a CV, especially if the professor doesn't know about some of your work or internship experiences
+ a list of your activities
+ copies of all correspondence you have had with targeted graduate programs
+ a copy of the latest draft of your statement of purpose
+ a list of the other professors you plan to ask for letters
+ suggested "talking points," especially if this professor is not in your primary discipline (for example, ask your theater professor to comment on whether your acting ability would be useful to you in teaching an introductory biology class for undergraduates, or ask your advisor to comment on your independent study project, or your tutoring of other students, or your service as a test proctor for a class or lab)

Help professors think of beneficial things to say about you, but remember: The professor will write about whatever they want. You can only offer suggestions.

Also see the handouts on pages 234 and 236.

1. Ask this question: "Dr. Johnson, would you be comfortable making a strong recommendation for me for graduate study in ______________?" If the answer is less than enthusiastic, consider your other options.
2. Ask this question: "Dr. Johnson, what will you be able to say about me?" This is a tough question to ask, but when do you want to find out? Before or after your first-choice graduate school does?
3. Always stress the date when you're going to apply, as in "Dr. Lee, I'll be applying to all my schools by November 5. Will you be able to have the letters ready by then?" Never talk about the deadline; talk about *your* deadline. Avoid needing a letter just before or after the end of the term. Allow a professor two to six weeks to write your letter. Otherwise, it may start out like this: "Paul, from what I can remember, was usually prompt, and had good handwriting . . ." This is even worse if your name is not Paul.
4. Check in with your professor every once in a while to see if the letter is done. Be nice about it, but don't fall off the radar. This is explicated more fully in chapter 10, Letters of Recommendation.
5. Be sure to give each professor a warm and sincere thank-you card once the letter has been submitted on your behalf.

Graduate admissions professionals consistently mention the following three activities as persuasive to them:

+ serving as a research assistant on original research while you're still an undergraduate, especially working in a laboratory where original research is underway;
+ serving as an instructional assistant to a professor, which can mean serving as a test proctor, grader, teaching lab assistant, tutor, or similar; and
+ serving as a residence hall advisor.

The most impressive academic activity, according to graduate admissions professionals, is any kind of extended, independent research project. However, even the relatively mundane task of verifying citations in student bibliographies qualifies as a highly regarded activity. Professors pick students for these jobs who are reliable, extremely thorough, and mature; these are qualities that graduate programs value highly. Deans usually pick residence hall advisors; these students go through formal training, and their behavior goes under a microscope for at least a year, so they are also regarded as mature and reliable. I know of one department chair who admitted a student to graduate school because he had been a house sitter for his undergraduate advisor, and the advisor had mentioned it in his letter of recommendation. "That's trust," said the chair.

Student government is also highly regarded. I know of one medical school applicant who got in a year early, before completing his premed program—and *before he even applied*—because of an odd confluence of events. To begin with, he had been a management consultant before returning to school to complete his undergraduate degree in a premed program. He got elected to student government, and at the same time started volunteering eight hours a week at the local hospital emergency room. The university had just launched a strategic planning phase involving considerable financial planning and, because the applicant was the only member of student government with heavy-duty financial skills, he was appointed to serve as the student member of the board of trustees. He did a great job, which also involved occasionally working with top officers of the university's medical school. He then heard about something called a "dean's admit," whereby, in very rare cases, the dean of the medical school could admit students directly. Since he knew the dean from his work as a trustee, it was easy to ask him for a dean's admit. The dean reviewed his background and admitted him, subject to a good MCAT. The applicant aced the MCAT and went to medical school a year early *without ever having applied and with no undergraduate degree.* This is, admittedly, an unusual and very talented student—but the point is that instead of trudging through his premed curriculum, he chose to get involved. It paid off handsomely.

Completely off-campus, nonacademic endeavors also count, sometimes more than the routine college-sponsored activities. For example, if you are a nationally ranked horseback rider in dressage, your commitment to excellence in this outside arena will be highly regarded by admissions readers. Any enduring outside passion is usually seen as positive, unless you reveal that you are unsure whether to become a professional soccer player or go on to medical school. If you are confused about your true priorities, your avocation or pastime could threaten your future vocation.

True commitment over a length of time to any charitable organization will make a favorable impression on reviewers. Do not overlook opportunities to make unusual contributions; students have performed as puppeteers and clowns at daycare centers and volunteered for whole summers at wildlife rehabilitation facilities located in the middle of nowhere. Less obvious activities will garner more attention than obvious and common ones.

Having your own work published is a recognized sign of intellectual and academic promise, and is somewhat easier than most undergraduates think. (It's impossible, of course, if you never prepare and submit an article for publication.) If you are working closely with a professor on research work that will be submitted for publication, you should brazenly ask to be included as a coauthor. The worst that can happen is that the answer will be no. On the other hand, if it's yes, the result *could* be even worse: a massive increase in your responsibilities on the project. This is often the price of one's early publications.

Most major universities and many smaller institutions have some sort of undergraduate research journal, in which student research is published in the standardized style for that field. The main purpose of these journals is not so much to disseminate the fascinating research of undergraduates as it is to teach students the publication formats and practices that will be required for success later in their academic careers. If there is no journal appropriate for your submission, start your own. Do a good job of it, because it is very likely the admissions committee will ask to see it.

Do not neglect the many undergraduate research programs and meetings throughout the country. These are outstanding opportunities for you to present your research as table topics or in brief presentations to a usually friendly audience. These experiences go in your application, too. An example of a table presentation submitted as part of an application to graduate school begins on page 181.

Stress your memberships in academic societies, but don't oversell social sororities and fraternities. If you are an officer or a committee chair, then stress these leadership roles. (If you are chair of the social committee of a fraternity, don't even mention it. That is tantamount to bragging that you are an expert—and an evangelist to others—in the fine art of drinking beer.)

Many students start their own activities, demonstrating initiative as well as organizational and interpersonal skills. It's never too late to found Students for the Elimination of Xeronisus. There are dozens of organizations waiting for your participation, so help them out while strengthening your own candidacy.

Although the example shown in the sidebar on page 39 is extreme, there are routine notices on the Listserv about falsified credentials and inflated claims, such as this one:

> **Alert: We have received an application from a student from ________ by the name of ___________. The certified translation of his transcript does not match the original transcripts provided by ___________. The English-speaking reference for his class ranking has been discovered to be his wife. The letter of recommendation from his professor has been verified by that professor as forged. If you need additional information, please call ___________ at __________.**

This message recently went out to every graduate admissions professional in North America. Don't be the subject of a notice like this!

The three most immediate ways to stand out

It's nice to develop yourself as a candidate from the time you are a junior in college, but suppose you are a senior or a graduate, and you've got to apply now. What are the best ways to stand out in the application process?

+ Write to the professors.
+ Visit the graduate program.
+ Submit an outstanding work sample.

You can write to the professors and currently enrolled students using the techniques recommended on pages 24 and 25. This approach is recommended more for academic and research programs than for business, law, or medical schools. Remember, the first goal is to establish whether this program is a good match for your interests, level of academic preparation, and work ethic. It is only a secondary benefit that this makes you stand out from the overwhelming majority of applicants who will not have established direct bonds with the program. (A very few schools—mostly doctoral programs—actually request that you name a faculty sponsor as part of your application process.)

You should visit your top-choice schools if you can. Although compulsory interviews have all but disappeared, almost all schools welcome visits from prospective students. A personal interview makes a deep impression on faculty and admissions counselors, much deeper than an essay and a file full of electronic data. However, a personal visit is a risky endeavor, as you may reveal more about yourself than you intend. A successful visit requires planning and due consideration of protocol.

First of all, it helps to look the part—that is, to look like somebody who belongs at the graduate school you are visiting. In some departments, students and professors will be wearing shorts and Birkenstocks, while at others, they'll look like they understand the phrase "sophisticated casual." (One grad student told me he wore a Hawaiian shirt to every interview, to stand out in interviewers' minds and to let them know he had a sense of humor. It must have worked; he got a very good assignment in a world-class lab.) My recommendation is to look clean, healthy, and comfortable, without pretending to be someone you're not. Jewelry should be kept to a minimum; avoid scents entirely; new clothes look better than old clothes. Try not to look fabulously wealthy or magazine glamorous.

Never, never, never just "show up" on campus and expect to be shown around. Call the departmental office or the admissions office well in advance of your visit, tell them you are very interested in their program and that you would like to visit, and respectfully ask if someone could meet with you while you are on campus. Always broaden your objectives beyond the main office. For example, make your appeal to a specific professor, or ask to meet with a currently enrolled graduate student whose work you've admired, or inquire about a tour of their famous electron microscopy laboratory, or some other special feature of the campus or program. In general, expect to book your own appointments with professors. Remember Asher's Law: Thou shalt not call, nor write, nor visit any professor without having read some of their works first.

A few days before your visit, email to confirm every appointment. This little act of courtesy is one of the most overlooked, and most appreciated, of polite gestures. It demonstrates consideration and maturity, and also helps ensure that you do not wait outside somebody's office for hours to no avail.

Before you visit, you should prepare yourself to be articulate about your choice of graduate studies and about your interest in the particular school you are visiting. You should also be ready to ask

ASHER'S LAW

THOU SHALT NOT CALL, NOR WRITE, NOR VISIT ANY PROFESSOR WITHOUT HAVING READ SOME OF THEIR WORKS FIRST.

intelligent questions about their program, facilities, faculty, research, and so on. (See the questions on the next page.) If you cannot do this, you should forgo the visit entirely. If you act like you are interested in a good fit between your needs and interests and what the program offers, you will make a more favorable impression than if you seem like a supplicant begging for any spot on next year's roster. Some applicants even ask admissions counselors or currently enrolled students to rank and discuss the *other* programs the applicant is considering, but I am not convinced that this is such a great idea. No one is going to enjoy saying, "Yes, their program is better than ours."

These are the types of questions you can expect:

+ So, have you read any good books lately?
+ Which theorists or thought leaders do you admire in our field?
+ Who have been your main influences as you have advanced in your understanding of the discipline?
+ What can you tell me that's not in your formal application materials?
+ So, why do you want to be a ___________________?
+ What do you know about our research topic and methodologies?
+ Can you tell me about your undergraduate advisor?
+ I see here it says you speak Portuguese. Que fantástico, eu também falo português, onde você aprendeu? No Brasil, em Portugal, ou você teve aula de português? Eu acho o português um idioma tão bonita, você não acha?
+ What do you do with your leisure time?
+ Could you describe how you study? What is your routine?
+ Could you tell me about a major failure in your life and how you dealt with it?
+ What are your career plans and how does our particular program fit in with them?
+ What other programs are you applying to now?
+ What will you do if you don't get in?
+ Why should we admit you over the many other fine and highly qualified candidates we have this year?
+ What makes you different?

The best advice is to be well prepared, and then just be yourself. Remember your interviewer's name, sit up straight and lean slightly forward in your chair, and pay attention. Do not be afraid to say those three magic words, "I don't know."

Ideally, you should show up a day or at least several hours early and walk through the campus to find the office and get a feel for the atmosphere. (Of course you will resist the temptation to "just pop in for a moment" prior to your scheduled appointment.) Show up for all scheduled meetings exactly four minutes early. Have a tablet with you in case you need to take notes, but don't let your notetaking interfere with natural conversation.

If you are a little different, in any way, interviewing can give you the edge you need. I know of an outstanding candidate who came from a small college in a rural area. He applied to top programs

Questions to ask any graduate program

WARNING: Do not ask any question you could have easily found the answer to yourself.

1. What would you consider to be the program's strengths?
2. What is the largest and the most typical class size for a graduate class? Are classes restricted to graduate students? To majors?
3. What would be the advantages and disadvantages to going to grad school immediately after completing an undergraduate degree? The advantages and disadvantages of waiting a few years? The best use of the interim time?
4. What are the criteria and process for selecting TAs, RAs, and fellows?
5. Will I get to develop my own topics, or will I be expected to work on a professor's ongoing research?
6. What facilities are available for graduate students? Are there any restrictions on access?
7. What are the key conferences and journals for this area of the discipline?
8. Which scholars and programs do *you* follow?
9. What is the mean time to complete (a) classwork, (b) research, (c) thesis or dissertation? (That is, what is the mean time to complete the master's or PhD?) Ask about the program as a whole, but perhaps more importantly, by professor.
10. What is your attrition rate? Of those who don't finish, what are their reasons?
11. What kind of student thrives in your program?
12. How reliable is your financial support year to year? Is the first-year offer always sustained, given attainment of academic goals?
13. What can you tell me about the age range, gender balance, ratio of married/single, race, LGBTQIA identity, and geographical origins of graduate students in the program?
14. Can you tell me who is launching new projects? Which professors have won awards and grants lately? (These presumably need graduate assistants.)
15. Can you tell me about your placement rates and types of jobs obtained by recent graduates? (Avoid relying on testimonials and anecdotal evidence.)
16. May I meet some currently enrolled students? (In person, or later via phone or email, be sure to ask about their research topics and be sure to take notes on specific professors mentioned.)
17. How can I be a strong candidate for a program like this?

all over the country. He took note of the fact that he was admitted at every program he visited and rejected by every program where he did not. I know of another candidate who wanted a coveted slot in a museum studies program, but had a spotty background. She called the departmental office but was told that she did not "meet the profile" of a successful candidate. She was interested in a particular curator who was a professor in the program and called him at his museum. He agreed to meet with her "briefly" as a courtesy, so she buried herself in the library to read up on his specialty before the visit. They had a three-hour meeting, leading to an offer from him to serve as her mentor. "I may not be able to get in," she said. "Oh, I can get you in," he said, and he certainly did. If you admire a particular professor, go meet with them.

Another way to stand out at the application phase is to submit a work sample. Some programs ask for them, but most don't. There are two rules for submitting a work sample:

1. It should be very directly related to the graduate topic.
2. It must be very good.

The best work sample to submit is a graded thesis, paper, or lab on the same subject you want to work on in graduate school, on which a professor has written, "A+. Julie, you're a genius. I never fully realized it until I read this. If you don't become a research scientist, it will be a loss for all humankind." Obviously, submitting your award-winning poetry would be the kiss of death in applying to a Lit Crit program, but some academic faux pas are so subtle that an undergraduate may miss them. Words can fall out of favor, sometimes very quickly, like "subculture" and "minority." In general, avoid submitting any work sample without running it past a faculty advisor.

Warning

If you choose to submit a video or film, it had better be very good right away. Any visual media should be submitted in universal and easily accessible formats, such as uploading PDFs or JPEGs, or providing a link to YouTube or to your own website. Follow instructions. Some art and architecture programs require submission of a portfolio; read the application carefully and submit your work in the format specified, even if it seems old-fashioned.

Some students take the time to further improve a class project before submitting it as part of their graduate application. Ask an advisor, "Is this paper good enough to submit as a work sample, or can you make some specific recommendations for improvement?" It's certainly within the bounds of propriety to submit published articles that relate directly to the program of interest.

Again, let quality take precedence over quantity. Admissions counselors have only so much time to devote to each application, so a smart applicant will, for instance, send in their *best* article and list the others on a bibliography. I know of one applicant for a theater MFA program who enclosed a copy of a play he had written. The head of the department picked up the play for a quick look and ended up reading it straight through in one sitting. He was so excited about this applicant that he called the candidate and basically admitted him over the phone. Now *that's* a good work sample.

In this same vein, an applicant to architectural school might submit a rendering, applicants to film school might submit a short, and so on. All students should consider submitting some sort of projects summary or research summary, such as the one described on page 71, Sample Undergraduate Research Projects. Note also the table topic work sample beginning on page 181. Also, do not substitute any unusual item for something officially requested. Follow the directions. If the admissions packet calls for a 2½-inch by 2½-inch color photo, then provide one; a self-portrait in pastels would be an egregious error. Some admissions people are amused by such shenanigans, but far more are annoyed by them.

4

What Happens to Your Application

Online application portals and applicant tracking systems usually work well. On most of these systems, you start by opening an account, for free. All they require is an email address. Then you have as much time as you want to draft and redraft your essays, upload information onto the forms, and peruse the workings of the site.

Once you hit "submit," however, you can't change another thing. It's game over, and the waiting begins.

Before we get to what happens on the other side of this process, let's really understand what you are supposed to be submitting, and how. First of all, try to submit everything through the portal. Avoid snail mail. If you have some big, amazing writing sample, scan it yourself and submit it online; do not mail it and hope that someone will scan it and match it up with your application. Admissions teams, be they faculty, admissions professionals, admins, or graduate students, are always understaffed and overworked.

Essays are submitted online either as an attachment or by filling in a window, and some programs allow either method. Forms are filled in online, from name to activities and honors and awards; that's a lot of typing and it has to be done perfectly. Resumes and CVs and writing samples can be submitted either as an attachment or by copying them into a window. A lot of questions in the application will request a narrative response, so you will be typing in paragraphs responding to these. Be sure to follow the instructions for each application, as there is no standardization in the design of application portals.

A major risk factor for applicants are the two things that others submit on their behalf: letters of recommendation, and transcripts. As Sartre said, "Hell is other people." You can control much of the application process, but you have to rely on others to get your transcripts and letters of recommendation to their destination.

Letters of recommendation are submitted online, which is good for reducing error, but has had the ironic consequence of increasing the workload for letter writers. Once upon a time faculty could just scribble "see attached letter of recommendation" on forms, and use a "To whom it may concern" salutation and *Bam!* A little work at the copier, an original signature on each, and the process was done. The online systems actually create more work per letter on the part of faculty, and a higher expectation of customization. (Be sure to read chapter 10, Letters of Recommendation, as soon as possible, certainly long before you approach your recommenders.)

The only part of the process that might involve paper is your official transcript. If your alma mater has an option to send your transcripts online, always take that option. There are some colleges and universities that still insist on mailing paper transcripts. These are sent to each school and then have to be matched to your application. That means there is a sender, there is a carrier, and there is a receiver. That is a lot of opportunity for failure. For reasons that are incomprehensible, universities often have just one person who sends transcripts (electronic or paper). If that person is sick, goes on vacation, is incompetent, or smokes too much pot on their lunch break, your entire future is at risk. The good news is that application portals have notification "check-off" boxes that will show when transcripts or letters of recommendation are posted. However, if you are sending transcripts from several schools, it is not always possible to know *which* transcripts have been posted.

Sometimes you have no choice but to call a program to verify that specific documents have been received and matched to your application. Phone calls about missing material are the most hated communication in any admissions office. This is one more reason to apply two to three or more weeks early. Asking someone to check something like this two weeks before the deadline is not as rude as calling right before the deadline. Plus, you might actually have time to resolve an issue if you discover a problem.

Here are some things to watch out for: If you are submitting an essay by filling in a window, my advice is to draft it in another program and then copy and paste only your final draft onto the forms. Although it is unlikely that an admissions person would have the time or inclination to observe your drafts, I have discovered that in most of these programs, they can if they decide to do so.

Second, some of these programs have character- or word-count features. If you write overlong, the bottom part of your essay may simply disappear. Verify that the entire essay is readable in the submission window.

Also, not all of these programs are fully compatible with even the most common word-processing apps. So if you copy and paste into a window, watch for apostrophes, quote marks, dashes, or scientific notations that become something very different when transferred into application windows. If you have diagrams, pictures, graphs, scientific nomenclature, or formulae, uploading a PDF version is safer, if that is an option.

What if you want to submit writing samples or research papers or copies of publications? If there are instructions on how to submit this material, then follow them, but sometimes there is simply no clear way to submit extra material, requested or not. As mentioned elsewhere, your awesome work sample can be a clincher for admission, so this really matters. If you can, scan it and send it in as an attachment. Pro tip: If an article or writing sample would be of particular interest to a specific faculty member, send it to her directly, as well. "I was not sure that you would see this additional material I submitted as part of my application, so I am forwarding it to you." Only do this if you are sure it would be "of particular interest."

If you really cannot identify another submission method, send it to anyone identified as the "admissions coordinator" and ask them to put it in your file. Do not assume that the admissions coordinator will actually log this into your application file, however. Maybe they will, maybe they won't.

Warning

Just because a school says your materials are complete doesn't mean that they really are. I interviewed a student who was told by two different schools that her materials were complete, but a professor had failed to submit a letter of recommendation. In both cases, she was denied admission.

Incidentally, if you are seeking a waiver of an application fee, you will need to know how that works online, which varies from school to school, and almost always adds some layers of communication and delays in time. Some offer a code to use in place of a credit card, and others have obtuse instructions that may or may not work. When in doubt, call them and ask. A shockingly high percentage of inquiries about waivers for application fees are simply ignored.

Then what happens?

Once you submit your application, what happens to it? Maybe nothing at all. If your application is not complete, most programs will not distribute it to reviewers. If you are missing a letter of recommendation or a transcript, or you left a required field blank, or, heaven forbid, your credit card was denied, you will fall into limbo. It is critical that you check the online check-off system to see if all your expected materials have been received and logged. Many programs will notify you via email, once your file is complete.

Most programs are totally paperless on the admissions side. Any physical items you send them (such as transcripts) will be scanned. A few organizations still print out everything you submit and create paper applicant files, just like in the old days, but that is rare. Paperless is definitely superior, because reviewers can access your documents from anywhere, anytime. This creates both a problem and an opportunity: If you do submit additional materials of any kind, such as a paper, an article, a lab write-up, or a research project, they may be invisible to remote viewers. *They may not realize these items are in your file.*

My recommendation is to alert key decision makers, when you can, that you have submitted something extra, whatever it is. This is not always possible.

Where the decision is made

A graduate program may expect you to meet several different sets of criteria. The regents of a major university may set general guidelines for graduate admissions. The specific graduate school—as a hypothetical example, the Graduate School of the College of Arts and Sciences—may develop another set of criteria. Finally, a department may set its own standards. When you apply, you are really applying to different constituencies, at least to the graduate school and the department. These are distinctly separate entities.

There are two models for making admissions decisions: a strong graduate school with a weak department, or a weak graduate school with a strong department. Under the weak graduate school model, the graduate school office serves a more administrative function: processing application files, making sure everything is in order, and forwarding applicant folios to the departments. The departments are in charge; the decision is made in the departments. Harvard is a classic institution with strong departments.

Under the other model, the graduate school is strong, and may set standards that are higher than, or just different from, what some departments may want. Large state universities tend to have stronger graduate schools than departments.

In professional schools such as those for business, law, and medicine, the authority is usually held entirely by the admissions staff, which almost always includes a good percentage of faculty. Faculty, and even currently enrolled students, will rotate through admissions assignments lasting a season or two.

To further complicate the matter, most programs reserve a small percentage of their admissions for people with special circumstances, who meet some but not all of their admissions requirements.

If you are trying to imagine what's going on with your application, keep these structures in mind.

Admit dances and wait lists

When all your materials are in place, hit that submit button. As mentioned, most programs now have online check-off systems, allowing you to monitor when each requested item goes into your portfolio. You can see for yourself what has arrived and what is still missing. Some programs will send you an email alerting you to missing materials, or confirming your complete application. At times, however, a professor may swear they uploaded a letter, and the portal says they did not. A school may report that your transcripts were submitted electronically last week, but the portal shows that no transcripts are matched to your application. If you do not receive confirmation, you must call the program and resolve discrepancies, and verify whether your application is complete.

Be very nice to the person who answers the phone. Get to know this person, as you may be calling them again. Say, "May I have your name, please?" Write it down on your activity log for that program. While you have this person on the line, ask when you should expect to hear about the admission decision. Be prepared to be interrupted and to be put on hold for long stretches of time. (See the story on page 28 of a student who was admitted while he waited patiently on hold.) Be considerate, be compassionate, and be sure not to alienate this communications resource. Many applicants underestimate the power wielded by academic admins. They are usually highly intelligent individuals who could make a lot more money working somewhere else. You may never actually succeed in speaking with the department head or the admissions director, but these people do every day. They can be your allies or your enemies in the admissions process; the choice is yours. (Incidentally, in smaller programs a departmental administrator often does the initial screening of graduate applications.)

Larger programs hate it when students call repeatedly without waiting for the process to work itself out. Call only when something seems amiss. Smaller programs are generally more receptive

Warning

Avoid sending anything gratuitous or weird. Many years ago an applicant gave a ship in a bottle to the Stanford Graduate School of Business. It was a very good ship, but it was not directly related to graduate business education. More recently a student applying to law school included with her application some kind of giant cookie that she had baked in a pizza oven. Her note said, "Please take a break to enjoy this cookie when you review my application." Another student used his AMCAS essay to write a country-and-western song he had composed about his desire to be a doctor. A law school once received an extra letter of recommendation for one applicant: a crayon drawing from the applicant's baby sister, stating "Please admit my big sister." All of these applicants were rejected.

to calls, but any time you become a pest it will sink your candidacy. Some programs with rolling admission will notify you within a few weeks. Some programs announce all admissions and rejections for the year on a single day, leaving you to bite your nails and wait along with everybody else. Most try to complete the process well before the official decision date of April 15.

Why are 4.0s rejected?

Students with a 4.0 GPA are routinely rejected by graduate programs. Grad programs value fit and match more than just capacity to perform. If a school can tell that they are a safety school, they will assume that the 4.0 will not attend even if admitted, so they will preemptively reject them. Some 4.0s are rejected because they are arrogant. This comes out in their essays or interviews. Some 4.0s do not customize their essays, and think that copying and pasting will get them into grad school. That is a red flag, especially for doctoral programs. Some 4.0s are feared to be unable to emotionally cope with the inevitable challenges of graduate study. To combat this last fear, write about some struggle revealing persistence and resilience, or say that you "accidentally" got a 4.0, but it was never a goal or requirement for you.

• • •

According to a resolution of the Council of Graduate Schools, most graduate schools have agreed not to make you declare your intentions before April 15. It is important to note that these are *graduate* schools, and this rule does not apply to medical schools, and may not apply to the other professional schools (for example, law). And the rule applies only to admission offers with funding, such as a fellowship or assistantship with a stipend. To see the resolution for yourself, go to https://cgsnet.org/resources/for-current-prospective-graduate-students/april-15-resolution or just search "Council of Graduate Schools best practices April 15."

Unfortunately, not every institution is a signatory to this agreement and some programs ignore the rule. Admissions seem to be running earlier every year, and in some cases students are receiving admission, and pressure to decide, before the deadline to *apply* has arrived. Science and engineering tend to run early, and social science and humanities tend to run a bit later. Nevertheless, you should be prepared for a little admissions dance, and that dance has everything to do with yield and funding allocations. Yield is the percentage of candidates who are offered admission who actually accept. The ideal yield is 100 percent. Every program wants maximum yield: it's more efficient, makes the program look more exclusive, and allows for more precise planning of aid allocation. So, you may have department chairs calling you up and asking questions like this: "We're intrigued by your candidacy. If we were to offer admission to you, do you think you'll decide to attend our program?" To which you say, "I'm intrigued by your program but, of course, it would depend on the specific aid package you might offer, and the ones that I anticipate from other programs. I think you have a wonderful program, or I wouldn't have applied, but I do need to make a decision based on all the

Pro Tip

If your safety school can smell that you consider it a safety school, it's not safe anymore. Put just as much zeal and attention into your applications for safety schools as you do for your top choices.

Throughout the application process, it is advised that you not tell a grad program outright that it is your first choice. Communicate that they are a close fit for your interests, or you would be delighted to be admitted to their program, and so on, but avoid that phrase "first choice." It reduces your flexibility, and in interacting with grad programs, students often discover that their first choice is actually a poor choice, and some other program on their list, perhaps even a safety school, can establish itself as a very desired option. A faculty mentor who takes a real interest in you can make a safe school the best school. Allow for discovery.

data. What aid offer did you have in mind?" Why do faculty make screening calls like this? To keep from writing down offers to students who they think are not going to choose them. If they give you a written offer, you can sit on it until April 15. If you do not show enthusiasm in a call like this, or if the school can smell that you consider them a safety school, you will not be getting a written offer. (Schools try to get first-round aid offers formalized by April 1, at the latest, but some will run late.)

What do you do if you get an "exploding offer," that is, an offer that expires prior to April 15? The Council of Graduate Schools best-practices agreement is an institution-wide agreement. A department cannot just claim that the agreement does not apply to them. Some overly eager and perhaps new faculty members genuinely do not know about the rule, and some recruiters just want to lock in the best talent by knowingly violating the rule. You can read the rules yourself at the Council of Graduate Schools' website. *A grad school candidate should not fight an exploding offer on their own.* It's not graceful for a candidate to go up against a graduate faculty member or university officer. If at all possible, you should enlist a mentor, a department chair, or some other authority to write the letter on your behalf. Here is an example:

I am advising Avery Tari on her applications to graduate school, and she is very excited about your offer of admission, which she shared with me. But I could not help but notice that the offer expires prior to the April 15th best-practices deadline established by the Council of Graduate Schools. This is an institution-wide agreement, and your school is listed as a signatory. (https://cgsnet.org/wp-content/uploads/2023/03/CGS_April15_Resolution_Mar122023-1.pdf). Ms. Tari would greatly benefit from being able to compare your offer with others she may receive, and having the time to review her options. What should I tell my advisee? Obviously, time is of the essence, so I would appreciate a quick response. May Avery have until April 15 to settle on a decision about your offer?

If you graduated some time ago and do not have access to a faculty mentor, you may have to write some version of this missive yourself. Be charming and overly polite.

No news is not necessarily the worst news; it may mean that you have been "wait-listed." There are at least two common kinds of wait lists. First, there is the "maybe" list that every program collects at the first sort. This maybe list turns into an informal wait list, and it can last for months, as the clearly outstanding are admitted and the clearly unprepared are rejected. This informal wait list can even go well past April 15, which is exactly why the friend I mentioned earlier got that letter on April 17 that began, "We are happy to extend an offer of admission to you for the fall incoming class. It is absolutely imperative that you respond by April 15th or your seat will be offered to another."

He, obviously, was one of the "anothers." If you have confirmed that you applied properly, and you don't hear by April 15, you are in all likelihood on this type of invisible wait list.

The other type of wait list is a formal wait list. You will receive a letter informing you that you are on the wait list—due, no doubt, to the unusually strong candidate pool this year, yada, yada, yada. These wait lists are bad, as they sometimes require you to wait around until the first week of classes to discover your status. Interestingly enough, you will probably have to provide another school with confirmation and a deposit.

If you are called up from the wait list, you face a dilemma. You have confirmed at one school, yet another is asking you to renege. *Relax.* No school wants a graduate student who is unhappy from day one. The first school also has a wait list, and they'll call someone up from it if you decide to jump. (Although they may not tell you this, and your deposit is a goner.) Your bigger problem is you have two offers, possibly from schools with very different reputations, and often the better school is coming up with the worse aid offer. On top of that, everybody wants you to decide *right now.* You simply have to weigh your options and make your best choice. Call your advisor, talk to your peers, discuss it with representatives of both schools, and make a decision.

Be very diplomatic and professional in declining offers. You may later do a postdoc, or need a faculty job, or be on a research project involving people from the institution. Academia is a small world, with a very long memory.

If you have any reason to believe that you have been wait-listed, do something! Send another letter of recommendation, send your midyear grades, get a professor to call and rave about your potential, get a family member to contact one of her friends at the target school. Above all, remind them of your interest in *their* program. One student I interviewed for this book was told that he was wait-listed at a top business school. They told him there was nothing he could do about it, and that he should not call, but just wait and see how the year's applicant pool shaped up. "When they said not to call, I thought that meant 'don't call more than once a week,'" he told me. He not only called fairly often to restate his interest in the program, but also drafted the following letter to update the admissions committee on his activities:

Dear Ladies and Gentlemen of the Committee:

I am writing to supplement my application to Stanford's Graduate School of Business.

Currently, I am on the waiting list for entrance for the fall incoming class. Because the scope of my consulting duties at Halperin-Smythe Associates has expanded considerably in recent months, I would like to make the admissions committee aware of some of my new responsibilities. Also, please find included four recommendations from my superiors at Halperin-Smythe.

The most important new project I worked on at Halperin-Smythe was an analysis of the unrealized value in patent holdings of technology companies (slightly redacted copy attached, with company approval). We found that many older technology companies were undervalued because their patent portfolios were undervalued. We identified and modeled four companies as particularly ripe for takeover, based on our analysis. They had stalled product lines and lackluster stock performance, but robust and deep patent portfolios. As a result of the study, we received an enormous amount of media exposure, including a write-up as the subject of a Heard on the Street column in the Wall Street Journal, a first for Halperin-Smythe Associates. Our findings have been used by a range of investors to reevaluate equities. Our study has generated substantial interest in business and academic circles. My supervisor, Richard Vines, and I designed the study. I then performed the analysis, produced the study's tables, graphs, and conclusions, and wrote the Methods and Example sections of the study.

This account of my activities over the past few months supplements the description, which you already have, of my duties at Halperin-Smythe (see original application). If you want further elaboration of any item, please write or call. Thank you for your interest.

Note how specific this candidate's update is. He is giving specific *new* evidence to influence the admission decision in his favor. Needless to say, his extra effort was rewarded by admission. If you are wait-listed, think of your application as suspended on evenly balanced scales, equally weighted on the "admit" and "reject" sides. Throw something, anything, onto the admit side.

This is an example of a "news item" that you can send after you apply and before you are admitted or rejected. A news item is something that happened after you applied that you think would impress the admissions committee were they to know about it. News items can be events like these: you are informed you will graduate with honors, your paper was accepted by the *Midwest Journal of*

Undergraduate Research, Prof. R. Johnson invited you to co-present your paper with him at an academic conference, Dr. A. Lee invited you to be his research assistant for the upcoming summer, you finished an interesting project at work that garnered high praise (as the example above), you have been named "outstanding biology senior," or you visited the program and have an update that can look like this: "I recently had a chance to visit your program and meet with Drs. Rayburn, Gubanski, and Lee, thus further cementing my impression that your program is an excellent fit for me, for the following five reasons: ________, ________, ________, ________, and ________."

If you fear you are on an invisible wait list, languishing in an aging "maybe" pile, you do not necessarily need some impressive news to report. Sometimes you can submit a supplemental *argument* for why you should be admitted. Here is the best one I have ever seen. This letter resulted in a second interview and an admission.

Dear Dr. X and Members of the Selection Committee:

Since I haven't heard from your program, either positively or negatively, I am going to assume that I am in the bubble of consideration. I can imagine the care and importance of your work, as you go through the "maybe" pile and decide who is and who is not going to get to become a physician. I would like to help you be comfortable with the decision to admit me to your entering class, for the following five reasons:

1. Where I am imperfect as a premed applicant, the cause is that I tried to do too much as an undergraduate. I did not need to get a master's degree and do real medical research on kidney cancer, but that has deepened my understanding of medical science. I did not need to compete on a volleyball team that became state champions, but I felt an obligation to my teammates, and I think it is important to pursue things to their conclusion. These activities took, literally, hundreds of hours. Had I taken the safe route of combining the premed core with fluffy classes, I am sure I would be a much stronger candidate, statistically. But would I be a better doctor? That is less certain. I learned a lot about people, about teams, and about medicine with these two time-consuming pursuits.

2. When I have a problem, I attack it relentlessly until it is solved. I earned a black belt in judo (shodan). I pursued lab work that requires tremendous investment in technique, but also the ability to go back to each step in a protocol, even the tiniest aspect of execution, to look for ways to overcome bad data and improve the integrity of findings. Research has taught me to be careful, and there is no more important aspect of practicing medicine than to be careful. I do not guess. I find out. I seek help. I verify.

3. My theory of the practice of medicine is in sync, I believe, with the future of medicine. The days of the maverick doctor, who goes off protocol on a "hunch," are coming to a close. The doctors of the future, my future, will be required to practice medicine in a complex and far-reaching system. AI will assist doctors in decision making. Doctors will be members of practice teams, and will need to really listen to nurses and technicians, and reach out to specialists, perhaps in the room and perhaps around the world. My ego is in check. I can be the right kind of care provider for this future medical workplace.

4. My ability to connect with people is broad. I am African American, from a family with a long tradition of valuing education. I grew up in Harlem, but also in the country. My mother is an engineer, and my father is a corporate lawyer. The polyglot world of my childhood makes me as comfortable with an undocumented Haitian as with a CEO. And I can speak fluent French to each. Doctors need to serve the public, and since I intend to be a PCP, it is critical that the public, all of the public, be comfortable in my office. I am confident that I would rank at the top on this criterion, the ability to connect with patients, compared to other applicants.

5. I can be an ambassador and a beneficial future representative of your medical program. I have served as an admissions ambassador for my alma mater all of the last six years. I've given lectures on college choice, been on hundreds of video chats, and answered countless emails and queries from prospective students. I take very seriously my role as a representative of all who have invested in me. Your decision to admit me will pay off in my diligence as a medical student, and as a practitioner, and as an ambassador for your program, well into the future.

I thank you very much for considering these points, and if there is anything I can do to make you more comfortable admitting me to your program, you can text or call me on my cell at (212) 555-0131 or email me at apex@grantonville.edu. I truly appreciate your consideration. Thank you.

What else can you do between the time you apply and the official notice of admission or rejection? If you are a senior in college, you can send in your fall grades. If you apply in the fall, most graduate programs will just make their decisions on the grades your transcripts show up until that point. They will require you to submit your final transcript, and they always verify that (a) you graduated and fulfilled any final course requirements, and (b) that you did not totally fall apart in the final year, thus requiring an investigation and reconsideration of your candidacy. But they do not see that document until the application process is completely over. If your fall grades come in strong, send them in. My counsel is not to send your updated transcripts. That's boring and has too much distracting information, and maybe reminds them again that you made a C in the freshman year. Instead, send them a table of just your fall grades, and compute your GPA for just that semester. This is an example of what psychologists call priming, and it can be powerful. Perhaps your GPA overall is 3.2, mostly due to a disastrous freshman year, but you take a light load and study hard in the fall of the senior year, and make 2 A's and 1 B. You can send a grade report that looks like this:

I'm an applicant for fall incoming doctoral class. My fall grades came in and I wanted to share them with the admissions committee. Here they are:

CLASS	*GPA*
Senior Symposium	*4.0*
Advanced Issues	*4.0*
Complex Applications	*3.0*
FALL GPA:	*3.67*

By the phenomenon of priming, you just became a 3.67 student. If you want to use an app to calculate your GPA, just search for "GPA calculator." There are several out there that can make the calculations super easy, or see the instructions and example on page 84.

You can also send in a continuing interest letter. As the admissions season progresses, you may receive some admissions and some rejections and some requests for further information and so on. You may have interactions of various sorts with the grad programs to which you have applied. Once this activity begins to occur, you can send a letter like this to those programs that have not revealed their opinion of you yet:

Dear Dr. Nguyen:

I have begun to hear from some of the other graduate programs, and yet I have not heard anything from you and your team. I am somewhat nervous, because I think your program is an excellent fit for my background, preparation, and interests, and I am hoping to hear good news from you. Most of all, I would not like to be forced to make a decision before I know where I stand with you. If there is anything I can address about my skills and abilities, I would be happy to respond promptly. You can of course reach me by email or text on (510) 555-0147. If there is anything I can do to influence the decision in my favor, let me know!

Standing by,
Zed Zealous

Don't copy this letter verbatim, but use it as an example to write a similar composition that is your own letter.

Also, after you apply and before you are admitted or rejected, you can have a faculty member inject themselves into the decision process by doing what is called a "faculty intervention." That is when a faculty member does more than write a letter of recommendation; they write an email or even leave a voice message that is a faculty version of a continuing interest letter:

> *My advisee has begun to hear from some of the other programs, and she reports that she has not heard anything from you. She is getting somewhat nervous, because it is getting late in the season. We've been very impressed by her here at Appelonia University, and I recounted some of her strengths in my letter of recommendation. I would hope that you would take a close look at her application before you make your final decisions this year. If I can further address her preparation, abilities, and interests, I would be happy to do so. I can be reached by cellphone at (210) 555-0141 or email at paultrego@appelonia.edu. Thank you for your consideration.*

Faculty do not direct other faculty. They use what is called senatorial language. It is overly polite. It may be circumlocuitous. They do not yell, "Hey! You'd be making a big mistake not to admit this one!" Instead, they nudge with "I would hope that you would take a close look at her application." That's the proper tone.

Timing for letters of continuing interest and for faculty interventions is important. These need to occur when university staff are actually doing admissions reviews. If you send them too early, they may have little effect. If you send them too late, all the slots and money are gone. My counsel is to send them when you know they are making decisions, and you know this because some schools will admit you, reject you, or ask you clarifying questions. Then you send these supplemental communications to the schools that have not indicated their plans for you.

You have to enlist a faculty champion to do a faculty intervention. I will warn you in advance that not all faculty will do this. They may say, "I wrote your letter of recommendation. You just have to wait now and let the selection process work its course." Some faculty never do this, some do it rarely, and some will do it for practically anyone who asks. I think there is no harm in asking, as long as you understand that many outstanding faculty, including faculty who may love you, may have a philosophical objection to this practice.

You may visit the program after you apply, and this is particularly useful if you are a borderline candidate, or you are an applicant from all the way across the country and you need to establish that you really are interested in moving to Orono, Maine. You can also visit before you apply. Grad programs have preview days and open houses, virtual and in person, usually in the fall. Get these on your calendar! Visits give you access to admissions officers and faculty and currently enrolled grad students, and the information they give you can create an invaluable edge when you apply. In your application you can quote a professor from a visit. You can mention visiting a lab. You can use inside knowledge that they gave you, such as, why they would admit someone who does not meet their published requirements or how to get selected for a graduate assistantship as an admissions coordinator (you can literally ask them).

You can visit on your own any time, but this requires a level of charm and decorum that many students simply do not quite have. A busy research faculty member is a busy research faculty member. Faculty at medical schools and business and law programs can be downright hostile to visits from prospectives. An introduction will help. Promising to "only take a moment of your time" will help. Enlisting the departmental admin for advice can help. Following Asher's Law can help (see page 44). Send thank-you letters to everyone who helps you or meets with you. Prepare answers to expected questions (see page 45).

Preview days and open houses are usually optional, but there is another type of visit that is not optional at all. If you are invited to visit a program in the spring, you must go. Even though they may call it by the same name, an "open house," for example, spring events are an entirely different animal. They may say that attendance is "optional," but really it is not. If you do not attend an event you are invited to in the spring, you are saying, "I don't like your program, and I am not going to come to your program, and I certainly don't want any funding." Let's call these events meet-and-greets, to differentiate them from open houses and preview days that happen in the fall (even though the schools themselves also use those names for these spring events).

If you are not admitted yet, meet-and-greets are protracted admissions interviews. Faculty or admissions officers want to get a look at you, see how you conduct yourself, or they may have a series of questions about your skills, experiences, and interests to see if you belong in their grad program. It can be awkward at a meet-and-greet if admitted students are mixed in with not-yet-admitted students, but this is common. If you are not admitted, to skip a meet-and-greet usually results in a default rejection from the program.

If you are admitted, meet-and-greets are about recruiting you, and drumming up your enthusiasm for attending their program. They are also about selecting you for assignments and possible funding. Think of meet-and-greets as speed dating for faculty. The faculty have a list of students that they might want to sponsor with an assistantship or have join their research projects. During the meet-and-greet, as soon as you leave the presence of a faculty member, they mark "yes" or "no" on their scorecard. Just like speed dating. A student with no yeses may not get the best funding, or may arbitrarily get assigned the worst assistantship.

In STEM, the tradition is for the program to pay for your travel to come to any in-person meet-and-greet. In professional schools, in humanities, and other non-STEM master's and doctoral programs, it is routine for them to expect the student to come up with their own funds to appear at these events. First of all, there is no harm in inquiring politely about a travel stipend. If you get no travel stipend, you can sometimes shame them into coming up with some funding for you:

> *Dr. Watson, I am an entirely self-supporting student and, as you can imagine, coming up with the funds to travel to grad school events like this is simply beyond my reach. Yet I very much want to meet the team and see if I would fit in, to see if I could become a valuable contributor. If you can assist me with airfare and accommodations, I would be eternally grateful. I would be happy to sleep on some grad student's couch.*

As always, all this has to be accurate and true, and don't copy this missive verbatim, but use it as an example to craft your own letter.

One of my friends called me up and said, "Don, my wife is due to have a baby right in the middle of meet-and-greet season. I simply cannot travel then, and I'm terrified the grad programs won't take me seriously." I said, "Scott, your wife will have other babies. You can't skip the meet-and-greets!"

No, that is not what I said. If you have an inescapable conflict like a due baby, for example, or invitations to two events on the same Saturday, or you have an important exam or presentation that cannot be moved, you will have to replace the meet-and-greet with an equivalent series of meetings. Tell them you have an inescapable conflict and cannot travel to be with them that week; you don't even have to say what the other obligation is. Then volunteer to seek out and connect with key faculty "and anyone else that you think I need to meet." Then follow through. This is a lot more work than simply going from meeting to meeting at a meet-and-greet, so you see why universities prefer the organized group process, whether virtual or in person. Scott had video meetings with faculty every night for a couple of weeks, and succeeded just fine in getting several offers of admission and full funding. And he got to be there when his daughter was born.

By paying careful attention to timing, by doing what you are supposed to do when you are supposed to do it, you should be one of the lucky applicants who begin to get admissions offers in February, March, and April. Admissions offers for professional programs (business, law, medicine, architecture, public policy, and so on) may not mention funding. It's an offer of admission, take it or leave it. But offers from doctoral and many academic master's programs may define particulars of funding, assistantships, fellowships, tuition waivers, health insurance, and all manner of terms and conditions.

Your application season is not over yet, however. You may have to juggle multiple offers, negotiate (sometimes), and make a final decision.

When you get an offer, acknowledge it right away. You do not have to say you are going to accept, but let them know right away that you got the offer and are considering it. Here's an example:

> *Thank you so much for the offer of admission and financial support. I am grateful for this opportunity. I will be back in touch if I have questions and I'll be sure to respond formally with my decision before the April 15th deadline.*

Short, simple, polite.

But suppose School B offers you a better financial deal than School A, yet you actually prefer School A. First, not all dollars are created equally. The cost of living in a locale also matters, and whether a stipend is for a nine-month or a twelve-month assignment also matters. A dollar in Manhattan, Kansas, a college town, goes a lot further than a dollar in Manhattan, New York, also a college town. A nine-month appointment allows you to earn extra money over the summers by working on contract with specific faculty or programs. If you decide to push a university for a more generous stipend, do not demand a specific number, never bluff, and be overly polite. Here is one example:

> *Dr. Hortzen, I am very excited by the offer of admission and funding to join your program next fall. Your program is an excellent fit for my background, preparation, abilities, and interests. I am particularly attracted by the opportunity to join Dr. Foster's lab from my very first semester. However, I need to let you know that I have an offer from another program that is more generous in terms of the funding, and is in a lower-cost area of the country, as well. What can we do? I really think your program is better, and a better fit for me, but I am*

a self-supporting student, and funding does matter to me. I just wanted to reach out to you before I make my decision, to see if you could help me with the funding.

As always, everything has to be true, do not copy examples like this verbatim, and craft your own version of this letter to suit your specific circumstances. My advice: Do not say how much more the other program offers, and do not ask for a specific dollar increase. Just say, "What can we do?"

They may ask to see the offer from the other school. They certainly will ask to know the numbers from the other offer. Whether you provide the actual offer letter or not, you do have to provide the competing offer's numbers and terms. And they may tell you there is nothing they can do. If they bring in ten first-year students all starting on the same day, they may have a policy to not adjust award offers to keep everything even and fair. Or they may give you more money. As long as you ask politely, do not at first mention specific numbers, and do not hint at any kind of an ultimatum, it is okay to push gently for more.

Never bluff in higher education. Everybody knows everybody. If you claim an offer that is not real, your chances of getting busted on this are high.

As mentioned, admissions offers with funding will usually expire on April 15 at 5 p.m. local time where the university is situated. My counsel is to turn in your decision a day or two early. Accept at one program, and gently turn down the other programs. Be graceful, because in a few short years you may need a postdoc or a faculty appointment from that school that you are declining.

• • •

If, after all of this, you actually do not get in, do not despair. Almost every one of the successful students I interviewed for this book had been rejected from other programs, and many had been rejected by *all* the schools they applied to in an earlier year. The first thing to do is call the admissions representative asking why you were rejected, and what you can do to correct any deficiencies in order to submit a successful application to them, or someone else, in the future. Don't be angry or upset or accusatory over the phone; say something like this: "I know you probably made the right decision, and I'm not calling at all to complain about that decision. I am just very committed to my goals, and I wonder if you would take a moment and tell me how to improve my chances in a future year, either with your school or another. Can you help me see which deficiencies I should concentrate on?" You may have to call a few times, but asking politely in this manner will often get a helpful response.

It is official NAGAP policy not to hide the decision rationale from rejected candidates, and the CGS also endorses this approach. If you have to, quote this: "When a student is denied admission, it is important that the specific reasons are stated in the student's file. A student who requests the information should also be informed of the reasons for the rejection" (*An Essential Guide to Graduate Admissions,* Council of Graduate Schools, p. 46). You do, however, need to know that sometimes the answer really is, "We had so many applicants that we are sometimes forced to accept some and reject others that are overwhelmingly similar in preparation and academic performance to date." *C'est la vie.*

Sample Timeline for Applying to Doctoral Programs

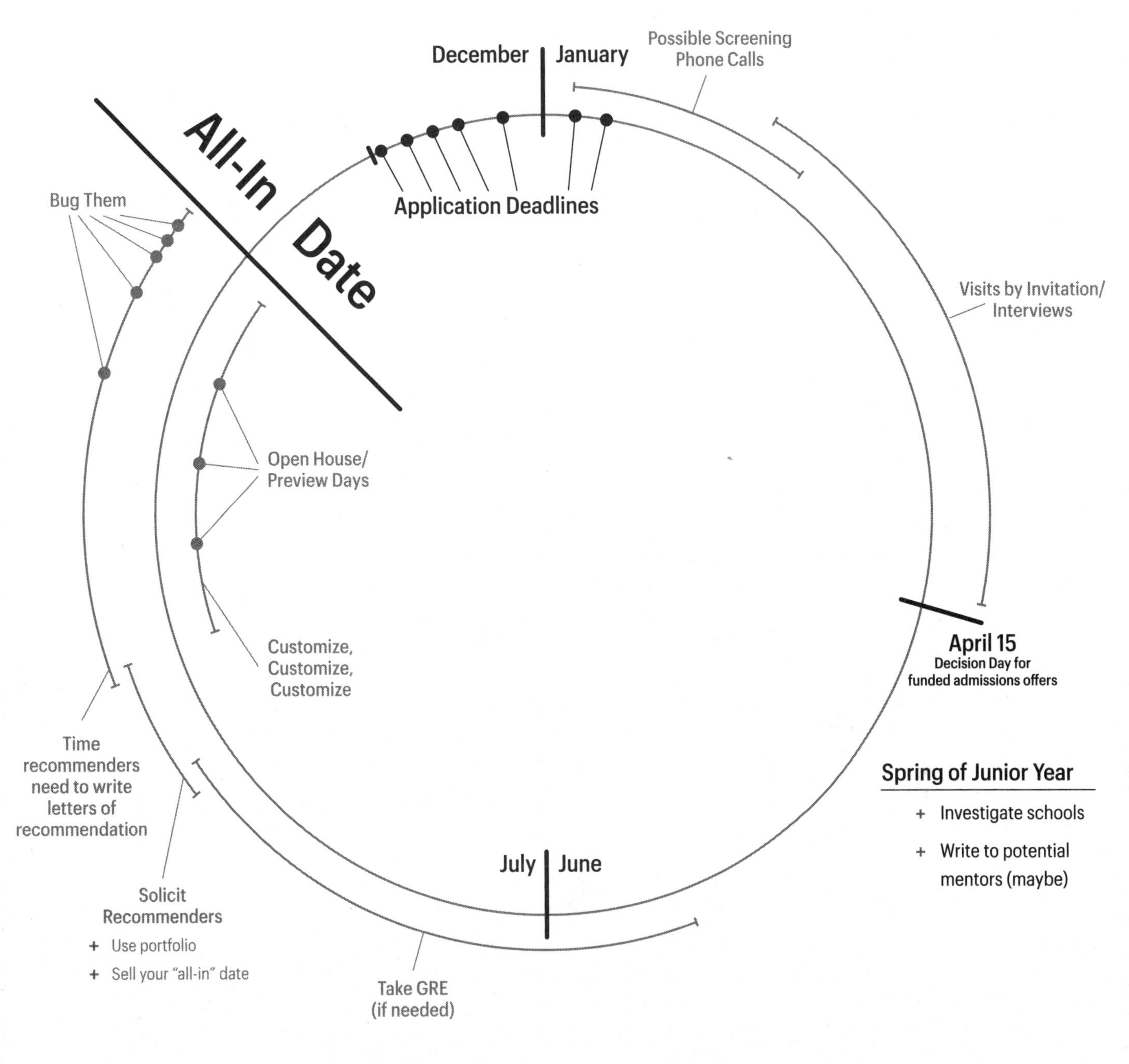

Summer: June - August

- Research experience or academically related experience
- Build list of schools
- Write core essays
- Write CV
- Spruce up writing sample
- Write to potential mentors about fit and match (maybe)
- Pick up a prerequisite or other needed class (maybe)
- Study for GRE (if needed)
- Assemble portfolio for recommenders

How to Shave a Year Off a PhD

1. Follow your program of study. Your program of study is the sequence of classes, milestones, and events that leads to completion. You create your program of study with your advisor. In graduate school, the milestones and events are more important than the classes. For example, if you miss a deadline to file a form, it can cost you a whole year. Update your program of study often, and post it over your desk. Look at it every day.
2. Come in the door with at least a vague dissertation idea, *but do not rigidly hang on to it.* Grad school is a transformative process, so your initial idea is a jump start, not a printed road map. Write all your papers for every class, as many as you can, on some aspect related to your dissertation interest.
3. Choose a mentor with a high completion rate. This is a professional relationship. It is irrelevant whether you are "buddies" with this person. Ask your mentor to suggest other people to serve on your committee. Start shopping, casually, for committee members right from the first day of grad school. Watch out for young professors out to make a name for themselves; they can be hard-asses. Watch out for old profs who might not survive your dissertation. Keep an eye out for your external reviewer; they are hard to find and hard to recruit, and be sure to check to see whether they dislike your mentor, school, topic, methodology, epistemology, or politics. In fact, check all members of your committee for reservations like this.
4. An appropriate dissertation topic is very narrow. Think of a question that can be definitively answered using your methodology, within your budget, in your lifetime. Most research has these three components: population, problem, theory (or topic, problem, theory). Remember, a dissertation is a training process. This is not supposed to be the most important work you will ever do. What's better—a perfect dissertation or a done dissertation? Duh. Do smart, good work, but most of all, get it done. It's nice if there are clever implications to your research, but the research itself can be simple and elegant.
5. Write a paper that is a dry run of your dissertation idea in the first two years. Ask a professor for (a) permission to do this, and (b) feedback on your idea, research question, methodology, and so on.
6. Students who finish theses have higher completion rates for dissertations. If your program offers a thesis as a master's option, take it. It may slow you down a bit at the time, but when you get to the dissertation you'll go faster. A master's thesis like this should be a one-semester project. One question, one method, one answer. Don't go overboard.
7. Do your own research before you get to the proposal stage. This sounds obvious, but a lot of students don't do this. They work on other people's projects, and

don't get their feet wet as the director of a project. Design, conduct, report, including IRB if needed (see next).

8. Go through the IRB (Institutional Review Board for the Protection of Human & Animal Subjects) process before you get to your dissertation project. Same reasons. IRB is like learning a new language, and you want to get through unscathed and with minimum delays. (A smart student *expects* IRB delays, by the way.)
9. Take an independent study and use it to do the entire literature review for your proposal *before* you submit your proposal. (Some proposals require lit review and methods chapters anyway, but you'll have the whole lit review done rather than a prelim version.) You'll probably have to rewrite your proposal (this is normal), but if you're smart you will be able to salvage almost all of your lit review even if you have to refine your question or methods.
10. Write your proposal before you take your comprehensive exams. Most places you cannot submit the proposal before passing comps, but this allows you to drop the proposal the day you receive notice of passing them. This, alone, saves as much as six months.
11. Stay on campus! If you stay on campus through your research and writing stages, you have a much higher chance of finishing in a timely manner, and you'll have access to your committee, campus resources, and so on. It may be tempting to go get "a real job" and do your dissertation while you work, but there is a much higher risk factor against completing.
12. Keep your eyes on the prize! Have a life plan that requires the PhD to be behind you. If you lust for that future, you will finish the PhD. If grad school is more attractive to you than that vision, or if you don't have that vision, you're at greater risk of not finishing.

These tips could shave a year, or more, off your process.

If you are still committed to your educational goals, then pursue them. Perhaps you did not apply early enough or to enough schools, and simply reapplying in a timely manner to a larger number of programs will result in success. Perhaps you need to apply to a lower rung of schools. If you applied only to top schools, you may very well have passed on an opportunity to study at a perfectly good school without such competitive admissions. Taking an interim degree was the source of success for many of the students I interviewed; for example, if they wanted a PhD in clinical psychology and were rejected for doctoral programs on their first round of applications, they would get a master's degree in psychology and apply again. Other students found success by taking a few additional prerequisites and related classes and concentrating on getting outstanding grades. You can sign up for classes as a nonmatriculated student at most universities, on a class-by-class basis, with instructor approval. I actually know of one PhD who, by using this method, never had to take the GRE; she had taken several graduate courses—always earning an A—and just wrote a letter saying she'd like to convert to full-time attendance. It was approved.

Still other students gained workplace experience related to their future career. Workplace experience can prove especially valuable for applicants to law and medical schools. (Many applicants are drawn to these professions without a clue as to the real challenges practitioners face on a daily basis, and admissions committees are more comfortable with applicants who know what they are getting into.) One student I spoke with discovered that one of his letters of recommendation was less than laudatory; when he replaced it, he found success on his next round of applications. Finally, I spoke with a few students who thought they were considered "too young." They did nothing whatsoever to improve their preparedness for graduate studies except to live for a few more years before applying again; nevertheless, they were successful in these later applications.

What to do if you don't get in

1. Apply to more schools.
2. Apply to more safe schools.
3. Apply earlier.
4. Get an intermediate degree.
5. Take one class at a time as a nonmatriculated student.
6. Go to summer school at one of your targeted schools.
7. Get an internship in the targeted field.
8. Get a "real job" in the targeted field.
9. Visit in person and wow them.
10. Get older and try again.

I know of one student who was rejected by all the schools he applied to on his first round of applications. Then he bought this book. Using the techniques I've shared with you, he was admitted to ten out of fourteen programs and was fully funded to pursue the PhD. He could have given up, decided that his academic credentials were not as worthy as he thought, and joined the wage grind for the rest of his life, but he did not. *He knew what he wanted and he tried again.* There are too many variables in the graduate admissions process to warrant giving up on your goals if you are not successful in your first round of applications. Try again, start earlier, and apply to more schools.

5

Getting Ready to Write

This chapter is a series of exercises designed to prepare you to write the first draft of your graduate admissions essay. Do not worry if much of the information generated by these exercises seems, at first, tangential to your educational goals or unlike what you had planned to include in your application. The goal is to build a pool of possible topics and points, most of which will not be included in your essay. You can draw both inspiration and details from this pool of data, and it will make your first draft flow more easily when you start writing.

No one student is expected to write detailed answers for every single exercise in this chapter, but you *are* expected to answer *every single question,* at least in your mind. Read and think and write as many notes as you can. You may even find yourself in the library or going through old labs and papers to find inspiration, but keep moving along so that you finish this section and go on to your first draft in a timely manner.

• • •

One of the complaints most admissions readers make is that "so many of the essays seem almost the same." Take a moment and imagine that admissions reader sitting down with twenty or thirty or a hundred essays from applicants. Can you see her eyes beginning to glaze over after several essays that all seem vaguely similar? Can you imagine her relief when she reads a first line like this?

> **I was taking out the garbage one dawn on the Serengeti Plain when I realized what had been bothering me . . .**

What makes you unique? Different? Unusual? I once interviewed a medical school admissions committee who let a woman into their school because she had been in a plane wreck. Is that a qualification for medical school? Perhaps not, but it is a qualification for getting noticed if you are otherwise qualified for medical school.

Sometimes the thing that makes a person really different is a personal or family matter:

> **At the age of forty-eight, I left my two adult children, my husband, and the dishes in the sink, and moved into a college dorm to become a freshman. And because I was a first-generation college student, I had no one to tell me that a college dorm is not the serene, academic refuge I had always imagined!**

With this opening, she immediately sets herself apart from the bulk of applicants. Many students turn something unusual about themselves into an interesting way to launch their essays. However, note the tones of such introductions—there should be nothing frivolous about these writers. They are as serious as can be, just different. They will not seem "just the same" as all the other applicants.

Take a moment right now, pull out a fresh notebook or piece of paper, and write down the most unusual things about you as a person—not you as an applicant or you as a student, but you as a unique and unusual person. Consider your whole life, and maybe even your ancestors' lives. Remember to include personal material, even if you know you would never include it in your essay.

Some students attempting this exercise have said that there is nothing unusual about them. One even told me, "I'm as typical as they come. I'm an average girl from the 'burbs. I know about SUVs, big dogs, yoga, and going out with friends." "Try really hard," I said. "It doesn't have to be something unique, just something that you've experienced or done or are that will not seem that common to the people who will read your essay." The workshop was in California. She came running up to me later: "I've got my first line! Here it is: 'When the earthquake struck, I was the only one in charge of my dorm. I got all twenty-two of my dormies out alive. . . .'"

Why didn't she think of this right away? Because all of her friends had gone through the same earthquake. It wasn't even that big an earthquake. Earthquakes are common in California, but on the East Coast they're pretty exotic. What's common in your town that might be interesting somewhere else. I've read great essays that mentioned peach farming in southern Missouri, going to the rodeo in central Washington, and being meticulously honest in New York City. Try to list a few things that are unusual about you, your family, your upbringing, your travels, your college, and your part of the country. You don't have to use any of this, but wouldn't it be an interesting challenge to list out ten things right now?

• • •

As you begin the process of applying to graduate schools, it is a good time to remember who and what your intellectual influences have been. The next set of exercises will assist you in tracing these influences. Answer each of the following questions with at least a full sentence but less than half a page:

+ What writers and which particular articles in your field of study have had the greatest influence on the development of your thought?
+ Who were your favorite professors in college, and why? How has each influenced you?
+ What is the best paper or exam you ever wrote in your major, and what makes it good?
+ What do you consider the most important book, play, article, or film you have ever read/seen, and how has it influenced you?
+ What is the single most important concept you have learned in college?
+ What are some trends you see in your discipline of interest?

If you can think of other educational milestones or guideposts, write about them in the same fashion—at least a sentence, but no more than half a page. Your goal is to generate ideas, some of which may be expanded upon later.

• • •

What are some of the encouraging words others have said to or about you over the years? Did a particular teacher or professor encourage you to pursue your studies, go beyond your abilities, or pursue a goal or dream? Write the *actual words* of the professor or teacher, and give the time and place you heard them. For example:

> **"Julie, you're good at math. Why don't you consider tutoring for the department?"**
> **—Dr. Lee, sophomore year, in front of the math building**

> **"Paul, you're really onto something here. Do you realize that if this works, intergalactic travel will be possible on a human time scale?!"**
> **—Prof. Wilson, in the theoretical physics laboratory, last year**

• • •

Where were you and what were you doing when you first thought of pursuing this particular direction of graduate study? One student told me that she was talking with her professor in an English class, and she suddenly realized that the whole class had become a dialogue between her and the prof. The other students were just staring at her, open-mouthed, as they scribbled furiously to get down what she was saying. In that moment, she decided to become a college professor.

I once interviewed a student who told a long story that started out like this:

> **There are a lot of doctors in my family, and I could never decide whether to be a doctor or go into zoology. I got this chance to be a volunteer for an ethology study in the highland forests of Tanzania, studying the behavior of the highland mangabey (*Lophocebus kipunji*) primate species. I spent six weeks staring up into the canopy and making marks on this waterproof clipboard with a grease pencil. Then I got a weekend pass, and went to town. I still couldn't decide—medical school or zoology. I thought about it every day. In town I saw this sign on a concrete building, hospital. No doors, no windows, tin roof. Typical. The sun is really bright in Africa. I couldn't see inside at all. So I stuck my head in the door. My body was outside in the sunlight, and just my head was in the shadows. I wanted to see, but I didn't want to disturb anybody. There were two rows of metal cots, all empty except the last one. There were no medicines, no supplies of any kind in sight, just a nun and this boy, maybe nine or ten, it's hard to tell, and he was surrounded by his entire family, and they were just moaning and rocking back and forth. That's when I decided I didn't care about monkey behavior. Right then, in that doorway, I decided to become a doctor.**

What were you doing when you decided to pursue this particular area of graduate study?

• • •

Now, answer these questions to build a historical overview of the etiology of your career choice:

+ How has your interest evolved, and what specific turning points can you identify?
+ What work experiences have led you to believe you would like to pursue graduate education?
+ What experiences as a volunteer or traveler have influenced your career direction?
+ What experiences from your family life have contributed to this choice?

Throughout all this, remember that you are building a pool of information from which to draw the first draft of your essay. Can you think of any other life experiences that you might want to include? Make a few notes on them and go on to the next exercise.

• • •

Not all applicants to graduate school have a specific career direction in mind when they apply. Although it is fine to be open to different possibilities, you might think twice before pursuing two to six years of specialized education without any plan to utilize it at all. (Incidentally, do not try to become a college professor just because you are smart and cannot decide what else to do with your life.)

Your next exercise is to define your career goal, as nearly as you can. Consider why you have chosen the particular path you are now pursuing, and make a list of your real reasons for doing so. What attracts you to this career? What do you hope to gain? Write these items down the left-hand side of a piece of paper. Be honest! Remember, nobody is going to see this list but you.

• • •

When this list of your true motivations is complete, use the right-hand side of your paper to write down other ways you could achieve or obtain each item. This is a way of getting you to consider your other career options, what they are, and exactly why you reject them, and perhaps to reconsider if you reject them. For example, if your goal is to be a college professor of English, you may have written, "opportunity to work with language around articulate and talented people" on the left-hand side of your paper; on the right-hand side, you might write, "online content provider or zine, advertising agency, publishing company, magazine, public relations," as other options that could satisfy that desire. Is your career choice really the best one for you?

• • •

Next, consider your academic background:

+ How have you prepared yourself to succeed in graduate school?
+ What body of relevant knowledge will you take with you?

+ What study or laboratory skills have you honed to date?
+ What personal attributes or physical characteristics make you particularly likely to succeed in your new career?

• • •

What is your biggest accomplishment to date? Take a little time with this one, as it may not be obvious. While you are thinking about it, make a list of "many things I am proud of."

• • •

What research have you completed to date? Make a list of major research projects and your role in them. If the research is published, look up the exact citation. If it is not published, devise a working title based on what it would have been named had you published it. This is good practice for when you start publishing articles regularly. (Be careful not to misrepresent a working title as a published work.) If you think the work is good enough to be published, get a professor to advise you, prepare it in the correct format, and submit it for publication. You have nothing to lose, and the practice will be educational.

Be ready to describe your level of participation in the research. On one project, you may wish to point out that you "designed experimental methods, scheduled and conducted experiments, analyzed the data, and drafted preliminary conclusions." In another, you may have done less, in which case you can still say that you "assisted Dr. B. Schottersly on a study of the effects of liposuction on porcine fat cell populations." Don't oversell something casual, however. Be ready to describe the hypothesis, methods, findings, and so on, or you should not be talking about the research in your essay.

It is also a good idea to spell out the ramifications of the research. Too often, students list research without indicating that they have any idea of its purpose. Link your inquiry into the light sensitivity of a certain barnacle to a possible treatment for a class of allergies and the reader will be more impressed.

Finally, list what you really learned from the research. Perhaps you gained specific knowledge of a concept, a technique, how to work with others, or even an emotion. For instance, you could have learned compassion, empathy, or even humility.

• • •

You have already noted the major writers and thinkers in your field and how they have influenced your development. Can you add any professors currently associated with your targeted school? One of the best opening lines is some version of this:

In my frequent correspondence with Drs. Wilson, Lee, and Wu, I have come to discover that your program and my academic interests align well.

An administrator once advised me that the best opening line of all time is this: "My uncle, for whom your library is named . . ." Now, *that's* an opening line!

The following excerpt is from a successful application for a scholarship offered by the Urban Land Institute (ULI). The gentleman named was, at the time, on the ULI board of directors:

I had the good fortune to hear Jon Q. Reynolds speak in a lecture this semester. At the end of his presentation, a student asked, "Do you see land development as a right or as a privilege?" Mr. Reynolds replied that it is a *responsibility*. I share this opinion; because of the longevity of land use and development decisions, they must be undertaken with a sense of responsibility to the public and to the future as well as to the investor. These decisions also . . .

An important note about this type of citation: You must be totally sincere or the reader can smell it. If you cannot be honest in your use of another's name, then do not mention it at all. Avoid featuring the most reviled professor in the program or the great leader who left last year; you need to know politics as well as names.

Of course, you will want to mention your major advisors to date, as well. It is standard academic protocol at the graduate level to do so, so show a little savvy and name your key undergraduate advisors. In graduate school, you are never a lone wolf; you are part of an academic department or a laboratory, and you operate under the supervision of an advisor or chief. Furthermore, you usually give their full title in any formal communiqué, including any honorary appointments. For example, you don't work for the Thin Film Laboratory, you work for the Thin Film Laboratory *under the guidance of Dr. Diana Centornella, Laboratory Chief and the Harlan J. Dansworth Materials Science Scholar.*

Names of major thinkers and theorists are a powerful addition to any essay. In many of the essay samples in this book, you will see frequent citations of those writers and thinkers who have most influenced the student.

Make a list of names you might want to work into your essay, but do not make any firm plans yet as to whom you want to include. Your list may include the following:

+ Influential undergraduate professors
+ Specific professors at the targeted institution who interest you
+ Major writers and thinkers in the field who have influenced you
+ Professors with whom you have visited or corresponded or spoken
+ Any other people you may have in common with the targeted institution

• • •

Can you describe an experience that demonstrates remarkable drive or perseverance? Are you involved in sports? What do you do with your leisure time? Do you have any hobbies or pastimes to soften the stress of graduate study? What can you tell someone that would lead them to believe they would enjoy your company?

Statement of Purpose Prewriting Exercise

Build a table of undergraduate research projects.

Suggestions:

- List projects in order of interest to your targeted reader.
- Use working titles to describe your research projects.
- Name your professor/advisor/supervisor.

EXAMPLE

Sample Undergraduate Research Projects

- Designed original research into the ultrafiltration of proteins, including developing a theoretical model for design, design and actual prototyping of cross-flow ultrafiltration unit, and experimentation to determine optimal settings for maximal permeate flux. A Biochemical Engineering Laboratory senior project under the direction of Prof. L. Hintzer.
- Designed a stream remediation project involving liquid-liquid extraction to remove *m*-zylene from contaminated water; also used EPA QUAL2E to model the effects of DO, BOD, and Nitrogen cycle, under the guidance of Prof. L. Hintzer.
- Conducted research into mathematical models of potential use for codifying chaotic systems such as watersheds, an independent study under NSF grant, supervised by Prof. P. Cenczynksy. Abstract and draft findings available at http://www.HarveyMudd.edu/~czynsky/models2.html.
- Designed and conducted original research into quantitative and qualitative properties of a meteorite sample using atomic absorption spectrophotometry, emission spectrophotometry, induction coupled plasma, and laser spectrophotometry under the direction of Prof. R. Hull-Wallace. Results presented at the Argonne National Laboratory during annual meeting of the International Association of Amateur Astronomers.

This is not just for science students! Similar descriptions can be written about papers and projects in the liberal arts and other fields. For example, "Designed and conducted an in-depth analysis of the use of lightness and darkness to convey moral authority in the Elizabethan poetry of Smyth, Hallbeck, and Colbin, resulting in a 28-page paper presented in summary to the Healdsburg College English Department Colloquium, November 1, 2025."

• • •

Students routinely "hide" information that members of the admissions committee would certainly consider pertinent. This can be a misguided approach. For example, one applicant to law school developed an undistinguished essay that failed to mention the fact that her father was a superior court judge. Her counselors told her to rewrite the essay and include her father. She crafted an incredibly powerful new essay centering on how her father used to drive her to tears in dinner-table debates, and how she grew to challenge her father and win, using his own rules of logic and argument. She wrote, "I feel as though I have ten years of litigation experience already." This new essay won her admission to all the top law schools.

Four Maxims of Graduate Admissions

+ Fit and match trump grades and scores.
+ Specificity plus flexibility leads to admission.
+ Capacity plus passion leads to admission.
+ Clarity of purpose is attractive.

Do not leave out the obvious. One of the authors of your recommendation letters may mention it anyway. Make a list of all those things you hope the admissions committee doesn't find out about you.

• • •

What do you know about the city, geographic region, or state where you will be applying? Have you ever visited? Did you like it? Is the weather there like the weather where you have lived in the past? Do you have close friends or relatives living near there now? Did your family live there in prior generations? How can you establish any kind of geographical connection with the location of the graduate schools you have targeted? Write down your responses to these questions.

You don't need to gush about how much you would love to live in __________, and you certainly don't want to say you want to live there because you'd like to ski or hang out on the beach. However, failure to mention the locale of the school, especially if it is far away, can be a deal killer. You have to show that you've thought about the move, and considered whether you will be happy there. For example, I was in an admissions dean's office in New York City, and he said, "If candidates don't mention New York City, we don't let them in."

"That's ridiculous," I said. "Suppose a 4.0 student applies to your program and doesn't say 'New York.' You really wouldn't let them in?"

"Absolutely not. I've learned over the years that students who don't mention New York haven't fully considered what it means to live here. And when they show up, they find it to be expensive, dangerous, and distracting. They have to say at least that they are looking forward to living here."

"What about people from New Jersey?" I asked. "Or does this only apply to people from far away, like Florida or New Mexico?"

He looked at me as if I were not very smart, then said, "Especially people from New Jersey."

• • •

Finally, consider the future as well as the past. Consider your immediate future—that is, the time between when you apply and when graduate classes start:

+ What classes are you going to take between now and your arrival at your targeted graduate school? What laboratory or research skills will you learn?
+ What research projects will you complete between now and when you begin graduate school? Will you complete a thesis or capstone project?
+ Will you present your findings at any type of conference or meeting?
+ Will you be going to summer school before graduate school starts? What classes might you take?
+ If you are working, what will you try to get accomplished before you depart for graduate school?

Students often fail to communicate important parts of their preparation that fall between application and matriculation at a graduate program. Be sure to cover this.

Also, consider your long-term future:

+ What are your specific postgraduate career plans?
+ How will this graduate education facilitate those plans?
+ What is your five-year goal? Your ten-year goal?
+ Will you be pursuing additional education or professional training beyond the program you are applying to now?

Envision as specific a future as you can, then write a few lines about where you see yourself going. If you cannot do this exercise comfortably, there's no need to force it. Many, many top students cannot see a specific career future for themselves.

• • •

As you have probably guessed by now, the miscellaneous notes you have been collecting throughout this chapter are, in fact, the basis for your essay. You may have painlessly drafted most of your essay without realizing it, and need only to string your notes together, or you may choose one single note and build your entire essay around it. Or, in a few rare cases, you may end up throwing all of these items away and writing something entirely new. In any case, if you have been thinking as you read this chapter, the self-assessment process *has* prepared you to write the first draft of your essay.

Warning

Again, the prewriting exercises in this chapter are designed to generate lists and a collection of rough draft paragraphs. This is not an invitation to include any of this material in your application essay without intelligent reflection. In the course of interviewing an applicant to top business programs, I discovered he was a belly dancer. In fact, he let me know, he was an *instructor* of belly dancing. I told him to be sure not to mention this in his essay. Another student confided to me that she was an exotic dancer and had paid her way through college with this occupation. I advised her that this was a classic example of something a candidate should *not* share with top law schools. There's more on this in chapter 8, Subsequent Drafts: From the Page into the Reader's Brain.

6

Types of Essays

The main types of application essays for graduate schools are:
Personal Statement
Statement of Purpose
Autobiography
Diversity and Adversity Statements
Statement of Research Intent, aka Research Proposal

There is quite a bit of overlap in what these essays cover and how to write them. This problem is compounded by the fact that universities will often use one term for the essay they are requesting when they actually want an essay and content from one of the other categories. In particular, they will ask for a personal statement when what they want is a statement of purpose, and vice versa. Or the prompts for the autobiography and the diversity statement will ask for the same content. The reason for this is that many universities will use one common application portal for over 100 programs. Departments have different wants and needs, but they have to compromise when it comes to the design of the admissions portal and application tracking system. This is one more reason to read prompts carefully and take them literally. If they ask for "two or three" sample projects, one is not enough and four is too many. If you have many relevant projects, feature two or three, and then include a sentence like this: "For four more projects relevant to this area of study, please see my CV submitted with this application."

You can turn in a personal statement in place of a statement of purpose, and it will still work in many cases. An autobiography can sometimes be perfect as an adversity statement. A little repurposing can help you hit the mark without starting over. But these are in fact distinct documents. To help you discern the features of each type of essay, here are quick definitions, explications, and writing tips you may be able to use for all these types of essays. You still need to read the next two chapters on first drafts and subsequent drafts, but this will help you see what schools are looking for when they ask you to write each different kind of essay.

Personal Statement

Personal statements are essays on your relationship to the intellectual endeavor that you are attempting to pursue in graduate school. Personal statements can have a timeline, that is, can be a description of how your interests have progressed and evolved over time. They are about you, but not in general. They are about *your engagement with a set of ideas* pertinent to your area of graduate study.

A huge problem with applicants' approach to these essays is that they are misnamed. "Personal" statements are not that personal, and that term often invites students to create self-indulgent ramblings that convey little of the content that admissions representatives are looking for. In your mind, every time you see the term "Personal Statement" let your brain read "Professional Statement." That will help you identify and present the most relevant content, and realize that your collection of concert tickets is not worth mentioning.

There is a structure of personal statement that is not beloved. I call it "my personal journey." No matter how sincere, it can come across as chatty, shallow, immature, and self-centered. "I did this . . . Then I did this . . . I discovered this . . . Then I learned this . . . And then I had this realization . . . Then this happened to me . . . Which caused me to do this . . . And now I see this . . ." and so on and on and on. A life story, in order, and compelling only to the author and their mother. A shockingly large percentage of medical school essays are organized like this, but I have seen this style used for every type of academic program.

Even in a "personal" statement, let larger ideas and concepts be the focus of many of your paragraphs, not just you and your perspective. Count the number of I's in your essay. Five or ten, no problem, maybe even more. But if every paragraph is organized around "I" statements and every sentence starts with "I," you should start over or attempt a major rewrite.

Here's an easy way to restructure sentences (and thus paragraphs) away from "I" statements and toward ideas and concepts. Remove the "I." Look for the idea or concept, and start your sentence with those words. Here's an example:

"I have always been fascinated by highly successful people."

First, strike out the "I."

"~~I~~ have always been fascinated by highly successful people."

Next, what's the idea or concept in this sentence? Answer: "Highly successful people."

"~~I~~ have always been fascinated by highly successful people."

So start the sentence with the words that represent the idea or concept.

"Highly successful people . . ."

Finally, salvage the sense of the sentence by repurposing "fascinating" away from being about you individually and to some more universal point of view.

"Highly successful people are fascinating."

Using this technique, you can make your essay more interesting, more intellectual, and less about your personal journey.

Properly, personal statements can be about how you think about your interests. They can also be about how your interests have evolved over time. A common theme in personal statements is the origin story of one's interests: What event, discovery, book, class, movie, or comment caused you to begin to think about this academic direction? What catalyst sparked this journey? *However,* a common error in writing and editing personal statements is to let a catalyst take over the essay. These essays are not stories, and they do not need to be literary. Convey content. Efficiently.

Suppose your interest in veterinary school originated when you were eight years old and your kitten was run over by your evil twin brother on a bicycle. Your parent snatches up your kitten and off you go to the veterinary hospital, a place you did not even know existed prior to this event. Whether the kitten is saved or not, you are now interested in being a vet. This event was the catalyst for your interest, and that interest endures to this day, although it may have passed through some interesting—or not so interesting—iterations.

You could spend one sentence or three paragraphs on this vet visit. I'm going to suggest that a catalyst is often best when short. "I originally got interested in oncology because my mother had cancer." That's a great line. Now you can follow it up in one of two ways. You can make this about your experience of your mother's cancer, trips to the doctor, grief, hair loss, fatigue, multigenerational power shifts, things the doctors said and did. Or you can pivot to what's really interesting to medical school admissions officers: cancer. "Cancer is a really fascinating cluster of diseases. In the book *The Emperor of All Maladies,* by Siddhartha Mukherjee, we learn . . ." and then you focus on your fascination with this medical phenomenon and its bewitching and bedeviling facets. You don't just have experiences; you actually know some things. *You make it about medicine.*

Finally, on this topic, I am also going to suggest that sometimes the catalyst adds little to the essay. It might just as well be deleted, especially if the event happened when you were young, or the event is one that is common or, most boring of all, universal (a young scientist with a telescope or a chemistry set). If you have an origin story, read your essay without it. Is it just as good, maybe even stronger? Then, strip out the origin story even if it helped you organize your thoughts and your essay. If the result is flat and abrupt, keep the catalyst in the essay.

Many prompts for personal statements will also ask you for specific information, such as what concentration you want to pursue, or how you intend to use the degree in your future career. If such queries are in the prompt, the answer needs to be in your essay.

Personal statements are favored by professional schools—business, law, medicine, public policy, architecture, public health, and so on. They will be interested in how you approach this future profession, what your motivations and interests are, and what skills you are bringing to the endeavor. Many other programs besides professional schools may ask you for a personal statement, and many doctoral programs will ask you for both a personal statement and a statement of purpose.

Statement of Purpose

A statement of purpose focuses on what you want to do in graduate school, and not so much on where you came from and where you see yourself going afterward. The reason for this is simple: In professional schools, a set or established series of classes leads to the acquisition of knowledge expected of someone with that concentration. An MBA in finance, an MPH in epidemiology, a master's in speech-language pathology have well-defined courses of study. But in a research-focused doctoral program, there are infinite interests, paths, class sequences, and research projects that could lead to the terminal degree. So, you have to specify what you intend to focus on in graduate school. Statements of purpose focus on that period of time you are actually in the program. What do you want to do, and who do you want to do it with? "I want to study X in order to do Y."

One graduate recruiter said it like this: "I want to know what you want to study, which specific faculty or labs you find attractive, and what you are bringing to the table. Tell me your skills, tell me your interests, and I don't need you to tell me a life story." You can make an excellent statement of purpose by concentrating on these three content areas: What are your skills, what are your interests, who do you want to work with?

Statements of purpose can be devoid of personal information. We may not learn the person's gender identification, undergraduate major, where they grew up, or anything at all about them personally. That's okay in a statement of purpose.

You will notice in the examples that follow this chapter that a lot of essays in this book do not actually follow this spare a structure. If you can tell a quick but interesting story, it can make a statement of purpose more compelling. But stories in statements of purpose are spice, not the main dish. Many scientists and technologists can write good and appropriate statements of purpose with zero personal information. See sample essays #5: "Nitrogen" on page 123, #16: "Iterated Mappings" on page 150, and #38: "Multifunctional Enzymes" on page 208, for classic statements of purpose—all intellectualism and zero personal content.

Statements of purpose need to be fully customized to each targeted program. This goes beyond responding to the prompt (about which more in the next chapter). This means every single sentence in a statement of purpose must be reconsidered in light of the specifics of the program it is for *and* the differences in the essay prompts.

Relate your skills and interests to the program and, for the doctorate, students will usually identify specific faculty of interest. For most master's applications, you do not have to name specific potential mentors in your essays. You establish that the program's strengths match your interests, but you do not have to tie your interests to individual faculty. But for the doctorate my recommendation is to identify a cluster of faculty who you are interested in, and name three or more of them in your statement of purpose. (Obviously, this is not possible in some programs; sometimes you really will be pitching your application toward just one or possibly two mentors.)

Faculty have warned me that students are doing what one called "cheap" name-dropping. Here is one faculty reviewer's note: "If you say, 'Of course it is the distinguished faculty at Columbia that most attract me to your program,' that's barely above a high school effort. That's insulting. Even if you say, 'I am most interested in working with Drs. Wilson, Karpinski, and Roy' you haven't proved it. Still an extraordinarily weak effort. Anyone can pick a few names off our website. What do you like about Dr. Wilson? What do you know about Dr. Karpinski? What do you believe about Dr. Roy? What do you see yourself doing here with them? That's context. We need that context to tell if you are sincere, and to know where to put you in the program. We need that context to assess your potential fit."

Some programs are perfectly happy if you are clear on a cluster of faculty of interest. But some programs actually require you to name a specific mentor as part of the application process. Successful applicants will often have communicated with or met that professor. In any case, the

Explore Fit and Match

Writing to professors and visiting help to establish fit and match. This is common for the doctorate, but not usually required for the master's. This student got meetings and eventually admission with this letter:

Dear Dr. Mabry:

When I look at the faculty at USC, you and Dr. Hall seem like the closest matches to my interests, but neither of you is listed on the departmental website as seeking possible graduate students. Only Drs. Stallman, Vost, and Bartoli are listed as seeking new students. Their areas of focus do not align closely enough with mine.

Would you be so kind as to consider whether there is a match with my background and your areas of interest, and whether there is any possibility at all that you could take on a new student next fall? Please hear me out . . .

essay should be structured to focus on that scholar's specific work, and how you would fit into that research focus. Read the websites and application portals really carefully, or you may not catch this very important difference.

Finally, on this topic of joining a doctoral program by targeting a narrow cluster of inquiry—and no one likes to talk about this—in many, many cases, *they don't actually hold you to it.* If you get to a doctoral program, you will usually have a year or even two of required courses, called rotations, and then you settle down with a particular mentor or PI (principal investigator). If, during rotations, you find some new and exciting topical area, or some captivating and dynamic mentor, you can switch. Do not tell anyone I told you this.

Autobiographies

Autobiographies are a common essay requested of applicants. Prompts for autobiographies usually give no guidance beyond a suggested maximum length. My counsel is to write an autobiography that is very nearly the same thing as a personal statement, that is, an *intellectual* autobiography. When and how did you get interested in this topic? How has that interest evolved over time, and due to what influences? Keep it professional.

Unfortunately, many students take this opportunity to go rogue. They write literature, when what is required is an argument. Be discerning. Let's suppose I grew up in a log home with no running water in Arkansas. Let's say I loved every minute of it; it made me who I am today. If I were applying to a top MBA program, I would not say anything about that at all. I would focus on how I got interested in business, some influential mentors, some business books and TED Talks that really shaped my direction. However, if I were headed for a doctoral program in rural sociology, my autobiography would be all about growing up in a hand-built cabin, and the nature of the multiple communities and social structures that surrounded and intersected with that supposedly isolated cabin. Make sense?

A student applying to a doctoral program in STEM prepared an autobiography that focused on her upbringing in a polygamous compound as a member of an independent sect of Mormonism. Her essay read like a TV pilot, complete with clumsy FBI informants, corrupt law enforcement, a work-from-home pyramid scheme, and more! I advised her to take all of this out. It was completely distracting from all the rest of her application materials, which focused on science, labs, research, and publications. She was imminently qualified, but this autobiography added nothing but sensationalism.

An autobiography can be a place to introduce information about adversity, and how adversity has shaped your academic record. Let us imagine two applicants. Applicant A has a 3.5 GPA. Her mother is the mayor of the city she grew up in, and her father is a renowned and beloved pediatrician. She has had a tutor for every class she ever took in school. She even had a coach who prepared her for her interview for preschool. All she cares about is skiing. In fact, she goes to Argentina every July and August to ski. She is an inattentive and easily distracted student, and her GPA is 3.5.

Applicant B also has a 3.5 GPA. She came to the United States six years ago, not speaking a word of English. She started community college without being able to understand everything her professors said. She has had a job every day of her young life in America. She struggled. But by dogged determination, her GPA has gone up and up. She made a 4.0 for her last three semesters, taking difficult upper-division classes and labs. But because of those early grades, her GPA is 3.5. This is why grad programs ask for autobiographies, diversity, and adversity statements, to give these candidates

Letter to a Prospective Faculty Mentor for Doctoral Study

(This letter is too long, but it is a good example of how to organize this type of email.)

Subject: Query from a prospective student

Dear Dr. Anderson:

My name is Lucia Cannondale and I am very interested in pursuing a PhD in anthropology at UC Santa Cruz. I graduated from Loyola Marymount University with a B.A. in communications and a GPA of 3.69 in May of this year. I am originally from Uruguay, in spite of my American name, and I moved to the US with a full scholarship from the Kilroy Foundation. Obviously I am fully bilingual, Spanish-English. My focus in communications was biculturalism, and I took enough anthropology courses to almost have a double major. I was fortunate that my senior thesis was selected by faculty nomination to be presented at Loyola's Undergraduate Research Symposium. This was a great learning experience that convinced me that a life of scholarship is attractive for me.

In the course of researching graduate programs, I was excited to come across your name and read about your work. My areas of interest for graduate study include diaspora culture, migration, singularities of culture along the border between countries, and disaster tourism. Some of this is closely related to your research interests and papers. I would be very grateful if you could answer a few questions to give me a better idea of your graduate program.

1. Do you agree that our interests are closely aligned, or am I missing something? I am open to new directions, and I truly appreciate your input on this.

2. According to your website your interests include transnationalism, diaspora, and Latin American area studies, but your last two papers were on incarceration in Texas. Are you still interested in those prior topics?

3. Are you accepting new advisees at this time? Would it make sense to mention you in my application?

4. If so, would I get to work with you from the first year, or are students expected to take a year or two of generalized courses before settling down with a primary advisor?

5. Is there any reading that you would recommend for me to do? Whose work do you find particularly promising at this time? Whose work should I be following methodologically, or for content focus?

6. How can I best prepare myself to be a strong candidate for—and student within—your program?

I would be truly grateful if you have even a moment to respond. As you can imagine, any help at all would make a big difference as I apply to graduate programs.

Respectfully submitted,
Lucia Cannondale

a chance to point out circumstances that are not obvious on a transcript. (There is much more on the issue of grades and essays in the section below on adversity statements.)

One thing to include is evidence of drive and grit and passion, even if it appears outside of academia. If you run marathons, or you mastered a martial art, or you hiked the Pacific Crest Trail, or you built a sailboat in a barn with hand tools from hundred-year-old plans, or you play stand-up bass in a jazz ensemble on Friday and Saturday nights, be sure that gets coverage. Grit, drive, determination, and perseverance are criteria for acceptance.

A few years ago at the University of California, Berkeley, a student fell asleep during a preprofessional advising meeting. Her advisor, who had met with her before, was quite perturbed. After the group was dismissed, he woke her up and demanded to know why she had even bothered to come to the meeting. She apologized, explaining that she had worked all night.

"Do you work all night very often?" he asked. She told him that she did, eight to ten hours per night, five to six nights a week.

"Why?" he asked, now concerned for her health.

It turned out her father had died, her mother was disabled, there wasn't any insurance, she was already a senior, and she decided to just tough it out and work to support herself and her mother.

"Why isn't any of this in your personal statement?" he asked.

"Well," she replied, "I didn't think they were really interested in the personal affairs of my life."

"Well, they are," he told her. "By the way, what kind of work do you do?"

"Oh," she said, "I'm a private detective."

Hmm. I wonder if a law school would be interested in that . . .

So, use your autobiography to make an argument. Present information that shows your development and your intellectual influences, and establishes that you have the skills, attributes, and attitudes that will allow you to perform in graduate school. Everything else is extraneous.

Diversity and Adversity Statements

How would you contribute to diversity of thought and experience if we were to admit you to our academic community?

Is there anything about your life experiences that the committee would need to consider to assess your ability to perform at the graduate level?

EXTENUATING CIRCUMSTANCES
If your grades and/or test scores are not strong, and you would like to provide an explanation, please do so here.

How, if at all, have your own experiences of race, socioeconomic status, sexual orientation, gender identity, ability status, immigration status, national origin, religion, accent, or appearance influenced your life in a positive or a negative way?

What are your own values concerning diversity, equity, and inclusion in contemporary society? Please define your terms and then address this question with your own, personal point of view. There is no wrong or right answer; we are seeking your opinion on these issues.

Diversity and adversity statements flummox many applicants. What goes in them? Unfortunately, almost anything you want. If the prompt gives you clear instructions for content, follow them. The prompts above are examples you can use if you need guidance to get started. Many applicants compose diversity and adversity essays that do not bolster their candidacy. More on that in a minute. And some applicants object that these essays can tokenize and exploit scholars of color and applicants who have been traumatized already by life experiences. Let's consider some ways to make diversity and adversity statements less daunting, and more of a positive addition to your application package.

First of all, what is the difference between a diversity statement and an adversity statement? A diversity statement is neutral to the idea that your experience of diversity has been beneficial or deleterious. It might have been one or the other or both. An adversity statement is explicitly about how your experiences, which may be uncommon among the graduate program's applicants, have been deleterious to you. That is, these adverse experiences have been an extra burden to you, that some other applicants may not have had to carry, along the journey to this point of applying to a graduate program. Diversity and adversity are different, but my advice is to ignore the name of the statement and follow the instructions in the prompt. The ideas and concepts from diversity and adversity can overlap, can be blended together, or can be treated separately. Let's explore this.

Let's focus on the diversity dimension first, then add in the adversity dimension. Any diversity and adversity essays can certainly contain elements from both. Starting with diversity, there are two approaches, which can be combined.

+ I come from an uncommon background, compared to the typical applicant to your program.
+ I support a diverse educational and socioeconomic world, in which all types of people can thrive and contribute.

Using the first option, you build an argument that your background would enable you to bring novelty to the academic endeavor. Properly, this is more than gender, racial and ethnic backgrounds, LGBTQIA identity, disabilities, immigration status, regional origin, socioeconomic status, and so on, although these can be dimensions of your argument. Try focusing on how who you are and your experiences along your journey to this moment will allow you to "contribute to diversity of thought and experience."

What can you see that others cannot? And, especially, how can that be an advantage?

I know of a researcher who studied curanderas and their influence on the attitudes toward allopathic medical treatment for cancer among Latine communities along the border of Mexico and the United States. To do this work, one needs to be bilingual, know what curanderas are, know how rural health care systems operate, and gain trust and access in communities that do not want to be studied by outsiders. Because she herself was from this community, she was asking questions that outsiders could not even conceive of.

Will you be able to help other students see new perspectives? Will you be able to pursue new goals in new ways? Will your disability or bilingualism or race or gender allow you to make a contribution to journalism? To medicine? To architecture? How is your status an asset to yourself, to others, to scholarship, to society as a whole? This is a different approach than laying out how your status will allow an institution to burnish its credentials as an inclusive place, an approach that some find patronizing and troubling.

Whether you are seeking an MBA, law degree, or a doctorate in ornithology, how does your gender, racial and ethnic background, sexuality, immigration status, socioeconomic status, regional origin, status as someone convicted of a crime, history with addiction and recovery, and so on allow you to ask questions no one else is asking, to see opportunity no one else can see? How can you contribute to diversity of thought and experience in your targeted graduate program?

The other approach to diversity is to answer these questions: How can you be an advocate for diversity? What are your values concerning the topic of equity and access in our society? How have you in the past created space for others to thrive who may not be part of the dominant sociocultural paradigm? How have you offered opportunity for underrepresented people? Anyone of any race, gender, background, etc., can build an essay around this topic. Again, this can be combined with the above approach; these approaches are in no way mutually exclusive.

A values statement is a place to start, but readers of diversity statements will be looking for behavior and experiences, actual prior actions related to diversity. If you have almost no experience working with people who would be considered diverse, a statement that you value diversity, and that you would create welcoming space in your classrooms, labs, workplaces, or whatever, may be a direction to take with these essays. However, many readers will not believe that you have not had any opportunity to interact with anyone besides people like you. Maybe if you are from an isolated village in Japan. Maybe then.

If you do not in fact value diversity, then my advice is to not make up performative beliefs and behaviors. There are some US states that have banned these types of essays in student selection and academic hiring. You can apply to programs in those states. You can also simply skip these essay prompts with no explanation—or write under the prompt, "I choose not to prepare a response to this prompt."

However, if you are going to prepare a diversity essay of any type, be very careful not to "other" the people you are claiming to value and support. The term "disadvantaged" others anyone designated with that term, and yes, "others" is a verb. I read an essay for a medical school application where the applicant bragged about working in a "slum" in Brazil, as evidence of her ability to work with all different types of patients. Her language certainly counted against her.

So, if you worked with unhoused people, talk about them as people, and not "homeless." There is a language structure favored by people who do diversity work: put people first. So, "people without housing," "people with disabilities," "people struggling with food insecurity." Put people first.

Be careful not to stereotype any group or person. Groups are rarely monolithic. Individuation will always exceed group norms, if there even are group norms.

Some applicants use a diversity and adversity statement to talk about their own challenges and struggles, and how they have overcome them. They may use this space to talk about their grades or learning disabilities or some aspect of their academic journey that deserves explanation. Just remember that these topics can also be covered in an autobiography, and the diversity dimension itself can have a positive message, like some of the ones suggested here.

Many underrepresented, marginalized, and minoritized applicants use this space to record and document injustices that they have endured due to power structures. They give examples of prejudicial treatment, microaggressions and macroaggressions, systemic racism, systemic misogyny, and institutional and personal instances of bias. I will not argue against this approach, and it is in fact common. People in power often have no idea how their power impacts and is perceived by others. Here is a sentence from one such statement; the rest of the essay went into detail.

My mere presence in these rooms is an experience of both triumph and frustration, triumph to be justifiably in that room, and frustration to be there alone with no guide and no friend to hold open the door.

Most people in power do not know the experience of being invisible. Or the opposite, having every head turn whenever they enter a room. It needs to be said that doing good work *while being an underrepresented gender* and doing good work *while being a scholar of color* entails an additional psychological burden, an extra cognitive load.

However, an entire essay with this focus misses a chance. At some point it is beneficial to segue into one's vision of the future, and how despite—or even because of—these experiences, one is enthusiastic about pursuing the graduate program.

"How would you contribute to diversity of thought and experience if we were to admit you to our academic community?" That's the question to answer.

Now let us pivot to focus on the issue of adversity as its own dimension, separate from but combinable with diversity. Universities do not often ask for "adversity statements" by that name, so let me explain why I am giving you a whole section on this. Universities want this content. They want and need it. Remember the case example above, of the two students with a 3.5 GPA? One who liked to ski and one who was a superstar? To properly do their job of evaluating student potential, admissions officers need to know which kind of 3.5 you are. This content could appear in personal statements, autobiographies, sometimes in a statement of purpose, or in a letter to a specific professor or department chair or dean. And sometimes this content is requested in a prompt hidden in the application form, let's call it Question 8-C, which might read like this:

Is there anything that the admissions committee needs to know to accurately assess your ability to perform at the graduate level?

If you have grades or test scores that do not represent your true potential, you should address that. As a general rule, it is better to keep your main application essay as positive as possible. But sometimes it is important to explain an issue rather than leave the reader to fill in their own guesses. Do not make long, involved excuses; keep it simple and devoid of drama; no whining and no feeling sorry for yourself. Details usually don't make the case better. For example, I read an essay that mentioned that the candidate's father was deported twice in his freshman year, and that was, of course, why his freshman year grades were a train wreck. The fact spoke for itself; it did not need a lot of detail or explanation. He persevered and excelled later in his program. It can be helpful to compute your GPA according to a formula that you devise. "My GPA after freshman year, once my family was stable again, was 3.8 overall." This student went to graduate school at Yale with abysmal grades from his freshman year.

Your problem must meet these criteria:

+ It has to be in the past.
+ It has to be resolved.
+ It has to be sympathetic.
+ It should be unlikely to recur in graduate school.

First of all, you need to get your transcripts and analyze your grades in the following categories: overall, in your major, in math and science, in math, in science, in everything except English and comp, year by year, semester by semester, over the last four semesters, not counting your freshman year, since you declared your current major, in classes that meet after noon, and so on, ad infinitum. Then, look for patterns. The best pattern of all is a perfect 4.0, of course, and second best is for your grades to go up each year. Then you can say, "My grades have improved every year. I feel as though I have not yet hit my stride as a scholar." Identify your worst semester and your worst grade, and ask yourself what was going on in that class or semester. Is this a problem you have permanently resolved? Can you assure the admissions reader that this was an anomalous problem?

My GPA took a tumble in the second semester of my sophomore year, when I had some difficulties that are now fully resolved. My GPA in political science, minus that semester, is 3.8.

You don't even need to say what the difficulties were. But it helps to say the matter is resolved. By the way, a clever reader will have noticed that the student above did two computations in a series on his GPA. First, he removed a period of time, then he calculated the GPA in the major, $f(f(n))$. By experimenting with GPA calculations, you can report a very different number than the one provided by the registrar. Just explain your work and give the outcome.

One student I interviewed was brought up to not defy his father. He was the first in his family to go to college, and his father did not really understand how college worked. The family owned a restaurant, though, and his father certainly understood

GPA Calculations

Want to calculate your grades? It's credit hours times GPA for each class, which gives you actual credit points. Then divide that sum by the maximum number of potential credit points. Multiply that result by the grade scale (in the US, almost always 4). That's your GPA for that set of classes. Or just search for "GPA calculator" and you can find many that are easy to use.

Example: If all the classes are 3 credit hours:

Class	Grade	Convert Grade to Scale	×	Credit Hours	Actual Grade Points	/ Max Potential Grade Points
Class 1	B	3		× 3	= 9	12
Class 2	A	4		× 3	= 12	12
Class 3	A	4		× 3	= 12	12
Σ					= 33	36

GPA = Actual / Potential $33/36 = 91.\bar{6} \times 4 = 3.67$ GPA

how restaurants worked: When the help no-shows, you call your number-one son. So his father kept calling him in to work when he had finals, when he had papers due, and so on. To solve this problem, the son transferred to a university at the far end of the state. His grades went up and stayed up. His problem was in the past, it was resolved, and, as long as he applied to graduate schools far from the restaurant, it was not likely to recur. Admissions readers want and need to know why this student struggled at his first campus.

Another young woman told me she had to work full-time when in college. "Gosh," I said, "that must have impacted your ability to study."

"Oh, yes," she said, "I hardly had time to study at all."

"Why did you have to work so much?" I asked.

"I like to buy a lot of clothes, and I ran my credit cards up. I didn't have any choice!" she cried.

I think you get it: This problem is not resolved, not sympathetic, and likely to recur.

Be careful of shining a light on a small problem and making it look like a big one. Students are always asking me something like this: "I made a C on organic chem. Then I retook it and made a B. Should I talk about that?" These are very common grade patterns, and unless something awful happened to you the first time you took the course, you are probably better off not to address the issue at all.

By the way, if your grades are more than ten years old, most admissions readers won't give them much weight, whether they were outstanding or abysmal. It is a good idea to get a few recent grades before applying to graduate school, so you can say, "My recent GPA is 4.0, including both graduate and undergraduate classes I've been taking in geography. As a mature adult, I'm looking forward to returning to school and focusing on my studies in a way I did not the first time around."

Should you reveal a learning disability, a physical condition, or mental health challenge? This has to be decided on a case-by-case basis. If your learning difference is accommodated or your health issue is no longer acute, probably not. Again, you do not always need to say what was going on.

I had some health challenges in the fall of my junior year, which impacted my grades. My GPA minus that semester is 3.4.

Here's how some other students have addressed adversity in their backgrounds, sometimes briefly and sometimes more fully:

I withdrew from three classes in the fall of my junior year due to the death of my mother.

I went to a very strict military boarding school when I was in high school, and when I came to college I am afraid I let the freedom erode my first year's studies. Please note that my GPA for the last two and a half years is 3.68 in my major. I feel that my test scores and my GPA in the last two and a half years are indicative of the performance you can expect of me.

Finally, I would like to address the issue of my academic career. As you have my transcripts, you can clearly see that I was not especially serious in my first few years as an undergraduate, and you can also see that I have improved dramatically. I have a 3.9 GPA in graduate school, and I expect to continue to do as well in the doctoral program.

I am writing to request that you disregard the first GRE score on my records instead of averaging it in with my second score (which I know is your practice). On my way to take the first test, I was involved in a major accident (see attached police report) and I was very emotionally agitated during the exam. I realize now that I should have just skipped the test, but I was in a state of shock from the accident and was not thinking clearly. As you can see, there is a big difference between the two scores. Thank you for your consideration.

Ever since I was little, I wanted to be a physicist. At least, that's what I wish I could say, but it is not the truth. The truth is, I was exposed to the harshness of the world at a very young age. The household I grew up in was rife with poverty, domestic abuse, drug use, and daily chaos. Combined with the lack of encouragement and mentorship to excel in my education—I come from a family where the majority didn't graduate high school, let alone go on to pursue higher education—my environment was not conducive to the molding of a scientific mind. Initially, this left me at a significant educational disadvantage. It took me many years to become enamored with physics. In fact, it was a chance encounter with a YouTube series, "PBS Crash Course Physics," that sparked my interest. Dr. Shini Somara made physics seem like the most interesting thing in the world. I, too, wanted to become a catalyst for others' passion. From there I started consuming as much information as I could and began constantly imagining myself conducting cutting-edge physics research and mentoring promising young students. I had the benefit of some wonderful mentors, especially Drs. R. Zhuang and L. Stevens (see CV and research proposal). My studies became my refuge, the one place where I knew I could excel, find respect, and outshine others. As corny as it may sound, I actually made a decision to break a generational cycle and pursue my undergraduate program with a zeal bordering on obsession. I have used my past as a tool to help me to succeed, take initiative, and build an exceptional work ethic. I believe my academic performance speaks to this. I have also used my misfortune to develop the invaluable skill that is adaptation, so that I may overcome any hurdle I face in the future. These past experiences have helped me to construct and mold a mind that *is* conducive for science and a passion for research. My early experiences have led to fierce determination, a sense of purpose, and curiosity, which will help me succeed in a research career.

My father experienced some unexpected business reversals in the spring of my freshman year, and I took a full-time job in order to complete the academic term. By the spring of my sophomore year, I qualified for financial aid, and was able to drop down to a part-time job. If you do not count the year when I was working full time and going to school full time, my GPA would be 3.35 overall and 3.53 in my major.

Though my undergraduate grades are less than average for graduate school applicants, I feel that the graduate climate is better suited to my type of academic personality. I have never been a good test taker in engineering courses, and exams always lower my grades for a course. However, my lab marks and other scores are always well above average, and I particularly excel at unconstrained projects, both within courses and in independent research. I think the lab write-up I provided and my letters of recommendation will establish that I can do the excellent work you expect of someone in your program.

Although I have always been a premed student, I would like to point out that I did not follow the premed strategy of taking only "safe" classes I knew I could make an A in. I took an overload for three out of eight semesters, mostly so I could take classes like "History of the US before 1865," "Greco-Roman Religion," "Native American Cultures," "Classical Greek Philosophy," and two years of Latin. My GPA in all math and science classes is 3.78, and I think that is representative of my ability to complete the medical school curriculum.

To make sense of my transcripts you will need to know that I changed my major four times before I finished my sophomore year, which is also why I extended my undergraduate career to a fifth year. I always made straight A's in math and science, but I just didn't connect that to engineering until . . .

Again, be careful not to lose more than you gain by bringing up negatives, especially if your rationale is not compelling. Unless you have a really good reason for mentioning weak grades or irregularities in your background, it may be best not to mention them at all.

You can also address weak GRE scores in language like the below. My counsel is to (a) provide alternate evidence of the skills the GRE purports to measure, and (b) to gently diss the test.

I don't want you to be concerned about my verbal GRE score. I was quite surprised that it was not higher. I've always been praised for my academic writing, but I am a careful composer, constantly looking up words and checking facts. I found it to be a very artificial way to measure my science writing skills, as almost none of the words on the GRE had anything to do with science, let alone chemistry. Also I was not used to working with a time limit and no reference resources. I believe my writing sample will put you at ease about my ability to deliver good papers and labs.

My quant score on the GRE was a surprise to me. I expected to score much higher. I earned an "A" in calculus, algebra II, and statistics. I've designed several quantitative research projects (see research sample). It is obvious I have no problem with quantitative reasoning. I'm not sure what happened with this test, and maybe I should have spent more time

practicing these skills in the test's format, but I think my performance in the real world more than establishes the needed skillset.

Concerning my GRE score, I think it is important for you to know that I did not grow up speaking English at home, and some of the vocabulary on the GRE was quite arcane. I don't know anybody who uses this type of language, at home or at school. I think my writing sample should put you at ease about this issue.

Just push back, even a little bit, against the idea that a GRE score defines your abilities. Provide alternate evidence, and gently question the validity of the test.

There are many more examples throughout the book of diversity and adversity statements inserted where they fit best in personal statements, statements of purpose, and autobiographies, not just in diversity and adversity essays.

One final warning on the whole topic of diversity and adversity: Avoid the temptation to trump up some small issue and claim disadvantage. Two of the worst pleas for special consideration I have ever read were (a) a student who claimed that he was uniquely disadvantaged because he was middle class, and his still-married parents were neither rich nor poor. I assure you this argument was not well received. And (b) a student who claimed she was discriminated against because she was too beautiful, and people did not take her seriously as a scientist. This was also very poorly received.

Statement of Research Intent, aka Research Proposal

Statements of research intent are not common in applications for master's and doctoral programs, but they are common in some elite scholarship applications and in postdoc applications.

The most important thing about these applications is to follow the protocols for preparing and submitting your research proposal. If your word count is wrong, or even your margins, that can be disqualifying. Deviating from the format is disqualifying. Failing to use the right citations format is disqualifying. Comply with every single direction provided.

The second thing to know about almost all of these exercises is that they are usually just that, exercises. Most programs do not actually expect you to execute the research project you have designed. Sure, you'll probably do something close, or related to what you are proposing, but these are admissions exercises. You are doing a pro forma research proposal, to show that you know something about a topic, and know something about how to design research. But you are not really proposing to do that actual research.

Avoid being grandiose. One reviewer told me about reviewing a really intriguing research project, smart and well designed. But he rejected the applicant. He told me, "You would need a $300,000 budget, multiple years, and a couple of graduate assistants to do that project. It was not doable." Make your proposed project affordable and doable.

Note that these proposals have multiple audiences. It pays to write something that is understandable to a smart layperson, or someone in your field but not necessarily an expert in your specific area of inquiry. This requires balancing the technical with the accessible.

In almost 100 percent of applications requiring a research proposal, you will need a faculty mentor to help you prepare your research design. For that reason, we will not delve more into the specifics. There are several statements of research intent in the samples, for example, Essay #21: "NSF Postdoc in Chemistry," Essay #30: "NSF GRFP—Neutrinos," and Essay #39: "NSF GRFP—Butterflies."

7

Your First Draft:

From Your Heart onto the Page

The topics for graduate admissions essays are usually specified by the school to which you are applying. The wording may vary, but the topic is usually some version of "Where are you coming from? Why are you coming here? Where are you going after this?"

Although most schools ask essentially the same questions, they each ask them in a slightly different way. Because of this, plan to write the essay for your first-choice school first, then modify it as needed for your other targeted schools. As a general rule, do not submit your first-choice school's application until you have finished three complete applications. Some of the ideas you use in other essays can help you fine-tune the application to your first-choice school.

The first thing to do is RTGDQ. One of my teachers in high school had a big rubber stamp, "RTGDQ," which he claimed stood for "Read The Gosh Darn Question." No matter how eloquent your exam answer was, if you failed to address the question directly, you could expect the dreaded RTGDQ to appear in your blue book. So open the application or catalog to the exact wording of the essay question, and RTGDQ. Then answer it. Truthfully.

Here is a common essay prompt for a personal statement:

Tell us how you got interested in this area of graduate study, why you would like to pursue graduate study in our particular program, and how this education will contribute to your future career plans.

Note that that prompt asks for three specific things.

+ How did your interest in this particular topic or field develop?
+ Why is our program attractive to you?
+ How will this education contribute to your career goals?

If you do not address each of the criteria they are asking for, you are not responding correctly. Remember, grad school is not like undergrad. You cannot copy and paste your way to grad school. Here's a prompt from one of the departments at MIT:

> **Please explain why you are a good candidate for graduate school. You should describe why you wish to attend graduate school, what you would like to study, and any research experience you have. Describe one or more accomplishments you are particularly proud of that suggest that you will succeed in your chosen area of research.**

Notice how specific this prompt is. There are five criteria in the prompt. Leave one out and you are not going to MIT. There are three dimensions in the last criterion alone: Fail to write about "one or more accomplishments" *and* "that you are particularly proud of" *and* "that suggest you will succeed," then you are not going to MIT.

Because students are using AI to help them with application essays, schools are asking more and more quirky essay questions, questions that don't lend themselves to a generic answer. They are asking more "why" questions, questions with answers unique to each applicant's mindset. They are asking more specific questions about your own experiences, and asking for details that cannot be filled in by AI, *and they are matching the content to your letters of recommendation and other material you submit.* They are also noting the tone, style, and vocabulary between the different essays you submit, say, a personal statement, a statement of purpose, a writing sample, and a diversity statement. If one has a different tone, style, and vocabulary, they may doubt that you wrote any of them.

There is no question that AI can generate essay ideas and outlines, and change the tone and sophistication of your vocabulary. AI can write your entire essay for you, but there are many good reasons not to do that. One professor said it this way: "AI will generate material that gets a passing grade, but it doesn't generate A work." I do not know that he is correct. Although faculty swear they can identify AI content, studies indicate they very often cannot. Should you use AI in your drafting, editing, and proofreading phases? Proofreading, for sure, but you will get better work if you do your own first drafts. You will get more authentic work. I'll return to the issue of appropriate use of AI assistants later in this chapter. For now, let's assume you are going to struggle along and do your own work. You will be glad you did.

How to Get Started

Your first draft should be honest and straightforward. Do not try to second-guess your reader at all. Let sentences come straight from your heart. Write like you talk if that helps you. Voice record your first draft, or pretend you are writing a letter to a friend, if it will jump-start the process. Keep the emphasis on content, not style; avoid pseudo-academese; don't think too much.

Write when you write, edit when you edit. In this chapter you will write, and in the next chapter you will edit. Do not let anybody tell you what to write, and do not let anybody see your first draft; read the next chapter and complete a second draft before you show your work to anyone. The first rule of brainstorming is to fill the whiteboard with ideas before evaluating any of them; as you draft your essay, do not critique it. Just keep writing and moving forward.

• • •

As general rules of style, avoid footnotes and minimize omniscient exposition. Omniscient exposition is that high-handed style of writing you learned in high school: "Should the student feel compelled to build labyrinthine semantical structures, and thereby disguise the relationship between modalities of meaning and the true self . . ." That really does sound like AI blather.

Be confident in your writing. Assume that you will be admitted.

• • •

An interesting first line or paragraph is a gift to your reader. If you are applying to a highly competitive preprofessional program, you will want to pay particular attention to your opening line or paragraph. You have already seen some interesting opening paragraphs in the last chapter. If you are an unusual candidate, or have had an unusual experience, launching your essay on that note can be a good idea.

One candidate told me her goal was to tell who she was in one sentence. She wrote, "I am the sixth of seven children from a large blue-collar Irish-Catholic family in the Midwest." Another candidate wrote, "As a member of the Pokagon Band of Potawatomi Indians, the seven grandmother teachings play a large role in my life. Honesty, bravery, love, truth, humility, respect, and wisdom take on a new meaning in my everyday life. The most important lesson that I have learned is to strive each day to gain wisdom." This is certainly an arresting opening line:

> **If this information were to fall into the wrong hands, I could be kidnapped and returned to my home country. If you cannot honor my need for confidentiality, delete my entire application immediately.**

Can you imagine coming onto that line while sifting through a stack of barely differentiable applications?

One of the best types of opening paragraph relates an epiphany. This can be the moment you decided to pursue your current goals or the moment you discovered just what might be entailed to pursue those goals. Look again at the "zoology or medicine" story on page 67. It's a classic epiphany tale. Here are two more epiphany openings:

> **I made an "A" in labor relations, but I learned more about labor-management issues in one summer working on a union construction crew than I learned in the class . . .**

> **When the old man urinated on my leg, it ran down my pants and into my shoe. I could not let go of him, as I was holding him up, trying to move him from a wheelchair onto the bed. That's when I first realized that medicine was not going to be just starched white lab coats and golf at four. I looked again at medicine, the actual practice of medicine on real people, and saw that it often involved messy fluids, imprecision, and an element of surprise . . .**

Don't be afraid to use vivid detail to make points. Most AMCAS (American Medical College Application Service) essays start out with some version of "I always wanted to be a doctor because I like science and I want to help people." If you are a medical college admissions reader, you come to hate this sentence. It is unbelievably common, in one version or another. Also, since the student has not *always* existed, they can't *always* have wanted to be a doctor, so they have proposed an ontological impossibility right in the opening phrase. Just for the record, the candidate in the last example above goes on to convey exactly that—that he likes science and wants to help people—but he conveys this message through a series of vignettes employing vivid detail. Try this subtle shift in the way you think about the medical school essay. Instead of writing "why I want to be a doctor" write "why I want to practice medicine." Let that sink in.

Avoid using words like these in your essay: *meaningful, challenging, beautiful, wonderful, invaluable, rewarding*. Say what you mean; either describe the event in question, or report your emotions and thoughts in more basic detail. Replace these vague words with a personal statement, something from your own unique point of view. If you have difficulty with this, start sentences with "I": "I felt . . ." "I realized . . ." "I saw that . . ." You might have to take some of these "I" statements out later, they may end up seeming indulgent, but it might help you get started on authentic content.

• • •

Some candidates take a bold position in their first few lines, implicitly promising their readers that there will be more to follow. Here are two examples:

"Why in the world do you want to go to law school? Heaven knows we don't need any more lawyers." Having worked for the large, prestigious law firm of Bells & Motley since mid-July, it continues to surprise me how frequently I have been asked that particular question.

Learning outside in a 9,000-acre forest was more engaging and exciting than sitting in a lab waiting for some bacteria to grow.

You do not need a fancy or arresting opening, but if one comes naturally to you, write it out. They are more common for professional schools and master's programs than for doctoral programs. Do not spend all day writing first lines; keep moving along. If composing a first line is a problem, just skip it for now. You can come back to it later.

• • •

Advice from a STEM Recruiter

+ Follow the instructions! It is astounding how many applicants do not follow our instructions.
+ Address each and every request for information. We ask specific questions that need specific responses. Answer the question we ask, not a question you would rather answer instead.
+ Work closely with recommenders. If your recommenders cannot match the detail and enthusiasm that you present in your application, that's a red flag for us.
+ The strongest applications provide the greatest detail. If you did work on a project that was later published, cite the publication and detail your contribution to it. What was your specific role and intellectual or task contribution in this larger project? If your work was part of a grant-funded project, report the actual grant number and title. AI cannot accurately fill in this type of detail, and it is easy for us to check.
+ Do not just claim skills. Tell us where and how you learned them.
+ Keep a portfolio of all your work throughout your career. This will help you incredibly at every stage, in grad school and beyond. Keep contemporaneous records. Start now with this habit.
+ The strongest candidates are strong in every one of our criteria. If you do not address a criterion, we will assume you do not meet it.

As your essay progresses, be sure to RTGDQ over and over again, and address the questions as asked, in the order asked. Be specific and provide details, details, details. You will discover that this approach to writing favors qualitative analysis over quantitative listings. In other words, it is far better to give a rich description of one incident than to cram your essay full of activities and accomplishments without any hint of what you learned from them and what thoughts and emotions they evoked in you during the process.

Of course your essay will have content that is also reflected in the rest of your application, for example, lists of honors and awards, or experiences on a CV you may have submitted. But do not be *overly* redundant with other parts of your application. If your complete work history is listed somewhere else on the application, mention a particular job, a particular accomplishment, or interactions with a particular supervisor only to give a new perspective or to let the committee know what one of these has meant to you personally. It is good practice to refer the reader to other parts of your application when they are important. Remind them that there is far more to you than you have room to discuss in this short essay. Tie your essay to the rest of your application with notes like these: "See letter of recommendation," "See resume for more leadership experiences," "See bibliography for additional articles," "See awards." You will notice this technique in many of the essays selected for this book.

• • •

Demonstrate that you have read their websites carefully, researched the program, and considered your reasons for applying to this particular school. The essay is never all about you. It is about you *and the particular program* and how the two belong together. Find a common thread, a point at which your philosophy and theirs meet in happy confluence, as in these examples:

> **I was especially impressed by Dean Jaedicke's statement in your brochure that the school "strives to imbue students with a sense of 'incompleteness.'" At Reed, we called it "learning how to learn," and finding out how much I don't know was the most valuable lesson I left Reed with.**

> **I want to enroll in the program at [major university] because of its excellent reputation in real estate and urban land economics; I have not found such strength at other MBA programs. I am also familiar with the admirable work of the Center for Real Estate and Urban Economics, and I particularly look forward to working with Profs. Edelstein, Rosen, and Wallace.**

> **The Government and Foreign Affairs graduate program at Virginia is attractive to me because of the faculty members' areas of specialization and my corresponding academic and research interests. I am particularly excited about the prospect of working with Profs. Ceaser, Milkis, and Sabato. Dr. Ceaser's *Liberal Democracy and Political Science and***

Reconstructing America have had an impact on my view of political science as a field. Specifically, I am intrigued with his view that political science should be a defender of liberal democracy and the implications of this. These books are also engaging because Ceaser uses the field of political theory to complement the field of American government, which I would eventually like to do. I am also interested in Dr. Milkis's use of historical examples to show that executive power has weakened the party system in his book *The President and the Parties.* Finally, I became familiar with Dr. Sabato's work as an undergraduate and would enjoy the opportunity to study the media and elections under him.

• • •

If the reader does not know of the quality of your undergraduate college, or the specific nature of an honor, award, or program for which you were selected, you may need to inform them, gently, about its awesomeness. Be careful with your language. You can't refer to something as "elite," because self-referential claims of eliteness fall flat, but words like "rigorous" are quite effective. Here are two examples:

I had the good fortune to be selected by faculty appointment for the Ronald E. McNair Postbaccalaureate Achievement Program, a program designed to prepare students for graduate research opportunities. While with the McNair Scholars Program, I received intense training in research methods and then had the chance to design and conduct an original research project under the supervision of Prof. L. Dodd. My project resulted in two presentations and one publication is currently pending (see CV for more details).

• • •

I had the honor of being selected for the Robert E. Cook Honors College. The Cook Honors College is a rigorous undergraduate program that has historically produced students who succeed in graduate environments. Indeed, every CHC student is expected to pursue graduate study. The Cook Honors College features a unique deontic curriculum, a series of core units organized around topical areas of inquiry designed to instill critical thinking and to address the question of what it means to be an ethical citizen of the world. Through these core courses, which replace liberal studies requirements, students are challenged to address "Big Questions" through reading a range of primary texts. We learn to synthesize ideas from several areas of study, and we present findings in a major unit paper and oral presentation. The program also allows us to develop rapport with top faculty in very small classes. These classes are, as I understand them, very much like your graduate seminars.

Do you see how much more impressive these reports are than to simply say "I was involved in undergraduate research," or "I was a member of the honors college"? You don't have to explain what Harvard or Princeton is, or a Fulbright award, but if your audience may not know the high value of your experiences, you can help by explaining a bit about them.

• • •

I like reductionism: (1) it is efficient, (2) it shows clarity of thought, (3) it is accessible to the reader, and (4) it makes for an easy transition from notes to paragraphs. The previous sentence is an example of reductionism, as is the following paragraph:

> **I of course know of the reputation of Tufts, which led me to investigate the school. The primary factors drawing me to apply are: (1) opportunity for clinical contact from the very first year, (2) opportunity for small group learning, (3) the "selectives" (pre-electives, as I understand them) available to first- and second-year students, (4) possibility of taking MPH-related electives or joining the MD/MPH program, (5) opportunity for overseas assignment from the International Affairs Office.**

A whole essay full of such paragraphs would feel disjointed and be tiring to read, so use this technique sparingly.

• • •

After you have addressed the specific questions asked by the admissions committee, you are free to weave in any specific additional points you may wish to impart. Check over all of your notes from chapter 5, Getting Ready to Write. Once you have given them what *they* want, you can give them what *you* want. Think of this as phase two of your first draft.

Whether they ask you to or not, substantiating your dedication to your career goal often makes for a strong essay. Saying you have "always wanted to be a ____________" is not as convincing as reporting specific actions that demonstrate the truth of that statement. Similarly, it is a good idea to demonstrate that you understand the real challenges and drawbacks to both the course of study and the eventual career you have chosen. Admissions committees are reluctant to admit candidates to rigorous programs leading to demanding careers if the applicant seems not to have a clear idea of what lies ahead. Dropout, burnout, chronic fatigue, divorce, alcoholism, drug abuse, and suicide plague certain professions in staggering proportions, and these problems are exacerbated when people join these professions for the wrong reasons. If you have a realistic understanding of what your life will be like (1) as a graduate student, (2) as a trainee in this new profession, and (3) as a skilled practitioner, then convey this to the admissions committee.

• • •

Some of the most thoughtful admissions readers told me that they like to learn something while reading applicants' essays. If you know a tremendous amount about something, whether it is a molecule or a minstrel singer, you might want to let the reader in on what is interesting about that topic. Don't make self-important and grandiose statements about the nature of chemistry, or folklore—instead, give the kinds of specifics that can only come from in-depth knowledge of a particular topic—ideally, one closely related to a professor's own area of specialization.

• • •

Although many essay questions do not require you to delineate your future career plans, a student with logical, clearly defined career plans often comes across as mature and directed. Your image of your future career goals and anticipated contributions to your field and to society in general may be of interest to admissions readers, especially when you seem to have a mission. Think of this as the "purpose" part of a "statement of purpose."

If you intend to use skills or talents in unusual combinations, be sure to let your reader know. For example, an applicant to medical school made no secret of his real ambition: to combine his knowledge of physics and electrical engineering with an education in medicine so that he could design a new generation of medical technology.

If you cannot imagine what kind of attorney or physician or educator you will eventually become, do not fake it. Your uncertainty will show through in your language or, even worse, your ignorance of realistic career options in your chosen field may offend an admissions reader. If you have a well-thought-out mission in life and in your career, state it; if you do not, you need not mention it at all (unless they ask you to address this).

• • •

Occasionally students will decide not to respond to the essay questions exactly as they are asked. If you deviate from the requested format, address the issue and let the admissions reader know your rationale for doing so:

> **Please note that I have combined questions A and B into a single essay, rather than submitting a separate autobiography. I have chosen to focus in detail on my particular experiences during the past two years in Africa—what I learned from them, how they affected me, and why these experiences have led me to pursue an MBA. I believe such a detailed description will give you a better picture of who I am than a general autobiographical essay of the same length could.**

I do not think it is wise to hijack the process, but if you do it, acknowledge and rationalize why you are doing so.

• • •

A difficult essay technique, which is definitely not recommended for everybody, is to build your essay around a theme. All essays have topics, but few have themes. A topic is *what* you are going to write. The topic of your essay is you: your intellectual preparation, your future goals, your rationale for picking a particular program. A theme is *why* you are going to write, the message or concept or point that strings all your paragraphs together into a comprehensive whole. Themes can include the high cost of medical services in a modern technological world, white-collar crime, the role of the teacher, how dance and physics are one discipline, and so on. In chapter 9, essay 17 deals with the theme of overcoming adversity as a means of strengthening character and motivation. Essay 32 develops the opposite theme, that *not* having to overcome adversity can also be an advantage. A theme can make a good essay a great essay. If this approach makes sense to you, you may wish to try it. However, some people have taken good, clean presentations and ruined them by trying to be more clever than the prompt required—or their writing skills allowed.

• • •

Although you should never just follow a formula, you can draw from a set of key ingredients that many successful essays share. They have great opening lines or paragraphs. They convey at least a glimpse of the applicant's personality, substantiate specific academic preparation and knowledge of subject matter, and demonstrate an understanding of the challenges as well as the rewards of a chosen career. They often give a sense of the candidate's maturity, compassion, stamina, teamwork skills, leadership potential, and general likability, usually *without addressing these issues directly.* They clearly catalog the student's technical skills and abilities; they establish that the student has the background and skills needed to excel at the graduate level. They name specific professors at the targeted program with whom the candidate is interested in working, and specific directions they expect to take with their studies. Then they go on to show how the applicant plans to use the graduate education in their planned career, and establish that the student has an understanding of their place in the "big picture."

The essay is an opportunity to tie all the disparate pieces of your application together into a comprehensive, coherent whole. Some admissions directors have told me that they are not always looking for new information in the essay; rather, they are interested in having the essay "make sense" of the rest of the application.

It is often better to describe one or two events in detail than to reproduce your entire resume in your essay. Give yourself some room to describe a project or issue, then refer to the rest of your examples. "See CV for other research projects," "See scholarships and awards for additional recognition like this," and so on.

Remember, there is no one right way to craft these essays. Students continually devise new ways to wow and amaze admissions counselors. Some of the most interesting essays will not follow the above formula or any other.

In your first draft, answer each question with complete and total sincerity. There is something about the reverberating ring of truth that cannot be faked and never seems overwrought. You will worry about the wisdom of your responses in the next chapter. For now, RTGDQ, let your heart do the talking, and just write down what it says.

Here are some random sample paragraphs to get your juices flowing:

I know now that I want to be a big-city, big-time, international lawyer. This is my goal, and I am not embarrassed by it. Washington is an amazing place to live, and the developing international environment is to me the most dynamic game in town. I love long hours and high stress. Give me an impossible job, a laptop, two Advil, and an energy drink, and I am where I do my best work. This is who I am.

From the aforementioned programs, I have gained experience with such biological techniques as electrophoresis, Southern blots, transformations, recombinant DNA techniques, PCR, chromatography, and sequence analysis.

Grasping Jeff's wrist, I could see his anguished gaze. His feet dangled from a 200-foot French citadel wall. If my grip failed, he would plunge into the evaporated remains of a rocky moat. There was no singular way I could pull Jeff from the edge. Just as my strength was fading, the third member of our trio, Kevin, grabbed my other arm and dug in his heels. The three of us managed to retrieve Jeff from the moss-covered ledge. The important lesson of this life experience was that individually each of us would have failed to pull Jeff from the edge. However, working together we were able to help Jeff help himself, and we achieved our group goal.

The historical periods in which I am considering working are ca. 1160–1400 (emphasizing Machaut), ca. 1575–1650 (concentrating on the Florentine Camerata), and the 19th and 20th centuries (especially Schumann, Berlioz, Berg, Varèse, Bartók, Messiaen, and Birtwistle). Within these periods, I am particularly interested in studying program music, opera, and sacred music—all genres with extramusical meaning. While the range of my interests is currently rather broad, I expect it to narrow with further study.

Finally, you should know that my uncle lives within a short bicycle ride from campus, and I have arranged to live rent-free for the first year of my graduate education. I grew up spending summers in Ithaca and already know every inch of town and campus.

I have a rather unusual connection to your school: I am named after it.

I finally got hands-on experience in biochemical engineering research when I was selected as a sophomore to serve as a laboratory assistant to Prof. Douglas C. Cameron. I found actual research to be different from my prior education. I had expected neat experiments with instant results, almost like a 50-minute television program with all the problems solved

Length?

How long should your essay be? If they give you no guidance, then make your essay somewhere between 500 to 1,000 words, maybe longer if you write well and are interesting. If they give you guidance, follow it pretty closely. For example, if they specify "5,300 characters including spaces and punctuation," or "no more than four pages," or 1,000 words, then that's the upper limit. Do not write one bit longer than that. However, it is considered disrespectful to write short, too! So get close to the limit, without surpassing it.

until next week. Instead, it took a great deal of time to do one experiment, often with an unsatisfactory result in the end. There were many false starts, many failures, wrong hypotheses, and some very long hours as experiments took an unforeseen turn. There is no greater satisfaction, however, than completing an experiment with good results. It is better than the feeling when you get the highest score on an exam.

Dr. Cameron is very demanding, an absolute zealot for precision in protocols and data capture. I am very proud to say that he has retained me each year, and this year named me as his laboratory manager. I am the first undergraduate in the history of the department to be so named. (See letter of recommendation.)

Really Short Essays

Specified essay lengths have been getting shorter and shorter, especially in engineering and the sciences. A thoughtful, serious person can play with 250 words, sure, but they cannot convey important, complex, nuanced information about their preparation for graduate study, the specific focus of their intended studies, and their understanding of the ecology of the academic field at this time in ridiculously short essays. "Omit needless words" only goes so far, and then you're cutting into the bone of your message. If you have to submit admissions essays in the 300-word range, consider putting critical information in other parts of your application, such as your CV, a table of undergraduate research projects (see page 71), a covering letter, some kind of "addendum," or by asking a recommender to convey specific content.

You should note that between now and my arrival at graduate school I will complete courses in statistics and research methodologies, and conduct an independent research project culminating in a capstone paper. My topic proposal is currently under faculty review, but I've been told it will be accepted as submitted. My intent is to investigate . . .

For these reasons, I particularly look forward to the opportunity to study with Profs. R. Walters and J. Brown for their work in twentieth-century topics of political and popular cultural history, respectively, and with Prof. T. Ditz, who discussed with me her work in women's and family history and cultural history.

It is my goal to become the superintendent of education for the state of California, or to become an educational theorist with similar potential to impact the lives of our future citizens.

Twelve years old, needle in shaky hand, sweat dripping down my forehead, I stood in front of a gaping tear on the chest of a two-thousand-pound animal. One of our horses had been chased through a fence by wild dogs and had ripped most of the skin off of its chest. My father was away on business and money was too tight for a vet. I had to decide

whether to try and suture up this beast with a small sewing kit meant to replace buttons on my Sunday shirt—or to pull out my pistol and use the 85-cent solution. After thirty-seven stitches and a lot of adrenaline, I knew what my new life goal was.

Topics to Avoid

I have alluded to some of these issues elsewhere, but there are several topics that it is wise to avoid. These are not hard-and-fast rules, just general guidelines.

With some noteworthy exceptions, avoid telling stories about your childhood or about the death of a grandparent. Many applicants to graduate programs are in the age cohort where grandparents are passing away, and, unfortunately, as traumatic and impactful as *your* grandparent's death may be to you, it's not a remarkable event for those reading these essays. As one professor commented on a blog, "I read a lot of personal statements for medical school. Please not another dying grandma story!"

You should avoid writing about childhood for a slightly different reason. Readers may be quite a bit older than you and already think anyone in their early twenties is not yet an adult. You know the type I mean, those administrators and faculty who call college students "kids." If you introduce yourself in the essay at an early age, relaying an experience from eight or twelve or fifteen, that image may stick in their creaky minds. You might be considered, unfairly, as immature.

There are some exceptions, some examples when a truly formative event did impact your development, but be forewarned. One faculty member actually wrote an article about this for the *Chronicle of Higher Education* called "Leave Dr. Seuss Out of It," in which she writes,

At the risk of sounding like a cranky old science professor, I will state emphatically that when I read an application to our graduate program, I do not want to hear about your second-grade teacher (with all due respect to excellent second-grade teachers). Neither do I want to read about a stargazing experience at age eight (even on a cold, windswept hill), a childhood chemistry set (no matter how beloved). . . . It's fine if an applicant mentions an early inspiration. I can deal with that, but it should not be the centerpiece of the statement.

The prompt for a PhD program at the University of Minnesota specifically warns applicants off of florid styles: "A broad flowery description about your interest in biology since you were 5 years old is not helpful."

Your essay should favor content over style. Your goal is not to impress them with your writing, but with your preparation and the clarity of your intentions.

(Oddly, in spite of the above, I interviewed one student who slayed in his interview for a PhD program in biology when he talked about getting his first microscope at nine. His faculty interviewer exclaimed, "I got my first microscope at nine, too!" And they became instant buddies. So, unfortunately, there are few rules that apply to all admissions readers—what one finds odious another may find charming, and vice versa.)

Avoid trashing your prior major or your school. It is not elegant and can reflect poorly on you. Do not reveal that you failed at premed before deciding to settle on medical administration. Say, instead, that you took several years of premed before deciding that you could have a more meaningful impact as an administrator than as a clinician. It is much better to say your interests evolved than to say your low grades pointed you in another direction. If your school did not have sophisticated applied physics labs, do not whine about it; tell how you got the most out of what you could access. If your first major was x and now you are interested in y, tell how your time with x will make you even better at y. "I started out in chemistry as a premed, but I came to realize that training for years in applied science was not that attractive to me. I want to work with people, and I want to help many people at once, not just one person at a time. In public policy, I can identify and influence structural issues that impact the lives of millions. My science training helps me see policy from an analytical perspective, to see it in terms of social forces and structures, and . . ." Something like that is best. Everything you have done until now makes you ready for what is next.

Do not make up falsehoods, but tell the positive side of the story. This is effective writing.

In applying for clinical psych programs, avoid going into detail on any family dysfunction from your own upbringing. You might mention it in a sentence, but I would not feature these experiences. Clinical psych is a science. Your precious essay space should be dedicated to research experiences, what you know how to do, where you learned it, what your specific interests are, and which particular research teams and labs at each program might be a good fit. Counseling psych, social work, social services, and similar are more open to descriptions of personal experiences, especially if they establish that you have empathy for constituent groups, but even there I would not go into great detail about your own travails.

Avoid writing about things that happened to other people. For example, a common theme is to write about heroic parents. Your parents' immigration or entrepreneurial or family of origin journey is their story, not yours. So, you can mention their journey, but do not let this take up several paragraphs. Turn the spotlight quickly onto you. Your story might be about what it was like to grow up with parents from other cultures, perhaps stricter and out of sync with United States norms and mores. Or your story might be about the responsibility you had to take on at home from an early age because your parents worked two or three jobs, or your role as an interpreter because your parents did not speak English. If your parents are Issei that's great, that's their story, but your story is the Nisei story. Do not let a fascinating tale about a client or a boss or a neighbor take up a lot of space in your essay. The part that matters is your relation to and experience of that parent, boss, neighbor, or client. Tell your story. It is okay to have a sentence or two, maybe even a quick paragraph like this:

> **My father crossed the Romanian border to escape a communist regime. He left everything behind. Despite studying at one of the top universities in Romania, his first job in America was as a dishwasher at a Coney Island restaurant.**

But then move on to focus on you and your journey.

For veterinary science, it is widely considered unwise to profess a deep love of animals, to be sentimental about animals, or to claim a zeal to "save" animals, especially the furry, cute kind. Veterinary science can be brutal. It is medical practice, with all its attendant blood, trauma, triage, and death. Wild or injured animals can kill you. Cows can kill you. Sentimentalists are considered poor candidates for the field. Exposure to animals is a plus, of course. But an attraction to petting them adds nothing to your candidacy. There is a vet essay on page 193 showing the right, slightly detached tone.

Avoid revealing a fatal flaw. A fatal flaw is a character flaw or preparation deficiency that would seriously call into question your ability to do the work. Don't reveal that you are not good at math, or that you are lazy, or that you have a tendency to sue your professors, or that your sobriety is tenuous. Those are examples of fatal flaws.

Avoid unnecessary politicization, but only the unnecessary kind. Do not use your essay to take shots at one end or the other of the political spectrum. Using code words or overt insults to other a group you do not like is almost always unnecessary and unwise. However, you do not at all have to hide who you are or pretend to be someone you are not. Writing about how your conservative point of view would enliven discussions and debate at a law school would be a good thing, or how your perspective as a member of the queer community could help graduate students in criminal justice see a wider range of needs among the constituencies they study and serve. Never assume that a reader of your essay has your political point of view. They may, or they may not.

These are guidelines more than rules. There are plenty of times that they might not apply to your particular case. Your childhood experience could be the best framing for your story. Your parents' journey might be critical to understanding the richness of your perceptions of an issue. But have a good reason for focusing on these topics; don't feature them just because you did not think it through.

A Few Writing Protocols

In general, in an academic setting refer to professors by their first initial and last name, so in your essays and emails and other communiqués you would write "Dr. J. Thompson," "Prof. R. Hernandez," and so on. This removes gender as an issue. One exception is if the faculty member is famous. So, Dr. Cecil West, not particularly famous, would be referred to as "Dr. C. West," but Dr. Cornel West, very famous, would be referred to as "Dr. Cornel West." I will let you struggle to decide who is really famous or not. While we're at it, it is sophisticated to use the plural of "Dr." and "Prof." when introducing several faculty members at once, so "Profs. Wilson, Lee, Sysilak, and Jones," or "Drs. Johnson and Wilson."

In American English the period or comma goes on the inside of quote marks. So, "this is correct," and "this is not". Engineers, who are taught to do it the other way to avoid miscommunication in presenting formulae and passwords and so on, have to be particularly warned to do this correctly in narrative writing. Canadians do it "the American way." The Brits do it "this way". To make this really complicated, the semicolon does go on the outside of the quotation marks.

A master's degree is always possessive, so, "I have a master's" is correct, and "I have a masters" is incorrect. This is an extraordinarily common error. PhD is losing its periods, so for now you can write Ph.D. or PhD, but whichever you use, do it that way consistently everywhere. MBA and MD usually do not have "abbreviation" periods. Same with some of the other professional master's, like MPH and MPP.

You get extra points in academic writing for using the semicolon correctly. The semicolon connects two independent clauses that are conceptually linked. "The rabbit hides in its hole; that is its safe space." But go with a period if the two sentences are not closely conceptually linked. "The rabbit hides in its hole. The hawk will fly right by it." The semicolon is also used in place of the comma if one or more members of the list also have commas in them. "The project involves travel to Atlanta, Georgia, Tokyo, Japan, Rotterdam, Netherlands, and Paris, France," should be written, "The project involves travel to Atlanta, Georgia; Tokyo, Japan; Rotterdam, Netherlands; and Paris, France."

The academy is old-fashioned and slow to evolve. That may be why it is full of excessive capitalization, which was common in proper writing about a century ago. You will see faculty making this type of mistake. Fall, winter, spring, and summer are not capitalized. The name of a discipline—humanities, biology, psychology, chemistry, mathematics—is not capitalized. When referring to a department, it is not capitalized unless it has a unique name, so "the physics department" is correctly not capitalized, and the "Maudie Jane Watkins Institute of Theoretical Physics" is correctly capitalized. English and French are proper nouns, so those would read "the English department" and "the French department." Titles that are attached to a name, "President Waldron," are capitalized, but "the president of the college" is not. "The office of the president" is not supposed to be capitalized, as much as you may want to do it. Likewise with "the office of the dean" and "the chair of the department" and "members of the board." All of these rules are broken daily in the academy, including by the president's office.

In academic writing, the serial comma, aka the Oxford comma, is preferred. So, the second-to-last member of a list gets its own comma. In casual or even journalistic writing, it would be fine to have a list like this: "squirrels, birds, bees and ants," but in the academy most people would prefer it be written this way: "squirrels, birds, bees, and ants."

Be sure to be consistent! If you use the serial comma, *use it every possible time.* Consistency is considered a sign of intelligence. Do not write "advisor" in one place, and "adviser" in another. Do not write "Smithtown, TX," in one place, and "Jonestown, Texas," in another. Don't indent a bulleted list one-half inch in one part of a paper and indent another list a full inch somewhere else. These types of small errors are noticed by academics, who perhaps should have more important things to worry about, but do not.

Avoid most contractions in academic writing. If you are telling a brief story in your essay, a contraction might be an acceptable choice there, but in narrative exposition avoid them unless the result is awkward.

Put any citations in the standard format for your field, which can be learned from style books. English, psychology, engineering, and physics all have their own style guides, and that's just for starters. If in doubt, ask a professor or librarian, or use Internet searches until you find definitive guidance for your academic field.

Subsequent Drafts:
From the Page into the Reader's Brain

In creating the first draft of your essay, the emphasis of the writing was all on you. This was to ensure the authenticity of your work—that it originate in you. Now it is time to introduce some admissions readers and hear what they have to say. The following points are all culled from my surveys and interviews with admissions readers at the top programs in the United States. You should pay close attention to these comments, but never forget that *every admissions reader is different.*

The essay hall of shame

+ "Errors and sloppiness, misspellings, inconsistent style. You have to wonder how they made the grades on their transcripts."
+ "Spelling errors, poor English."
+ "Anything that starts out, 'I've always wanted to be a ___________.'"
+ "Sometimes they don't really answer the question. We ask each question for a reason."
+ "When they just seem to be saying what they think we want to hear. We can pick up on that right away."
+ "Our application is a little different. We change our questions every year, and we ask a lot of short essay questions. We want original work. I hate it when I can tell that they're recycling material they wrote for other schools."
+ "The essay sounds like they want to dedicate their life to saving the world, but there's nothing in the rest of the application to back up any claims of altruism."
+ "We ask for dates on activities. It's a red flag if all the activities are brand-new."

+ "A whole essay on deep personal problems or excuses for past performance. It's amazing how common that is. The essay should be upbeat, convincing, persuasive."
+ "Too long. It shows no discipline."
+ "Every year there is always at least one essay from someone who tells us how proud he would be to be admitted to ____________, but this isn't that school."
+ "Students are so afraid to take a risk that they don't really tell us anything. That throws us right back on the numbers."
+ "Don't tell me what ____________ is. I know what my own discipline is! What can they be thinking? Tell me what ____________ means to you or what you want to do in it."
+ "Some students think they can use the essay to manufacture a person who doesn't exist. It doesn't work."

Review your essay in light of these comments. Would it earn a place in the Essay Hall of Shame? How would you like to read a whole lot of this:

> **I have been fondly looking forward to a bright entry at your faculty. In making this assertion, I hope I am not just facile enough to make a claim, for, the facts about my academic antecedents vouch for my superior academic credentials—if I should borrow a phrase out of the vernacular parlance. In this regard, let me crave your indulgence in what I furnish below, concerning my prospective career related to Graduate Studies.**

This is from an actual application, and it went on like this for pages.

Admissions readers are actually quite forgiving—every year they admit people in spite of serious errors. I reviewed one law school essay that had two grammatical errors in the first sentence, yet the student was admitted to Harvard, Michigan, Chicago, NYU, Columbia, UC Berkeley, and Stanford law schools. This is because those two errors in the first sentence were followed by an inspiring essay. (On the other hand, I sat in with a law school admissions committee while they sorted the maybe pile one last time. They did not read beyond the first mistake. The first error in spelling, punctuation, syntax, semantics, word usage, or consistency of style, and they pushed a "reject" button on their tablets. If the error was in the first line, they didn't read the second line. Late in the season the decision-making process can get brutal.)

• • •

I know I told you to write like you talk in your first draft. Now, however, you have to make a very important editing pass to turn all casual language into academic language. Readers of these essays are looking for graduate-level language, the same language a scholar would use when writing to a colleague. So, your first draft may have stated, "I had a part-time, work-study job in the biology department." That's okay for a first draft, but that's not graduate-level language.

Deconstruction of casual language:

I	Oh, I guess it's all about you, eh?
had	The whole thing's in the past, I see,
a	and it only happened once.
part-time	"Part-time"? Well, that's not very serious.
work-study	Oh, a work-study student. We have a lot of poor students already.
job	So, they had to pay you to get you to do it, eh?
in the biology department	Puh-lease! We are bio-*chemists* here.

It would be much better to convert your first draft into the type of language that one scholar would use with another: "I assisted Dr. R. Simmons on a study of possible medicinal derivatives of the venom of the southern copperhead, *Agkistrodon contortrix*." That's grad level.

By the way, although it is true that MFA, law, and medical essays can be a bit more conversational than some of the examples here, it is also true that MFA essays are often improved by sophisticated conversation of artistic concepts and artists, law essays are often improved by fairly technical citations of legal concepts and issues, and medical essays are often improved by mention of medical terms in the same way one doctor would mention them to another.

Review your entire essay and see where you can ramp up the language effectively. I like to think of this editing pass as a black box called the "Academizer." You take your first draft and ram it through the Academizer, which has a dial on it turned up to 11. You will probably need to review some textbooks, look up some citations, double-check your terminology to be sure you're using it with precision. But this is often the difference between a good essay and a really good essay. Think of your essays as an open-book test. You are allowed, *expected,* to use every resource to make your essays impressive.

First Draft →

"So this one time, at STEM camp . . ."

9 10 11

Academizer

Final Draft

"I assisted Dr. Simmons on a study of . . ."

If your first draft was truly written from your heart, the material will represent the real you. Now, however, it is time to make sure there is not *too much* of the real you in your essay.

One of the things an admissions committee is evaluating is your judgment. If they ask you to explain how your presence on campus will improve diversity, be prudent enough not to say you have been discriminated against because you are a male. If they ask you about your biggest challenges as an undergraduate, have the good judgment not to explicate your ongoing litigation against your advisor and his dean. Got it?

Write your second draft as though you were sitting in the reader's brain. In other words, really *read* each section of your essay and ask yourself, "How will the reader respond to this?" The problem with this editing approach is that students tend to overanalyze and overanticipate their reader. In your first-pass edit, just look for the obvious. For example, one student applying to business schools drafted an essay about how her greatest accomplishment was moving away from her family. She had a very close family, and this was her honest response to the essay question "What is your greatest accomplishment?" In editing her draft, she decided to replace that first response with another one citing her proposal of contract terms that saved her company a considerable amount of money. This was not what she considered her greatest accomplishment, but to a business-oriented admissions reader it was certainly more encouraging.

Warning

Read your essay as though you were sitting in the reader's brain, and correct only the obvious gaffes. Do not overanalyze!

Incidentally, one of the best "greatest accomplishment" essays I ever read was not about success, but about dealing with failure. This is a risky approach, but in this particular case, it worked. As you retreat from the gut honesty of your first draft, do not revert to entirely safe and boring responses.

As mentioned, you may wish to think twice about responses that criticize past professors, denigrate other programs, espouse intolerant religious beliefs, or feature trendy political concerns that have nothing to do with the rest of your application. It is usually not a good idea to reveal that you are singularly motivated by money (although if you are eloquent enough about it, it might work). Writing about your triumph over past personal problems can result in a powerful essay, but do avoid writing about ongoing mental anguish. Finally, you might bear in mind what one admissions reader told me: "I am simply not moved by the claim that someone's status as a Christian is a qualification for medical school."

Watch for displays of arrogance and omniscience, as exemplified in such statements as "X *must* Y." Choose less inflammatory language, such as "X *would greatly benefit from* Y." Sometimes just a few word changes can fix an overly certain tone. "I know I would be an outstanding addition to your student body" might be better rendered as "I would love to become a tireless and valuable contributor to your program." It is fine to disagree with the entire profession you are about to join, but do not insult your reader with high-handed narrative exposition. "Buildings will never make sense until architects learn to . . ." should be rewritten into a first-person personal statement such as "as an architect, my passionate interest will be to improve the . . ." There are many revolutions going on right now in medicine, anthropology, business, climate science, energy, and other fields, and you can be part of those revolutions, but not by alienating the first admissions reader you come across. Give them a chance to be on your side.

Avoid the words "perfect" and "prove," as in "I know I would be perfect for your program" or "I want to prove that X causes Y." They will be the judge of your fit, not you. Research cannot and should not be designed to reach a predetermined outcome. Academics in general avoid superlatives.

Avoid writing anything like "My longtime friend died, and after I saw how he was treated in the hospital, I wanted to become a doctor so I would never let that happen again." Such sentiments reveal a lack of sophistication, a certain solipsism, a lack of understanding of the harsh realities and tough decisions that go with a career in medicine. Read your essay from an admissions counselor's point of view, and see if you want to change or remove any unintentional self-revelations.

Be especially wary of revealing character weaknesses such as sloth, dishonesty, or egocentricity. Unfortunately, some secondary essays actually ask questions like "What are your weaknesses?" Try to describe weaknesses that are actually strengths turned inside out, such as "I study too much and forget to have fun," or "I try to do too much," or "Sometimes I spend a lot of time in the library just looking up interesting articles and forget to apply myself to the task at hand." Unfortunately, admissions directors report that they have heard it all on this front and are a little weary of this approach. However, anybody who says "I drink too much," or "I am not as motivated as I could be," or "I get depressed a lot" is simply begging for a rejection.

Finally, it is very important that you audit your essay for insensitive or sexist language or points of view. This is taught in high school, so there's no excuse for getting it wrong.

• • •

If sitting in the brain of your reader causes you to throw out the majority of your first draft, you are probably being too critical. This is only an editing exercise and should not cause you to start over. You will lose the integrity and authenticity of your essay if you write only what you think the reader wants. This is specifically what admissions directors do *not* want.

Once you have taken a pass at the draft using the above methods, the bulk of the material before you is probably going to make it into your final draft. It will become better written as you go through more drafts, but the points presented will probably remain the same. Only now might you show your draft to another human being, but my recommendation is to wait until you think you have a final draft.

• • •

The next editing exercises are more fun than sitting around in someone else's brain pretending to be an admissions reader. First, read your draft for lines that you can "spice up." Try to infuse your essay with another dose of life. For example, "I worked as a teacher's aide at a day-care school" sounds rather mundane and onerous. Using both detail and accomplishment, and by putting your experience through the Academizer, here is another way to represent the same fact:

> **Last spring and summer I was a teacher's aide at a day-care school espousing the principles of Rheikofkian development theory, using only positive interaction. I was commended by the head teacher for devising new games that exemplified Rheikofkian theory in practice and for reaching a particular student who had been diagnosed as borderline emotionally disturbed. After one semester under my tutelage, this student was able to be mainstreamed when she entered the public school system. (See letter of recommendation.)**

If your essay is too long, resist the temptation to keep all the points, saying less about each. It is better to throw out some points and topics, and perhaps even enrich your presentation of those that are left, than to turn your essay into a brutish list of activities. Trust your reader to look over the rest of your application and see supporting material, especially if you refer to it with citations like "See resume for additional leadership experience."

Avoid self-promotions such as "I am an intelligent, compassionate, and caring individual" in favor of describing scenes and events where you act in an intelligent, compassionate, and caring manner. If you feel compelled to self-describe, soften the statements with qualifying clauses such as "I think of myself as . . ." or "people have often said that I am . . ." or "I have often been told by others that I am . . ."

If you still have the phrase "I have always wanted to be a ____________" in your essay, remove it. You have not always *anything.* If you want to take this approach, try telling a story about the moment at which you first became interested in your future career. Do you remember that moment?

If "I" is the first word of your essay, restructure the sentence. For example, turn "I have always been fascinated by highly successful people" into "Highly successful people have always been fascinating to me." Also, get the target school right. Every year I talk to students who apply to "John Hopkins" and "Colombia." Somehow, they never get in.

Watch out for possible negative connotations that can sneak in with the words you select! We are becoming a society seemingly unaware of connotations, as I see advertisement after advertisement with as much negative emotive impact as positive. You should not fall for this sloppy way of communicating. Words are rich signifiers, bringing a whole baggage of extra meaning with them wherever they go. If your essay is full of words like "work," "study," "laborious," and "exhaustive," your reader may be tired and exhausted by the end of the essay. If you write, "I practice piano for three hours every day no matter what," you are certainly getting a message across, but a better message might be "I enjoy music a great deal, and I play the piano for three hours or more every day. My favorite composers are . . ." So read your essay again, and see if there are word selections and phrases with negative connotations that you could turn into more positive constructions.

• • •

There is a range of essay styles, and an autobiography for a social work program is going to be very different from a statement of purpose for an economics program, and an essay for medical school is going to be much more personal and introspective than that same student's essay for a doctoral program in chemistry. RTGDQ, and craft an appropriate response.

Edit to make sure that you get your message across. Do not worry about composing a work of art. Rough transitions and a few belabored sentence structures are fine as long as you convey the message you want. Do not let your language draw attention to itself; it should be a medium for your message, not a message in itself.

Your spelling and grammar should be perfect, however. Absolutely perfect. You should have a final draft of your essay proofread by somebody you consider to be an expert in grammar and spelling, but do not seek such expertise until you have a final draft. In my opinion, this is an excellent and appropriate use of AI. Get an AI assistant to proofread your final version. But don't slavishly believe its revisions and suggestions. AI often introduces error. See the writing protocols on pages 102 and 103; I have seen AI mess these up repeatedly by applying rules from a totally different type of writing. Don't surrender good judgment.

Be careful not to edit the life out of your essay. A grammarian and a stylist would have a tumultuous marriage. It is hard for some grammarians to accept, but the English language is like a snake, and it is always getting away from them. The erosion of the distinction between "that" and "which," the acceptance of "like" for "such as," dangling participles sneaking in, and, horror of horrors, the begrudging acknowledgment that splitting an infinitive is sometimes the way to best wring the exact meaning out of a sentence—all of these cause dilettante grammarians to have sphincter-tightening paroxysms. If you are applying to a graduate program in English, you may wish to be hyperconservative, but otherwise, take the advice of an overly picky grammarian with a grain of salt.

Write your essay first, as it is far more important that your creative and intellectual energy be expended on content than on worrying about stylistic details. Once you have your essay, though, be sure that you do attend to stylistic details—every last one of them. In my research for this book, basic errors in spelling and usage were cited by admissions readers more often than any other specific complaint about applications essays. However, if you find an error after the application is submitted, it is probably better just to live with it than to send in a "corrected" version; doing so only adds insult to injury. Do not call attention to your own errors.

• • •

You absolutely can get help with your application essays. In fact, you are expected to get help. Your essays should be reviewed by faculty, the writing center, your most trusted mentor, and so on. Application essays are examples of public, academic writing. What does that mean? Think about how an academic article gets crafted. A scholar comes up with an idea and sends an outline to a friendly colleague. That colleague writes back with suggestions. The scholar incorporates the suggestions and sends a draft of the article to another trusted colleague. Then the scholar sends the essay to an expert in statistics, to make sure their tables and analysis and data are presented correctly. Then they submit to a peer-reviewed journal. Those peers may accept it, reject it, or ask for revisions and resubmission. This is a public, academic, iterative process.

I recommend you write your own first draft, but then pursue the right kind of help. If someone starts writing paragraphs for you, that's too much help. If you use AI to create essays that you did not write, and could not write, that's the wrong kind of help. But if you show your essay to someone and ask for suggestions, that is not just allowed, it's expected. Use AI for proofreading, but with the warnings I gave elsewhere about making sure it applies the right style parameters. (AI can also be useful for shortening essays—for example, suggesting edits to turn a 1200-word essay into a 1000-word essay—but that is not the same thing as creating content.)

To illustrate this a bit further, one of my correspondents recently told me about guiding a student who was the "lone wolf" type, a student who thought he was supposed to do it all himself, like some monk in a cave. She corrected this misconception, then helped him form a team to help him with his essays for a major scholarship. The student was in an undergraduate research program, so he worked with his program director to plan the application process. He worked with his academic mentor on the technical aspects of his essay, the nomenclature and the underlying science. He worked with a STEM editor from the university's writing center on multiple iterations of the essays. And finally, he paid a proofreader recommended by the chair of his department to perfect his grammar, spelling, layout, and consistency of style. Again, this is not unusual. You are entitled to get help with developing your first drafts into your final versions.

There is no correct or ideal number of drafts, but fewer than three is probably too few. Once you have what you consider to be a pretty good draft, you can begin to road test it on people you respect. When you think your essay is perfect, submit it.

A DISCLAIMER EVERY APPLICANT SHOULD READ!

Before we launch into the chapter of samples, you need to know of four major cautions. First, this book is not designed to take the place of faculty advice and counsel. It is designed to complement faculty advice and to make you savvy on the mechanics of the graduate application process so that you can get the most out of your contacts with faculty. The sooner in the process you can involve faculty, the better. Seek out faculty guidance, and do not disregard it. If your advisor disagrees with advice in this book, they are probably right. This book is designed to address the essay-writing needs of a very wide range of applicants, and your faculty advisor knows more about *your particular case.*

Second, it remains for you, the reader, to adjust the suggestions and information contained herein to your particular goal. At one end of the spectrum are doctoral and postdoctoral candidates in highly technical areas. Candidates for such programs need more focus on substantiating their intellectual preparation and specifying their research goals, and less on the personal details of their lives. For some of these applicants, an appropriate application may be devoid of personal information.

At the other end of the spectrum are candidates for fine arts programs, candidates for non-subject-specific scholarships, and occasionally a candidate for a preprofessional program such as law or medical school. For some of these candidates, a fully appropriate essay may contain *only* personal information, or it may consist of just a scene or vignette, providing virtually no information about the applicant's academic preparation and career plans. You should be sensitive both to the range of possibilities and to what would be considered an appropriate mix of information for your own particular type of application. One correspondent wrote: "My sense is that graduate programs in some areas are not concerned much about an individual's life story. Rather, they need to know that the applicant is mature and devoted to his or her field of study; the applicant needs every opportunity to prove his or her writing to be in the academic style. The difference might be that some need to write *statements of purpose,* while others need to write *personal statements.*" The samples that follow run the gamut from autobiographical sketches (personal) to summaries of research (as impersonal as you can get).

A third caution: although this book is in places irreverent, nothing presented here should be construed as an invitation to be flippant, flighty, glib, or "cute." Such a tone would be a huge mistake in a statement of purpose. Although I have tried to reveal a greater range of approaches to these essays than students normally consider, I most certainly do not encourage you to write anything that does not reveal a proper respect for the admissions process. Although the other books in this genre often say something like "and a little humor never hurts," in the essays I read I find that humor falls flat rather often. One admissions director called humor a "high-wire act," and said that he appreciated it when applicants could pull it off, but that they did not seem to be able to predict when it would work. You should take risks in your writing, but take them in the areas of revealing personality, revealing whatever about you is unusual or unique, or taking a well-presented controversial stand. If you choose to make a joke, make it a subtle one, indeed. Humor should be a garnish, never an entrée. Humor that fails is often interpreted as immaturity, and immaturity is almost universally believed to be detrimental to success in graduate school. Be different, take a risk, but in general be serious and purposeful.

Finally, do not measure yourself against the samples and examples in this book. Statistically, it would be *much* easier to be admitted to one of the most competitive programs in the nation than to be selected for a book such as this. I have selected these particular essays according to two criteria: either I found them to be almost perfect stylistically or I found the candidate to have a particularly strong application, or both.

Many of the candidates selected for this book are a little different. One of the priorities of most graduate admissions professionals is to create and/or preserve diversity in each year's incoming class. This means racial and socioeconomic diversity, certainly, but it also means recruiting people who have had different life experiences and people who have unusual career plans. However, you do not have to go to Africa or join the carnival to have a successful graduate application. If the most unusual thing about you is how utterly normal you are, then maybe you should build your essay around that. No matter who you are, you can follow the principles outlined in this book, take a risk, and make your best application.

As soon as you are done with your essay, feel free to email it to me for consideration for the next edition of this book at don@donaldasher.com. Be sure to include both an email address and a permanent address and telephone number. All such correspondence shall be considered submitted for publication and subject to editing and revision. Recompense is limited to a copy of the new edition. I look forward to hearing from you, and *best of luck*!

9

Samples, Samples, Samples

Read several essays to discover what style may be best for the unique combination of your objective and your background. All forty-seven essays are listed by a number and a "nickname." You should check the index beginning on page 251 for mention of specific academic subjects that may appear elsewhere in the book.

Having said this, I urge you to begin by browsing the entire collection of samples without regard to a specific subject matter, stopping to read essays that interest you. Do not just flip to the ones in your field, or in fields most like yours, to see what others have done. Take time to explore a number of essays. Some of the stories represented there are so fascinating that another whole book could be written on them.

Whatever you do, remember this: *Do not even think about modeling your essay closely on one of the examples in this book; essays in this book are provided so that you may learn how to write the best statement for your own unique background. Admissions people have also seen this book, and if you copy material, they will notice it right away.*

Having trouble finding an essay?

Check the index on page 259.

ESSAY #1: "HEALTH CARE ADMINISTRATION"

Allow me to explain why this essay is the very first example provided. This essay ignores several writing suggestions provided in this book. It has too many "I"'s in it, it even begins with the pronoun "I," it does not have an arresting opening, and it has very straightforward narrative exposition throughout. It is not fancy. However, this essay is truly excellent because it conveys the information the admissions reader wants, and does so efficiently. The language does not call attention to itself. The content drives the power of the essay. So even though many of the essay examples that follow have narrative techniques from the best of creative nonfiction, remember what your goal is: to convey that you have the preparation, skills, abilities, interests, and passion to excel in the targeted graduate program. If you do that efficiently, you will have a great essay. This is a great essay. With this essay, the applicant received offers from all ten of the MHA programs to which he applied.

I am pursuing a graduate degree in health administration because it enables endless opportunities to serve in the health field. While completing an introduction course for health care management, I learned about opportunities in health administration and how impactful it can be in changing health care as we know it; I knew that this industry was right for me. Through health administration, I can improve the quality of life for all by serving health care providers, reducing disparities, and reducing costs. Being able to help and serve others gives me purpose and motivates me internally. Pursuing graduate studies in health administration at Johns Hopkins University will allow me to achieve my goals sooner, address systemic inequities, and positively impact the US health care system.

The curriculum and environment at the Bloomberg School of Public Health, a nationally top-ranked program, will help launch my career. With this degree, I can create effective retention strategies for medical staff, making an impact on the administrative side that will positively affect the clinical aspects of health care. I want to learn how to create and implement policies that will enable medical facilities to operate efficiently; the MHA program at JHU will equip me with the leadership, planning, decision-making, and financial-management skills to do so.

Two years ago, I served as a student volunteer at Tidelands Georgetown Memorial Hospital, assisting clinical nurses and patients with basic needs, managing the telemetry log, and performing clerical work. In some instances, I was alone at the nurses' station with the responsibilities of answering the phone, patient calls, and visitor questions, sometimes all at once. After noticing how burned out some nurses were, I wanted to identify what factors influence nurses' decisions to leave or stay at their job, and determine whether burnout was a factor. I was able to conduct research under the mentorship of J. R. Jackson, PhD, MSN, RN, through the Ronald E. McNair Postbaccalaureate Achievement Program at Winthrop. I conducted a mixed-methods study that used a concurrent triangulation design titled *Perceptions of the Current Nursing Shortage and Strategies to Increase Staff Retention*; this approach allowed me to capture the perspective of over 400 nurses and five nursing leaders. At the national McNair research conference, my oral presentation received first place in the business category. Additionally, it has been accepted at the Sigma Theta Tau International Honor Society of Nursing research conference and submitted to the AcademyHealth Annual Research Meeting (ARM). Currently, my mentor and I are preparing the manuscript for publication.

These experiences challenged me to be flexible and patient and improved my time-management skills as I completed multiple high-impact projects simultaneously. This contributed to my academic success, as I have had to balance my coursework, leadership roles, work, and social life, which later helped me earn a spot on the President's List. Furthermore, I was selected for one of the highest honors Winthrop has to offer: Winthrop University Student Marshal, for distinguished

ESSAY #1: "HEALTH CARE ADMINISTRATION" (CONTINUED)

academic performance. As student marshal, I serve at Winthrop's commencement and convocation ceremonies. These opportunities played a significant role in my success as an undergraduate student and will aid me as I continue my studies.

I have had additional experiences that have helped me develop useful skills for graduate school and my future career as a hospital administrator. On campus, I was recommended by the faculty to work as a business statistics peer tutor for the academic success center. I assist my peers in developing skills to become independent learners and succeed in their classes. In this role, I can teach my peers, improve my quantitative skills, and focus on being an effective listener. I was also selected to serve in an additional role as student project coordinator. My duties include coordinating and conducting interviews with candidates who could serve as effective peer tutors and running reports in TutorTrac, the data management system. These reports ensure tutees' compliance with attendance policies for tutoring privileges and help the program track individual tutees' resource use. Before I began managing this information, there were no procedures on how to organize and analyze the reports. As a result, I developed an approach to capture and analyze data efficiently, requiring me to be independent, attentive to detail, and creative.

One of my proudest accomplishments was being nominated and elected as secretary and treasurer for Winthrop's chapter of the National Society of Collegiate Scholars. Previously, our chapter was dormant and essentially nonexistent for over a year. One of our main goals was to increase the number of members. After strategically working with fellow officers, we developed and facilitated an array of recruiting events that increased our membership to 300 members. As a result, we received the Platinum Star Status Award from the national office for demonstrating strong leadership and providing community service and networking opportunities for members. Furthermore, I was elected to serve as the executive vice president because of my leadership capabilities. Another accomplishment was participating in the 2nd Undergraduate Case Competition for Health Administration Programs hosted by the Medical University of South Carolina (MUSC). Along with three other teammates, we developed and gave an oral presentation on a program focusing on patient- and family-centered care and reducing central-line associated bloodstream infections. Among eleven teams, including the other finalists (Auburn, Penn State, and Central Michigan), we placed first in the competition.

My past experiences have equipped me with the ability to succeed in graduate school; moreover, my undergraduate studies at Winthrop have cultivated my ability to apply concepts I have learned to unfamiliar situations. I appreciate how the MHA curriculum at Johns Hopkins focuses on optimizing performance in health care organization, strategic leadership, and negotiation. The Bloomberg School of Public Health is one of the few schools that offer courses with this focus. This piqued my interest because the program is dedicated to developing health care professionals

ESSAY #1: "HEALTH CARE ADMINISTRATION" (CONTINUED)

who will be able to fulfill health care leader roles and can elevate health care facilities. Furthermore, the administrative residency requirement also attracted me to this program since I will be able to gain invaluable experience and apply what I have learned throughout my coursework.

My interest in leadership aligns with the MHA program's faculty research. I am particularly interested in Dr. M. Bittle's research on leadership and organizational performance improvement and Dr. C. Fabuius's research relating to strengthening the direct care workforce. As an undergraduate researcher, I have learned that research is a rewarding process that allows me to make significant contributions to my field. Employment shortages in health care is my primary interest; however, I look forward to working with faculty members and seeing how my research evolves in graduate school. Determination, with my other qualifications, will lead to my success as a student in the MHA graduate program at Johns Hopkins University.

ESSAY #2: "SCHOOL OF EDUCATION"

UCLA Teacher Education Program (TEP)

Each morning, I arrive at work in a button-down shirt and my hair in a close-cut fade. I'm a substitute teacher in conservative rural Iowa, where I'm temporarily living. Children often ask me, "Why do you look like a boy?" If another adult overhears, their instinct is to quiet the student and apologize to me. But I'm never bothered by young people's genuine curiosity. As a masculine-presenting gay woman, I do look like a boy and children should not be punished for acknowledging that. Attempts to invisiblize my queerness are another form of erasing it. Our plural identity markers are not always wearable or self-evident. But each visible and invisible ingredient of our selfhood should never be something to be ashamed about or ignore.

The very first line on the website for this program is: "*UCLA's Teacher Education Program* (TEP) prepares aspiring teachers to become social justice educators in urban settings." The applicant knows her audience, and knows herself.

My daily experience as a queer educator encourages me to invite students to live bravely and resiliently as themselves too. My professional and personal endeavors demonstrate this invitation. I've built queer safe spaces at my college as a fitness coach for gender-diverse students and as facilitator of a creative writing group for queer-identifying students and staff. As a leader of the Latinx Student Union at Reed, I nourished intersectional self-reflection and healing by leading workshops to unpack issues salient to LGBT students of color. And with The Flame, a grassroots LGBT-centered Christian ministry in Portland, I've also taken part in several activist projects to help marginalized communities. Recently our team helped the Oregon synod of the Evangelical Lutheran Church of America fund an initiative for the Poor People's Campaign.

Being a Latinx educator from an economically disadvantaged background, I will serve communities like the one I grew up in. As an openly queer person, furthermore, I want to be a guiding light for LGBT youth, for whom seeing themselves reflected in their leaders can be crucially life-sustaining. Educators should share identities in common with the students they serve, and I will offer myself as a resource for other underrepresented students and their families. When students know that their classrooms are safe, and when they maintain dialogue with their educators about their needs, they are better able to become their own self-advocates and agents of growth.

My immediate intentions will build the foundation for my long-term goals. During and after the TEP, I will instantiate myself in a community of social justice–oriented California educators. The TEP's union of relevant theory with care-based site work will provide me the skills needed to enact substantive, lasting change in my classroom, school, and district. My fundamental goal, in whatever iteration it may bloom, is to support and ensure the safety of those I serve. I will use my TEP on-site work to empower and prepare students to be their world's own change-makers, responsibly invoking intellectual frameworks alongside experientially developed teaching strategies. I will accomplish these imperatives through a position that most provokes direct impact, whether as an administrator or lifelong instructor. I will wear this liberatory pedagogy as I do my queerness: with honesty, openness, and resilient pride.

This essay has an excellent use of a metaphor, walking across bridges, as a theme. It is not overstated, not overwrought, and that is why the theme works well. It has the same author as the prior essay. The essay prompt was just these three words: "Personal History Statement." This is an excellent example of how the same content can be used for personal statements or diversity statements or autobiographies. This essay could have been submitted, verbatim, for any one of those three types. The program she is applying to has a commitment to "centering issues of equity and justice," so the essay matches the tone and priorities of the target audience.

Note the place-names attached to personal experiences. This type of detail is an indicator that a real human wrote this essay.

ESSAY #3: "BRIDGES"

Personal History Statement–Teacher Education Program (TEP)

Every foggy morning during middle and high school, my twin sister and I would scramble inside our father's truck, loaded with the gear he'd use for the day as a house painter. We'd commute the 20 minutes from our Hispanic suburb with no sidewalks to the cleaner, wealthier community of Albany, California, for class. As kids, we checked our playgrounds and motel bedspreads for used sharps—while our classmates drove to Tahoe for their vacations. While they were skiing, we knew to sleep on the floor at night on New Year's Eve in case shots were fired through windows.

Like the stretch of I-80 that carried my sister and me to Albany each morning, I consider the spaces in my life as a series of dualities across which I walk a perpetual bridge. The two sides of my bridge have been Albany and my neighborhood of El Sobrante. They have been my California hometown and my Oregon college town. They have been family in living rooms and peers in college classrooms. They've been choices, between self-destruction and the pursuit of bodily wellness; as an individual who comes from a family where alcoholism devastates and kills, my wellness is both an action and a mechanism of resistance. As a bridge-walker, I have developed various access points of community, resources, language, and selfhood. Receiving a graduate education at Berkeley will prepare me to incorporate this unique position into my teaching philosophy. The TEP's liberation-oriented program will impart tools I'll use to uphold cultural plurality and mutual support as pillars of student success.

As a young student, I poured myself into reading and writing as an escape from my family's tumultuous struggles with mortgage payments, jobless winters, and substance addiction. In high school, I became a diligent volunteer and cross-country team captain, utilizing the community offered by my wealthy school to create leverage against the other areas in my life where support was lacking. During this time, the neighborhood around UC Berkeley became my playground. I raced Saturday invitationals with the Albany track team at Edwards Stadium. I slurped Hokkaido boba from U-Cha on nerve-saturated first dates at the Shattuck theater. UC Berkeley's campanile shone like a beacon, a knowable point from the view at Indian Rock, where my friends and I would bundle together around cardboard bowls of Korean takeout and watch the sun descend to melting on the glittering Bay Area horizon.

I am also a kid from El Sobrante, just east of Wildcat Canyon. In my neighborhood, Saturday mornings meant crushing cans on the backyard pavement for five cents apiece, and weeknights signaled the smell of *barbacoa* and *al pastor* filling the air around hot concrete tables with their bright familiar richness. This is one bridge that I walk: I have developed an affinity with the communities of Albany and Berkeley while maintaining my roots in El Sobrante, embodying the cultural and class plurality of two East Bay microspheres. My experience as a bridge-walker traversing these sociocultural divides has taught me to always honor multivariate spaces and modes of moving through the world. I am seeking a graduate degree with Berkeley, furthermore, because I deeply value its formative role in my personal life and identity.

ESSAY #3: "BRIDGES" (CONTINUED)

My sister and I were the first in our immediate family to graduate from a four-year college. Through our time together at the same college, we established not only a set of tools to approach our world critically, but also a highly sharpened understanding of how we can use such tools to enact direct change in places we love and care about. I envision these tools as most immediately usable in the classroom. This bridge, between collegiate frameworks and real communities, is another that I will inhabit as I construct a pedagogy rooted in tangible, generative care for compromised Bay Area neighborhoods. I am pursuing a graduate degree to learn how to most responsibly provide this care. As a queer student, furthermore, I found sanctuary and restoration in my alma mater's substantial LGBT community. School has been a life-saving space for me to manifest my own wholeness and goals, and TEP will help me provide the same space for other underrepresented students.

I have sought to advance spaces of resilience and resistance for marginalized young people within various workplaces. As a house advisor at college, I served one of the school's several identity-based living communities, within which all residents identify as non-male. In collaboration with my residence life supervisor, I initiated a campaign to change the name of our Women's Floor to Gender Minorities Floor, in order to support trans and gender-diverse residents. As the leader for this specific residential community, I often found my work emotionally costly and challenging. My training in mental health first aid, intervention and mediation, and restorative justice prepared me to provide trauma-informed care. I handled residents' substance use issues, eating disorders, gender identity crises, Title IX cases, and multiple cases in which residents moved into my floor to escape abuse. Growing up low-income pushed me to cultivate self-advocacy and personal resourcefulness at a young age, and I employed these life-saving tools to support students. I learned how to accommodate the requests of vulnerable residents, how to direct peers to salient resources, and how to foster a cohesive community dynamic based in a mutual dialogue. I see this cultivation of dialogue as a bridge too, crossing between residents' demonstrated needs and my direct action taken to meet those needs. In the classroom, I will further utilize these assets to furnish safe environments and provide holistic support to students.

During the two years in which I did not serve as a house advisor, I worked at Lane Middle School, a Title I school in southeast Portland, Oregon. As a freshman in college, I worked in a language arts class of thirty sixth graders. When I returned as a senior, I was the chef's assistant in a cooking class within the Schools Uniting Neighborhoods after-school program. In both environments, many of the students had disabilities, used adaptive learning plans, or faced an array of other circumstances that created learning barriers. I helped them complete assignments and supervised their use of cooking utensils, while making sure to stay in dialogue with them about how to best accommodate their varying visible and invisible needs. I found that the young people at Lane shared more identities in common with me than many of my peers at my elite college down the street, and my time with them

ESSAY #3: "BRIDGES" (CONTINUED)

felt like coming home. At the same time, I understood my privilege as a bridge-walker between my academic community and the teenagers I served. Both ends of this bridge belonged to me. This dual positionality allowed me to utilize the tools I cultivated in my college classrooms to promote an atmosphere of safety, tandem investment, and intellectual curiosity among young learners at Lane.

I have also fostered spaces of advocacy and mutual support among my peers, both within and beyond my college campus. As a club leader of my college's Latinx student union, I helped organize the first- and second-ever Latinx Heritage Celebration Months on campus. We contracted speakers, planned social events, and hosted potlucks that fed five hundred students and neighbors with food from local Hispanic vendors. My school's majority-white population, Eurocentric academia, and toxic elitism from wealthy students all contribute towards a very challenging environment for Latinx and other students of color. My lived experience as a young Latina transfer student, and my skills as a peer mentor, equipped me to furnish the channel between Latinx students at this college and this new space of healing and joy for our community. When I teach, I will similarly build bonds within and across my school to provide the access and care necessary for students' sense of belonging.

Classrooms contain infinite potential as sites of resistance to oppressive structures, not simply through education but also through their capacity to be centers of support for families. Impactful educators have a responsibility to model their schools as critical social spaces. In so doing, we uphold our own bridge between underserved communities and resources for their children. These maintain a crucial link in the informal networks of care and dependability that keep so many marginalized people alive when other systems of social infrastructure fail to meet our needs. A bridge framework is furthermore useful in reimagining classrooms virtually. We have learned that pandemics and wildfires and power outages of uncertain duration may keep students out of classrooms, but we can envision our pedagogies as links that connect us to our students, using a variety of tools to extend beyond the classroom and into the world. With my graduate education I will be able to deepen this practice, to reach across physical distances to prepare fulfilling learning environments in ever new and unfolding ways.

When I teach, I will continue crossing and building these connections. I will be an interlocutor between the real communities that have shaped my understanding of the world, and the intellectual theoretical underpinnings that have sharpened and deepened my locus as a thinker and worker. Walking both sides of this bridge will allow me to serve as an ethical, self-critical agent of change and growth for the next generation. With my TEP training, I will uplift the community that raised and empowered me. I will cultivate children's ability to forge their bridges across all the beautiful multiplicities of their own worlds.

ESSAY #4: "THE SOUND OF KITTYWAKES"

While my coworkers stared at the amazing sight of thousands of black-legged kittywakes exploding off the cliff face, I closed my eyes and listened. I had been working in Prince William Sound, Alaska, for a number of months and had noticed that when a colony of these seabirds was flushed by a predator, they made a particular descending warble vocalization. In fact, in the hectic life of a kittywake colony with up to sixteen thousand birds coming and going, this distinct call seemed to be the trigger for the only coordinated activity in which I ever saw them participate. Later that afternoon, I practiced making the "flush call" until the researchers with me were sick of it, then climbed onto the colony and did my best imitation. The thunder of the entire colony lifting off, as other birds picked up the call, cemented my long-held intention: I want to work with sound. My purpose for undertaking doctoral work in acoustics and animal behavior is twofold. First, my professional goal is to contribute to the existing research on biological systems that use sound. Second, my personal goal is to convey in-depth understanding and love of these systems to the students I teach.

With regard to advancing current research, the concept of coevolution has always held special fascination for me. Its importance to the theory of evolution, so central to the study of biology, is made more relevant by vivid examples in the area of echolocation. Certain bats and moths have evolved for so long in their predator-prey relationship that the moths have actually developed acoustic countermeasures to help them evade bats' echolocation.

The highly specialized nature of these countermeasures, which include Doppler shifts and both broad and narrow band interference, reveal how strong an evolutionary pressure the predation of the bats must be. Though my reading of articles has turned up extensive research with regard to bats, I have not found any work dealing with any similar predator-prey relationships among marine organisms. I plan to explore whether cetacean predation over thousands of years has caused prey species such as squid or fish (which are heavily preyed upon by sperm whales and dolphins respectively) to evolve acoustic evasive techniques similar to those utilized by moths on land. This work may show us not only how coevolution has influenced marine echolocation, but how convergent evolution may have led both marine and terrestrial prey to similar defense mechanisms.

I have strong preparation to help me realize both my personal and professional goals. Since completing my undergraduate degree, I have participated in NSF-funded research in Alaska and National Parks research on endangered species in Hawaii. I successfully brought this active participation in research to the students I have taught. Classes I have designed and taught have varied from public education programs to high-school-level courses in biology, evolution, chemistry, and physics. These teaching experiences have confirmed that I have the desire and aptitude to

Science essays can be somewhat personal, such as this one, or highly impersonal, such as the next one. One style is not "right" and the other "wrong"; you need to pick the style that matches your background, your interests, the assigned topic, and the institution to which you are applying. This student has done considerable work to identify alignment between his academic preparation and interests, and the focus of this particular graduate program. Even if you apply to fifteen programs, try to make each application as focused and specific as this one.

Graduate school is an excellent place to combine two disciplines that might not be so easily combined as an undergraduate. Teaching, tutoring, and proctoring experiences are important for winning assistantships and are in general highly regarded by graduate programs. Be sure to mention them. This candidate not only has teaching experience, but he also has a teaching philosophy, as mentioned here.

ESSAY #4: "THE SOUND OF KITTYWAKES" (CONTINUED)

convey my knowledge of the sciences to others. Though my position running the science department for a private high school provided significant teaching satisfaction and latitude, I want to teach upper-division college courses to advanced students. My willingness to sacrifice this rewarding position should be seen as a reflection of my desire to pursue a career in higher education.

The departmental philosophy at UCSC parallels my own. I was pleased to read of the biological sciences department's requirement that all graduate students teach for a number of quarters. This stems from my firmly held belief that you may possess information, but that it has not yet become knowledge, and thus truly yours, unless you can teach it to others. Doctoral study at UCSC would be an opportunity for me to work directly with Drs. Costa, Oritz, and Williams in developing my research interests, and the teaching requirement will provide an opportunity for me to hone my instructional skills. It is this kind of departmental commitment to developing multidimensional graduate students that I am looking for.

In conclusion, the combination of my two goals—to contribute to the existing research on biological systems that use sound, and to convey in-depth understanding and love of these systems to the students I teach—has led me to pursue an advanced degree in biology. In return for UCSC's commitment to provide an environment conducive to higher learning, I would like to offer a young man confident in his ability to take advantage of all you have to offer. I would like to offer you an experienced teacher and researcher who would like to contribute to the body of work you are producing.

I would like to offer myself.

ESSAY #5: "NITROGEN"

Summary of Current Research

My current work with Dr. T. Raganasik is on the activation of nitrogen-regulated promoters. Earlier work in this laboratory has shown that transcription of the *glnALG* operon of *E. coli,* coding for glutamine synthetase and two nitrogen regulatory proteins, is initiated at *glnAp2* by σ^{54}-RNA polymerase. Under nitrogen-limiting conditions, the regulatory protein NR_i is phosphorylated by NR_{ii}. NR_i-phosphate (NR_i-P) binds to two sites, located 100 and 130 bp upstream from the transcription start site, and catalyzes the isomerization of the closed σ^{54}-RNA polymerase-*glnAp2* complex to the open complex. We have now shown that NR_i-P cannot activate a σ^{70} promoter, like the *lac* promoter, containing NRI_i-binding sites but can activate other σ^{54} promoters like *nifHp.* These results suggested that the activation by NR_i-P is not solely dependent on the presence of the NR_i-binding sites but also on the nucleotide sequence of the downstream promoter region. In collaboration with Dr. V. White, we studied the effect of phosphorylation of NR_i on its DNA binding properties. Our results showed that phosphorylation greatly increases cooperative binding of the activator to two adjacent binding sites, and that the interaction between two NR_i-P dimers is required for activation.

Furthermore, I am studying the activation of *glnHp2,* also a nitrogen-regulated promoter, of the glutamine permease operon of *E. coli.* I have shown that open complex formation at *glnHp2* is activated by NR_i-P, and that the activation is stimulated by integration host factor (IHF), a DNA-bending protein. IHF binds to a site between the NR_i-binding sites and the promoter. A single nucleotide mutation in *glnHp2* (T to G at position -14) increases the affinity of σ^{54}-RNA polymerase for the promoter. Using an *in vitro* transcription assay, I showed that the stimulation by IHF takes place only in promoters that form weak closed complexes with RNA polymerase. Activation of the mutant promoter is not stimulated by IHF. On the other hand, when the binding sites for NR_i or IHF were placed on the opposite side of the DNA helix, IHF inhibited the open complex formation. We conclude from these results that the stiffening produced by the IHF-induced bend can facilitate or prevent interactions between the upstream bound NR_i-P and the closed RNA polymerase-promoter complex, depending on the relative location of the binding sites for these proteins. In this manner, a regulatory protein, IHF, can stimulate or block transcription without itself contacting either the RNA polymerase or the activator.

Recently, we have found that σ^{54} binds specifically to the *glnHp2* promoter in the absence of the core RNA polymerase subunits. In collaboration with Drs. W. Carson and M. Blick (AFRC Nitrogen Fixation Laboratory, University of Sussex, England), we have demonstrated a new role for core RNA polymerase in transcription: that it assists the binding of σ^{54} to promoter DNA. An altered form of σ^{54} with a deletion within the N terminus showed increased DNA binding properties. Our results suggest σ^{54} has a latent DNA binding activity that is revealed by core RNA polymerase.

Graduate applications may require a statement of purpose, an autobiography, an essay or two or six on assigned topics, a summary of research, or all of the above. All these writing assignments are slightly different, and you should be sensitive to the instructions. Remember, RTGDQ. This two-part essay is in response to the essay prompt: "Describe your research experience to date."

Research summaries are a common part of laboratory science applications. The focus should be on the science, not the scientist. Presenting your research in a clean, impersonal format—as this candidate did—is the best approach.

Be sure to name your advisors, as it is bad form to imply that you did high-level work all by yourself, without any advice or counsel from a senior scientist.

ESSAY #5: "NITROGEN" (CONTINUED)

Summary of Previous Research

As a postdoctoral associate in the laboratory of Dr. A. Kirschner, I was involved in two research projects. One project was to characterize the *ams* gene, which is involved in decay of *Escherichia coli* mRNA. I cloned the *ams* gene by complementation, mapped the transcription start site, and determined the size and the N terminus sequence of the *ams* protein. We used a T_7 RNA polymerase-promoter system to overexpress the *ams* locus. We determined the nucleotide sequence of the *ams* gene, and these data showed that the C terminus of the protein has homology to a mitochondrial ribosomal protein of *Neurospora crassa*. More recently, it has been shown that *ams* encodes RNase E, an endoribonuclease that plays a general role in the chemical decay of *E. coli* mRNA. The other project was the characterization and secretion of protease III (*ptr*) of *E. coli.* I mapped and sequenced the *ptr* promoter and determined the N terminus sequence of protease III. This N terminus contains a signal sequence that is needed for secretion of protease III to the periplasm. Using the cloned *ptr* gene and protease III-alkaline phosphatase fusions, we found evidence that protease III is also secreted to the growth medium.

In my PhD work, I studied the chemistry and ultrastructure of the spore wall of *Aspergillus nidulans* conidia, and the effect of cell wall components in the uptake of chemicals. I used electron microscopy to study the ultrastructure of the conidial wall and found that it is composed of several layers. The outer layer is covered by regularly arranged fibers (rodlets) which can be removed by sonication. Chemical analysis of purified conidial walls from a wild-type strain showed the presence of neutral sugars (glucose, galactose, and mannose), protein, chitin, melanin, and small amounts of lipid. Chemical fractionation experiments showed the presence of alpha-1,3-glucan in the electron-dense outer layer. Conidial walls of a white mutant strain lacked melanin and alpha-1,3-glucan. I also purified the rodlets, which contain protein and melanin in equal amounts and some carbohydrate. Histidine, aspartic acid, glutamic acid, glycine, and alanine are the most prominent amino acids of the rodlet protein. The presence of melanin and possible cross-linkages between it and amino acids like aspartic acid, glutamic acid and glycine make the rodlets resistant to proteases. I also studied the effect of conidial wall components on the uptake of sugar analogs and amino acids by conidia. Conidia were first treated with sonication to remove the rodlet layer, and then with proteases or glucanases. The removal of glucan and protein from the outer layer of the conidial wall allowed an increased uptake of 2-deoxy-D-glucose, 3-O-methyl-glucose and L-alanine. These results indicate that certain components of the conidial wall act as a barrier to penetration of chemicals.

ESSAY #6: "LAW SCHOOL ESSAY OF B. T. BALDWIN"

Law School Personal Statement

"So this is police work," I thought, sitting at a shaky table in a downtown pancake house one freezing afternoon three years ago. Beside me sat a deputy DA with little experience in the courtroom. Across from both of us sat our case's star witness, Scottie Wasserman, an unhoused person in tattered and worn clothing. The bulk of the restaurant patrons had migrated to the other half of the establishment upon our entrance. Whether this was due to Scottie's appearance or my police uniform, I didn't know.

Weeks earlier, Scottie had been the only person around to witness an unhoused woman being thrown against a fence and strangled. As the DA saw Scottie walking into the courthouse that day, I could see the horrifying visions in her head of an intoxicated unhoused man taking the stand, slurring his speech, and repelling the jurors out of a guilty verdict.

As the initiator of this lunch, I sat wondering how it would feel to be the DA in charge of such a case, being responsible for a witness like Scottie, and helping in the defense of a woman who was impoverished and living rough. Your tax dollars at work, some might think in a cynical tone, but I could still recite those words without cynicism.

All of my college peers were still working through their senior year, while I had decided to race to earn my degree in three years in order to join the police academy sooner. My high GPA should be viewed in light of my class load at the time. In a way it was a sacrifice, but by joining the police department early, I was able to see the difference I could make—differences like that day in the pancake house with Mr. Wasserman.

The table continued to tremble under Scottie's arms and legs as he tried to balance his fork and ignore his condition. Seeing him and his compatriots on a daily basis on my beat had given me an insight into alcoholism and the dependence on addiction that the people sleeping rough are often burdened with. I thought about how the elements of my education and my life experience could help the situation. As a community patrol officer, I was supposed to be quick on my feet, a problem solver, as well as a humanitarian. Being raised in a police family meant knowing the limitations and realities of social services. Having gained the outlines of the criminal law and justice system in college, I thought I had forged a bit of a unique vision of the crucible. I thought I understood where theory met practice.

I had already tried out my most idealistic side. I tutored freshman undergraduates in college. I helped build a criminal justice forum to aid those who wanted to help. I volunteered as a field investigator for the Personal Recognizance Program, verifying employment, church, and family ties, to get cash bails waived. And I volunteered at a police assistance program on weekends.

ESSAY #6: "LAW SCHOOL ESSAY OF B. T. BALDWIN" (CONTINUED)

Vivid depiction of a scenario or event can be a powerful essay for professional schools. The underlying and *unstated* theme to this essay is "where theory meets practice."

None of those things seemed to matter, though, to Mr. Wasserman. He flattened the hair on his head, trying for presentable with whatever will he could muster. Scottie's blood alcohol content was always more than three times the legal limit for drivers. The DA tried to smile. I could tell she was calling on all her law school training, all her knowledge. This was to be her first case. From her recent studies, she knew the law she would be trying, she knew how to handle a jury. But she didn't know how to present someone like Scottie.

Sitting there, I envied her challenge and considered what I could bring to the table in such a situation. I thought about the transition from enforcing laws to studying law to *using the law*. I watched as the DA grew more and more nervous. "Why do you shake like that, Scottie?" she asked, faking a calm demeanor.

She didn't appear to know why we were sitting in a pancake house, feeding Scottie a heavy dose of sugars before he testified. Scottie knew. "It's withdrawal, ma'am. Officer Baldwin knew I wouldn't be any good at the trial if I was drinking. I don't think it's right, hitting someone for nothing, and I want to be sober for this. I haven't had a drink since last night, and I wouldn't have been able to hold it past lunch if given the chance. Officer Baldwin has been with me all day now so I don't drink."

I knew that my upbringing and my experience on the department had provided me with a knowledge base that few lawyers would have the luxury to attain—the ability to understand the people who go through our legal system, the ability to reason as they would reason in times of crisis. Whether civil or criminal, almost every US citizen who is involved in our legal system is experiencing what for them is a crisis. I wanted to be able to understand what they were going through.

Scottie stayed sober and gave the testimony that earned the DA her win, a unanimous guilty, and the two of them together took a dangerous criminal off the streets. I drove Scottie to the west side that evening and let him out, and watched him walk into the corner store to buy what he needed to stop his shaking. I don't have a bleeding heart. But I understand a bit about nuance and complexity, about what it means to be a human.

It's not enough to simply believe in people, or hope for the best, or throw around platitudes that are at their root condescending. I think driving a black and white all day has given me a perspective of the gray area that most people don't get to see.

I am hoping that my police career gives me a greater understanding of the laws that I will someday enforce and the statutes that have been fought for in our judicial system. I'm eager to take what I've learned so far and add it to a rigorous education in the law. I know this combination can be used for a greater good. It is my goal to be of service.

ESSAY #7: "LIBRARY FLOORS AND LITERATURE"

Personal Statement

It happened two years ago as I lay sprawled out on the floor of the library lounge at the Université de Grenoble in Grenoble, France. I was working on an *explication du texte* of Guillaume Apollinaire's poem "La Loreley" for my *Poèmes et Proses du XXe Siècle* class when I suddenly put it together: this was *my* approach to literature. Close reading, formalism. Staying close, very close, to the text. I was certain.

Certainty, however, proved rather unstable. I knew it was important not to close myself off from other approaches to literature, so when I returned to Swarthmore from Grenoble, I took two courses that I knew would be highly theoretical—Women Writers 1790–1830 and Feminist Literary Criticism. These courses brought me around to a kind of hybrid approach to literature that I find rich, effective, and enjoyable. In this approach, I maintain a close connection to the text while I apply theoretical work.

I am using this approach to literature in two major projects this year.

First, I received a $2,400 National Endowment for the Humanities Younger Scholars Summer Research Grant. I proposed to expand on a prior research project, looking at the use of silence in the novels of Elie Wiesel, and at the ways Wiesel both demonstrates and gets around the fact that conventional language simply breaks down when it is used to talk about the Holocaust. I plan to expand on the same project for my senior English thesis. For this thesis, I am studying the ways Wiesel uses silence in the literal content of his novels and in his writing technique, and am working toward explanations as to how he gives these silences meaning. My fluency in French from my semester of study in Grenoble has been invaluable since most of Wiesel's works were originally written in French. My thesis involves close, formalist readings of Wiesel's novels, and is enriched by theoretical work. (This thesis appears as "Senior Essay" on my transcript; that designation will change next semester to "Thesis.")

My second major project this year is a self-designed research project sponsored by the Swarthmore English Department, under the supervision of Prof. L. Sturman. I am working with British poetry immediately following World War I, looking at how these poets write about a kind of war that truly had no precedent since it was the first war in which death could be so effectively and impersonally mass-produced. I am focusing on my observation that a surprising number of these poems rely heavily on biblical or mythical images, as though more contemporary images simply were not applicable anymore.

I have known for several years that I want my graduate work to be in the field of English, but my approach to literature has been enriched by my double major in English and sociology-anthropology. Twice my interest in anthropology has led me to study literature of non-European cultures, both times with great personal satisfaction. My papers for the *Black African Writer* combine theoretical research with a good deal of formalist textual analysis and close reading. I had several long

This is a great experiential opening. The reader can "see" the student "sprawled out," and the essay offers an exotic setting. This candidate displays amazing breadth while leading the reader through distinct phases in her intellectual development. The masterful way the candidate weaves in theorists, theories, authors, and names of works lightens what could otherwise be heavy exposition. The essay as a whole amounts to an intellectual argument, the point of which is this: this candidate's background points to the inevitable conclusion that this student is ready to excel at the targeted graduate program.

ESSAY #7: "LIBRARY FLOORS AND LITERATURE" (CONTINUED)

conversations about these papers with Prof. W. Mann, the R. Talbot Sondheim Professor of African Studies at Swarthmore.

My second excursion into less-traveled territory was a paper I wrote for Introduction to Hebrew Scriptures. I chose to do an exegesis of Isaiah 65:17–25. I worked from the original Hebrew text since I had taken a course in biblical Hebrew (Religion 93) and have a moderate level of reading comprehension of the language. I had a marvelous time digging so deeply into each word, and sometimes even individual letters, as is required in an exegesis of a Hebrew passage.

My two major projects this year—my thesis and my senior project—are related by the theme of war literature, and my work on one project gives me new ideas for the other. I feel fortunate that this has worked out, and at the University of Colorado Boulder I want to continue studying twentieth-century literature. However, I am also ready to start widening my base, casting out in some new directions. I have found over and over that if I have a long-standing, gut-level enjoyment of some kind of literature, I almost invariably have a wonderful time and do a good job taking an academic approach to that literature. Old English literature is in this category for me.

I have never done academic work in Old English literature, but for years I have treasured a recording in Old English of the stories of *Sir Gawain and the Green Knight, Caedmon,* and *The Wedding of Sir Gawain and Dame Ragnell.* And when I am feeling particularly harried, I often go to the Swarthmore library and treat myself to an old, scratchy LP of a reading of *Beowulf,* following along in the Old English text and in a modern English translation. By imitating the voice I hear and following in translation, I have taught myself a tiny amount of this language. I want to follow up on this interest.

These paragraphs show the depth of specific interest this student has in this specific graduate program. Be sure to customize your essays to this level of detail. Also note the liberal use of professors' names, both at the undergraduate alma mater and the targeted graduate program.

AI cannot draft an essay like this. At least not accurately, and not yet.

My interest in studying at the University of Colorado Boulder has grown out of conversations I have had with numerous people, including Prof. L. Langbauer, who had a lot of specific information since she taught there one summer. When I spoke about my interests with Dr. A. Blum, another professor of English at Swarthmore, she recommended that I call Prof. M. Ferguson. I did so, and had a wonderful conversation that helped me to confirm that I would feel very much at home in the department. I am especially excited about the department's strength in twentieth-century, Renaissance, and Old English literature.

I am also pleased about the distribution requirements, since they will help me to explore areas that I did not or could not at Swarthmore. By doing that, I will continue to learn new things about literature. I do not want my experience in the Université de Grenoble library to be a unique experiment in my development. I want to continue changing, refining, playing around with the ways in which I approach literature. This ever-changing, ever-learning approach will help me to be a lifelong scholar and lover of literature.

ESSAY #8: "64,000 MILES TO LAW SCHOOL"

I have known since junior high that I would be a lawyer. But I did not take the traditional road to law school.

I finished my undergraduate coursework at UC Davis and was awarded a BA with a major in political science/public service and a minor in Spanish. I did not consider applying to law school immediately, for I felt that I had lived a sheltered life in a middle-class suburb of Sacramento, and that I knew little of the real world. So I packed my bags, put two thousand dollars in a money belt, and took the train to Guadalajara, Mexico, determined to make a new life and face whatever rigors it had to offer. I knew no one in Mexico and had no connections, but I got a hotel room and began to look for work the next day.

I was to remain in Mexico for three years. One of my first jobs was as an English teacher at the Tourism School of the state-run University of Guadalajara. Ostensibly set up to give free educational opportunities in a career in tourism to Mexicans with low income, the school was as much "real world" as I could have asked for. The directors would delay our payroll checks and then offer personal loans, at high interest rates, so that the teachers could cover expenses until the checks "arrived." Student union strongmen packed pistols on campus and hijacked city buses when they grew tired of waiting at bus stops. Leaders of the student union passed my classes regardless of their failing grades or lack of attendance. My outrage, frustration, and helplessness left a deep impression on me; for the first time in my life, I was a foreigner with no civil rights.

Despite a low salary (US $650 per month) and poor working conditions, I stayed on in Mexico, resolved to become truly bilingual in Spanish, for I felt certain that it would be important in a legal-related career in California upon my return. I eventually found work at the Instituto Anglo-Mexicano de Cultura, a private English institute under the auspices of the British Council. I studied there in a one-year program and received a teaching certificate. My work consisted of writing the curriculum for and teaching six English classes per day to groups of thirty teenagers and adults. In my free time, I studied Spanish, Portuguese, French, and Latin in a program I developed for myself. On holidays, I traveled around the country by bus to familiarize myself with different dialects and to see the wonders of Mexico.

When I returned to California, I immediately began studying for the California Court Interpreters examination in Spanish. I did not yet feel ready for law school, and decided that court interpreting would be the best way to be in contact with the law and at the same time use my Spanish and work with the people for whom I had developed a deep appreciation.

I passed the exam on my first sitting, the first candidate to pass in Sacramento in two years, and began working freelance in the Sacramento municipal and superior courts. From the first day, I was thrust into interviews between attorney and client and onto the witness stand in cases ranging from family law disputes to

This student involves the reader in a fascinating life story—in this case, an adventure that the student voluntarily pursued. Note that he conveys his rationale for pursuing each stage of the adventure, and doesn't just drag the reader along for a travelogue. This essay exemplifies the writing edict, "show, don't tell"; for example, rather than telling us that he has compassion, intellectual curiosity, uncommon drive, and that his journey resulted in the maturity he was seeking, he shows us all these points without ever mentioning them directly. This is an impressive presentation for an uncommon candidate. Note how this student took a circuitous route to his goal, but without ever once losing sight of the object of his intentions.

ESSAY #8: "64,000 MILES TO LAW SCHOOL" (CONTINUED)

forcible rape and drunk driving to first-degree murder. In the interpreter's position, literally between the lawyer and his Spanish-speaking client, I saw the criminal lawyer's job as it really is: the frustrations, the heartache, the human element, the tactical considerations, the negotiations with opposing counsel, the grinding work and long hours, the hard-won victories, and the saddening defeats.

In my first year as a court interpreter, I worked in conjunction with the UC Davis Extension college to develop a training course for court interpreter candidates in Spanish. I wrote the curriculum, and the California Court Interpreters Association provided some of the materials. I gave the course solo for the first spring and fall semesters, and then team-taught the course with federal interpreters and colleagues Yolanda Portal and Carol Meredith. I am proud to say that six of the students from those courses went on to pass the state interpreter exam; they now make up an important segment of the court interpreter pool in the northern Sacramento Valley.

Provide context for accomplishments, as this student did by citing the pass rates for these exams. Isn't this more impressive than simply writing that he passed? The context lets us know this is an impressive accomplishment.

I then passed the Spanish interpreter examination for the US federal courts. This exam has an overall pass rate of 3.9 percent; of the 11,457 candidates who have taken the exam since its first offering, 442 have passed. (Official statistics provided by Ramon Castaneda, Staff Interpreter, US District Court, Sacramento.) I began working as a freelancer in the Sacramento federal court. The work was high-pressure and fast-paced, and I learned much about the changing state of sentencing under the recently approved federal guidelines. I stood beside young men accused of trafficking hundreds of kilos of cocaine and interpreted their tear-choked pleas for mercy as judges handed down sentences of twenty and twenty-five years in the federal penitentiary.

For three years, I divided my work between the Sacramento federal courts and the California state courts in a ten-city area stretching from Stockton to Shasta Lake and the Nevada border at Lake Tahoe. In my extensive travels, I saw how the law was applied differently around the state, and I became especially aware of the tremendous shortage of bilingual, bicultural attorneys to serve the needs of California's Hispanic population.

In legal interviews, despite my best efforts to convey the meaning of the words, I sensed a lack of understanding at a deeper level. I wanted to break in and explain to the attorney the realities of Mexico's legal system; I wanted to explain to the defendant how our judicial system was different from theirs. But I could not. I saw more than a few Spanish-speaking defendants walk through the system as if in a daze. I grew frustrated and more convinced than ever that if I wanted to make a real difference, it would have to be as an advocate.

But there was one more step to be taken on the long road to law school before I would feel ready. After three years of saving and extensive planning, I set off in a 2004 Subaru Outback wagon with 150,000 miles on it, with the goal

ESSAY #8: "64,000 MILES TO LAW SCHOOL" (CONTINUED)

of driving overland to the tip of South America and back up to the Arctic Sea in Alaska. Twenty countries, thirty months, forty border crossings, and sixty-four thousand miles later, I achieved that goal.

Along the way, I gave interviews on Brazilian television in Belo Horizonte, Goiania, and Santa Rosa. I made presentations to school groups of twenty to two hundred students in Brazil and Canada. I interpreted at a judicial conference between Justice Edward Panelli of the California Supreme Court and members of the Supreme Court of Bolivia in Sucre, Bolivia. Throughout Latin America, I negotiated prices with mechanics, immigration officers, customs officials, policemen, soldiers, and on one occasion with armed men wearing masks. I had to make my way through red tape and bureaucracy in Spanish, Portuguese, and French. I managed a thirty-two-thousand-dollar budget through countless ups and downs and returned the Outback safely to California last September. In sum, I gathered the real-world experience I felt was necessary to be an effective lawyer. At present, I am writing a book about my experiences, *A Passage to Patagonia: 64,000 Miles of Driving the Americas.*

I look forward to working as a lawyer in areas where I can employ my language skills and my court experience together with my law school education. I am particularly interested in the Jerome N. Frank Legal Services Organization's immigration project and the immigration-level services course at Yale. My interest has a personal facet as well, for my wife is an immigrant from Uruguay. I am also very interested in your course "US–Latin American Relations and the Pressures of Globalization." This will be an important field of law in the years ahead as US and Latin American ties evolve, the regional human migration crisis due to economic collapse and civic failures continues to worsen, and the boundaries of the law in many specialties will be stretched and redefined. I intend to be a part of this dynamic process going forward. How will law address these issues? How will law help forge solutions?

I think others would say that I am a hard worker, a good organizer, an enthusiastic speaker, and an avid student. I believe I can make a positive contribution to the student body of the Yale Law School, and with a Yale Law School degree, I can make a positive contribution to the legal profession and to the welfare of immigrants in the years of change that lie ahead.

Note how the candidate makes this more than an adventure, by pointing out how this adventure relates to law. Predict success for yourself as a graduate student, and later as a professional practicing in your chosen field. This is a highly effective close to a personal statement.

ESSAY #9: "LAB SCIENCES AND CHINESE"

This student mentions a *long* history of interest in science, going back to "childhood chemistry kits," but notice that she does not dwell on this genesis, but moves right along into a significant adult experience. This is much stronger than building an essay around a childhood experience. As one science recruiter said, "Let's leave Dr. Seuss out of it."

From childhood chemistry kits to PCR and cloning, I always knew I had a passion for science, but it was an experience while conducting research in a laboratory this last summer that finalized my decision to attend graduate school. It was 4 a.m. in my Princeton internship laboratory where I experienced my biggest *Eureka!* moment. I had been building on a series of experiments that led to that defining moment at the fluorescent microscope. I was extremely meticulous while preparing the slides. This was it! I thought. Several weeks of experiments were about to yield a conclusive answer. The experiments were designed to determine if there was a direct interaction between a RAS protein and the MAPK pathway, and the fluorescent intensities would tell all. That morning, not only did I know that the RAS protein did not have direct contact with the MAPK pathway as the conventional pathway portrayed, but I knew that I had discovered this myself. Yes, Dr. R. Nuñez had set up this lab and supervised it, and yes, three postdocs had helped me hone my skills but, in the end, I had discovered the finding—I did the experiments, I interpreted the results, and I realized I could advance knowledge in the field of biology. Laboratory research has always appeared to match my intellectual interests very well; the end result of gaining knowledge is captivating. Research epitomizes what I find most enjoyable and what I would most like to pursue as a profession.

Always cite your mentors by name.

I have been fortunate to have the opportunity to take part in a number of different research projects over the last few years. I was first exposed to research my freshman year of college by taking on an independent project concerning the extraction of metals from acid mine drainage water samples by an *Amaranthus* plant species under the supervision of Dr. A. Kondo. The following year, I conducted research using the plant pathogenic fungus, *Rhizoctonia solani,* examining viral-like particles (dsRNA) that were unique to disparate isolates of the fungus with the goal of creating a biosensor to detect bioagents with Dr. N. Bharathan. The summer after my junior year, I participated in the Princeton University's Summer Undergraduate Research Program in Molecular and Quantitative & Computational Biology, working with Dr. J. Broach, where I requested to work on two separate projects since one project did not suffice for the amount of time I wanted to spend in the laboratory. For one of the projects, I focused on examining nuclear localization of the transcription factors MSN2 and MSN4 in response to sources of stress, such as nutrient deprivation and osmotic irregularities in *Saccharomyces cerevisiae*. For the other project, I tested the conventional method of RAS protein's direct interaction with the MAPK pathway to determine its accuracy. After these research experiences, I found that my interests lay in the field of molecular biology, so I began my senior biochemistry research project in a laboratory involved in studying circadian and ultradian rhythms in *Paramecium tetraurelia* with Dr. R. Hinrichsen. My project focuses on using RNA interference to determine the function of genes involved in the regulation of calcium flux in the calcium storage unit.

I am particularly interested in graduate studies in the molecular mechanisms involved in embryogenesis and morphogenesis, the development and function of stem cells and chromosomal and protein behavior in regard to these biological

ESSAY #9: "LAB SCIENCES AND CHINESE" (CONTINUED)

processes. I find that the types of research interests I have are in correspondence with several research faculty members at Yale University, including Drs. V. Horsley, D. L. W. Wells, and W. Zhong. All of these faculty members have research projects that involve the molecular mechanisms of developmental processes. I am greatly intrigued by Dr. Horsley's research in epithelial stem cell proliferation and its applications to regeneration, Dr. Wells's research in the biochemistry involved in dendrite synaptic plasticity, and Dr. Zhong's work in studying molecular mechanisms of stem cells that go through asymmetrical divisions. Yale University would provide me with a great opportunity since its faculty research matches so well with my academic interests.

A future career goal of mine is to work in partnership with developing countries in the biosciences to enhance knowledge in the scientific field. As an undergraduate, I have consistently studied Chinese language and culture, and have traveled abroad for a language intensive program in Chengdu, China, an unusual experience for a lab sciences major. These classes have made it possible for me to graduate with both an Asian studies and biochemistry bachelor's degree. Also, for next semester, I have set up an independent study course to learn scientific terminology in Chinese. China is a major contributor to the sciences, as seen by their development of the Beijing Genomics Institute along with their advanced twenty-year bioscience plan for the stem cell and genetic engineering industry. Science is a collaborative subject that requires knowledge and resources from what should be an international level. I think it is important that scientists keep enduring international channels for communication and collaboration open, no matter what disruptions or agitations the political class may choose to foment at any given moment. I consider myself a useful student not only for the scientific background I can bring to Yale University, but also for my proficiency in the Chinese language that I can use to enhance international collaborations in science.

Upon completing the graduate program, I look forward to continuing my education through a postdoctoral fellowship, after which I plan to conduct research at an institute of advanced studies involved in medical and therapeutic treatments of developmental abnormalities. Eventually, I would like to obtain a position in academia to focus on advancing applications to stop abnormal differentiation of embryonic stem cells. Along the way, I would also work to encourage international collaborative efforts to work on scientific issues in today's global society. The program at Yale University would serve as a vital foundation for obtaining knowledge in my intended field.

Throughout my experiences as an undergraduate researcher and research assistant, I have learned that research is a rewarding process. This direction matches best with my interests, skills, and goals. I realize that as a graduate student, I will be expected to spend countless hours in the laboratory performing research; however, I also realize that this is my passion. I believe my determination and tenacity in the pursuit of knowledge, along with my other qualifications, can lead to success as a student in the graduate program at Yale University. It is my goal to become highly skilled, and to contribute real value to the projects of the faculty at Yale University.

Each essay should read, from first line to last, as if you only wrote the essay for this one application. That establishes fit and match. This student does a worthy job of matching her background and interests to the specific program, specific labs, and specific faculty members.

ESSAY #10: "HOW WILL YOU ADD DIVERSITY TO OUR PROGRAM?"

This white student wrote that it was hard to come up with a response to how she would add diversity to the campus, but she succeeded. She establishes that she will contribute to diversity of thought and experience in her academic community. She goes on to write: "Thanks so much for writing such a great book! It really helped me get through the application process with ease and I got accepted to every school I applied to. The essay writing advice was great and I think it really enabled me to write some winning essays—people on the admissions committees were quoting them back to me in my interviews!"

After an hour of constant rubbing, my hands were covered in blisters and I still could not produce a spark from the stick. But I had intentionally hiked to the bottom of this canyon equipped with only a sleeping bag and my wilderness skills, determined to either catch my dinner and cook it with only the resources available to me or spend the night hungry. The first task had been a challenge in and of itself, wading in the cool creek until my legs were numb while I tickled the bellies of fish hiding in the banks, waiting for the right moment to snatch one with my hands. With the fish caught, I now needed fire. At my current rate the task seemed impossible, but when the stakes are high, the motivation to succeed is strong. I painstakingly went back to work until finally, a wisp of smoke and a spark combined to produce the best tasting and most satisfying meal of my life. This experience and others similar to it have given me a deep understanding of the natural world and a unique perspective on the relationship between humans and the environment.

Since graduating from the University of Minnesota, I have sought out an intimate relationship with the natural world. Through this approach, I have come to appreciate natural resources in an uncommon way that I believe brings a nuanced perspective to the field of conservation biology. I have spent months in the deserts of the Southwest living out of a tent and teaching myself survival skills in the barren canyons. I have lived in the woods of the Midwest in a rustic cabin with no running water, washing up either in the creek down the hill or the faucet next to a wood-burning sauna across the adjacent field. Living this type of life requires constantly overcoming obstacles just to obtain basic necessities: food, shelter, water. These solitary experiences, indeed struggles, have deepened my appreciation for the value of "land" in a way that I would like to share with my classmates if accepted to the graduate school at the University of Minnesota.

This journey started when I saw a poster at my high school announcing that local Native elders were opening tribal youth classes to non-tribal youth. I gained a whole new way of looking at the world. I have gone on to study with various Midwestern herbalists and the Lakota healer, Paul Red Elk, learning about diverse Native American belief systems and how they relate to the Upper Midwest's natural resources. Learning some of the ancient traditions of the Lakota people gave me a more intuitive way of looking at plant communities, a view that has the knowledge of centuries behind it. I was taught the difference between knowing the Latin name of a plant and really knowing the plant—where it was found historically, the folklore surrounding it, which animals depend on it for survival, what medicinal uses it has, and how it can be used for food or other material; in essence, the spirit of the plant and its historical relationship to humans. This unique perspective toward ecology, which has strengthened the foundation of my undergraduate degree, is one that I am eager to offer the University of Minnesota's conservation biology program.

ESSAY #10: "HOW WILL YOU ADD DIVERSITY TO OUR PROGRAM?" (CONTINUED)

If accepted to the graduate school at the University of Minnesota, I will bring a unique way of understanding Midwestern ecology through the Native American and survivalist lens. In any research or interventions I do, I will invite tribal herbalists, ecologists, and political leaders to collaborate and participate. I would like to use the same drive it took to spark fire in that Southwest canyon to motivate myself and others in the program to succeed. I would like to use my understanding of Lakota traditions to view the natural element in terms of its history, cultural value, role in community ecology, and function in supporting human survival. I offer the university my blend of the typical conservationist perspective and a deep, intimate understanding of the natural world.

Notice that a short essay can also be highly effective.

ESSAY #11: "CHEMISTRY INTO LAW"

Personal Statement for Law School

This is an outstanding and humorous opening paragraph, bringing the reader right into the story. An opening like this makes a promise: "I promise not to be boring, no matter how many essays you've read today and how tired you may be of brilliant, accomplished candidates."

The second paragraph traces the origin of the candidate's interest in law. This is always a good topic to cover in an essay.

Always name your advisors.

This student provides a rationale for her transition from studying chemistry as an undergraduate to studying law as a graduate student. She follows two tracks to explain the transition: first, explicating her personal transformation from being interested in chemistry to being interested in law, and second, exploring how her chemistry education could be useful in a legal career.

I waited patiently by the bench in what all Harvey Mudd chemistry majors call the "Super Lab," staring for what seemed to be hours at a small flask bubbling with something that looked like a cross between Pepto-Bismol and whipped cream. I was waiting for the color to turn just the right shade of blue before I could go home for a late dinner, but it was obvious that this solution was as far from blue as baseball is from rugby. I realized then that Super Lab was not so Super, and neither was a career as a chemist.

Every summer since high school, I worked at Lawrence Livermore Laboratory as a research assistant. One of my major projects involved working on a team to develop probes for the detection of radioactive substances. When I turned in my final report, a computer program that would give the same results in five minutes as four people would in a week, my pride turned into disappointment when my supervisor took credit for all of my hard work. Unbeknownst to me, somewhere in tiny print in the contract I signed as an employee, it said something to the effect that as an employee I would relinquish all rights to everything that I developed at Lawrence Livermore National Laboratory. I felt that it was unfair for a company to claim such rights to its employees' innovations and wished to learn more about the issues that surround intellectual property.

I was introduced to the field of intellectual property law in industrial chemistry, taught by Prof. G. van Hecke. For my final report, I researched the development of the Gore-Tex fiber by procuring its patent from an online patent service. At that time, I was considering a career in the management sector of the chemical industry because I wanted to be able to use my knowledge of applied chemistry while at the same time work with people. However, once I was introduced to industrial chemistry law, I realized that a career in law would not only incorporate all of my skills but would give me more breadth than management in a chemical company. Whereas management would limit me to a particular industry, IP law would expose me to a number of industries. IP law would also not confine me to a particular strategy in dealing with problems but force me to develop different strategies based on the industry and the problem that I am dealing with. Law school suddenly became a very attractive career path to me, especially because it would allow me to use my education creatively to help protect the product of people's ideas.

Although I am an applied chemistry major, what I have learned as an undergraduate can be applied in many ways to law. Because I have a strong technical background, I have been trained extensively in solving problems both alone and in teams. Although the problems themselves have been technical, the analytical skills that I have acquired in solving such problems can be applied to the world of law. Harvey Mudd's unique engineering clinic program allowed me to work on a team

ESSAY #11: "CHEMISTRY INTO LAW" (CONTINUED)

of five students to develop a project plan for General Electric Nuclear Energy to bring the concentration of toxic organic compounds in their waste system down to environmentally safe levels. I have also worked on student teams to solve problems for Habitat for Humanity, and during my summer internships to solve problems for the government. Because I am an applicant from a nontraditional background, I can provide a different perspective to problems encountered in law, and can even introduce vastly different but equally effective approaches to solving these problems.

My technical background is not the only factor that sets me apart from the traditional law school applicant. Because Harvey Mudd balances its technical program with an equally strong emphasis in the humanities, I am not only leaving Mudd with a great education in chemistry, but I am also leaving Mudd as a technically educated student who is skilled in writing and communication. In addition to possessing a liberal arts background that is unequaled by most technical applicants to law school, I also possess a background that is unique even for a Harvey Mudder. The typical Harvey Mudd student studies at Mudd for four years, then pursues graduate school in a science or engineering field, and then works in either industry or academia. Unlike the typical Mudd student, I have managed not only to perform well academically, but to take advantage of nonacademic opportunities in order to better balance my life. My experience as the resident assistant of my dorm has given me tools that are necessary to a lawyer such as time management, interpersonal and conflict resolution skills, as well as the ability to effectively deal with crisis situations. Having to juggle my responsibilities as a resident assistant, a student, and an athlete has increased my organizational skills by orders of magnitude. As freshman and sophomore class president, and team leader of an engineering project, I learned how to be more assertive and gained valuable leadership skills in the process. In addition, my membership in the National Forensics League and participation in Lincoln-Douglas debates have provided me with the skills of impromptu speech, oral communication, and the art of persuasion using sound facts as the basis for arguments.

I finally managed to completely break the mold of the typical Harvey Mudd student by attempting to study abroad for one semester. This was the greatest challenge of my undergraduate career because not many science and engineering majors, let alone Harvey Mudd students, leave to study at foreign institutions. Many attribute this to the specificity of the science curriculum and the resulting difficulty in finding compatible curricula at foreign institutions. After making use of all the resources possible, I realized that although it is indeed an arduous task to find a university abroad that matches our curriculum to a tee, it is not impossible to do so. After one year of persuading some reluctant administrators to make it easier for a Harvey Mudd student to leave for one semester, I found myself at the University of New South Wales in Australia, where I had some of the most valuable experiences

Finally, note how she reveals herself as an interesting and independently willed person by recounting her experiences in debate and foreign study. To really grasp this essay, it helps to know that Harvey Mudd is one of the most elite and difficult engineering colleges in the United States. This student can afford to poke a little fun at herself because she has succeeded in a program renowned for its intellectual rigor.

Once you prove you can do the work, *then* you can address the issue of whether you are a nice or interesting person.

This is a nice summation of her entire argument.

ESSAY #11: "CHEMISTRY INTO LAW" (CONTINUED)

in my life. I returned much more independent, and especially aware of the world around me. Upon my return, and due in part to my own example, I discovered that the school had proposed many changes to allow more flexibility in the students' education so that studying abroad would be possible for others who follow me.

I once had the misperception that those who are educated in disciplines such as political science, public policy, or prelaw are more likely to be prepared for a graduate education in law than most other students. Now I believe that a student coming from a more nontraditional background can contribute in many ways to society as a lawyer. In a world where technology is the dominant means of progress and is advancing at such a breakneck pace, it can be a great advantage to society to have knowledgeable people working with laws concerning technology. I not only believe that I am qualified to perform this service to society as a lawyer, but I am convinced that [school withheld] possesses the quality of education and diversity in student body that can best help me fulfill these goals.

ESSAY #12: "PHD IN PHILOSOPHY—EPISTEMOLOGY"

"The progress of philosophy, at least, is dialectical: we turn up to old insights in new and, we hope, improved forms."

—P. F. Strawson

My primary areas of interest in philosophy are epistemology and the history of analytic philosophy. In epistemology, I'm most occupied with questions regarding the epistemology of testimony. In particular, how are we epistemically dependent on other agents? What is the epistemic import of beliefs in other agents, or in Edward Craig's term, informants? How are those beliefs different from propositional beliefs? Looking into these questions will shed light on interesting features unique to testimony as a source of knowledge. In addition, I have a long-standing interest in topics such as external world skepticism and responses (such as dogmatism, Wittgenstein's hinge commitments, contextualism, inference to the best explanation, and pragmatic encroachment), theories of knowledge, epistemic justification (particularly immediate justification), perception, self-knowledge, social epistemology, and religious epistemology.

Be careful when putting an epigraph at the top of your essay. Several academics responding to my surveys said they want to see *your* thoughts, not quotes of someone else's. Nevertheless, a quick quote from a respected thought leader that sets the tone for your essay might be acceptable to most readers. This one works just right, and is referenced later in the essay.

In the history of analytic philosophy, my interest includes but is not limited to the works of Wittgenstein (both early and later), G. E. Moore, ordinary language philosophers—Ryle, Austin, Strawson, Grice—as well as Anscombe, Sellars, Bernard Williams, Gareth Evans, and John McDowell. I'm greatly influenced by their thoughts on metaphysics, epistemology, mind, language, and action. I have developed a general interest in prominent themes of 20th century analytic philosophy, such as truth, meaning, reference, thought, representation, intentionality, and philosophical methodology. To appreciate these thoughts more fully, I try to see them in the historical continuation. I'm also interested in the history of modern philosophy, particularly in figures such as Descartes, Pascal, Leibniz, Berkeley, Reid, Kant, and Kierkegaard.

Think of your essays as an open-book test. This applicant does an excellent job of taking us on a survey of the discipline, and where he would like to land within it.

My secondary areas of interest are moral psychology and philosophy of action. I have always found interpersonal interactions and relationships fascinating. Recently I began to notice the philosophical significance of action-theoretic concerns, which explains why some of my favorite philosophers spent so much time writing about questions in moral psychology. I would love to learn more about this area in my graduate studies. In general, my interests are liable to change in this early stage of my career. I often find myself thinking about free will and moral responsibility, immunity to error through misidentification, perceptual content, the myth of the given, Christian ethics, the good sense of the scientist (especially intuition and creativity), mereology, and the role of common sense in philosophical theorizing.

I'm a historically minded student of philosophy. All of my nonhistorical interests are heavily informed and inspired by the thoughts of philosophers from the early modern era onward. I aspire to become a philosopher fluent in the history

ESSAY #12: "PHD IN PHILOSOPHY—EPISTEMOLOGY" (CONTINUED)

These wide-ranging lists of interest would be particularly supportive of the career goal of being a professor of philosophy. Professors often need to develop coursework outside their narrow area of inquiry.

It is risky to mention just one professor as "of interest," but this candidate's enthusiasm and understanding of the department's focus and strengths help him be convincing that he does see fit and match with the rest of the faculty.

of philosophy, who can critically engage with old insights and bring them to bear on contemporary issues, as Strawson remarks in the epigraph. I'm convinced that this fluency is a prerequisite for later original contributions, as we stand on the shoulders of giants that come before us. Ultimately, my career goal is to obtain a professorship in philosophy.

As a double major in philosophy and mathematics, with a minor in classics, I believe I am well equipped for graduate education in philosophy. I have a solid foundation and appreciation for the analytic tradition from origins to contemporary discussions. Upon successfully defending my senior thesis, I expect to graduate with honors in philosophy. My extensive math background with advanced completed coursework in topology, mathematical logic, real analysis, and abstract algebra allows me to understand, and to a certain extent, critically engage with the more technical works in logic, metaphysics, formal epistemology, and philosophy of science. On the applied side, I have been auditing computer science classes (the letter grade "Y" in my transcript means I audited that class), and my coding skills also contribute to my versatility as a prospective researcher. I am comfortable working with R, MATLAB, and Latex, and I am capable of teaching myself other tools as needed. I believe I can stay current and relevant and change along with the discipline and trends in student foci over time.

Given my goal and interests, the University of Pittsburgh is an exceptionally good fit for my graduate studies. Pitt is simply the hub for theoretical philosophy, particularly with a focus in its history. This is what makes Pitt stand out most to me from every other program. As a historically minded student of philosophy interested in theoretical philosophy, I consider this feature especially important. There are many faculty members whose research and writings I'm interested in, and I'm incredibly excited by the idea of working with them. Although I do not know in advance my area of specialization, I eagerly anticipate the opportunity to study with Prof. J. McDowell. His works have left a great impact on my own thoughts in topics as diverse as disjunctivism, Wittgenstein, communication, and philosophical methodology. I really anticipate exploring further with him his thoughts on dualism from *Mind and World*. I am sure other faculty will help me find my own best journey to in-depth studies.

I am confident I have the capacity to be successful as a graduate student at Pitt. I would be deeply honored to continue my philosophical pursuits there. Thank you for your consideration.

ESSAY #13: "SPORTS, PRESIDENTS, AND PUBLIC RELATIONS"

The Question:

"What are the reasons you wish to pursue the graduate program and how does it relate to your career goals?"

Master of Arts, Strategic Public Relations
University of Southern California

The Catalyst A burst blood vessel in the brain of my former university president provided the tragic high and low point in my young public relations career.

It began with a jarring call at six a.m. on a Sunday. The president of George Fox University—where I serve as assistant director of public information—had suffered a life-threatening stroke caused by a brain tumor. I was called in to deal with the news media. For this very newsworthy emergency, I served as the university spokesperson, doing all media interviews, writing press releases, and recording a daily voicemail line with health updates. The situation was made even more hectic by the fact that two of my university relations colleagues were out of the office.

I found myself hurting for our president and his family but caught up in the action. Even when the director of public information returned, I remained as the media spokesperson. A year later, cancer claimed the life of our president, and I was asked to summarize the personality of this remarkable man in our alumni newspaper. (See writing sample.)

That was one experience which has led me to apply to University of Southern California for further training in public relations.

Beyond Age 30 Although I am assistant director of public information, much of my time is consumed by my work as sports information director for George Fox's athletic program.

Not long ago, a coworker asked me, "Are you going to be a sports information director when you're sixty-five?"

My instinctive reply surprised even myself: "I don't plan to be one when I'm thirty."

Since I'm twenty-six today, I can feel that clock ticking.

I feel I've gone about as far as I can in small-college sports information. Since graduation—when I moved from a twenty-hour-a-week student position to full-time employee—I've elevated the coverage of nonrevenue sports by improving their publications and press releases.

When I began, media guides were produced only for men's basketball. Now all thirteen varsity sports have a media guide. Many guides have received national honors. My women's basketball guide is perhaps my favorite. Created from scratch,

Here's an arresting opening line.

This essay is a little chatty, but it does an outstanding job of conveying the enthusiasm and decency of this remarkable man. One gets the impression that if life served him a pile of lemons, he wouldn't start a lemonade stand, he'd start a franchise. Also, he has done a good job of adopting the writing tips espoused by this book, such as referring to supporting documentation (as in "See writing sample"). His essay traces the history of his decision to pursue graduate education and details his preparations to succeed. This is a natural theme on which to organize any essay.

Feel free to spice up your essay with direct quotes from real people that support your points or advance your narrative.

ESSAY #13: "SPORTS, PRESIDENTS, AND PUBLIC RELATIONS" (CONTINUED)

it has been honored as the second best in the nation among colleges at our level of athletic competition. (I've enclosed the most recent copy.)

With the assistance of student assistants, I produce weekly news releases for each sport. They often are used verbatim by local newspapers. While speaking about athletic media relations at a recent conference, a sports reporter from a Portland radio station declared George Fox, the "King of News Releases."

At George Fox, we strive to stand above the crowd. While most schools at our level photocopy their basketball programs, my office puts together a twelve-page program that generates about $27,000 in advertising revenue.

This year, I supervise a staff of up to seven students who assist me in stat keeping, ticket selling, ad selling, news release writing, and office work. I also recruit and manage about a dozen volunteers to staff games during basketball season.

I enjoy my job. I like working with my student assistants and seeing them mature as writers and persons. It's fun to be part of the "team" with coaches and student-athletes. I still find my palms sweaty in the ninth inning of a tight baseball game, but the amount of coverage available to small colleges is frustratingly small. So much work for so little return.

Stepping Outside the Sports Arena Although I often find myself consumed with the promotion of my athletic department, I don't want to be pigeonholed as a sports fanatic.

After earning a number of state awards as a high school trumpet player, I received a music scholarship at George Fox. I continue to play occasionally at weddings and church services, and I teach lessons.

The death of a college roommate from leukemia led me to volunteer at a camp for kids with cancer run by the American Cancer Society. For the past six summers, I've been known as the bugle-blowing counselor "Mr. Toad."

My Destination I still tell people I don't know what I want to be when I grow up, but I'd like it to be in the public relations field.

I believe I have the talent for it.

I was recently honored with the "Rising Star" award in the field of communications by the Council for Advancement and Support of Education (CASE) District VIII. It's an award given to professionals in their first five years in the field. The district is made up of development, alumni, and public relations professionals at educational institutions in five states and six Canadian provinces. George Fox University—with twenty-three hundred students—is one of the smallest colleges in CASE.

I take an active role in George Fox's weekly university relations meetings, where we discuss potential news stories and a wide variety of PR issues. Topics

ESSAY #13: "SPORTS, PRESIDENTS, AND PUBLIC RELATIONS" (CONTINUED)

have ranged from "How can we improve internal communication on our campus intranet system?" to "What do we put in our alumni newspaper when one of our newly admitted freshmen has been arrested for a double homicide?"

I personally started and got buy-in for the Crisis Initiative, where we decided to model responses in advance to a series of possible scenarios: "Racial Incident," "Earthquake," "Sexual Assault," "Embezzlement," "Sexual Scandal," and so on. This had never been done before, and involved taking turns doing research and making mini-presentations monthly. Unfortunately, we did not model "President stricken ill."

I get a thrill out of trying to capture the interest of the news media with a story tip and have achieved local and national success. *U.S. News & World Report* used one of my submissions about a unique George Fox campus tradition in its annual college ranking guide.

Although I don't believe I want to be a full-time writer, I consider writing one of my strengths. My story about a record-setting female pole vaulter this summer was used by the National Association of Intercollegiate Athletics (NAIA) in its online magazine *NAIA News*. (See writing sample.) Another feature about a women's basketball senior citizen fan club received a national award from the College Sports Information Directors Association.

Note that this writer has a conversational tone throughout, so his use of contractions is acceptable.

An Itch to Explore After eight years as a student and administrator at George Fox, I feel very comfortable here, but I want to broaden my horizons. It's an itch. Perhaps I picked it up from my father, who packed my family up when I was twelve and took us to live in Brazil for a year. Twenty countries later, I'm still hungry to explore. In the last three summers, I've had coffee at the home of a Bosnian war widow; seen Belfast, Northern Ireland, during a commemorative march; and crossed from Hong Kong to China with a relief worker to see her work on an island inhabited by people with leprosy. Travel has opened my eyes to a world larger than a basketball game.

After you've established intellectual capacity, it's okay to throw in a human-interest section.

I enjoy the academic environment. Going back to school excites me. Education always has been a part of my life. My parents are both teachers. Since I have an interest in possibly following in their footsteps later in life, I would appreciate being considered for a teaching assistantship. (See separate application packet.) I believe I would be an excellent candidate since I have spent the last seven years editing sports and general news releases written by college students.

Why USC? I believe USC would provide me with excellent training in my profession. After discovering its high ranking, I visited the school's website for more information. The idea of receiving hands-on training from LA's PR professionals is

The more persuasive your answer to "Why here?" the more likely you'll be admitted. Students who do not customize their essays waste an opportunity to impress admissions decision makers.

Preparing yourself fiscally for graduate school is just as important as preparing yourself intellectually. When you've made prudent financial preparations, let readers know.

ESSAY #13: "SPORTS, PRESIDENTS, AND PUBLIC RELATIONS" (CONTINUED)

extremely attractive. I contacted Alan MacDonald, who earned his master's degree in PR from USC, and current journalism graduate student Jennifer Prosser to ask about their experiences. Both gave the school and the professors high marks.

Although I could see myself returning to a public relations position at George Fox, I'm intrigued by the variety of options that would be available to me after graduation. Alan MacDonald told me that USC stood for University of Social Connections. In addition to my current experience, a degree from USC would give me additional credibility. During my January visit to USC, I met with Tim Burgess and was impressed that the Annenberg School of Communications had its own career advising office.

I have done quite a bit of research on master's degrees in communications, but USC's public relations program was the first and only one to excite me. I am applying to no other program.

I do not go into this application process halfheartedly. This has been my passionate intention for over a year. In preparation for the cost of full-time graduate school, I became frugal. I decided to continue driving my twelve-year-old car, and I moved out of a house where I rented alone to save costs in a shared duplex with four roommates.

I feel that I am ready to perform in your program—mentally, financially, academically—and that I have honed the skills necessary to excel. I would like the opportunity to fulfill my capacity at USC.

Thank you for considering my application.

ESSAY #14: "PERSONALLY RELATED TO GOD"

Statement of Purpose for Architectural School

Leon Battista Alberti is my great, great, great . . . great-uncle on my mother's side. His name is neatly inscribed in a genealogy contained in one of our family Bibles. It was only after I became interested in architecture that I discovered who my relative was, although it is common knowledge that everyone on this side of my family can draw or paint, as if by genetic decree.

This opening paragraph is powerful and auspicious, since Leon Battista Alberti is the Leonardo da Vinci of architecture.

I grew up in a lower-middle-class neighborhood in Detroit, one of three girls. My father was a blue-collar worker who instilled in me a strong work ethic and a respect for all creations of manual labor. He taught me how to take things apart, fix them, and put them back together again. He taught me to be proud of any job well done, no matter how trivial or how complex. He taught me to be honest.

This essay is wonderfully honest and forthcoming, and for several reasons it is a nearly perfect application essay. The applicant puts a "spin" on her essay, featuring her intent to pursue a specialized career and demonstrating how her rather unusual background is uniquely suited to achieving excellence in that career. Finally, her essay ties together the rest of her application in a compelling manner. The candidate has clearly thought about her goals and plotted a serious path.

My sister has a developmental disability. This fact sensitized me at an early age about learning to live with disabilities. My mother went back to school in her thirties to become a deaf-education teacher. So I grew up with an unusually strong feeling of social responsibility, of obligation to help others. Instead of being angry about my sister, we responded by "going to work."

I took my interest in drawing, painting, and sculpting and decided to pursue a career in occupational therapy. Occupational therapy helps teach basic living skills to those with a range of mental health challenges; people with developmental disabilities; and those who have suffered a stroke, trauma, or other serious central nervous system conditions. My specialty was occupational therapy using art as a treatment modality. I especially preferred three-dimensional media, such as ceramics, woodworking, handicrafts, and horticulture. I was also taught to use skilled observation techniques in order to develop an activity analysis, or a breakdown of the minute, specific steps needed to successfully complete a basic task.

As an occupational therapist, I also designed and fabricated adaptive equipment for use by patients. I learned how to manipulate and structure a patient's immediate environment in order to promote their highest level of independence and functioning. I designed treatment aids, detachable wheelchair fixtures, and for one client I designed kitchen modifications to allow her to return to her role as a homemaker in spite of her disability from muscular dystrophy (I obtained funding for the work, as well). I have often been the staff member called upon to repair the furniture, fix the Ping-Pong table, fine-tune the equipment, wire the new stereo. . . .

All of this experience, I feel, will be directly applied in my future career as an architect with a specialty in universal design.

In my experiences as an occupational therapist, I was often struck at how poorly designed clinic and treatment areas were for the patients they were supposed to serve. In Michigan, I was a consultant to Easter Seals on a group project to

ESSAY #14: "PERSONALLY RELATED TO GOD" (CONTINUED)

evaluate buildings for barrier-free design. For the same organization, I contributed to a project to create a map of wheelchair-accessible Kalamazoo, Michigan.

At one program where I served, the physical surroundings were so austere that I launched a project to paint children's hospital corridors, wards, and gymnasium in colorful wall graphics. At another program, a psychiatric facility, a "decorator" with good intentions had painted the ward in electric orange complete with vinyl floors to match. The colors proved overly stimulating and disorienting for some patients, and the nurses and I succeeded in lobbying the director for a more appropriate and calming color scheme. I have seen nurses scramble to fill dozens of medication trays with 100 percent accuracy, while spinning and turning and reaching around in a dispensing room that is only 4′ by 6′ in dimension. I have seen shower rooms too small to accommodate the patient and the nurse. I have seen grab bars installed at useless angles and levels, doorknobs that someone with arthritis in their hand cannot turn, chairs for patients that tip over easily or are hard to get out of, counters and corridors that are invisible to the visually impaired (they lack a simple border line; how easy it would have been to do it correctly). So I have observed the pleasures that simple, inexpensive design can bring to patient populations and staff, and the heavy-handed errors that are all too commonly committed by designers who have no real awareness of the hospital environment.

I have come to believe that humanity will be better served if health care facilities are renovated or built by individuals who have some sensitivity to the people actually working in them and some knowledge of patients' specialized needs. I am very interested in universal design of medical and treatment facilities, design of hospice environments, and residential design for people with disabilities and for the rapidly increasing geriatric population. I view these as exciting areas for change and growth in modern architecture. The design training that I would receive at Berkeley, combined with my knowledge of the needs of these population groups, would allow me to bring a unique perspective to my career as a practicing architect.

This applicant, like the last one, is applying to only one school. Although this is always risky, any time your reasoning for doing so is due to a complete confluence of your interests and the offerings of that particular program, mentioning that fact can only strengthen your candidacy.

To facilitate a smooth entry to your program, I have been taking the prerequisite math classes (which will be completed by July). I have a straight "A" average in these classes, and I find myself very eager to return to full-time studies. I have selected Berkeley as my program of choice because of its reputation for commitment to accessibility, universal design, and related areas of modern architecture and design. Some of the other programs I investigated relegated universal design to a single elective. Berkeley is right for me. I am applying to no other program.

ESSAY #15: "ARABISM AND ISLAM"

Statement of Purpose

In 1933, the Syrian-Egyptian scholar Muhammad Rashid Rida, emphasizing the importance of Muslim Arabs' loyalty to the greater Islamic community, wrote that "each man must be a member of a body greater than his own nation." Almost a hundred years later, in a very different context, these words are relevant to my own life. They capture the essence of my principal academic interest, the hierarchy of allegiance to nation and religion in today's Egypt. In addition, Rashid Rida's words convey the basis of my attraction to a career centering upon the Middle East: my desire to reach beyond my own society to help build closer ties between the United States and the Arab world.

I am applying to UCLA's Islamic studies program to prepare for a career in US-Mideast relations, focusing on Egypt. UCLA's interdisciplinary training, with its emphasis on foreign language, is ideal preparation for such a career. Although I intend to seek a PhD in modern Middle Eastern history, I first would like to complete a master's in Islamic studies. I view the MA program as an opportunity to fill in gaps in my knowledge of Middle Eastern history (economic history, for example), to strengthen my Arabic and French skills, and to focus my research interest before pursuing a PhD. Because of my interest in early-twentieth-century Egypt, the opportunity to work with Prof. L. Marsot is a primary factor drawing me to UCLA. I have had meetings with Prof. Marsot and she is expecting my application.

Living in rural Turkey as an AFS student during high school first exposed me to the Middle East and Islam. I entered college planning to concentrate in Middle Eastern history, but, as my transcript suggests, Yale offered few courses in this area. Thus in courses that on the surface seemed to have little to do with the region, I found every possible Middle Eastern angle. For example, for a seminar on British history, I contrasted the British colonial administrations in Egypt and the Sudan; for a course on medieval Europe, I wrote about the characterizations of Arabs in twelfth-century German literature. Reading in my spare time also helped me develop a solid background. Once, to my friends' bewilderment, I took Yvonne Haddad's *Contemporary Islam and the Challenge of History* on a vacation in Florida. A summer internship in the Middle East studies division of the Brookings Institution strengthened my knowledge of contemporary Middle East politics. At Brookings, I researched the role of nonviolent resistance in *intifadas*, prepared a bibliography on the history of the Sudanese civil war, and wrote a position paper on how the Arab Spring created a temporary reconsideration of the role of women in public life. Finally, my undergraduate training included three years of modern standard Arabic at Yale and a summer at the Arabic Language Unit of the American University in Cairo.

My interest in the early-twentieth-century Islamic reform movement in Egypt began with my senior thesis on Muhammad Rashid Rida. Living in Turkey and Egypt interested me in relations between Arabs and Turks, and the larger issue of

This post-Fulbright essay is from an accomplished scholar well into her specialty. Notice how the impact is at once both personal, in the sense of being straightforwardly egocentric, and abstract, in the sense of focusing on the realm of ideas. The writer passes what business school students call "The Airport Test," as in "Is this someone I'd want to spend eight hours stuck in an airport with?" If you are interested in Arabism and Islam, you'd find her company most interesting indeed.

Whenever a professor is endorsing and expecting your application, you can say so in your essay. It may help your application sail through screening processes.

Note how the candidate points out her early focus on Middle Eastern history even though her college didn't have many courses in this topic.

ESSAY #15: "ARABISM AND ISLAM" (CONTINUED)

the role of nationalism in Islam. For my thesis, I translated Rashid Rida's articles on Arabs and Turks from 1898 to 1916 to examine his views on the connection between Arab political strength and Islamic reform before the collapse of the Ottoman Empire. In contrast to most historical interpretations of Rashid Rida, which categorize him either as a pan-Islamist or the first Arab nationalist, I found that Rashid Rida advocated both Muslim unity and Arab supremacy among Muslims as keys to reforming Islam. He emphasized one or the other according to external political factors. I concluded that Rashid Rida's significance lay in his attempt to resolve what many of his contemporaries, as well as subsequent Egyptian intellectuals, held to be a theoretical conflict between Arabism and Islam.

My experience as a Fulbright scholar in Cairo last academic year was a turning point in my study of the Middle East. First, I improved my Arabic skills dramatically in an intensive program. I am now quite comfortable conducting research in Arabic and am proficient in the Egyptian dialect.

Furthermore, I continued my research on Rashid Rida at the Women's College of al-Azhar University. My project entailed translating a series of Rashid Rida's articles on Arabs and Turks written just before and during World War I to determine how the imminent dissolution of the Ottoman Empire influenced his view of the political role of Arabs in the *umma* and led to his calls for an Arab caliph.

I then became interested in the Muslim Brotherhood in Egypt, and shifted the focus of my project to investigate how Rashid Rida's ideas about Islamic reform influenced the Egyptian Brotherhood's ideology. My affiliation with al-Azhar was essential to this research. As the only Western woman at the university, I had an unusual opportunity to become well acquainted with a group of female students who belonged to the Brotherhood and the "Islamic Group." In discussions about my research, these young women echoed many of Rashid Rida's articles when they spoke of trying to resolve the "conflict" between their Muslim and Egyptian identities. They brought to mind Rashid Rida's calls for the caliphate when they emphasized the Muslim world's need for a Muslim-Arab leader to foster greater political and spiritual unity. These conversations, along with research on Hassan al-Banna and the Brotherhood in Egypt today, demonstrated to me that Rashid Rida's ideas are not, as some have charged, obsolete. Rather, I believe that the early-twentieth-century Islamic reform movement offers an excellent basis from which to analyze Egypt's current complex relationship with Islam and Islamism. Researching the connections between Muhammad Rashid Rida and this movement will be the core of my graduate study.

Finally, the Fulbright helped to focus my professional goals. Living in Egypt convinced me that a more accurate American interpretation of the Islamic revival movement is central to the long-term success of American-Egyptian relations and spurred my interest in a career in diplomacy or development work focusing on

ESSAY #15: "ARABISM AND ISLAM" (CONTINUED)

Egypt. Though some Western analysts argue that the rise of "militant" Islam in the region, and the anti-Western sentiment that often accompanies it, diminishes the possibility of good relations with the countries of the Middle East, I believe that the geopolitical importance of the region (especially Egypt) precludes severing any ties. Rather, Americans must explore ways to strengthen our relations with Arabs, especially in light of Islamist movements. Whether I pursue a career in development or diplomacy, I hope that Arabic will be an integral component of my day-to-day work. (See FLAS fellowship essay, enclosed.)

I recognize the challenges of a career in US-Mideast relations. Discussions with my former professors and other experts, as well as my own experiences, have elucidated the potential limitations for women in this field. I have also weighed the personal implications of devoting my professional life to another part of the world, while there are compelling problems in this country. However, my belief in the need for better mutual understanding between the United States and the countries of the Middle East assures me that I've made a worthwhile choice.

I look forward to graduate study at UCLA as an exciting, and essential, stage in my scholarly career. I'm eager to apply my academic preparation and enthusiasm in UCLA's program, and I'm certain that Rashid Rida's words about the importance of reaching beyond my own society will continue to guide me.

Always mention your language skills when they are pertinent to your graduate subject. Don't overstate them; rate them on the scale of native speaker, fluent, proficient, or basic; or use the US State Department scale (I, II, III, IV, V).

Like many essays that focus on science and laboratory research summaries, this essay is about mathematics and nothing else. It could be written by a wealthy urban socialite or a tattooed body builder. It either succeeds or fails based on the math within it.

ESSAY #16: "ITERATED MAPPINGS"

Statement of Purpose—PhD, Mathematics

Over the past few years, I have become interested in the dynamics of iterated mappings. As an independent research project, I have been investigating the dynamics of the quadratic map, $Z_{n+1} = Z_n^2 + C$, when it is applied to algebraic structures other than the complex field, which is used to generate the classic Mandelbrot and Julia sets. I began by exploring the three-dimensional sets that are generated when real-valued 2 × 2 symmetric matrices are used for Z and C. Later, I extended my investigation to include the four-dimensional sets produced by general real-valued 2 × 2 matrices, using a basis that is compatible with the matrix representation of complex numbers. To gain intuition into the dynamics of the quadratic map on these structures, I wrote several computer programs to generate slices of these sets and to calculate orbits for given values of Z and C. My original "Mandelbrot set" program starts Z_0 at 0 and lets C range over 2 × 2 matrix space, which is the same type of algorithm that is commonly used to generate the classic Mandelbrot set. The first programs defined an iterate to have escaped when its Euclidean distance from the origin was greater than or equal to an escape value (usually 2). This is the same escape condition that is used with classic Mandelbrot and Julia sets.

My research has already yielded several interesting results. It is well known that the complex plane is isometric to a two-dimensional slice of 2 × 2 matrix space. I found that lines in this slice that pass through the origin serve as lines of rotational symmetry in the matrix Mandelbrot set, and the matrix Julia sets are all symmetric about the origin. The images that I have generated have shown an incredible variety of structure depending on the slice viewed, and, in the case of the matrix Julia sets, the value of C. The boundary of the matrix Mandelbrot set is chaotic in some places and perfectly smooth in others. I have been able to calculate the precise shape of the boundary for some of the slices with smooth boundaries. Some of the slices of the matrix Mandelbrot set are perfect squares, circles, or sections of hyperbolic solids. Others are narrow bands that stretch as far as the edges of the circle defined by the escape value will allow. The presence of "arbitrarily bounded" slices such as the hyperbolic solids and the narrow bands reflects the fact that the matrix Mandelbrot set has fixed points whose Euclidean distance from the origin exceeds any escape value. Many of the matrix Julia sets also have arbitrarily bounded components.

The presence of arbitrarily bounded slices raises the question of how to determine whether a particular escape criterion is reasonable for a Mandelbrot or Julia set. The purpose of the escape criterion is to classify orbits as either bounded or unbounded. In the case of the classic sets, all escape conditions that contain the disk of radius 2 centered at the origin will classify all orbits in the same way. This is true because all cycles of the quadratic map on the complex field are contained inside this disk, and all orbits that leave this region tend toward infinity in such a way that each iterate has a greater Euclidean modulus than its predecessor. But for the

ESSAY #16: "ITERATED MAPPINGS" (CONTINUED)

quadratic mapping on matrix space, any escape condition that relies on a Euclidean metric will exclude some cycles. Based on the images I have seen and an analysis of the quadratic mapping on 2×2 matrices, I conjecture that an escape criterion based on a metric that is half hyperbolic and half Euclidean will provide a better test of boundedness for the matrix Julia and Mandelbrot sets. Although computer images seem to indicate that my candidate for an escape criterion will be effective, a proof of this demands that I have a better understanding of the dynamics of matrix Julia set orbits. I will also need to consider the mathematical implications of using an escape criterion based on a non-Euclidean metric.

For an analytic mapping on the complex field, all attracting cycles must attract a critical point of the map. Since the quadratic map has only one critical point, $0 + 0i$, a quadratic map with a fixed value for C (corresponding to a specific Julia set) can have at most one attracting cycle, and if one exists it must attract 0. If there is no attracting cycle, then the orbit of 0 escapes to infinity. The Mandelbrot set therefore shows which values of C induce an attracting cycle and which ones do not. Classic Julia sets can be defined equivalently as the closure of the set of repelling periodic points.

I would like to establish whether each of these features of the complex quadratic map can be generalized to the matrix quadratic map. If there is at most one attracting orbit in a matrix Julia set, and if the orbit of 0 is necessarily in its basin of attraction, then an escape condition that respects the dynamics of the Julia sets will also respect the dynamics of the Mandelbrot set. In order to prove that the orbit of 0 behaves in this way, a means of identifying critical points and determining whether a cycle is attracting, repelling, or neutral is needed.

Following the approach used for the complex quadratic map, I have been able to prove the appropriate attracting and repelling cycle theorems using the modulus of the Fréchet derivative. Based on the orbit calculations that I have done, it seems that attracting cycles so defined do attract the orbit of 0. It also seems to be true that there is at most one attracting cycle. For functions of the real numbers, a proof that a critical point of the map must be in the basin of attraction of each attracting cycle can be obtained by using various characteristics of Schwarzian derivatives. This proof cannot be adapted to functions of complex numbers because of the presence of imaginary numbers. The proof in the complex case is a "deep result" that depends on Montel's theorem and the analyticity of the map. One way that I might be able to prove this result for the quadratic mapping on matrix space is to examine matrices that have an imaginary component separately, and use a Schwarzian derivative approach with the symmetric matrices. Another possible approach would involve using the specific dynamics of the quadratic mapping on matrix space to show that there is at most one attracting cycle and that it attracts 0. It is also possible that this conjecture may need to be modified before it is true.

ESSAY #16: "ITERATED MAPPINGS" (CONTINUED)

It is possible to recast the quadratic map on 2×2 matrices as a Clifford algebra. Thinking about the dynamics of the map in relation to the algebraic structure of the system will allow me to generalize my results to higher-dimensional spaces that result from larger matrices or from matrices with complex entries. I am also interested in exploring the connection between the dynamics of the matrix quadratic map and the quadratic map acting on the quaternions, which form the more famous four-dimensional Clifford algebra. One of the principal differences between these two algebras is the presence of zero divisors in the matrix case. I am interested in investigating the implications of this aspect of the algebra on the dynamics of maps on matrix space.

One of the best aspects of doing research is being able to share what I have learned with others. I also enjoy hearing about other people's research at seminars and research conferences. It is especially gratifying to read or hear about work that gives me new insight into my own projects, or to be able to share my results with others who are interested in the implications for their research. I plan to obtain a PhD in mathematics and become a professor. My best professors use what they have learned through their research to make their classes more exciting and to communicate the relevance of important concepts to their students. They also use their knowledge of current research in their field to give students a sense of mathematical history and a sampling of interesting open problems. I look forward to learning more about a wide range of mathematical ideas in graduate school. I am pleased that I have been able to incorporate concepts from many different mathematical fields into my current research project, and I plan to use a similar approach in the future.

Only once the technical material is well established does this candidate turn to more personal topics.

ESSAY #17: "HIGH WATER"

When you grow up in a place where isolation is a way of life, just getting to town can be a challenge. Throughout my school years, my family lived on a gravel road with only three outlets to "civilization." One way was across a dry creek bed, another was over a small brook, and the last was a low-water bridge on the Meramec River. When we had a hard rain, each one flooded and we had no way to get to town at all. As a result, I missed many days of school over the years. In a rural area like ours, twenty miles from the nearest grocery store, blocked by three swollen waterways and nearly impassable roads, traveling to another country seems like an impossibility. Yet despite the odds facing a first-generation student with working-class parents, I have been able to surpass my small town boundaries in my struggle to build my own bridge to a better future, plank by plank.

In researching the works of Annie Ernaux, a French working-class woman who forged her own bridge to academia, I came across a phrase that sums up my experiences in education. She said that at the beginning of her academic career, she had believed that education was a land of equality, fraternity, and liberty, but she soon found out that some girls were freer than others. Those of us who start out on the bottom just have to work a little harder to find that one way out. As a freshman in high school, I took the one foreign language offered by my high school, which just happened to be the language my mother had learned in high school and the one I most wanted to learn. I made the most of what I was offered, taking all four years of French and reading French novels lent to me by my teacher on the side. At the same time, I chose the most challenging courses offered in all subjects and became as involved as possible in the few activities available at our school. I earned a full scholarship to Truman State University as a result. That was my ticket out and I have never regretted my difficult departure.

Not only did my scholarship offer a bridge to Truman State, but it also provided the means to cross the Atlantic, in the form of a stipend for study abroad. I had no difficulty deciding where to go. France had always been a magical place in my imagination. Throughout my studies in high school, I pictured myself in the lavender fields of Provence, on the beaches of the "Méditerranée," and under the Arc de Triomphe in Paris, without ever believing I would one day visit these places. Now I had the chance to make my fantasy a reality. The five weeks I spent in Provence and my week in Paris were real eye-openers for me. The culture was so different from anything I had experienced in Missouri that at times I wanted to catch the next plane back to the States. But when I translated for a group of fellow American students and our new French friends complimented me on my language skills, I felt like a vital link between people of two different cultures. I realized I could adapt to a foreign environment because this connection with people who were not as foreign to my experience as I had assumed eradicated my perception of "us" versus "them."

Notice that this applicant weaves a unique adversity narrative perfectly into her intellectual story.

This is the type of candidate that admissions professionals are looking for: someone who can transcend her environment and reach for a goal; someone who is primarily, if not overwhelmingly, motivated from within; and someone who will appreciate and capitalize on opportunity. This candidate is vastly preferable to one who may appear statistically similar (vis-à-vis grades and scores) but has been coached and prodded and supported and tutored her whole life.

By quoting historical figures, "some girls were freer than others," you can say things you might not dare to say directly yourself.

Name your key advisors.

ESSAY #17: "HIGH WATER" (CONTINUED)

Back at Truman, I was able to connect the assorted planks that are my intellectual interests (linguistics, literature, international studies, and women's studies) in a cohesive pattern in the study of French and francophone culture. I consider myself lucky to have studied under Dr. B. McLane-Iles in courses such as Francophone Women Writers and Francophone Literature of Quebec. Besides encouraging my interest in francophonie and feminism, Dr. McLane-Iles has always challenged me to draw everything I can from each literary work I read or each experience I have with the language. Her assistance has been invaluable in broadening my perspective so greatly that I decided to strive for the PhD in French literature with a focus on francophone women instead of my original goal of a teaching certificate for high school French. With the PhD, I will be able to integrate my diverse educational background in research as well as teaching. An entire school year of direct interaction with francophone culture will give me the firsthand knowledge that I will need as a professor to help students traverse the cultural chasm between the United States and the rest of the world.

ESSAY #18: "NURSE BOUND FOR MEDICAL SCHOOL"

AMCAS Essay for Medical School

When I was an undergraduate at the University of California, Davis, I wanted to be a physician. Although I always excelled in the life sciences, I had to work twenty to thirty-two hours per week throughout my first years of college, and I graduated without honors status (BS, human biology, a premedicine major I designed in collaboration with the faculty).

I was very dissatisfied with this performance, as I was sure I could have excelled had I had more time for my studies. I reaffirmed my commitment to health care as a career, and I studied nursing at the University of California, Los Angeles. There I applied myself and graduated *magna cum laude* (BS, nursing).

I then pursued a nursing career with zeal, selecting a path that would allow me to stress medicine, autonomy, and decision making in my work. After serving a year on a medical-surgical floor, I accepted a position with the Kidney Transplant Unit (KTU) at the University of California, San Francisco, Medical Center (UCSF Medical Center). This position allowed me to gain in-depth knowledge of a specific patient population and gave me opportunities to advance my assessment skills. My nursing skill was acknowledged in formal and informal ways, including my nomination for the Sophie Robinson Award for excellence in nursing, and I served on many in-service and quality assurance committees.

Next, I was selected for the position of physician extender for the Renal Transplant Service at UCSF Medical Center, where I was hired by the department of surgery to assist house staff in meeting patient needs. I attended twice-daily rounds, followed up on radiographic, laboratory, and consult reports, performed routine house staff procedures, and occasionally assisted in the OR. This was a custom-designed nursing position, and I was allowed to define the role to the extent that I oriented and worked side-by-side with interns. I was also invited to serve as research assistant, collecting data on drug side effects under direction of Dr. J. Melzer, UCSF Medical Center, on a project with the working title of "Investigational drug study on MALG (Minnesota Anti-Lymphocyte Globulin)."

After eighteen months of this experience, which I enjoyed thoroughly, I decided to obtain critical care experience and began to apply for competitive positions in this area. I obtained an appointment to the Cornell University Medical Center at New York Hospital as a post-anesthesia care nurse. In this position, I provided post-op care for cardiac, neurologic, pediatric, trauma, burn, and vascular patients. This was exciting work, with a diverse patient population. This is also when I decided once again to become a physician. Because of the following event, I realized that the intellectual challenges of nursing were no longer enough for me, and I made my decision to go on to medical school and become a physician.

I received a forty-two-year-old female with a newly placed peritoneal shunt. (She had had an eleven-year history of ovarian cancer, and a chronic ascites problem

This is an AMCAS essay for medical school. If schools are interested in the candidate, they will request additional materials, known as secondaries.

Notice the straightforward coverage of the candidate's grades in her first undergraduate career.

If you are not admitted to medical school on your first attempt, you should note that many students are admitted after strengthening their backgrounds as this candidate did.

Note the proper use in this essay of working titles to describe research in progress.

Put some medicine in your application to medical school. It positions you as an insider.

ESSAY #18: "NURSE BOUND FOR MEDICAL SCHOOL" (CONTINUED)

requiring frequent paracentesis.) She awoke combative, and was quickly extubated by the anesthesiologist. Her recovery deteriorated, as she developed pulmonary edema, a temperature of 40 degrees centigrade, and right-sided heart failure. I provided the critical direct nursing care to this patient for hours while the interns consulted on approaches to her treatment. I was acutely aware that my abilities and knowledge were limited to nursing, and I very much wanted to be able to contribute meaningfully to the intellectual debate I was witnessing among the interns.

The attending physician was summoned to survey the problem. He clamped the shunt and put her on antibiotics, recognizing that the patient's heart was not strong enough to handle the large fluid load. The patient went to the ICU, and I decided to go to medical school.

I returned to the Kidney Transplant Unit of UCSF Medical Center and began to study for the MCATs. I also took a course in hematology from San Francisco State University and served as a research assistant on two additional projects: (1) I conducted GFR studies as an assistant to Nephrology Research Fellow Dr. C. Stempl, UCSF Medical Center, on a project with a working title, "Does Verapamil improve GFR in transplant recipients?" and (2) I am currently research assistant under the direction of Dr. W. Amend, UCSF Medical Center, performing the retrospective arm of a two-armed study, "Incidence of Cytomegalovirus in transplant patients and the efficacy of Acyclovir prophylaxis."

This ending shows confidence, determination, and poise. Remember, you are someone who is going to succeed whether you're admitted to their particular graduate program or not. This person is a medical doctor today.

My ultimate career direction is to practice infectious disease medicine. Witnessing the devastation these organisms can cause on immuno-compromised patients has given me a great appreciation for the role of the physician, to intercede in and reverse the course of infectious disease. I would find this work immensely interesting and rewarding, and I look forward to the opportunity to pursue it.

With more than enough energy and stamina to succeed, I am intellectually, emotionally, and financially prepared for medical school. I will admit no more impediments to my goal. I am eager to begin the process.

ESSAY #19: "TOBACCO MOSAIC VIRUS AND THE EIFFEL TOWER"

"What is the most important difference between tobacco mosaic virus and the Eiffel Tower?" my professor asked on the last day of my introductory biochemistry class, as he put two slides of the structures up on the screen. "Both are made of precise building blocks that elegantly come together to form the whole unit," he explained, "but only the virus knows how to put itself together." At this point, I had a *Eureka!* response. I truly recognized the beauty and complexity of life at the molecular level. That's when I first knew that I wanted to undertake biomedical research.

Here is a superb example of using an experiential opening for a science-oriented essay.

There are many career paths and research opportunities related to medicine, pharmaceuticals, and biotechnology that do not involve an MD degree. This PhD candidate in medical pathobiology will have many exciting opportunities to contribute to medical science, without suffering through a few years of eighty- and hundred-hour sleepless clinical internships.

Since then, my decision to pursue graduate study has been confirmed by both my undergraduate course work and my research experience. While studying immunology in my sophomore year, I learned for the first time not only the facts about the workings of the immune system, but also the ideas and experiments that led to their discovery. As I became exposed to the experimental side of the information found in the textbook, I began to appreciate the sophisticated thought processes and energy required by scientific research.

Trace the history of your interest in the topic.

The most influential experience in persuading me to attend graduate school, however, has been my current independent research project, which will culminate in an honors thesis. I am examining the antigenicity of a protein in a novel drug delivery system. (Please see the accompanying research summary.) I am eager to bring the concepts I have learned in my project to the level of a graduate program of study. First, I discovered how the power of perseverance can overcome obstacles. When my experimental system, the ELISA, suddenly stopped working, careful troubleshooting led to the discovery of a minor technical problem. Through this experience, I learned how to critically dissect an experiment to find the root of error. In addition, the graduate student with whom I have been working for almost two years, Jorje Soares, has taught me the ability to take an idea and follow it while at the same time demonstrating to me the balancing act involved in allocating time, money, and energy to a project when the direction your results will take you is unknown. My research sponsor, Dr. R. Martinez, with her contagious energy, has also influenced me with her enthusiastic approach to attacking new research areas, and has motivated me to work harder to reach my goals and the goals of the lab.

The pathobiology graduate program at the College of Physicians and Surgeons of Columbia University is of interest to me for several reasons. First, the affiliation of the university with Presbyterian Hospital, Milstein Hospital, the Institute for Cancer Research, and the Institute for Human Nutrition provides students with the opportunity to combine basic scientific studies with clinical applications. The resources available at the hospitals and centers aid students in immediately applying what they learn in the classroom and laboratory to situations where disease demands immediate attention. In addition, the location of the college in Manhattan is attractive because of its proximity to other research institutions and medical schools.

This is a model answer to the question "Why here?" Every program wants an answer to this question, whether they explicitly ask it or not.

ESSAY #19: "TOBACCO MOSAIC VIRUS AND THE EIFFEL TOWER" (CONTINUED)

Such a dynamic group of scientists provides many opportunities for the exchange of fresh ideas and collaborative efforts. Finally, the range of research conducted by the faculty is appealing. The studies of Dr. N. Sucio-Foca are of particular interest to me because they involve the creation of peptide vaccines, an area of immunological research that has much potential for the treatment or prevention of many diseases.

Once in graduate school, I hope to pursue studies related to the development of vaccines. My interest in this topic stems not only from my course work specific to immunology but also from an additional academic experience in the course The Burden of Disease in Developing Nations. In this class, I learned that although vaccines are currently available to treat a myriad of diseases, some of these vaccines are useless to people in the developing world because they degrade under the conditions of high temperature or humidity that are often found in these countries. Multiple lines of research can thus address both the development of new vaccines and the improvement of currently existing vaccines so that they may be useful to the greatest number of people.

In trying to create new vaccines for diseases for which they are currently not available, several approaches from immunology, biochemistry, molecular genetics, and organic chemistry can be considered. For example, an understanding of whether a humoral or cell-mediated immune response is best suited to fight a particular disease is needed. Immunologic techniques involving animal models and cell culture studies can be used to determine how B and T cells interact to fight disease. Furthermore, specific pathogenic macromolecules can be used as the antigen in a vaccine rather than an entire protein. This method requires the isolation and purification of protein subunits using biochemical assays such as gel electrophoresis, column chromatography, and protein sequencing. In addition, the gene encoding an antigen can also be used to develop a vaccine. Recombinant DNA techniques such as screening of genomic cDNA libraries, gene sequencing, and the polymerase chain reaction can be used to isolate, characterize, and amplify a specific gene. Finally, specific protein antigens can be chemically synthesized. This method requires not only a rigorous use of synthesis design from organic chemistry, but also principles from biochemistry to determine protein sequence and folding, as the conformation of a protein domain and not just its amino acid sequence is often recognized by antigen presenting cells. Thus, X-ray crystallography and FTIR must be employed. All of these lines of research can lead to the development of new vaccines.

After graduate school, I will consider a career in the pharmaceutical industry. The ability to see an idea about a molecular process evolve into a product that will help make people's lives healthier is my motivation for this choice. However, I am also considering a career in academia because I am interested in the possibility of combining research with teaching and interacting with undergraduates. I am

ESSAY #19: "TOBACCO MOSAIC VIRUS AND THE EIFFEL TOWER" (CONTINUED)

currently tutoring genetics students and have previously tutored organic chemistry students, and the one-on-one interaction has enabled me to teach and learn at the same time. Through my involvement in Women in Science and Engineering as a biochemistry affinity group leader, I have been able to advise students about the selection of courses, summer jobs, and potential professors with whom to do an independent study. The teaching experience that has proven to be the most challenging is serving as mentor and instructor for a ninth-grade girls' science club for the past three years.

I have prepared my own lessons and led discussions with a group of twenty, sometimes less than enthusiastic, fourteen-year-olds. Trying to capture their attention has forced me to be creative in my style and presentation of material.

My past experiences have well prepared me to pursue graduate education at the College of Physicians and Surgeons. My undergraduate education in the competitive atmosphere at Brown has enabled me to not merely reiterate ideas stated by my professors but to apply the concepts I have learned to unfamiliar situations. During my four years here, both my study skills and my ability to process information have sharpened, as evidenced by an improvement in my grades within my major from a 3.0 grade point average freshman year to a 3.6 junior year. The lack of self-confidence that plagued me during my first two years here was induced by both insufficient study skills and an unusually rigorous course load, wherein I completed my inorganic and organic chemistry courses in three semesters rather than four and took physical chemistry, a course usually reserved for upperclassmen, my sophomore year. In addition, my interactions with people within the Brown community outside the classroom have prepared me for the intellectual atmosphere at Columbia. The need to write and speak effectively on issues of importance, whether it involves a change in the housing policy or creating a new concentration, are requisite to enact positive change. One initiative that I undertook was the creation of a website, Women in Science and Engineering, which has worked wonderfully to connect women scientists at Brown and at other top universities across the country and, indeed, the world. By combining my diverse undergraduate experiences, I will be able to grow as a researcher in your pathobiology graduate program while contributing my ideas about both the research interests of my colleagues and issues facing the Columbia community.

When your grades have markedly improved, always point that out. Readers may look at your GPA without noting your GPA *trend*. Help them see what you want them to see.

Service to your academic community, and the other "communities" to which you belong, is almost always regarded as a positive sign of character and maturity.

ESSAY #20: "IDITAROD DOGS AND MOLECULAR BIOLOGY"

Statement of Purpose

Note that this applicant chose a very personal tone for this science essay. He also could have chosen to focus only on his science background and used a much more detached tone. This is a style choice. He pulls this off very well, but many scholars without such exotic life experiences would be better off adopting the tone and voice evident in many of the other science examples in this book.

This applicant also told me that he wore a Hawaiian shirt to all his interviews, to stand out from the crowd in the minds of interviewers who may meet with a dozen candidates in a day. These techniques worked for him, but only because they matched his effusive personality.

They call it the last frontier. Last summer I set out for Alaska, to see the true wildness left in this world. This spirit of adventure took me to Homer on the Kenai Peninsula, where I became the "dog handler" for Iditarod musher Jack Berry and his sixty huskies. Although I came to Alaska to live among the wild, I found myself spending all my free time teaching English pronunciation to a Brazilian doctor and arguing plant physiology with the dedicated women of the Homer Garden Club, when I wasn't hitchhiking the fifteen miles to the Homer Public Library. For better or for worse, I'm obsessed with learning, and I want to take my pursuit of knowledge to a far greater scale.

Theoretical physicists are in pursuit of the grand unifying theory, the set of equations that will make compatible all of this world's macro- and microcosms. As I see it, there is a similar grand objective in the world of biology. I feel a drive to elucidate the mechanisms of life through molecular studies. There are ways, paths, lines of thinking that converge the realm of the biological with the domain of chemical logic. I know that a solid understanding of the physical function of proteins can be that unifying link.

Now it is the rainy winter of my fourth and final year at college. I have been an enthusiastic biochemistry and molecular biology major enrolled in what is possibly the best program of its kind. This past spring I worked independently on a project to determine the preferred conformation of dehydrated isosorbide. While this was interesting in its own right, I think that the knowledge obtained through studies of organic chemistry is most relevant when applied toward macromolecules. Aside from being fascinating structures, they have a significance reaching far beyond the laboratory. I've chosen the topic of my undergraduate thesis with these greater interests in mind. For this thesis, I am pipetting toward a crystal structure of xylose isomerase that contains a single active site mutation. I find it absolutely amazing that proteins can catalyze reactions and am obsessed with the relationship between their function and structure. Enzymes catalyze reactions, but an amino acid polymer is also capable of much more. Motor proteins, G-proteins, the amalgamations in the SNARE hypothesis—cells have created proteins for an intense diversity of uses. I am lucky to be a structural biologist at a time when the techniques necessary to decipher the form of these proteins are uncovered. I am intrigued by the functional structure of proteins, and value any laboratory method that can provide molecular insight. I chose to apply to Scripps because I have been uncommonly impressed by the structural research I've seen published by Scripps researchers. Drs. O. Gilula's and N. Unwin's investigations of the structure and functional mechanisms of gap-junction and ion channels are especially intriguing. I find ion channels to be wondrous edifices. Ion channels are contraptions straight out of a Dr. Seuss storybook: one massive protein that

Notice the answer to "Why here?" and the mention of specific researchers of interest to this candidate. Customize your essays, or lose out to the candidates like this one, who do.

ESSAY #20: "IDITAROD DOGS AND MOLECULAR BIOLOGY"
(CONTINUED)

chooses to allow specific ions through it, if and only if it is satisfied with the chemical and electrical environment surrounding it. This, truly, is a level of chemistry where biological decisions are made.

I could drone on for pages about the research that I find fascinating, as Scripps has a collection of amazing resources. I would love the opportunity to work in a laboratory with this talent. I am enrolling in graduate school to learn more and to understand greater biological systems so that I will be able to apply my molecular knowledge to my own research. I'm fascinated by the biology of the cell; with a thorough understanding of the techniques available to the protein scientist, I will finally possess the ability to address the basic hows and whys of cell function.

Two years ago, I spent a semester abroad with the School for Field Studies in the Pacific island nation of Palau. With every mangrove and coral reef transect we took, I wanted to know: "Why do these angelfish live here? How can these trees grow out of the salt sea?" The only answers my professors could give: "Because the fish do best in this biotic environment . . . because they've evolved and adapted for longer than you can imagine." The answers available are just not satisfactory, but I know that with more training I could find those answers for myself. I want answers with a mechanism: answers that resemble not statistical spreadsheets, rather blueprints of ingenious design; answers that might detail how membrane proteins balance harsh extracellular conditions with a cytoplasm that is conducive to life. These are answers I need to find, and I'm too stubborn to quit now. I need to go to graduate school, for I've only just learned the principles of protein structure and function. I want to be an expert. The MCSC Program holds the resources that can enable me to continue my quest.

When using a conversational tone, contractions are more acceptable.

Notice how different this essay is from the last one, even though both these candidates are applying for laboratory science opportunities. Although the title for this postdoctoral essay, as requested on the application form, is "Personal Statement," there is not a shred of personal information in it. The essay contains a proposal for formulation of a chemistry lab and research project, and mentions several prominent chemists who support the proposal. This type of application entails a whole lobbying campaign and extensive personal contact in support of the project, and this essay needs to be considered in that larger context. The ability to make and utilize personal contacts becomes ever more important as your academic career advances.

ESSAY #21: "NSF POSTDOC IN CHEMISTRY"

Personal Statement for National Science Foundation

Postdoctoral Research Fellowship in Chemistry

The training conducted under this grant would be geared toward establishing a new academic laboratory in which biological, chemical, and physical techniques are focused on elucidating the fundamental forces and principles of bioorganic and bioinorganic catalytic mechanisms. The strategy of this laboratory would be to elucidate chemical structure/reactivity properties of enzymes and enzyme-bound intermediates leading to the design of experiments that test the nature of transition state stabilization for a given reaction. As chemical systems, some proteins provide excellent, surprisingly tolerant, structurally definable scaffolds for holding probes of the ground states and transition states of catalyzed reactions. Mutant proteins are truly chemical analogues of the wild type structure, and genetics provides an excellent way to generate and test a large number of these analogues (10/8 structures, which would result from randomizing seven amino acid positions, could reasonably be tested genetically). X-ray crystallography and NMR spectroscopy provide powerful, essential, yet incomplete characterization of enzyme chemistry. Fruitful interpretation of good structures can be limited by a paucity of functional information. Therefore, the proposed laboratory would be primarily responsible for generating functional information through the preparation of enzymes, random and site-directed mutant enzymes, inhibitors, and chemically and isotopically modified substrates and cofactors, and through the characterization of the chemical reactions of these reagents. Characterization of the reactions would routinely include genetic function, reaction product analysis, kinetics, and at a minimum, the preparation of suitable samples for X-ray crystallography, NMR spectroscopy, and any other informative techniques. How far the work of the lab extends into the physically oriented techniques will be determined by the extent of the training I am able to accomplish as well as by personnel in the lab; however, collaborations with specialists in crystallographic or spectroscopic techniques will always be preferable to provide as many perspectives on a given project as possible. To the extent that good, effective mathematical models are available, they will be highly considered during the interpretation of results and tested by the design of experiments, e.g., the AI-based MAN-3 has proven itself a useful analytical tool for electrostatic forces in proteins. It generates volumes of possible findings that still need to be tested in the laboratory. The laboratory would study many different enzymes with different chemistries at various stages of development. The study of established enzyme systems would provide the most rigorous testing ground for our knowledge of enzymatic chemistry. The analysis of enzymes with undefined mechanisms would include therapeutic targets where much may be presumed about the chemistry of the enzyme, but where satisfactory, functional inhibitors are still wanted. The social raison d'être for

ESSAY #21: "NSF POSTDOC IN CHEMISTRY" (CONTINUED)

this laboratory would be the development of new therapeutic inhibitors based upon the chemistry derived from pursuing an understanding of catalysis. The study of enzymes with unknown mechanisms should provide fertile ground for the discovery of new chemistry.

The proposed postdoctoral work provides an excellent opportunity to establish a project that has much in common with the future work of the proposed laboratory. The enzyme is a therapeutic target with an unknown mechanism. The project hinges on the synthesis of substrate analogues as inhibitors and involves chemical and kinetic characterization of the inhibition, aspects of enzymology in which I am not well trained. In addition, chemical characterization may involve the preparation and analysis of protein crystals.

The proposed scientific advisor, Prof. R. Abeles, has established a laboratory where compounds are routinely designed and synthesized with the intent of testing bioorganic and bioinorganic enzymatic mechanisms. As a consequence, he provides expertise in an environment where the results of such experiments are routinely analyzed and interpreted. He actively seeks to train his postdoctoral fellows in science while teaching chemistry as it pertains to the analysis of enzyme mechanisms. In short, he operates a laboratory with the focus with which I would like to operate my own. His recommendation would indicate my suitability as the director of such a laboratory.

This candidate has already been involved in detailed discussions with the researchers named.

Brandeis University presents an excellent faculty. In addition to Dr. Abeles, the biochemistry faculty includes Dr. W. P. Jencks, who is also a particularly lucid and careful chemist and enzymologist. As a sign of the continuing support of penetrating enzymology, the university has recently added to the faculty two noted crystallographers, Drs. G. A. Petsko and D. Ringe, whose collaboration with Dr. Abeles is very strong. Their crystallographic program now includes the Laue diffraction technique, which allows structural characterization of enzymatic reactions on a millisecond time scale.

Note how engaging this future scientist's writing is. Her enthusiasm is palpable. And she tells a story in which a professor is the hero, the source of wondrous knowledge and light. Remember who is going to read an essay like this? Exactly.

Grad school involves lots of teamwork, especially in engineering. Telling a story about a successful team project is a great idea.

Point out interpersonal skills, cross-disciplinary experiences, and project management skills. The ability to design, create, launch, and manage a complex, multiperson project can really set you apart from other candidates who may have technical excellence but lack these "real world" skills.

ESSAY #22: "SYSTEMS ENGINEERING"

Statement of Purpose, PhD in Systems Engineering

A large chart is slowly unfurled in front of the class as the professor offers excitedly, "This will give us some perspective on what you've been learning these last three semesters!" The chart displays a descending continuum of linearity to nonlinearity on the y-axis. On the x-axis is the number of variables in a system. I sit up attentively, anticipating my professor's introduction to what would become my favorite class, Systems Simulation. The professor directs the laser pointer to the top left corner, highlighting the first- and second-order topics such as radioactive decay and RLC circuits: "We've spent all this time learning the basics of these linear systems." His laser pointer drifts to the lower right and he enthusiastically narrates, "Now this is where it gets interesting. Limit cycles. The immune system. Economics." As his pointer travels to the lower right-most item, he says eagerly, "And finally: *Life*." It occurs to me then that although I have taken four courses in my intended specialty, I have only begun to learn systems engineering. I am eager to cross the frontier to begin learning about life. This revelation motivated me then, and it motivates me still, to pursue a PhD in systems engineering with a specialization in nonlinear control and simulation of interdisciplinary systems for my graduate studies.

I have sought out many opportunities to work on multidisciplinary engineering projects in my undergraduate career. In my most recent summer research position, I had the opportunity to work in a team of three undergraduates under Prof. J. Rossmann in designing and constructing Harvey Mudd College's first large-scale subsonic wind tunnel to allow for visualization and quantification of external flows.[1] I had a range of responsibilities within the team that involved a full spectrum of research, design, and construction. These included calculating the necessary specifications of the settling chamber, exit diffuser, and axial fan. Furthermore, I worked with a limited budget to design a cost-effective structural support system, negotiated with vendors, and helped assemble and build the test section and flow-straightening screens. This experience gave me a real-world taste of how elegant systems engineering could be—I had the tools to beautifully integrate mechanical, structural, electrical, economic, and project management aspects in order to design a successful wind tunnel. The greatest challenge during the project was completing the design and construction of the wind tunnel over a ten-week period; our team learned the value of efficient time management, maintaining focus, and good project planning. I look forward to coordinating the documentation of our design and construction process of the wind tunnel in a forthcoming publication by the end of the spring semester.

Last year, as part of a larger project to explore the development of a GPS–Loran-C integrated navigation system, another engineering team I was on investigated the

1. Rossmann, J. S., Hsu, Y. J., Schauer, J., and Stratton, C. "Design and Construction of a Subsonic Wind Tunnel." UC Santa Barbara: Fluids Mini-Symposium. Santa Barbara, CA.

ESSAY #22: "SYSTEMS ENGINEERING" (CONTINUED)

viability and characteristics of Loran-C (Long-Range Aid to Navigation Type C) as an air-traffic navigation and positioning system.[2] My responsibilities within the four-person team were to determine and model the sources of error contributing to the relative inaccuracy of Loran-C. I assisted in experimentally testing daily and seasonal variation and the effects of Earth's conductivity and terrain. Moreover, I helped develop a MATLAB model for errors due to transmitter station synchronization. For an initial guess within a 6-kilometer radius of the true position, the average absolute accuracy of the model improved from 460 meters to approximately 2 meters. This project enabled me to demonstrate my ability to maintain good working relationships with my team members and advisor. I also discovered the importance of independent motivation and drive within a team in contributing to the success of the project.

Notice how this writer differentiates her contributions from the overall project.

Working on these research projects involves organizational and leadership skills. As president of HMC's Society of Women Engineers (SWE) for three years, I head the coordination and execution of SWE's annual Women Engineers and Scientists of Tomorrow Conference. Over 160 high school girls and parents attend this one-day conference to interact with current women in the sciences and participate in workshops in engineering. The numerous accomplishments of SWE during my term, such as initiating engineering department gatherings and arranging fund-raising activities, demonstrate my leadership skills and ability to plan and complete successful projects. My motivation also is evidenced by my involvement with our collegiate chapter of Tau Beta Pi (TBP). As TBP president, I organize tutoring sessions for the seven engineering core classes and participate in TBP community service.

Nice, straightforward, effective discussion of leadership and service.

That captivating chart that plots the complexity of systems presented in my systems simulation course symbolizes the path I hope to pursue. So far, I have managed to edge my way toward a better understanding of the dynamics of nonlinear systems; I have modeled fascinating systems ranging from the romance of two lovers to the limit cycles of oscillating chemical reactions. At Caltech, I intend to further study nonlinear systems modeling and simulation. I am especially interested in continuing my work in interdisciplinary engineering systems with applications in robotics and the automotive industry. I hope to bring my previous research modeling the Loran-C navigation system, my most recent nonlinear variable structure robust control project in systems simulation, and my experience in hands-on experimentation techniques from my wind tunnel research to the development of modeling these systems. The proximity to the charming city of Old Town Pasadena has also factored into my consideration to attend Caltech. To be in this rich environment would be a tremendous opportunity.

2. Boyd, C., Ahle, K., Hsu, Y. J., and Thatte, G. "Modeling the Existing Loran-C Radionavigation System." Harvey Mudd College Clinic Final Report. Claremont, CA.

ESSAY #23: "WHERE DRIVE AND TALENT CAN TAKE YOU— THE FULBRIGHT"

Personal Statement for the Fulbright Scholarship

Every candidate faces many choices when writing an application essay. These next two essays were written by the same candidate, who did win the Fulbright and then took a deferral on his PhD studies. The point is: You also can write a more or less personal essay, a more or less technical essay. This candidate's prudent choices resulted in success in two very different directions. Had he switched his essays, it's probable that neither would have been effective. You might try more than one approach to your essay before choosing the one you think will serve you best. You may have one background, but you have many stories to tell and many ways you can tell each story.

When I first saw a skeleton hanging on the window of a house, I shrugged and wondered what type of neighborhood my family had moved into. What else could I think? I was a recent immigrant from Israel and the concept of Halloween was one of those American cultural entities which I had yet to learn about. It was the start of several years' worth of an interplay involving mutual ignorance on my part, regarding American culture, and on my American peers' part, regarding mine.

In fact, this was not the first immigration in my family's history. Both of my parents emigrated from Romania to Israel. The consequence was that sentences in our household sometimes started in one language (e.g., Romanian), were interjected with a phrase from a second (e.g., English), before finally being terminated in a third (e.g., Hebrew).

When I arrived to the United States (where I was later naturalized), I was "fluent" in only one word in English (the word "no"), inappropriately clothed (with respect to the fashion of the time), and culturally inept. Thus, I was cast out by many of my classmates as an outsider at first. Through hard work and determination, I strove to excel academically and initiated extracurricular involvement as I began to overcome the language barrier. With time, I believe my classmates also learned a lot about me and my previous country's culture.

Based on my experiences, I realized that the most effective way to rid oneself of ignorance of other nations (and to learn from them) is via complete immersion in the foreign culture. This is why I am so excited about the Fulbright program's general premise. How else can we gain each other's trust to the extent that we can collaborate on ideas and projects that will shape our future?

My experiences have left me with as many questions as answers. I now wonder which traits are innate to humans and which are cultural. For example, while a kiss signifies love in one country, it can serve as the equivalent of a handshake in another. Winking is considered rather impolite in some non-Western cultures. If such seemingly innate nonverbal forms of communication are interpreted differently, then certainly there must be many other differences that we can learn about.

Every point in this essay is chosen for its relevance to the published scholarship criteria.

As an individual who has seen two very different cultural worlds, I feel that I am in a position to better understand such cultural issues. It will be especially interesting for me to explore Canada, where I can see a culture that is not as different from America as that of my native land. Even though it has fewer cultural differences vis-à-vis the United States than more distant countries do, I have already witnessed several of them firsthand on a couple of trips to Canada, including a visit to the University of Toronto. It will be interesting to see how American and Canadian cultures retained some characteristics and yet differentiated in others as they split from their original British roots.

ESSAY #23: "WHERE DRIVE AND TALENT CAN TAKE YOU—THE FULBRIGHT" (CONTINUED)

I think that a Fulbright experience will help me as I look toward the future. My career goal is to apply computer and engineering methods to biology (specifically biochemistry), in order to facilitate the design of better drugs. I would also like to encourage governments to provide cooperative research funding opportunities for drug design efforts. Such opportunities would divide the cost of researching new drugs among North American companies and the government and involve North American academic institutions in the research process. Working together across national and commercial/academic boundaries would be especially rewarding in this field. Drug research is expensive, yet people all over the world realize immense benefits from each new type of drug that becomes available, no matter what country it originates from. I hope that I can be a part of the process that improves the quality of life for citizens everywhere. For, while we may be different in how we communicate and in the traditions we cherish, surely we are all made of the same "stuff of life," as the astronomer and public scientist Carl Sagan once put it.

ESSAY #24: "WHERE DRIVE AND TALENT CAN TAKE YOU—BIOMEDICAL ENGINEERING"

This essay was written by the same person as the last one. Although there is a modicum of overlap, notice how different this presentation is from the prior example.

Molecular Biophysics Essay

Ever since I was young, I have wanted to understand not just how the body solved complex engineering problems, but also how these mechanisms worked at a fundamental level. In particular, I am interested in applying computer and experimental techniques to biological problems (and vice versa). Of particular interest is the use of computational tools in analyzing issues relating to sequence analysis/protein engineering, protein folding (and the reverse problem).

I think this is why I find the pursuit of a PhD almost a necessity, given my need to satiate my mind's curiosity for seeking deeper knowledge in this area. In fact, I think this methodology has been reflected throughout my life, as I have always strived to challenge myself to find answers and overcome obstacles. When I arrived in the United States, I knew only one word in English (the word "no"). Yet, I was determined to work hard in order to catch up. Graduating valedictorian of my class in high school and serving as copresident of Science Olympiad proved that it could be done.

I went on to Carnegie Mellon University, not because of the merit-based scholarships, but because I wanted to gain deeper understanding of computer modeling applications in biology/medicine. While I majored in electrical and computer engineering with a minor in biomedical engineering, I took as many relevant biology and chemistry courses as I could within the curriculum, including advanced courses like 03-510 (Computational Biology) and 42-680 (Bioinstrumentation). This spring, I am scheduled to take a biochemistry and second organic chemistry class. My senior symposium will focus on the absolute latest in use of AI and machine learning in biomolecular chemistry. I will more than fulfill your necessary prerequisites for advanced biochemistry study by graduation.

I am confident that I will succeed in advanced courses given my background. I also feel that I have some rather unique advantages as a nonbiology major. Having a heterogeneous entering class composed not only of biology/biochemistry majors allows for more diversity in thought processes. Having undergone a similar curriculum with similar experiences, biology majors will likely have similar perspectives when encountering a novel problem. In contrast, an individual like myself may have a unique, novel contribution. Many of the breakthroughs in the past have come from interdisciplinary study resulting in a link between two previously unknown areas that went on to serve as the basis for an invention (and a new area for research). Recent examples include the invention of DNA-based computers, biochips, and synthetic life. In each case, a biologist or an electrical/computer engineer working alone could not have carried the project to fruition.

I have always strived to complement my education/experiences in computational approaches with fundamental biology. I have gained experience with biology both at the molecular level and at the systems level, which allows me to

ESSAY #24: "WHERE DRIVE AND TALENT CAN TAKE YOU—BIOMEDICAL ENGINEERING" (CONTINUED)

see the big picture. When chosen by the Ohio governor to represent the state, I went to the Lawrence Berkeley Laboratory for a program called "Life Sciences and Biotechnology." Here, I attended both lectures and did lab work involving biotechnology. Professors included Dr. M. Diamond, Nobel Prize–winner Dr. Glenn Seaborg, Dr. S. Spenger (on the Human Genome Project), Dr. M. Bissell, and Dr. J. O'Neil (Calgene). At a summer course at Case Western Reserve University entitled "Biotechnology and Genetic Engineering," I gained additional knowledge in experimental techniques.

Name your advisors.

From the aforementioned programs, I have gained experience with such biological techniques as electrophoresis, Southern blots, transformations, recombinant DNA techniques, PCR, chromatography, and sequence analysis. Through class/lab work and various programs, I have become knowledgeable in computer techniques used in biology such as coding region identification (via base composition, codon bias/preference, etc.), BLAST/FASTA algorithms for sequence match scoring methods, multiple sequence alignment, general similarity and homology methods (e.g., dynamic programming, dot-matrix methods, usage of hashing), secondary structure prediction (methods like Chou-Fasman, Garnier-Osguthorpe-Robson, SOPMA, etc.), and hydrophobicity analysis.

Make a laundry list of laboratory skills. Don't assume your reader will know what you can do.

In terms of bioinstrumentation, I have learned about NMR, IR, and techniques for novel instrumentation design. This past summer, I worked on a signal processing project in the Tachycardia Research group of St. Jude Medical's Pacesetter (a company formerly owned by Siemens). I designed and built a stimulus waveform generator. Then, I initiated a research study with the group's manager involving pain thresholds (in over thirty individuals) and coauthored "Sural Nerve Sensory Thresholds of Defibrillation Waveforms," which has been submitted and accepted. It will be presented at the next American College of Cardiology Scientific Session and published in the organization's peer-reviewed *Journal of the American College of Cardiology*.

One example where I applied computational/engineering techniques to biology (as I hope to do in my career) goes back to the first semester of my freshman year. I independently wrote my own grant proposal based on an idea I thought of while at the Lawrence Berkeley Lab that involved application of neural networks to the classification of DNA fingerprints. When my proposal won a SURG grant, I carried out the project independently under mentor Prof. J. Moura, editor-in-chief of *IEEE Transactions on Signal Processing*. This endeavor, combined with academic achievements, resulted in my recognition via honorable mention as part of the all-USA College Academic Team competition (published in *USA Today*). Only one Carnegie Mellon student is known to have ever been recognized in this competition. Since it involved novel coding techniques deployed on a PC and supercomputing environment, the work also led to an article (which I wrote) in the "Cross Platform Strategies" section in five magazines in eighty-two countries.

Trace the history of your interest. This applicant is able to trace this particular idea back to freshman year.

ESSAY #24: "WHERE DRIVE AND TALENT CAN TAKE YOU—BIOMEDICAL ENGINEERING" (CONTINUED)

For the past several semesters, I have been working on a research project on the "system level" at the University of Pittsburgh Medical Center. It involves analysis of EEG signals from brain waves and design of a barbiturate drug infusion system with Dr. M. Bloom, the director of neuroanesthesia at the University of Pittsburgh's medical center. The results of my project are rather exciting. The control system was tested on a live rhesus monkey and later revised. We are currently discovering and classifying relations between various patient variables and the sedative state and already have some interesting correlations. As we approach the next phase, this information will be combined "to establish an entirely new approach to patient modeling and the use of control in bioengineering systems" (as originally stated in the NSF grant from a group of three professors that I helped to form last semester).

I believe I can make a significant contribution to the current literature during graduate school and eventually lead efforts in innovation upon graduating from the University of Pennsylvania. I think the result from my experience at Google's Speech Technology Laboratory is an example of such an endeavor. Not only did I put forth a new idea, I also implemented it in a prototype and wrote the first draft of the patent (which I presented to the other coinventors for input). The patent was submitted to the patent office in July after approval by the review committee.

I also have experience in writing, a skill that is obviously imperative for researchers who wish to communicate their findings with others. As a writer for several newspapers, I have had the chance to interview people such as Ohio's governor, a US congressman, a CEO (FORE Systems), three current and past presidents of Carnegie Mellon, and a managing editor from *U.S. News & World Report.*

Address the question, "Why here?" This candidate wrote different, and successful, applications to Caltech, Stanford, MIT, Berkeley, and others. Customize, customize, customize! Of course, it helps to be as accomplished as this scholar.

I have found several faculty who share my interests at the University of Pennsylvania. In Prof. Lewis's lab, I am interested in the work going on related to computational methods used for studying protein-nucleic acid complexes. Papers from Prof. Sharp's research in structure of protein at the molecular level (using computational techniques as an option) also piqued my interest. I see a possible match with Prof. Wroblewski's work involving image processing and protein structure. I am open to working in other labs involving a combination of computational and experimental techniques in biochemistry as well.

ESSAY #25: "BRINGING POLITICS TO LIFE"

Personal Statement

As the United States launched yet another small war in a distant corner of the globe, Senator Everett McKinley Dirksen returned to life and captivated a hometown audience in Pekin, Illinois, with the folksy eloquence that made him nationally famous. Unlike Thucydides, George Washington, and Theodore Roosevelt, who all proclaimed that the best preparation for peace is war, Dirksen (performed by local journalist and actor Dave Watters) spoke to a group of teachers and community leaders about the power of words to assuage conflict, whether on the floor of the Senate or in the conduct of American foreign policy. The relevance of Dirksen's speech to the approaching war was a gratifying coincidence; indeed, his reflections on *spoken* language seemed deliberately ironic as our country began bombing near the birthplace of *written* language. But for me the greatest pleasure of the evening was playing resurrection-man to the senator, selecting and arranging the findings of my archival research and then watching it unveiled in an educational dramatic monologue. That night I witnessed the power of the scholar to breathe life into the historical record.

The invention of the Dirksen persona, now used as an educational tool at schools and community festivals throughout central Illinois, was just one of the many Dirksen Center projects I worked on intending to educate the public about the history and legislative procedures of Congress (see attached resume, also see the video at Dirksen/schools/8/trailer.com). During my three-year tenure, I researched and wrote dramatic monologues for portrayals of Abraham Lincoln and John F. Kennedy; cowrote an essay presented at a historical conference on civil rights; and helped write a syllabus and plan readings for an advanced college seminar on the US Senate. Although the Dirksen Center had previously awarded me fellowships for study in Washington, DC, and at the Institute of International Affairs at Bradley University, I believe there was one other factor that especially prepared me for research at a nonprofit educational institution. While in college, I joined the forensics team, the national speaking champions for the last sixteen consecutive years. As an extemporaneous and impromptu speaker, traveling to weekly competitions all over the country, I followed current events daily and read and filed dozens of publications every week in order to speak on any foreign or domestic policy question that I might draw. I thus acquired an active comprehension of world affairs that extended far beyond the college classroom. But my earliest knowledge of international affairs began as a child when my parents would recount the many years they spent abroad in the Peace Corps and working for a Greek import/export company. From my parents, I also learned that one of my ancestors was one of three Greek citizens granted transportation contracts to help fortify the Greek-Bulgarian border against Nazi invasion during World War II. I have consequently remained fascinated with modern Greek history and US foreign policy toward postwar Europe.

This understated essay reveals a highly accomplished candidate, with considerable post-undergraduate education and experience relevant to this application. The writer reveals a life steeped in academia, and this next program is but a logical next step. The tone is confident but respectful, which is a very good choice for an application essay. Also, this essay is fairly short. One gets the impression that other complete essays could be written about items selected from any paragraph.

ESSAY #25: "BRINGING POLITICS TO LIFE" (CONTINUED)

As a makeweight to my daily absorption in public policy at Bradley, my intellectual curiosity began to broaden while encompassing politics in ever more subtle ways. In the course of reading about Italian fascism during World War II, I became intrigued with the polemics and poetry of Ezra Pound and grew puzzled at the relationship between the literary avant-garde and reactionary politics in Italy, France, and Germany. This interest led me to leave Bradley for the intense scholarly environment of the University of Chicago, where I wrote an honors thesis on Ezra Pound's *Cantos* that synthesized poetic analysis with history of religious methodology and inquiry into the antidemocratic politics of literary modernism. Because I studied religion as much as politics during the course of my research, and because I thought that further religious study would assist me in the revision of my thesis for publication, I decided to attend the University of Chicago Divinity School to study Greek religion, sacrifice, and ritual theory, an academic opportunity I had never previously envisioned. As a student at the University of Chicago, I was also able to study educational public policy with literary critic Dr. Gerald Graff and to conduct research and write monograph chapters for a World Health Organization study on international oral health care policy.

I am applying to the Fletcher School because I hope eventually to work for a government or nonprofit institution (such as the US Senate, National Endowment for the Humanities, or the Dirksen Congressional Center) where I can integrate my public policy research with my scholarly training in the humanities. Of the international affairs programs that I have researched, Tuft's offerings in US foreign/diplomatic policy and political theory seem especially strong, and I am specifically looking forward to courses on US foreign relations since 1918, American Constitutional history, and the development of political theory, which should allow me to build upon my existing knowledge of scholarship on political leadership and archival sources for US legislative history. Tuft's curriculum is also very appealing to me because of its emphasis on economics and quantitative methods in the social sciences, two areas in which I would like to receive more training before beginning a public policy career. Given my experience as a lecturer at Bradley, Vassar College, and the George School in Philadelphia, I also hope to teach one day.

If you cannot name specific professors you are attracted to, then mention specific classes or areas of study in which you know the program excels.

Working at an educational research institution such as the Dirksen Center has shown me that ideas can be put into action, a notion expressed in ancient Greek as *paideuma,* coincidentally the title of the journal in which my Pound essay will soon be published. However, it was Senator Dirksen rather than Ezra Pound who persuaded me that reverence for study and civic responsibility are compatible goals. Bringing the senator back to life on that January eve of war gave him the voice to do so.

Be sure to mention pending or submitted publications, as well as those already released.

ESSAY #26: "TO BE A COLLEGE PROFESSOR"

Statement of Purpose, Combined Application for the Doctoral Program and Teaching Assistantship

I had never had the opportunity to teach before; graduate assistants at Baylor rarely teach, and so I was still quite nervous and unsure of myself when I stepped to the lectern that first night at Ouachita Technical College as the new adjunct political science instructor. I had prepared my lecture; I knew my subject; I certainly had the desire to teach, but until that moment I still didn't know if I had what it would take to be a college professor. When the class ended three hours later, I knew.

This essay is attractive because it reads so well. It may not be as flashy as some, but it is a clean, efficient presentation of a serious and thoughtful candidate. If you want a teaching assistantship, as does this candidate, be sure to discuss your teaching, tutoring, and proctoring background.

Ever since I left Baylor with my master's, I have known that I eventually would return to graduate school to continue my work toward a doctorate. I have always considered my time in the "real world" to be a preparation for this return to graduate school, an opportunity to mature and to broaden my experience in government and politics beyond the theoretical and the textbook.

Toward this end, I have spent the past three years with the Arkansas Historic Preservation Program, a state government agency charged with the enforcement of the National Historic Preservation Act. I was initially hired to oversee the development and publication of *A Foundation for the Future: The Arkansas Historic Preservation Plan,* a comprehensive statement of the agency's mission, goals, and objectives over the next five years. On the completion of this project, I was asked to stay on as the agency's staff planner. This has been a most valuable experience for a student of government and politics, a chance to apply my education and skills in a public policy area with national, state, and local implications.

Over the past three years, I have had the opportunity to work on a number of interesting and diverse projects with federal agencies including the National Park Service and the United States Postal Service, with other state historic preservation offices, with state and national historic preservation interest groups, and with city and county government officials all over Arkansas. I have researched and written on numerous historic preservation public policy issues, including an intensive study on the effects of post office relocation policies on historic downtowns that resulted in a US Senate subcommittee hearing here in Little Rock. My efforts at developing comprehensive preservation plans and land protection strategies for Arkansas's Civil War battlefields through the Secretary of the Interior's American Battlefield Protection Program have been commended by officials of the National Park Service. My main goal was to update Civil War signage and displays, remove or downplay Lost Cause sentiments, and recenter these presentations around the experiences and concerns of contemporary citizens, including communities of color. This was a major undertaking involving extensive research, outreach, and negotiating the concerns of multiple constituencies that did not always agree on much.

Use your essay to explain your decision-making processes, to tie all your other experiences together, and to "make sense" of data that may also be provided on a CV or other parts of your application. This candidate's background might have seemed disjointed, running from academia to government and back again, but this explication of his intentions lays such concerns to rest.

My time in state government has been an invaluable experience. I have witnessed firsthand the interactions and relationships among federal, state, and local governments; I have developed a better understanding of the intricacies of

ESSAY #26: "TO BE A COLLEGE PROFESSOR" (CONTINUED)

government bureaucracies; and I have broadened my education through extensive research and writing on Arkansas's political and social history. Through my professional connections, I had the opportunity to serve as a regional campaign manager for a gubernatorial campaign, and I was also active in the last presidential campaign; these experiences have given me valuable insights into modern political campaigning and the electoral process. I believe that these experiences have served to complement the very fine education that I received at Baylor and to strengthen my fascination with government and politics.

In August of this year, I accepted a part-time position with Henderson State University as adjunct political science instructor at Ouachita Technical College in Malvern, Arkansas; my experience teaching "American National Government" to a diverse class of nontraditional students has been transformational. This experience, more than any other, has forced a personal reassessment of my goals and strengthened my resolve to leave a position that I have found both professionally challenging and personally rewarding, and to return now to graduate school to earn a doctorate and to pursue an academic career.

The entire remainder of this essay explains why the candidate chose this particular graduate program.

For the past two years, I have collected information from a variety of PhD programs in the southeastern United States, and I have slowly narrowed my choices to a handful of schools. I visited Vanderbilt's department of political science last summer, and was impressed with the friendly faculty and their willingness to speak with me about my educational interests and goals. I was already familiar with Vanderbilt's excellent reputation, but I felt that I should experience the program firsthand before I applied for admission. Academically, I feel that I am better suited to a smaller, more intimate educational environment. It was this atmosphere that I found so rewarding at Baylor, and its absence led me to leave the University of Virginia. Based on my discussions with Drs. Gare, Bennett, and Halestrap, I hope that I have found it again at Vanderbilt.

At Vanderbilt, I hope to pursue a course of study involving the nature, formulation, and implementation of American foreign policy, specifically toward Europe, Russia, and the states of the former Soviet Union. The recent global reevaluation of NATO and the surprising global backsliding in democracy and democratic ideals represent both challenges and opportunities for American policy. What is our role in encouraging the growth and maturation of new or faltering political systems? Will we move into a new period of unipolar stability, give way to China, or devolve into a patchwork of unstable and temporary bilateral alliances and agreements? To be clear, I do not disregard the importance of China, but I am interested in European-facing interests while taking a global perspective. That global perspective will necessarily involve China, but also a number of international public policy issues: climate change and the environment, economic interdependence and free trade, refugeeism, and the continuing political and economic instability in the developing

ESSAY #26: "TO BE A COLLEGE PROFESSOR" (CONTINUED)

world. How will these issues play out in the American political process, how will the president and the Congress address these foreign policy concerns, and what factors and pressures will influence their decisions? These are the issues that I hope to address in my studies at Vanderbilt.

I am therefore applying for admission to Vanderbilt University's political science doctoral program with the teaching assistantship option. The experience, the education, and the degree that I hope to earn at Vanderbilt will enable me to pursue a career in teaching and research at the university level, and to make a lasting contribution to this fascinating discipline. I am confident that my academic and professional experiences have imbued me with the depth and maturity that your program demands, and that, given the opportunity, I could be a valuable asset to your department. I hope that you will seriously consider my qualifications and arrive at the same conclusion.

ESSAY #27: "ECONOMICS—WITH FIT AND MATCH"

Mention faculty by name, and mention context for each connection. Have you met them? Read their papers or books? Corresponded with them? Do your current professors recommend them, or is your undergraduate mentor a protégé of a targeted graduate advisor? These are important data points.

Customize your essays right from the top, so that the readers know you wrote this essay for this program and these faculty readers. Most students seem to put their customization near the bottom of the essays, which makes the bulk of the essay seem canned. As always, naming specific faculty members and their research foci is one of the easiest and best ways to customize. It shows fit and match.

Always parse your grades in your major if they are high, and especially when they are this high.

I want to study economics because I want to understand human action, and the most quantitative way to accomplish that goal is in the field of economics. Similarly, I want to study development economics and microeconometrics because a powerful way to understand human action is to study the places and situations in which human systems fail. In order to achieve a nontrivial grasp, I must be competent in using the proper methods of analysis that can help me to uncover the trends that underlie specific types of failure. There are few better examples of economic systems than the missing and imperfect markets pervasive in developing economies. The Leonard Volstachen School of Economics is an excellent fit for these goals. I appreciate how the curriculum emphasizes current applied research in economic development with an econometric rigor that advances the ability of researchers to attain valuable results. I have been corresponding with Dr. James for a few months, and she has been quite encouraging about the match between my interests and your program's overall strengths. I met Drs. Willcox and Fine at a conference in Chicago last summer sponsored by the *American Economic Review*. I found Dr. Willcox's paper on the risk profile of farmers to be compelling, and Dr. Fine's online lecture of panel data techniques helped me to understand the subject in a superior way. I look forward to meeting the entire faculty of the department.

I first became interested in economic graduate study with my first taste of econometric research. The culminating goal of the class was an econometric research paper, hopefully fit for publication and presentation. It fired my imagination when I read academic papers on whether access to formal credit constrained agricultural production decisions, and the methods various economists used to answer that and similar questions. The precision of the analysis and the soundness of the methodology impressed me, and I realized that sort of stimulating work—conducting quantitative research and then articulating one's findings to economists and noneconomists alike—was a career that I could pursue. Those economists I was reading were, in important ways, the final product of the person I now saw myself as being able to become.

I have a good knowledge of statistics from my minor and from conducting research. I am able to manage large and multipart research projects independently; I also collaborated with a peer coauthor to craft a research paper. I know statistics software. From my work at a financial services consulting firm and a bank, I am comfortable managing complex data sets and analyzing them. I have maintained a 4.0 GPA in my major, and a 3.84 overall. In addition, I was fortunate to attend an undergraduate institution—the Cook Honors College at Indiana University of Pennsylvania—that combines a rare mix of analytical thinking and an emphasis on the students' obligations to act on the knowledge received. The unique curriculum revolves around "Great Questions" (in contrast to the "Great Books" liberal arts curriculum), in which each question (e.g., "How can we tell the good from the bad?") is followed by the equally important "What, therefore, should we [the students] do?" The analysis half of the question is one of the primary drivers of my

ESSAY #27: "ECONOMICS—WITH FIT AND MATCH" (CONTINUED)

desire to understand economics and the tools that economists use to understand human action.

I am further grateful for a second major in philosophy, which has enabled me to think carefully about the structure of good thinking and soundly constructed argument, how to be careful in the foundations and assumptions one makes—whether it is in evaluating the assumptions behind philosophers who subscribe to Bayesian confirmation theory or economists who hold that access to formal credit constrains agricultural production decisions of farmers. My peer coauthor and I were honored to receive the Best Undergraduate Paper Award at the Pennsylvania Economic Association for our paper on the credit constraints and the production decisions of rural farmers in India. Our paper was also published in the peer-reviewed *Pennsylvania Economic Review*. The faculty of the College of Humanities and Social Sciences selected me for the Margaret Flegal Harte Scholarship, a merit scholarship for outstanding students in the humanities and social sciences. As a student-elected member of the Board of Directors for the IUP Student Co-operative Association, I learned how to enter the fray of a political debate with real consequences for students, faculty, and administrators.

Mention major accomplishments in your essay even if they are mentioned in your CV or elsewhere in your application. Assume that your essay is read all by itself, without the rest of your portfolio at hand.

In terms of my research interests, I am specifically intrigued by the determinants of the decisions of farmers in developing economies, untangling the empirical relationship and determinants of formal and informal lending in developing economies, as well as deepening my understanding of microeconomic development and econometric measuring techniques. I understand that in the course of my graduate studies my interests will be refined and may change, but at the moment those are the topics that most interest me.

I would enjoy spending my time in Athens, Georgia, which is far warmer and inviting in its climate than Western Pennsylvania, where I currently live. In the spring, I will be working on further research projects with my coauthor, using the data we have already gathered and structured to answer different theoretical questions, perhaps about the determinants of the demand for formal and informal credit and how each differs and is similar to the other. I will continue interning at Stewart Capital Advisors, conducting quantitative and qualitative research. I also plan to assist Dr. J. Jozefowicz in conducting research on the impacts of the change in the Gini coefficient in West Virginia on the state's unemployment rate.

Nice geographical connection! Mention it but don't belabor it.

There is nearly a year between the time you apply and when you arrive at a graduate program. Be sure to mention your projects that will be ongoing or completed during that year.

After receiving my PhD in economics, I plan to find a faculty position at a research institution, where I can spend time teaching students—both economics majors and nonmajors—as well as conducting research, primarily on the choices of rural farmers, those living unhoused, and other individuals who do not have access to ideal, or, in many cases, any market at all for goods, and how that impacts their decision making. I hope to promote the discipline through research, be able to use that research to help the subjects of that research, and impart to students the passion of pursuing the study of human action that is the wide and profoundly relevant field of economics.

ESSAY #28: "AEROSPACE ENGINEERING"

It is okay to mention a past failure as long as (1) you don't dwell on it, (2) you don't whine or complain in any way, and (3) you use it as a demarcation point for growth, achievement, and perseverance.

Sometimes, a rejection is the best thing that can happen to you.

When I first applied to graduate school, six years ago, I was rejected. Instead, I went to work in the creative, multidisciplinary defense R&D industry, where I had the opportunity to learn the realities of the engineering vocation. I also learned my strengths, my weaknesses, and most importantly, what I wanted to do next.

A turning point in my professional life occurred as I looked into the sky to watch a sixteen-foot remote-controlled aircraft about to attempt a first-of-its-kind operation. The aircraft was flying over an inactive military airfield, preparing to turn and approach a prototype system to catch and land unmanned aerial vehicles on Navy ships. As program manager, I had led the effort to develop the system for two years. As I watched the aircraft circling around for its first attempt, I realized that I was about to experience a moment of closure over a great amount of work by me and our entire team. What happened next was out of my hands. The success of the tests would be decided by the remote pilot and the quality of the hardware our team had built.

The pilot turned the aircraft in a tight arc. I remember that it seemed to float directly in front of me, before pulling out of its bank and continuing toward the recovery system, its tail-hook directly on target to snag the arrest loop that would initiate engagement.

As the aircraft passed over the recovery system, there came a loud noise like several trucks shifting into low gear at once. The event was over in the blink of an eye, but what happened was this: the aircraft snagged the arrest cable and was then yanked out of the air onto the wheeled landing pad, which was already moving at synchronous velocity thanks to the innovative design of our engineers. The recovery pad absorbed the aircraft's vertical impact and then, as a single unit, the aircraft and cart rolled just ten more feet to halt under hydraulic braking.

If the implications of your research are important, make them plain. Don't expect the reader to infer them.

The system had plucked the drone out of the air and brought it safely to rest in less than sixty feet overall. Our team had just demonstrated a new means of landing an unmanned aircraft. The practical implications were enormous. We had just changed the definition of an airfield!

Fifty minutes later, we achieved a second successful recovery.

That day gave me a lot. I walked into my company with renewed self-confidence. Of greater value was the benefit I would discover in the months to come, when I felt the pride of standing in front of a room full of engineers and presenting the new capability that we had made real. VTOL drones get all the press, but our system increases the versatility of fixed-wing UAVs that have massively greater utility overall. Those in the room knew the value of this development, and the applause was enthusiastic and genuine.

My work with this landing and recovery system has had the largest impact on my career to date, but I did not plan it that way. I have also worked in space

ESSAY #28: "AEROSPACE ENGINEERING" (CONTINUED)

systems, on projects I started on my own initiative. A few years ago I wrote and won a SBIR proposal topic in satellite thermal control. The goal of this project has been to develop thermal control equipment that can be rapidly assembled onto a satellite bus to control heat flow between the bus and a piece of onboard hardware. This thermal control project gave me my first presentation and publication opportunities, as well as the chance to write and win additional proposals and build my own area of expertise. The activity I will remember most is working with Lockheed Martin to put the hardware through vibration testing on the same equipment used to test multimillion-dollar satellites. Working with the Lockheed engineers and being treated as an equal by them was greatly inspiring and helped to boost my confidence as an engineer.

Like many in the aerospace field, my passion is to expand human activities in space. I originally wanted to do a graduate program in space-based life support systems, because I was most inspired by the specific topic of human survival in space. However, my experience in the defense community forced me to conclude that a focus on the human-crewed aspect of space systems may not lead to the highest-potential discovery. With the disclaimer that what follows is my own opinion, I have seen in the defense community the emergence of a vision of human-machine interaction in which every human war-fighter is surrounded by a team of unmanned systems. The human will serve as the commander, while the unmanned systems will perform supporting operations that vastly multiply the human's capability. This model is how I believe future space exploration will occur. Both technical and budget considerations suggest that unmanned systems should lead the way. To an extent, they already have. I expect our space community to continue to extend that model in the years to come so that unmanned autonomous systems become an inseparable and, in some aspects, a dominant aspect of human-crewed operations.

I also share the view of many in the space industry that economic benefit is necessary to sustain progress. It is now absolutely proven that the profit motive beats command-and-control development at this stage in our species' relationship to space. My overall goal is to develop and deploy new systems that will foster immense economic activity in space. As these systems and their economic uses increase, they will inevitably draw us humans outward as well.

Having discussed my long-term goals, I'd like to address my undergraduate transcript. I entered undergraduate studies with high native intelligence, poor study skills, and a lack of direction. When I realized that my college career was not succeeding, I went on leave and spent a year developing software for a technology startup and pursuing my interest in technical writing. When I returned, I came with the intent to succeed academically. With this in mind, please note that my GPA for my upper two years was 4.0 in my major.

Excellent explication of a GPA. It is okay to get a rough start as long as the trend lately is positive, and especially if the trend lately is positive *and* consistent.

ESSAY #28: "AEROSPACE ENGINEERING" (CONTINUED)

I am excited about completing a PhD program in aerospace engineering for three reasons. First, I want to shape my fundamental engineering skills, acquired in my undergraduate studies and in my work, into expertise in my specific interest of space systems.

Second, I want to hone my skills for original research. In industry, the technical quality of a proposal is only one factor that contributes to its award. I know that I have used strategic positioning, as well as simple salesmanship, to give my proposals a boost. While there is nothing wrong with this, it is important to me that I drive my technical skills to their absolute maximum, so that when I do utilize my instincts for strategy and salesmanship, I will do so knowing that my technical approach is the best that it can be.

It is almost always a good idea to mention several specific faculty members whose work matches your interests.

My final goal in graduate school is to work hands-on with spacecraft technologies that make it out of the laboratory. It was Texas A&M's research projects involving the design, fabrication, and operation of small satellites (AggieSats) that first drew me to the program. Visiting the A&M campus to meet with Prof. H. Reed, AggieSat lab director Mr. J. Perez, and the student members of the AggieSat team further assured me that A&M would offer the excellent aerospace education and research opportunities I am looking for. The challenge of Autonomous Rendezvous and Docking (ARD) that will be addressed in future AggieSats is an excellent fit with my long-term goal of designing autonomous space systems, and I believe that several of my skill sets such as thermal management, mechanical design, and systems engineering will be useful to this challenge. I thank you for your consideration.

ESSAY #29: "TABLE TOPIC"

This table topic, also known as a table presentation, is a work sample submitted in addition to a statement of purpose. Table topics are presented at scientific meetings. The author/researcher stands in front of a presentation board and represents her research to interested parties, who most usually browse through an auditorium full of such exhibits (sort of like a science fair for grownups). This particular topic won "Best Chemistry Presentation" at a regional conference, which was of course mentioned in detail in this student's statement of purpose.

The Synthesis of Thiaporphyrins as Possible Photodynamic Cancer Therapy (PDT) Agents

Amy L. Gryshuk*, Dawn Cox*, Ryan J. Howard*, Lynn E. Maelia#, Edward P. Zovinka*
*Dept. of Chem., Math & Phys. Sci., Saint Francis College, Loretto, PA & Div. of Natural Sci., Mount Saint Mary College, Newburgh, NY

I. ABSTRACT

The study of thiaporphyrins is of interest because of their potential use as Photodynamic Therapy (PDT) agents for cancer treatment. When light activated, the photosensitizer excites the oxygen in the cell to its toxic singlet state, which kills the cancer. Prior experimentation on the insertion of molybdenum into a thiaporphyrin ligand has shown bands at 717 nm, which is in the desired red region (630–800 nm).[1]

The goal of this project is to efficiently and affordably synthesize thiaporphyrins according to a "3+1" Synthesis of a thiotripyrrane dicarboxylic acid with 1-H-pyrrole-2,5-dicarboxaldehyde. The thiotripyrrane has been successfully synthesized according to ^{1}H NMR data and we are currently preparing 1-H-pyrrole-2,5-dicarboxaldehyde.

II. INTRODUCTION: WHAT ARE THIAPORPHYRINS?

Unlike the porphyrin, the thiaporphyrin (SPH) consists of 3 bridging pyrroles and one thiophene ring. The dithiaporphyrin (S_2P) consists of 2 bridging pyrroles and 2 thiophen rings. The addition of the S atom to the macrocycle core is of particular interest because the core modified porphyrins are a relatively untapped resource. The core size is smaller in comparison to the normal porphyrin and the aromatic character is modified due to non-planarity of the macrocycle.[2] The N···N distance is 4.383 Å in tetraphenylporphyrin, the S···N distance is 3.585 Å in thiaporphyrin, and the S···S distance is 3.069 Å in dithiaporphyrin.[3]

Our current research includes inserting early transition metals since metals later in the transition series, such as Cu, Fe, and Ni, have been previously studied with the SPH ligand. While the structural and reactivity changes brought about by modification of the core may be of interest for catalytic uses, the main purpose of this research project is to study metallothiaporphyrins for possible use as Photodynamic Therapy (PDT) agents for cancer.

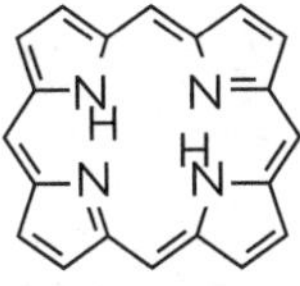

PORPHYRIN

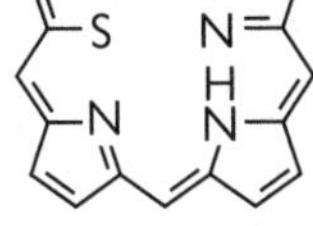

THIAPORPHYRIN

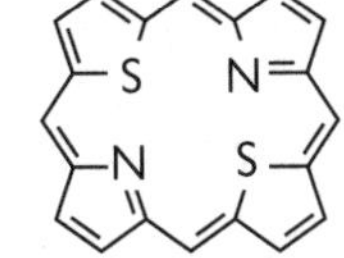

DITHIAPORPHYRIN

When submitting work samples, be sure to comply with these two rules: work samples must be very, very good, and they need to be directly related to the targeted area of graduate study. You should have a professor review any work sample you plan to submit, both to review the quality of the work and to assess the appropriateness of the submission. This one is a winner.

ESSAY #29: "TABLE TOPIC" (CONTINUED)

WHAT IS PHOTODYNAMIC THERAPY (PDT)? PDT is a medical treatment for solid cancers in which photosensitizing agents such as porphyrins are administered and then activated with light (630–800 nm).[1] It is a safe, noninvasive treatment for cancer that is based on the "phototoxicity of photosensitizing agents like porphyrins which are the natural precursors of hemoglobin."[4] Porphyrins have been chosen because of their similarity to hemoglobin, which carries oxygen in red blood cells throughout the body including to the cancerous regions.

The photosensitizer is inserted into the body where it accumulates near cancer cells. In the ground state, the oxygen present in the cells is in the triplet state. When light-activated, the porphyrin excites the oxygen in the cell to its toxic singlet state, which kills the cancer. Light with wavelength in the 650–800 nm range is preferred because of its ability to penetrate up to 3.0 cm (over 1⅛ inch) deep into human tissues.[4]

PDT eliminates the need for surgical procedures because of the possibility of irradiating the tumor through the skin, through topical applications of porphyrins, or through endoscopic laser therapy.

The Basic Idea of Tumor Phototherapy Is To:[5]

1. Select a good photosensitizer with selectivity for photodamage to tumor tissue.
2. Inject the photosensitizer and wait until the tumor region fluoresces to denote the presence of porphyrin.
3. Irradiate the tumor with the visible light (650–800 nm).

PDT[5]

Advantages

+ Painless
+ Noninvasive
+ Able to treat multiple lesions with topical porphyrins in one sitting
+ Good patient acceptance
+ Good cosmetic results
+ Not cytotoxic unless irradiated with light
+ Can be repeated as often as necessary without damaging healthy tissue

Disadvantages

+ Impure compounds currently in use

ESSAY #29: "TABLE TOPIC" (CONTINUED)

+ Compounds remain in the skin for 4–6 weeks, causing cutaneous sensitivity
+ Still experimental—research is continuing

PRELIMINARY EVIDENCE According to Marcinkowska, et al., "Modification of the core of porphyrins, by the introduction of various heteroatoms in place of one or two pyrolle-NH groups, allows preparation of new heterocycles that show interesting properties in terms of their aromatic porphyrin-like character and the marked difference in the electronic spectra."[6]

Following this suggestion, we have prepared thiaporphyrin (SPH) and have inserted a molybdenum atom into its core. The electronic spectrum of this molybdenum thiaporphyrin (MoSPH) shows the absorption of light at 717 nm.[7] This is in the target 650–800 nm wavelength range for PDT use.

I have read this research presentation over 100 times, and I have come to the conclusion that this is a very, very good presentation of a fairly straightforward research project. It is neither complex nor profound. Do not be intimidated by this example. Endeavor to present your work with similar sophistication and precision.

III. EXPERIMENTAL

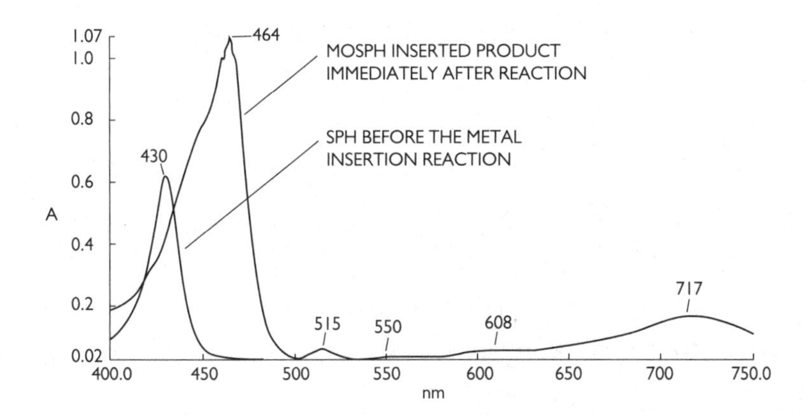

Step 1: Synthesis of 2,5-Acetoxymethyl-thiophene

Thiophene —(1. CH_2O HC(g))→ 2,5-bis(chloromethyl)thiophene (Cl, S, Cl) —(1. NaOAc)→ AcO, S, OAc

Reference: Griffing, J. M.; Salisbury, L. F. J. Am. Chem. Soc. 1948, 3417.

ESSAY #29: "TABLE TOPIC" (CONTINUED)

Step 2: Synthesis of Thiotripyrrane

AcO OAc + N H CO_2Et → EtO_2C N H S N H CO_2Et

Reference: Boudif, A.; Momenteau, M. J. Chem. Soc., Perkin Trans. 1, 1996, 1240.

I. LiOH

HO_2C N H S N H CO_2H

Reference: Sessler, J. L.; Cry, M. J.; Burrell. A. K. Synlett 1996, 127.

Step 3: Synthesis of 2,5-pyrrole-Dicarbaldehyde

H_3C N H CH_3 → $Pb(OAc)_4$ PbO_2 HOAc Room Temp 3 hrs → OHC N H CHO

Reference: Boudif, A.; Momenteau, M. J. Chem. Soc., Perkin Trans. 1, 1996, 1239.

Step 4: Synthesis of Thiaporphyrins

HO_2C N H S N H CO_2H + OHC N H CHO → S N H N N

OR

HO_2C N H S N H CO_2H + S O O → S N N S

Reference: Boudif, A.; Momenteau, M. J. Chem. Soc., Perkin Trans. 1, 1996, 1241 & Broadhurst, M. J.; Grigg R.; Johnson, A. W. J. Chem. Soc. (C), 1971, 3689.

ESSAY #29: "TABLE TOPIC" (CONTINUED)

Synthesis 2,5-bis-chloromethyl-thiophene

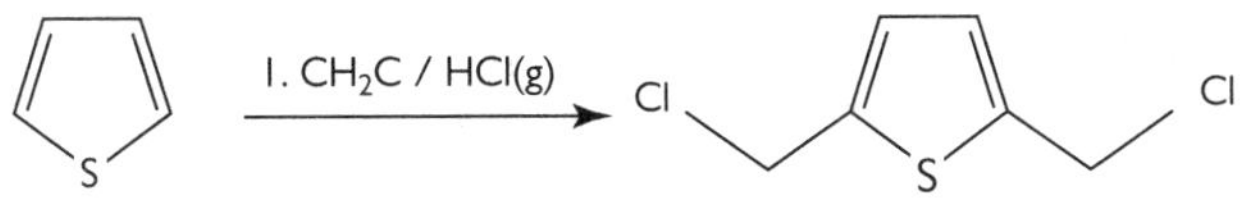

I. CH_2C / HCl(g)

Reference: Griffing, J. M.; Salisbury, L. F. J. Am. Chem. Soc. Vol. 70, 1948, 3417.

To a 3-neck 500 mL flask with stir bar and thermometer was added 45.0 mL 37% CH_2O and 11.5 mL conc. HCl. HCl gas was bubbled through the stirring solution for 2 hours until a specific gravity was reached, 1.1797 g/mL (literature suggested 1.185 g/mL). After 2 hrs. bubbling was stopped and an ice/water bath was added to cool the 3-neck flask (kept stirring). Distilled thiophene (15.0 mL) was added dropwise at 1 drop/sec. The temperature remained between 30°C and 0°C. After the thiophene was completely added, the yellowish solution was stirred for an additional 20–30 minutes. After 20–30 minutes, the stirring was stopped to allow the solution to settle into 3 layers (kept on ice/water bath). Three layers were visible: top—cream/white; middle—light yellow; bottom—larger dark-gold yellow (oil). The 3-neck flask remained on ICE at ALL TIMES (polymerizes at R.T.). The lower oily layer was siphoned off, placed into a separatory funnel, and rinsed twice with ~25.0 mL COLD distilled water. The oily layer was extracted into a 100 mL r.b. to refrigerate overnight to form crystals.

2,5-bis-chloromethyl-thiophene oil polymerizes at R.T. so it was kept on ICE at ALL times. Next day, noticed a lower dark oily layer and light golden water layer with possible para-formaldehyde solid. The flask and glass frit used for vacuum filtration were chilled. The filtrate flask was placed into an ice bath while filtrating. Solid golden para-formaldehyde was present on frit surface (discarded). Water globules present in filtrate were siphoned off and discarded. The oil filtrate was pipeted into a 25.0 mL r.b. and refrigerated.

Synthesis 2,5-bis-acetoxymethyl-thiophene

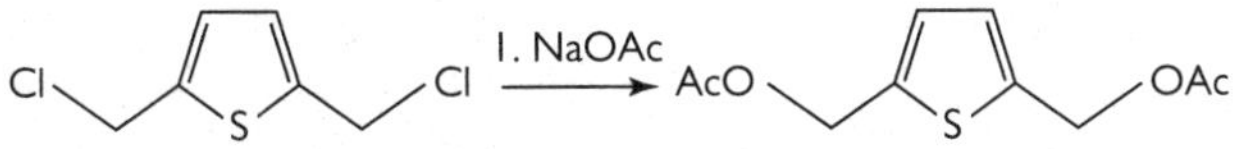

I. NaOAc

Reference: Griffing, J. M.; Salisbury, L. F. J. Am. Chem. Soc. Vol. 70, 1948, 3417.

Transferred 49.0 mL glacial HOAc into 100 mL r.b. Measured out 13.8053 g NaOAc and added to stirring HOAc. The solution started to solidify so a glass stirring rod was used to break up the solid chunks. Slowly 14.09 g 2,5-bis-chloromethyl-thiophene was added to the stirred suspension (kept 2,5-bis-chloromethyl-thiophene r.b. on ice

ESSAY #29: "TABLE TOPIC" (CONTINUED)

while waiting to add—polymerizes at R.T.). The temperature was kept steady at ~60°C. The golden yellow slurry was stirred for 5 hours. After 5 hours, the solution was cooled at R.T. for 16 hrs. to form two layers. Two layers were present: top—brown/rust clear liquid; bottom—yellow solution w/white solid on bottom. Next day, oil settled out (¾ maroon oil on top & ¼ yellow on bottom). After 16 hours, the solution was vacuum filtrated. A white solid remained on glass frit. The white solid was tested for solubility and presence of chloride ions. The rich, brown oil filtrate was transferred to a 100 mL r.b. via pipet. The r.b. was rotovapored on a hot water bath.

After being rotovaporated, a chunky, crispy, golden-orange caramel solid with white chunks remained. COLD Na_2CO_3 was added to 100 mL r.b. to neutralize. The white solid settled on the bottom leaving the brown oil layer on top. Excess Na_2CO_3 was added. The contents were transferred to a beaker where excess distilled water and ethyl ether were added. Then, the solution was placed into separatory funnel and the oil layer was extracted into a 50.0 mL r.b. (dark brown oil). The r.b. was not capped to allow the ethyl ether to evaporate off.

Synthesis of Thiotripyrrane

AcO S OAc + N H CO_2Et → ETO_2C N H S N H CO_2Et

Reference: Boudif, A.; Momenteau, M. J. Chem. Soc., Perkin Trans. 1, 1996, 1240.

Added 0.9541 g distilled (Fraction #3) 2,5-bis-acetoxymethyl-thiophene to 100 mL Schlenk flask. While stirring and under nitrogen, 1.2883 g ethyl pyrrole-2-carboxylate was added to flask. Approximately 30.0 mL denatured ethanol to golden, clear solution was slowly added. Lastly, 0.1663 g p-Toluenesulfonic acid was added to the stirred solution. At first the solution was pale yellow and/or slightly cloudy. For 7 hours the mixture was refluxed under nitrogen to produce a dark, golden/tan solution. Nitrogen was blown over the top of the flask while cooling. Once cooled, the flask was placed in the refrigerator overnight.

The next day there was a clear brown liquid above a dark "caramel" oil. The clear brown liquid was decanted to evaporate off the EtOH. CH_2Cl_2 was added to the Schlenk flask to dissolve the dark "caramel" oil. Oil was transferred into large glass vial and weighed. An IR (salt plate) of the thiotripyrrane oil and EtOH oil from thiotripyrrane were taken.

The crude thiotripyrrane oil was columned using silica gel and eluted with CH_2Cl_2.

ESSAY #29: "TABLE TOPIC" (CONTINUED)

Synthesis of Thiotripyrrane-dicarboxylic acid

ETO$_2$C N H S N H CO$_2$Et → HO$_2$C N H S N H CO$_2$H

Reference: Boudif, A.; Momenteau, M. J. Chem. Soc., Perkin Trans. 1, 1996, 1241.

10.0 mL of 1.0M NaOH in water and 5 mL of absolute ethanol were added to 0.2130 g of thiotripyrrane-ethyl ester with stirring. After 22 hours of stirring at room temperature, the solution was refluxed for 4 hours. The solution was allowed to stir for another 18 hours at room temperature. Unreacted starting material was extracted into 10 mL CH_2Cl_2, the NaOH solution was neutralized with 1.0 M HCl, and the resulting carboxylic acid was extracted into CH_2Cl_2 (3 × 10 mL). This was dried over $MgSO_4$ and filtered into a round bottom without purification for further reaction to the dithiaporphyrin.

Synthesis of 2,5-pyrrole-Dicarbaldehyde

H$_3$C N H CH$_3$ → (Pb(OAc)$_4$, PbO$_2$, HOAc, Room Temp 3 hrs) OHC N H CHO

Reference: Boudif, A.; Momenteau, M. J. Chem. Soc., Perkin Trans. 1, 1996, 1239.

Carefully weighed out 0.515 g $Pb(OAc)_4$ and 1.0476 g PbO_2 into 100 mL r.b. Approximately 30.0 mL HOAc was added to the r.b. Originally the stirred solution was black. To a 50.0 mL beaker was added 0.5166 g 2,5-dimethylpyrrole. HOAc (16.5 mL) was added to the beaker to make a slurry. When the slurry was added to the stirred solution of HOAc, $Pb(OAc)_4$, and PbO_2 the color turned to dark brown/coffee. The solution was stirred for 3 hours at R.T. and capped with a stopper. After 3 hours, 20.0 mL distilled water was added to the r.b. The mixture was refluxed for 30 minutes and allowed to cool (kept stirring).

Distilled water (100 mL) was added to the r.b. and placed into 500 mL separatory funnel. The r.b. was rinsed with 100 mL CH_2Cl_2 and added to funnel. A dissecting light was used to distinguish 2 layers: top—dark maroon water; bottom—CH_2Cl_2 dark/light red-maroon layer. The CH_2Cl_2 layer was extracted into a 250 mL Erlenmeyer flask. Water layer was rinsed with CH_2Cl_2. CH_2Cl_2 layer was transferred back into separatory funnel and 10.0 mL Na_2CO_3 was added. CH_2Cl_2 layer was extracted into a 500 mL Erlenmeyer flask. The dark, plum, maroon colored sol'n was transferred back into the separatory funnel and rinsed with 100 mL distilled

ESSAY #29: "TABLE TOPIC" (CONTINUED)

water (3 times). The CH_2Cl_2 layer was extracted into a 500 mL flask and dried over Na_2SO_4. The liquid was decanted off into a 500 mL r.b. and rotovapored on hot water bath.

The crude 2,5-pyrrole-dicarbaldehyde residue was columned on 3.0 cm diameter Silica Gel and eluted with $ChCl_3$. Fractions #1–10 were collected in 50.0 mL integrals. TLC plates and IR were taken.

IV. DISCUSSION

Literature procedures were followed for the synthesis of 2,5-bis-chloromethyl-thiophen (41.4% yield), 2,5-bis-acetoxymethyl-thiphene (61.8% yield), thiotripyrrane (33.6% yield), thiotripyrrane-dicarboxylic acid (??), and 2,5-pyrrole-dicarboxaldehyde (3.4%). Step 1 (2,5-bis-chloromethyl-thiophene) and Step 2 (2,5-bis-acetoxymethyl-thiophene) were successfully synthesized while Step 3 (2,5-pyrrole-dicarboxaldehyde) is still being studied. All materials were characterized by IR and/or ^1H NMR spectra.

V. FUTURE PLANS

Future research will involve the synthesis of thiaporphyrins (SPH) and dithiaporphyrins (S_2P) according to the "3+1" Synthesis. Once successfully synthesized, early transition metal thiaporphyrin complexes of SPH and S_2P that absorb in the desired 630–800 nm wavelength range will be prepared. These compounds can then be used in studies as possible PDT photosensitizers for cancer.

The last few weeks of summer research will focus on the synthesis of dithiaporphyrin, followed by the thiaporphyrin. The dithiaporphyrin can be synthesized more easily because the thiotripyrrane-dicarboxylic acid can react with the commercially available 2,5-thiophene-dicarboxaldehyde. Once the 2,5-pyrrole-dicarboxaldehyde is purified, the SPH reaction can be attempted.

Once S_2P and SPH are synthesized on a small scale, they can then be attempted on larger scales. Our focus will then be on inserting molybdenum and/or tungsten into the S_2P and SPH ligands.

VI. RESOURCES

1. Pandey, R. K.; Ressler, M. M. "Creating New Photosensitizers for Cancer Therapy." *Chemtech* March 1998, 35.
2. Lato-Grazynski, L.; Lisowski, J.; Olmstead, M. M.; Balch, A. L. "The First Structural Characterization of a Nickel (I) Macrocyclic System: Structure of Nickel (I) Diphenyldi-p-tolyl-21-Thiaporphyrin." *Inorganic Chem.* 1989, 23, 1183–1188.

ESSAY #29: "TABLE TOPIC" (CONTINUED)

3. Lato-Grazynski, L.; Lisowski, J.; Olmstead, M. M.; Balch, A. L. "21-Thiatetra-p-tolylporphyrin and Its Copper (II) Bicarbonate Complex. Structural Effects of Copper-Thiophene Binding." *J. Am. Chem. Soc.* 1987, 109, 4428–4429.

4. Luma Care. Http://www.lumacare.com/ 1997 MGB Technologies.

5. Bonnet, R. "Photosensitizers of the Phorphyrin and Phthalocyanine Series for Photodynamic Therapy." *Chemical Society Reviews* 1995, 19.

6. Chmielewski, P.; Lato-Grazynski, L.; Marcinkowska, E.; Pacholska, E.; Radzikowki, C. S.; Ziolkowski, P. "The New Sensitizing Agents for Photodynamic Therapy: 21-Selenaporphyrin and 21-Thiaporphyrin." *Anticancer Research* Vol. 17, 1997, 3313–3314.

7. Zovinka, E. P.; Howard, R. J. Unpublished data on MoSPH, 1997–98.

ACKNOWLEDGMENTS Donors of the Petroleum Research Fund, administered by the American Chemical Society (ACS) for partial support of this research; the following institutions:

Mount Saint Mary College
Saint Francis College
United States Military Academy at West Point

This is a research proposal submitted for the National Science Foundation Graduate Research Fellowship Program. College seniors and first-year graduate students can submit proposals for the NSF GRFP. It is important to know that this is a pro forma proposal. You are showing that you know how to design a research project, but are not expected to necessarily conduct the project you propose. Your topic, obviously, should closely match your graduate programs of interest. You can even focus your proposal on one institution, as this candidate does here, and then elect to pursue your degree path at a different institution. Faculty guidance is essential to prepare these documents. This candidate enlisted the assistance of faculty at UC Berkeley, the target institution, as well as at his undergraduate institution, in the design and drafting of this research proposal.

This is only one part of the application. Candidates will also provide a personal statement and other supporting materials. The award comes with a large fellowship for the student, and an award to their department.

ESSAY #30: "NSF GRFP—NEUTRINOS"

Background: From the postulation of the neutrino by Wolfgang Pauli, to its discovery by Fred Reines and Clyde Cowen [1], to the experimental evidence of neutrino oscillations by the Super-K and SNO collaborations [2-4], this particle has been the subject of great interest amongst physicists. Today, the neutrino sector is a quickly growing field, as there are many questions that still need to be answered. There is significant motivation to determine the mixing angle, $\Theta 13$, which was shown to be non-zero [5] and could give insight into charge-parity violation. Additionally, searches for neutrinoless double beta decay ($0\nu\beta\beta$) [6] hope to prove the Majorana nature of the particle, and show violation of lepton number conservation. Despite the large interest in neutrinos and significant theoretical and experimental efforts, relatively little is still known about the elusive particle. Its elusiveness is, in part, due to being extremely light and having no electric charge, making it a challenge to detect directly. Current techniques include using neutrino detectors that rely on a clear liquid scintillator [7], while others make use of Cherenkov radiation [8].

Scintillation detectors require the use of a scintillator material, which produces photons in response to incident radiation, and can operate at low-energy thresholds. The produced photons are, generally, detected by a photomultiplier tube (PMT) and converted to an electrical signal with a distinct peak. Scintillation detectors are particularly good at detecting high energy photons but are indiscriminate in terms of the direction of the detected photons, and so lack the capability for event reconstruction. Additionally, scintillation events happen over a broader range of times and narrower range of wavelengths, when compared to Cherenkov radiation events. Cherenkov radiation is produced when charged particles move through a medium faster than the local velocity of light, and travels in the direction of the particle. These events happen at much higher energy thresholds, but the intensity of the radiation is much lower than that of scintillation radiation. Thus, Cherenkov events require much more sensitive PMTs, but are directionally sensitive and can be used for event reconstruction and particle identification. Therefore, it can be understood as to why scintillation and Cherenkov techniques are more suited for low-energy experiments like Daya Bay [7] and high-energy experiments like IceCube [8], respectively.

As stand-alone techniques these two approaches are limited in their physics scope and there exists a need to overlap these methods to achieve enhanced sensitivity to a broader range of physics. The project I propose to work on is the Eos-Theia project [9], led by Dr. G. Orebi Gann at the University of California, Berkeley. The aim of this project is to combine these techniques to provide a test-bed for the next generation of hybrid detectors. The goals of my proposed GRFP project are to utilize a water-based liquid scintillator (WbLS), 200 high quantum efficiency fast-timing R14688-100 [10] PMTs, and dichroicons [11], to:

Goal (1)—Construct Eos, a tonne-scale scintillation-based detector. *Method:* The construction of Eos will take place at UC Berkeley, beginning Summer of 2023. The primary structure will be a stainless-steel tank that houses an acrylic vessel. The acrylic vessel will be filled with the WbLS and surrounded by approximately

ESSAY #30: "NSF GRFP—NEUTRINOS" (CONTINUED)

200 high quantum efficiency, fast-timing PMTs. These PMTs will also be placed above and below the vessel, for increased coverage. The WbLS will reduce the overall scintillation light, when compared to pure liquid scintillators. Furthermore, the fraction of scintillator in the WbLS can be controlled and thus the target medium optical properties can be fine-tuned. This will allow us to increase the ratio of Cherenkov to scintillation photons being detected. Additionally, a water buffer will be placed between the steel tank and the acrylic vessel, which provides a medium in which Cherenkov radiation can occur. Lastly, a calibration source will be placed at the top of the tank, to enable testing, once construction is complete.

Goal (2)—Test novel R14688-100 PMT photodetectors and dichroicons, and advanced reconstruction algorithms for Cherenkov and Scintillation separation. *Method:* The R14688-100 photodetectors are an essential part of Eos. They have a maximum quantum efficiency of about 35%, which is the ratio of the number of photoelectrons produced to the number of incident photons. They are also capable of achieving a transit time spread of 900 picoseconds, providing a fast-timing response to consecutive photon detections. The dichroicons use a shortpass and a longpass dichroic filter at the aperture which allows for spectral sorting of short- and long-wavelength photons. An important mechanism for discerning Cherenkov and scintillation radiation. The dichroicons are likely to be placed at the top and bottom of the detector, while the 200 R14688-100 photodetectors will be placed around it. Testing of these novel photodetectors will require the deployment of radioactive calibration sources to produce the Cherenkov and scintillation photons. The use of these sources and photodetectors will help to verify detailed WbLS optical models, as well as test advanced reconstruction algorithms that use both Cherenkov and scintillation photons for event, energy, and direction reconstruction. This will be achieved by separating the arrival times, wavelength spectrum, and directionality of event photons.

Intellectual Merit: The scope of this project is the construction and commissioning of a novel hybrid detector. Eos will provide a test-bed for many novel technologies and has the potential to push the boundaries for future neutrino event detections by providing unique imaging capabilities for both low- and high-energy neutrino measurements. Additionally, Eos is imbedded in a large-scale multi-institution, international project, Theia. The success of Eos would give promise to future ktonne scale hybrid detectors, like Theia, which aims to achieve a broad and sensitive scientific program. This will include long baseline neutrino oscillation measurements, searches for charge-parity violation, and extended reach of neutrinoless double beta decay searches. Additionally, Eos would represent a large step in advancement for other fields, by demonstrating a broad range of capabilities. This may allow future detectors to observe Diffuse Supernova Background flux, perform measurements of geo-neutrinos with unprecedented statistics, conduct tests of Grand Unified Theories via nucleon decay, and probe for physics beyond the Standard Model.

Broader Impacts: I will be involved in outreach, recruitment, and mentorship of undergraduate students to assist in the Research and Development (R&D) of Eos.

You must follow application protocols for programs like the NSF GRFP exactly. The wrong-size font or margins can disqualify an applicant. The wrong citation formatting can disqualify an applicant.

This essay almost did not get into the book, as the editors found it "too intimidating to readers." The applicant responded: "I suppose readers might see it as intimidating if they haven't experienced much physics writing. However, I spent a lot of time and effort making it very readable for the targeted reader." The effort paid off. The essay won.

He also said, "The GRFP is much more prestigious than I had originally thought, and it opens a ton of doors. I was able to secure a better offer for funding from my institution, once the GRFP funding ends. It's also going to offer me *much* more flexibility in graduate school in selecting projects, starting research earlier, and being able to focus first-year courses onto my trajectory."

ESSAY #30: "NSF GRFP—NEUTRINOS" (CONTINUED)

An important aspect of this large-scale project is to specifically involve underrepresented minorities (URM) and work closely with Minority Serving Institutions (MSI) and Hispanic Serving Institutions (HSI), in order to engage students that would not otherwise have these opportunities. I will actively involve URMs that are less common such as, low-income, first-generation, and non-traditional students. One way that I can achieve this is via recruitment through the UC Berkeley McNair Program. The aim is for these students to gain R&D experience in fundamental nuclear and particle physics, with the goal of improving STEM retention and diversity within the local MSIs and HSIs and beyond. This will be an opportunity for many students to make contributions to a multi-institution, next-generation project through work in Department of Energy national laboratories, like the Lawrence Berkeley National Laboratory. I will also work to assist in the proposed General Education course, "Discoveries in Physics," which aims to provide a conceptual overview of experimental and theoretical physics. Lastly, a barrier for many students is having to work to support tuition costs. This project seeks to fund students year-round at several MSIs and HSIs, in the hopes of alleviating some financial burden in their pursuit of an education.

References

[1] C. L. Cowan Jr., F. Reines, F. B. Harrison, H. W. Kruse, A. McGuire, Science 124, 3212 (1956).
[2] Y. Fukuda et al. (SuperKamiokande Collaboration), Phys. Rev. Lett. 81, 1562 (1998).
[3] Q. Ahmad et al. (SNO Collaboration), Phys. Rev. Lett. 87, 071301 (2001).
[4] Q. Ahmad et al. (SNO Collaboration), Phys. Rev. Lett. 89, 011301 (2001).
[5] K. Abe et al. (T2K Collaboration), Phys. Rev. Lett. 107. 041801 (2011).
[6] W. H. Furry, Phys. Rev. 56, 1184 (1939).
[7] F. P. An et al. (Daya Bay Collaboration), Phys. Rev. Lett. 129, 041801 (2022).
[8] M. G. Aartsen et al. (IceCube Collaboration), Phys. Rev. Lett. 120, 071801 (2018).
[9] M. Askins et al. The European Physical Journal C 80, 416 (2020).
[10] https://www.hamamatsu.com/eu/en/product/type/R14688-100/index.html.
[11] T. Kaptanoglu, M. Luo, B. Land, A. Bacon, and J. Klein, Phys. Rev. D 101, 072002 (2020).

ESSAY #31: "RANCH REALITIES"

Personal Statement for Veterinary School

As I was growing up, our house was always filled with an assortment of animals—dogs, cats, birds, and reptiles. In the summers, I worked on my grandparents' cattle ranch in central Oregon, and there I participated in the planting, irrigating, and haying operations. My true preference, however, was working with the livestock. I rode on the cattle drives and helped in the brandings (which included dehorning, vaccinating, and castrating). Through these experiences, I came to understand the relationship between rancher and livestock, and the often harsh reality of animal husbandry.

This essay is simple and direct. In its own style, it is overwhelmingly articulate. It reveals that rarest of creatures, an idealistic candidate devoid of naïveté.

Notice the straightforward expository style. It is easy to read, and the words don't distract at all from the message.

At my grandparents', too, I became interested in horses. My first horse was an unbroken quarter horse, who quickly educated me on the trials of owning a large animal. I have owned two other horses, both Thoroughbreds, which I trained, showed, and later sold. As a horse owner, I have experienced my share of colics, wire cuts, and mysterious lameness, as well as learned how to handle and cajole an animal that weighs eight to ten times more than I do. I have taught English and Western lessons, anatomy, general horsemanship, and first aid to Sierra Club members and summer camp children, and have been responsible for the care of fifteen lesson horses. No matter what the experience, the companionship, enjoyment, and sense of responsibility I have gained from growing up around animals has convinced me that veterinary medicine offers me a way to combine my love for animals with my interest in biological science.

More recent events have also directed me toward a career in veterinary medicine. After graduating from Duke with a bachelor's degree in biology, I accepted a four-month internship near Naples, Florida, working at a wild animal rehabilitation clinic. In contrast to my experiences with domesticated animals, the wild animals I encountered did everything in their power to flee or fight their way to freedom. We worked in cooperation with local veterinarians to provide emergency care to injured wildlife, nursing care to convalescing animals, and physical therapy to animals that were potentially releasable. I participated in all aspects of these procedures and gained invaluable experience handling raptors, seabirds, and other native species. My daily responsibilities included medicating, weighing, rescuing, and providing emergency care, as well as preparing food, cleaning cages, and answering public inquiries.

My internship ended in January, and I moved back to Seattle, where I was hired by a major dog and cat hospital. The hospital provides general and specialized veterinary services, employing an oncologist, a neurologist, a radiologist, and an internist. When I started at the clinic, my responsibilities included restraining animals during procedures, cleaning cages, and medicating hospitalized cases. I now am the technician to Dr. V. Petrakis, the neurology specialist (see letter of recommendation), and my duties include placing IV catheters, drawing blood, monitoring

ESSAY #31: "RANCH REALITIES" (CONTINUED)

animals under anesthesia, and preparing for joint/spinal taps and myelograms. In addition, I have been trained to operate a CAT scan, which the hospital is fortunate enough to own.

In my present position, I am not only learning new procedures and techniques, but also gaining experience in seeing how a veterinary clinic operates. I realize that in order to maintain high professional standards it takes solid managerial and financial skill. The hospital runs smoothly only when inventory is well stocked, kennels well maintained, and a positive rapport exists between the clinic and clientele. Based upon conversations I have had with veterinarians and on my own observations, I sense that the profession of veterinary medicine is undergoing rapid change. Advancements (in both human and animal medicine) have created new dilemmas for veterinarian and client. While care has improved and previously incurable conditions can now be treated, the costs for such procedures can be prohibitive. I believe veterinarians must approach their clients honestly when discussing the benefits and costs of treatments and offer alternatives to the client whenever possible. The increasing prevalence of pet insurance only complicates the matter. It seems that a vet has to navigate a complex clinical landscape to conduct an ethical practice.

Having a clear interest in a niche implies maturity and a sophisticated understanding of your future profession. However, it will increase your chances of admission only if the program you have targeted has some special expertise in that area.

After working in several areas of the animal care industry, I have begun to narrow down my potential career goals. While I enjoy working with small animals, my interests really lie with large ones. My experiences working in central Oregon have enforced my desire to work in a rural area and treat livestock. I am also interested in wildlife and marine mammal medicine. In addition to my work in the small animal clinic, I work as an ecology teacher on a research vessel on Puget Sound. This experience has reinforced my commitment to environmental issues. Wildlife veterinary medicine seems to offer a way I can help preserve wildlife and fulfill my own professional goals.

ESSAY #32: "A HAPPY CHILDHOOD—THEN ARCHITECTURE"

Autobiography for School of Architecture

I was born in Port Harcourt, Nigeria, to a middle-class African family. I feel fortunate to have had a beautiful early childhood. I attribute most of my success as an adult to a strong foundation made in early life by a warm and loving family that nurtured, guided, enforced discipline, inspired excellence, established norms and value systems that were ethical and humane, and instilled a good sense of judgment. Above all, there was endless love. On the other hand, though, the school (elementary, high school through college) was a big partner in this enterprise. They reinforced and complemented some of these efforts. And for me, it was a pleasure to seek, wonder, and learn, combined with the splendor of meeting new friends, each of whom had a meaningful significance in my life. Subsequently, I developed a very good social, moral, and intellectual base that enhanced my capacity to succeed in a competitive and dynamic society.

As time evolved, my decision to attend undergraduate school in the United States was a major one. First, there was the thrill of adventure, the joy and excitement of discovering the "New World," the United States of America, and the enthusiasm to begin college work. America has fascinated me, especially as portrayed by Mark Twain, Ernest Hemingway, Emily Dickinson, and depicted in the paintings of Norman Rockwell. Of course, I was also aware of the superior design education available in the United States. After graduation, I emigrated to the US to study architecture, attending Hampton University in Hampton, Virginia, a beautiful college by the sea with a committed and informed faculty, rich in resources.

Architecture was a challenging and demanding major; however, my interest to seek involvement in building human habitation and improving the quality of the environment was a strong one. In addition, it is my nature to accomplish and excel. I have particularly liked the works of valued, appreciated architecture, an architecture that makes impression and quality statements, that provides refinement and distinction. To this effect, quintessence and excellence in design leadership reinforced my inspiration and commitment to the study of architecture.

At Hampton, I completed a rigorous five-year program that emphasized concept development and design. I graduated top of my class with my first professional degree, bachelor of architecture (BArch), three years ago last May. I was elected chairman of the Design Council by my fellow students of architecture and was appointed to the visiting lectures committee by the student body president. I was elected president of the International Students Association, was initiated into Alpha Kappa Mu honor society for distinguished scholars, and served as a peer counselor and a mentor to architecture majors. I was the director of the visual aids department within the university's architecture department, including supervision of work-study students, and by invitation of the professor, served as a teaching assistant for

If you read a lot of admissions essays, you may grow weary of the "victim mentality" of applicants. I've read essays from candidates who claimed they were victimized because their parents were middle class, because their pet bird died, or because they had to ("Gasp!") work while they went to school. This is not impressive to adult admissions readers. Strife is when your mom dies in your arms from a horrific and excruciatingly painful disease the day of your comprehensive exams. Strife is when you can't afford to buy postage stamps, much less something so expensive as food. Strife is when you grow up in an active war zone where attending school is an act of extraordinary bravery. That's strife.

This essay is an absolute slap of fresh air. This candidate had a happy childhood, is well adjusted, and promises to bring this optimism with him to graduate school. Wow!

The prompt was for an autobiography. Note that this content could just as well be a personal statement.

Autobiographies should focus on your life experiences that molded you into a good candidate for the targeted graduate program. Be honest and forthcoming, certainly, but don't forget that this, too, is an admissions document.

ESSAY #32: "A HAPPY CHILDHOOD—THEN ARCHITECTURE" (CONTINUED)

"Architectural History," for which I also gave lectures on African art, architecture, and aesthetic influences.

During this period, I was the recipient of distinguished academic and professional awards, including (a) the American Institute of Architects' Scholastic Award: The Certificate of Merit for Excellence in the Study of Architecture, (b) the Virginia Foundation for Architectural Education's O'Pendleton Wright Scholarship to a Distinguished Architecture Student in Advanced Standing, two years in a row, and (c) the Adrian Freeman Scholarship prize and citation awarded by the Hampton University president to the "outstanding graduating senior who has shown excellence and promise."

During my college years, I also came to appreciate coffee instead of tea, discovered the hamburger, learned to play golf, played on the varsity table tennis team (competing in an ad hoc mid-Atlantic conference), and continued to pursue my interests in photography, nature, fishing, sailing, and surfing. Hampton is well situated for such sports, as it is at the mouth of Chesapeake Bay. During the summers, I traveled extensively throughout the United States, and attended summer sessions at Virginia Tech and the University of Texas at Arlington.

In professional practice, my involvement evolved from working as a junior gofer and plan-check corrections clerk through assisting in various efforts of the design and working drawing process to leading the production crew, interfacing with principals and consultants, and agency coordination for reputable design firms in the Los Angeles area. I last worked as project manager with the RL Atkins Company, a Beverly Hills–based design-build land development company.

Even though my career was advancing rapidly, I felt the need for continued, specialized education to achieve my ultimate goals. I left practice to pursue my second professional degree, the master of architecture degree (MArch) at UC Berkeley, which I selected for its preeminence in design leadership and on the recommendations of my professors from Hampton and my mentors from my professional career. At Berkeley, I am doing quite well, currently ranking a 3.88 GPA, and expecting to graduate with high honors.

Upon completion of my current studies, I hope to begin study immediately with the PhD program. During the course of my experience of architecture, both as a student and as a professional in practice, I have considered the terminal degree as an appealing option, both to achieve the fulfillment of my intellectual interests and to serve as the foundation of my later career. My objective is to serve the practice of architecture in a leadership role and ultimately to contribute to research and education in my chosen field.

ESSAY #33: "MD/PHD—AMCAS ESSAY FOR MEDICAL SCIENTIST"

It is fine to trace your interest in an academic discipline to a college course, but think twice before starting with a childhood experience.

Many science majors at Truman State University loathe Introductory Biology II. It is commonly known among students as the biology major "weed-out" course because of its difficulty, and as a "survey of life" course, students must spend long hours in the lab looking at different species of protozoa and algae under microscopes as they try to make sense of these unfamiliar organisms. However, my Introductory Biology II experience convinced me that I wanted nothing more than to pursue a career in the biological sciences. This course opened my eyes to the amazing diversity and complexity of life on this planet. As we moved through the course, I loved seeing how different taxonomic groups, although each adapted to their individual environment, were still related to each other via shared ancestors throughout evolutionary history. The laboratory component, which I had been dreading, became my favorite part of the class. Every week, I went to extra "open lab" hours to take a closer look at all these remarkable organisms, and they never failed to enthrall and fascinate me. At this point, I knew there must be some niche within this vast discipline to which I could dedicate my life's work.

From that point on, I have taken every opportunity possible to gain exposure to my chosen field. Starting in the fall of my sophomore year, I worked with my Introductory Biology II professor, Dr. A. E. Weisstein, to develop a mathematical model of how an infectious disease epidemic could possibly disseminate throughout the United States. The model is now finished, and I am currently coauthoring a paper analyzing the pedagogical efficiency of introducing mathematical modeling into the introductory biology classroom. This past summer, I had the good fortune to be selected for the Summer Undergraduate Research Program at the University of Massachusetts Medical School, where I investigated virulence mechanisms of the plague bacillus *Yersinia pestis* in the laboratory of Dr. J. Goguen. Currently, I am conducting original research of my own design concerning antibiotic resistance of *Escherichia coli* isolates from man-made reservoirs in northeast Missouri under the auspices of Dr. C. Cooper at Truman State University. This work was originally funded by a Merck/AAAS grant last summer, but I have now transformed the project into a longitudinal study to analyze resistance patterns over time. The preliminary results were presented at the American Society for Microbiology Missouri Branch Annual Meeting. These experiences, along with many others, have cemented my desire to seek further education in the life sciences.

But why medicine? I have stated that I want to continue study within the life sciences, and there are plenty of other fields that fall within this designation; however, there are many reasons that draw me to the study of medicine in particular.

First and foremost, a formalized study of medicine allows me to study the human being in great detail. As a student who is quite interested in science, this fascinates me to no end. The human being is arguably the most interesting organism

ESSAY #33: "MD/PHD—AMCAS ESSAY FOR MEDICAL SCIENTIST" (CONTINUED)

on the planet, and I would very much enjoy the opportunity to learn more about how our bodies are able to function on a day-to-day basis. In addition, my plan is to perform research as a physician scientist, specifically in the field of infectious diseases, and a background in medicine would help me to better understand these diseases in a clinical, instead of purely scientific, context.

Second, medicine is an applied science, and it allows me to make the most immediate impact on society. There are many fields in the life sciences that have little application to human society, and although I know that I would, and do, find many of those fields interesting, I would prefer to dedicate my life's work to a topic that had more direct human benefit. Since I know that I want to study science, medicine gives me the tools to maximize my individual contribution to humanity as a whole.

Third, I am excited for the opportunity to work with patients. Although my primary interest is in becoming a physician scientist, I still want to work with patients, and interpersonal interaction is a very important part of this work. I believe that I have the personal skills necessary for these interactions. In the course of my volunteer work through Blue Key, a service organization on campus, I have had the opportunity to volunteer at multiple nursing homes in the Kirksville, Missouri, area. These experiences have shown me that I do enjoy working with patients, and I look forward to the clinical training aspect of medical school.

Always assume that readers are only looking at your essay. Of course this student's outstanding grades and scores are listed elsewhere in the application, but listing them here is just smart—and impressive.

Finally, I am convinced that I have the qualities necessary to succeed in medical school. My perfect GPA and 42T MCAT score demonstrate my intellectual ability, while my campus involvement and athletic pursuits show that I possess the social and personal qualities to succeed. In addition, my research background displays my interest in, and passion for, research. All of these attributes are essential for success in the study of medicine.

I wish to study medicine in preparation for a career as a physician scientist. Medical school promises to be quite the journey, and personally, I am ready for the journey to begin.

ESSAY #34: "COSMOPOLITE"

Robert Lewis

Statement of Motivation—Peace Corps

"Of Bedouins and Bulgarian Circuses"

Like many people who are both idealistic and practical, I sometimes have struggled with my goals, my intentions, with the very heart of the question "What is important to me?" So for many years, I mixed occasional traveling and trekking with a career in the financial services industry. In one world, I am a tough negotiator, able to iron out operations problems in an environment where many, many thousands of dollars are involved in every transaction. I consume and synthesize a massive amount of data, facilitating the profit motive of others. Sometimes it is like consuming sand.

This is an essay submitted as part of an application to the Peace Corps. The applicant is already an accomplished and widely traveled citizen of the world. This type of candidate is more common than the average academic advisor might believe, setting a high bar for acceptance.

In the other world, I always feel I am the guest, the one whose invitation is a gift, the one who strives to learn the house rules and be the ideal visitor. My tough veneer is left behind (except for solving crises), and I am a student in a classroom without walls. It is clear to me that this is better living, and this is what I want to do for years at a stretch, rather than just months.

Traveling runs in my family. My ancestors were barrel makers from a village near Tokaj, Hungary, before they came to the United States early in the last century. One of my sisters married a Swede and lived in Sweden for three years. Another is a photographer, who often works and lives abroad as well. I have lived in England for six months, in Rome for ten weeks, and have traveled throughout Europe, Africa, and the Middle East. Wherever I go and no matter how short the stay, I tend to put down roots almost immediately. I learn the local grocer's name. I discover the intricacies of the town, the hidden nooks and shops the locals use, who knows the best gossip, how to get fresh fruit, and so on.

I have worked in almost every country I have been to, also. Jobs I have held have mostly been manual labor, the sort of jobs that people get when they have no papers: apple picker, waiter, tomato picker, dishwasher, gardener, cook, painter. Some of the jobs have been quite interesting, however, such as staff at a popular nightclub. Of course, I have taught English on several continents. Ironically, in London I even tutored the English on British English. I taught American English to Russian immigrants in Israel. I really enjoy this type of work and find it to be an ideal way to become really well acquainted with locals.

Being willing to work is good. Being willing to work with your hands may be better. Having skills related to growing food or building or mechanical equipment repair may be best of all.

In southern Egypt, I passed from Bedouin tribe to Bedouin tribe like a token for four bizarre and yet serene months. I took to the nomadic life rather well, but I preferred riding a horse to riding a camel. After months of seeing no one from my own country, I crossed the Nile and entered Sudan. There I ran into aid workers who could not believe I had been traveling overland.

ESSAY #34: "COSMOPOLITE" (CONTINUED)

Bulgarian Circus? Nothing could be better.

Once while waiting to use an international phone in Israel, I listened while an acrobat from the Bulgarian Circus tried to get a connection to Sofia. His Russian was not very good to begin with, and it was clear that the operators were totally at a loss. I stepped forward and offered my services as a translator, and speaking Russia to the acrobat and English to the operator, I got the call put through. This led to several weeks in which the Bulgarian Circus provided me with room and board—not to mention lots of entertainment—and carried me around with them in return for translating and dealing with local authorities.

Here's the rationale that reveals the candidate to be a serious and thoughtful person, not just an adventure seeker.

Although it is great to have adventures, I do not want to misrepresent my interest in the Peace Corps. I could easily just continue my double life of travel and work, but my main goal is to combine these two lives, to bring my work in line with my true interests. I believe that helping others is the root of all true meaning in life, and I want to help others in an endeavor more meaningful than increasing the wealth of the already wealthy. I grew up in a small town of six thousand, mostly "gentleman farmers," where the center of town was literally a combined general store and post office. I would be comfortable anywhere you may wish to assign me, and I look forward to any assignment. I am experienced, and I think skilled, at teaching English, but I would be happy to pursue agricultural or development projects as well. I have no preference as to geography, either. I am interested in Poland, Hungary, and the rest of Eastern Europe, because I believe history is in the making there, but I would most certainly welcome an assignment anywhere in the world.

The Peace Corps has many different assignments and is subject to trends in its selection criteria. Ask around before you apply, to see if you can discover what they are most interested in this year.

As to my future after the Peace Corps, I would want to incorporate my Peace Corps experience in a new career in the United States, or perhaps with an international development or international aid organization. Career possibilities include teaching, social services, or perhaps serving a development organization with my financial skills. I look forward to these new directions with eagerness and the certainty that my future holds a more integrated life, with work and leisure, heart and mind, involved in all my endeavors.

ESSAY #35: "BLUE COLLAR TO PSYCH SCHOLAR"

Statement of Purpose—PhD in Psychology

Following nearly ten years of employment as an aircraft mechanic, I took a hard look at where my life was going. Although I was responsible for important work, requiring extensive technical knowledge and mechanical skills in manufacturing and maintaining aircraft, I felt compelled to include myself in a larger arena. Each airplane that I repaired and that flew away was a poignant reminder that I was standing still. Consigned to the tedium of long commutes and time clocks, my daily routine was empty of genuine enthusiasm and curiosity. Predictable, the content of my days offered little beyond another paycheck, another weekend, another Monday. I realized that in order to redirect my life and fully experience the world, I would have to confront the uncertainties that change would bring.

Note that this statement of purpose has many of the elements of a personal statement.

My first step was to face an embarrassing truth—reenrolling at the age of thirty, I earned my high school diploma. I could have forgone this step of earning a diploma but I was compelled to alter how I approached my past, and in doing so, how I would meet my future. Resigning as an aircraft mechanic and enrolling full-time at my local community college, I attained my associate of arts degree. Unquestionably, these initial accomplishments contributed to my deep-rooted curiosity about human behavior and motivation. Focusing my academic direction, I then earned a bachelor of arts degree in psychology from California State University, San Bernardino (CSUSB). While working part-time and attending college full-time proved exhausting and at times frightening, nevertheless, the decision to change my life was revealing itself as the correct path. In preparing for a career within psychology, I recognized that a doctorate in this field would be essential. With this goal in mind, I resolved to strengthen my academic and practical background by entering the master's program in general/experimental psychology at CSUSB.

This man is matter-of-fact about having made a major error in his first career choice. His bravery in returning to school is admirable.

Having proposed my master's thesis on the perception of family resources and the psychological adjustment of parents caring for a child with autism, I expect to defend by October and earn my master's degree. Data collection for my thesis topic was based on protocols created during my work as a research assistant at the University Center for Developmental Disabilities (UCDD) at CSUSB. The UCDD has over 120 families with children with developmental disabilities who receive behavioral treatments and family services. The opportunity to work directly with these families was sobering when considering factors affecting family dynamics. However, it offered practical as well as conceptual understanding within this area. Additionally, involvement with the UCDD was fundamental in understanding the steps of setting up a research investigation from its earliest stages. During my time there, I was able to research literature related to the field of autism and developmental disabilities, evaluate measures used for test construction, write test items, pilot test questions and testing administration procedures, and interview parents and siblings for data collection. Seeking to expand my research experience, I also participated in a study

Be sure to run laundry lists of skills, techniques, and even equipment you can operate, as this writer does here and on the next page.

ESSAY #35: "BLUE COLLAR TO PSYCH SCHOLAR" (CONTINUED)

investigating the effects of amphetamine on glial cells. This study, utilizing an animal model, offered the chance to learn laboratory techniques related to handling, injecting, surgery, profusions, cryostat brain slicing, slide mounting, and finally digital microscopic cell counting. This study will be published this year.

This student is establishing teaching, writing, and statistical skills, virtually ensuring that he will get an assistantship. Teaching, writing, and statistical skills are the trifecta for graduate assistants.

Eager to complement my basic course requirements for the master's program, I have completed two extra upper-level statistics courses (multivariate and structural equation modeling) as well as two additional clinical courses (family dynamics and pervasive developmental disorders). Moreover, having been selected from among many candidates to instruct an introductory experimental course, I have just completed a full academic year instructing a laboratory section. My responsibilities included facilitating experiments and teaching the associated APA writing style and content format to upper-level psychology students. Additionally, following my teaching assistantship, I was hired as a writing consultant for my university's MARC Scholars Program. As a writing consultant, I am responsible for reviewing students' research content and writing styles across a range of disciplines including physics, economics, geology, as well as diverse subjects within psychology. Though these opportunities to interact and advise undergraduate students require long hours of detailed review, I found them extremely rewarding and they have made me, I feel, a more well-rounded person.

To understand the application of psychology, I have sought out volunteer opportunities as well. As a crisis counselor for a local suicide/crisis hotline for over three years, I have assisted individuals who were overwhelmed by the burdens of stress. In addition, as an unpaid assistant at Patton State Hospital, a state forensic treatment facility, I assisted staff in reintegrating patients for release into community halfway programs after many years isolated from society. Currently, I have begun training to volunteer at a rape crisis center that will require that I meet with victims and act as an advocate and assistant during their initial hospital and police investigation. Moreover, employing my expertise as a photographer, I have documented artwork and activities at a local museum.

In changing the direction of my life, I also decided to reenlist in the United States Air Force Reserves. Reenlisting as a photographer rather than in my previous military career as an aircraft mechanic has opened an esthetic outlet fostering creativity and even fun. As a supervisor in a combat photography unit tasked with visual documentation of worldwide military activities, I have been able to pursue my interest in people and travel through a medium that integrates aspects of both psychology and art—a rare opportunity in the military. The experiences and paths I have led are diverse: adopted as a child from Korea, living and working in Europe, traveling around the world, as well as the life of a student have all etched their marks within me. I believe the breadth and depth of my life experiences are my best qualities. Through them, I can appreciate how perspectives are influenced

Combat photography? Wow. That's a conversation item.

Notice how he mentions this adoption bombshell in passing, without elaborating at all. Another great example of how sometimes less is more.

ESSAY #35: "BLUE COLLAR TO PSYCH SCHOLAR" (CONTINUED)

through ethnicity, culture, geography, and even history. My competence in the laboratory, as a teaching assistant, as a researcher for the UCDD, as a paid writing consultant for the MARC Scholars Program, volunteer efforts helping people during crises, and even my work as a photographer with the USAF have solidified my dedication to the field of psychology as a career choice. My goal is to complete a clinical PhD program, commit my life to the field of psychology and learning, and be of service to others.

I am highly interested in the topic of psychotherapy and anxiety and would be excited to work under the direction of Dr. Tehanson. Additionally, Dr. Lehman's work with anxiety and depression would be particularly interesting. I would be an enthusiastic member of either one of these professors' research teams.

This essay needs more "why here" than this. Strive in your essays to make a close connection to faculty, especially research faculty.

The general rule is to identify three or more with whom you have affinity.

ESSAY #36: "UNDERWATER ARCHAEOLOGY"

This candidate is clearly going to be an asset to any department he might join. In the second paragraph, he has articulated his reasons for selecting a school stronger in archaeology than in marine archaeology, and it would seem that any school would be interested in his affiliation with Oxford's Marine Archaeological Research Expedition (MARE). This is another example of a student who is going to excel regardless of whether he is admitted to any particular program.

A student who brings intellectual queries with him is more interesting than one who expects to be told what to investigate.

Of course Brown would love to be told why it is a better choice than Oxford.

Personal Statement for Doctoral Program in Anthropology (Archaeology)

The peculiar fact that archaeology is both a social and physical science forms the basis of my attraction to the study. The process whereby information gained from chemistry and geology is transformed into statements about human culture and society fascinates me. I have chosen to study archaeology because it is one of the few fields I have found that demand a knowledge of metallurgy in order to make statements about trade networks, or of religious forms to understand settlement patterning—in short, an open and enquiring mind into all aspects of the past and present world as a basis for an understanding of humankind. I am applying to Brown University because my investigations have led me to believe that I will find an atmosphere of intellectual interest and diversity in faculty, students, and course work paralleling those I would like to see in myself.

An overworked catechism among marine archaeologists is that "there is no such thing as marine archaeology, only archaeology under water," but after four years of exposure to the field I am skeptical. The dichotomy in archaeology between technique and technology on the one hand, and the questions of human social processes that these try to answer, is not fully appreciated by many. My experiences on projects in Jamaica, Bermuda, and Italy, and my personal research into the matter, has led me to believe that technique exists in marine archaeology apart from any humanistic component and that most researchers follow the Hollywood adventure movie school of "shoot first, ask questions later." Even after thirty years, most of its intellectual parameters continue to be defined not by the archaeologists, but by the artifacts themselves. Although there is no doubt that other institutions in the United States and abroad offer fine education in the techniques of marine archaeology, techniques, in and of themselves, hold little interest for me. These techniques should only be a means, and my studies at Brown will be directed toward understanding and defining an end.

In general, therefore, what I would like to do while at Brown is to examine the nature of the interaction between human social processes and the maritime environment and to see what light marine archaeology can throw on existing questions of human culture change. On a more specific level, I am currently interested in the following questions: Did the deforestation of Crete lead to the decline of the Minoan civilization as a sea power? Was the site of Troy an inevitability given the nature of the Hellespont and the abilities of Bronze Age shipping? And at what point in time, if at all, were the Mycenaeans able to penetrate the Black Sea to the Danube, perhaps for tin from Bohemia?

Given the nature of these questions, it seems logical that I should stay at Oxford. My professors are pleased with my work to date and have asked me to stay on to complete a DPhi. There are two reasons for which I have chosen to apply to Brown

ESSAY #36: "UNDERWATER ARCHAEOLOGY" (CONTINUED)

instead of staying on. On a pragmatic level, I have financed my year here without any financial aid by working for two years; I am unwilling to spend the equivalent of a small condominium or two BMWs for three more years. Money aside, I enjoy teaching and intend to make a career of it at the university level. Oxford does not emphasize teaching for its graduate students, and I feel that an important part of my education is lacking. Although I will be leaving Oxford, I will maintain my ties here and I expect that my involvement with MARE (the Marine Archaeological Research Expedition) will continue, allowing both myself, and hopefully other students at Brown, an opportunity to do marine archaeology in the Mediterranean.

In conclusion, I would like to say that given my interests and concerns, I feel Brown is the best place for me to be. The facilities, scholarship, and traditions of the institution, combined with the caliber of the student body, make me confident that I will be stimulated throughout the course of my studies. I feel confident of my ability to succeed and hope that I have demonstrated a commitment to, and some ability in, the study of archaeology.

ESSAY #37: "ADVANCED NURSING"

Goals Statement for Advanced Program in Nursing

When my sister Michelle first told me of her anticipated career choice, I was less than enthusiastic. "Nursing," I said with typical teenage disdain. "Why would someone as intelligent as you want to change bedpans for a living?" My image of nurses was one formed by television. Nurses were always running around with a gurney, answering phones behind a counter, or handing something to the real action heroes. Such TV nurses were merely filler for dramatic scenes of doctors making profound observations and brilliant diagnoses. However, nursing as a profession and I as a person have grown a lot over the past decade. I now see that the options for nurses are as diverse as the health care system itself and that nurses are finally being given the credibility and respect they have deserved all along.

As an early college undergraduate, I put aside my original ambitions in art and literature to explore a burgeoning interest in life sciences and psychology. I was fascinated by the intricacies of the human brain. I anticipated graduate study in neuropsychology and perhaps a career in research. However, I realized that a life spent in a research lab, however edifying, was not for me. I knew that I would sorely miss human interaction.

Upon graduating *summa cum laude* with a degree in psychology, I took a position as a resident advisor in a group home for adults with developmental disabilities. The clients were considered profoundly disabled with severe cerebral palsy and a host of other health problems. It was difficult at first, both emotionally and physically. But in two years I learned a lot about health care, nurturing, and empowerment. Over the past six years, I have worked and volunteered in a variety of social service positions (see enclosed curriculum vitae). I am currently employed as a family counselor at a multiservice center for people without reliable housing, Freeman House, that caters mostly to people with mental disabilities. However, as a social worker one is often frustrated by the many limitations of an overburdened, inefficient system. I find nursing appealing in that it provides more concrete, tangible aid. Nursing skills are specific, and results more directly observable. In addition, I have retained an avid interest in the life sciences and have been taking science courses for the past three semesters to give myself a firm grounding for graduate study. (See NYU transcript.)

I would like advanced specialty preparation so that as a nurse practitioner I will have more autonomy to make decisions about a patient or a program as a whole. I'd also like to have the option to teach, both in-service at a medical center and at the college level. Working closely with the nurse practitioner who heads the mobile clinic that attends to the health problems of our clients at Freeman House, I have had an excellent opportunity to observe her role and responsibilities (see letter of recommendation). This observation has solidified my career objective.

My projected specialty is adult primary care with a minor in mental health nursing. This appeals to my keen interest in community health issues, as well as

This essay has a lot of "I"'s in it, but it does not fall into solipsism and a version of "my personal journey." It succeeds because she keeps talking about ideas and concepts much bigger than her own reaction to them. Her mature perspective and clarity of purpose carry the essay forward.

This essay starts off with a bold and challenging statement that is bound to alert the reader. The rest of the essay is an excellent example of clear and concise writing. The reader is carried along by the text, and the points are made so smoothly that anyone would have to agree with the last line. With the ascendance of advanced nursing and physician assistant specialties, it is important to note that the top-ranked nurses are earning more than the bottom-ranked doctors, and it's cheaper, faster, and easier to become a top-ranked nurse.

Pursuing a few courses specifically related to your graduate interest is very persuasive to admissions professionals. This is especially important if you've been out of school

continued >

ESSAY #37: "ADVANCED NURSING" (CONTINUED)

my belief in the value of preventive health education and prescreening programs. I see a strong need for more health education in the population that I work with; specifically alarming is the lack of knowledge on such basic issues as birth control, HIV/AIDS, wound care, and nutrition. I feel that as a nurse practitioner, I would have greater impact on an economically disadvantaged community. A mental health minor would allow me to deal in a more holistic fashion with the complex problems of this population. Upon graduation from this program, I would like to use my nurse practitioner license to practice in a clinic that provides both on-site services and outreach care. This may include home or shelter visits, or school and community health education seminars.

I am enthusiastic about your Master's Entry Program because it is the ideal way to achieve my goals. I feel the accelerated pace is appropriate to my level of preparation and ability to perform. I feel confident that my academic and practical background would allow me to excel in the program.

for some time. It can also help you overcome any prior grade liabilities. A handful of recent A's may overcome any problems from the past. Refer to supporting documentation, as this candidate does, "See NYU transcript." This reminds the reader there's more to you than would fit in an essay.

Nursing schools and dental schools want people who want to be nurses and dentists, not people who used to want to be doctors.

ESSAY #38: "MULTIFUNCTIONAL ENZYMES"

This is an example of a highly technical essay detailing research projects in chemistry. The reader will be a specialist in this area of chemistry. Note the total lack of personal information.

Research Summary in Application to Doctoral Program in Chemistry

My first research project involved determining whether the enzyme Uridylate Synthase "channels" the intermediate Orotidine 5′-monophosphate. This is a multifunctional enzyme and explanations for the evolution of this multifunctionality have been somewhat widespread but conflicting throughout the literature. This project then questioned the basis of these explanations and offered new hypotheses as to why such multifunctional proteins have evolved. I wrote the computer modeling programs that integrated, through recursion, all of the relevant Michaelis-Menton rate equations. This analysis proved that a channeling argument was unnecessary to explain the available experimental evidence. I also performed some related enzyme assays in order to check several related hypotheses developed by Dr. R. McClard at Reed College and myself.

Last summer I worked on an organic synthesis project that involved synthesis of one interesting analogue of a potent, possibly the most potent, regulator of the gluconeogenesis glycolysis pathways fructose 2,5-bisphosphate. The key to the synthesis of the analogue shown below is control of the stereochemistry of the previously anomeric carbon. My work was involved in the reactions with I_2 and Br_2 and creation of the "halogenonium" ion of the Wittig product from the starting protected arabinofructoside sugar, also shown below.

BzO O BzO OH BzO → $(Ph)_3P{=}CH_2$ BzO OH BzO BzO → I_2 BzO O I BzO BzO

→ → $^{2-}O_3PO$ O PO_3^{2-} HO HO $^{2-}O_3PO$ O O PO_3^{2-} HO OH HO

Analog

Fru 2.6 bisphosphate

ESSAY #38: "MULTIFUNCTIONAL ENZYMES" (CONTINUED)

My current research project, my senior thesis, is related to the one I was involved in during the summer. In this case, I am attempting to synthesize an analogue of phosphoribosylpyrophosphate (PRPP), which is the molecule that provides the sugar portion in the *de novo* pathway of pyrimidine biosynthesis. This work utilizes the same synthetic scheme as shown above with the exception of starting with the ribose sugar and several changes in the phosphorous portion of the molecule. The synthetic scheme below shows the route I hope to exploit in synthesizing the target molecule. These projects were all carried out with Prof. McClard.

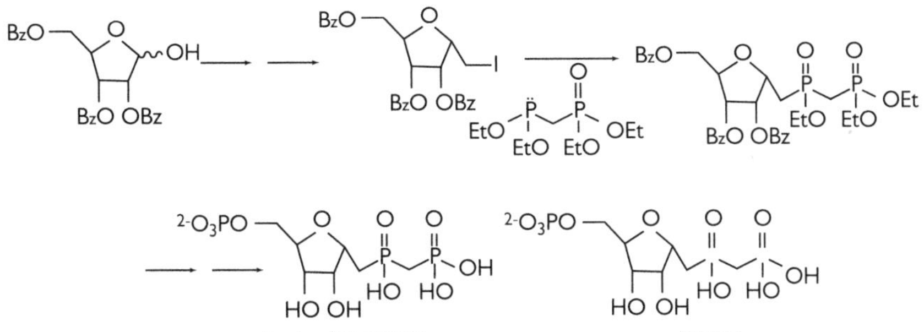

Analog (PRCPCP)

(PRPP)

This is a research proposal for the National Science Foundation Graduate Research Fellowship Program. Be sure to also see the comments accompanying Essay #30 beginning on page 190, which is also an NSF GRFP proposal. Advice there is not repeated here.

The author of this proposal demonstrates outstanding command of science writing. The tone and voice are perfect.

This successful candidate's advice for other applicants: "I would start as early as you possibly can. . . . When you are reaching out to potential advisors mention that you are applying for the GRFP. They might offer to read it for you or even help form a project, since it is in their interest for you to get this grant. . . . For your proposal, it is important to have a clear hypothesis/question formulated for each of the projects stated within the proposal. It shows the reviewers that you understand the project and potential outcomes. It is also better to go with a project that connects with your experience and not something too novel or

continued >

ESSAY #39: "NSF GRFP—BUTTERFLIES"

Background: Butterflies include over 18,500 species,[1] and they are perhaps some of the most charismatic insects. With nearly 3,500 species, the skippers (family *Hesperiidae*) are one of the most speciose, but poorly studied butterfly families[2]. Relatively few studies have applied modern molecular techniques to build an evolutionary tree of skipper species, and most of those that have are focused on the evolution of the family as whole[2,3]. Furthermore, few studies have examined their biogeographic patterns despite the fact that skippers may be one of the most threatened butterfly families, due to their specialization to host plants and selected habitats[4]. Distribution data on skippers remain hidden in museum collections, and without the mobilization of records and an understanding of their historical population boundaries, effective conservation measures cannot be designed or conducted. These data can be mobilized through digitization efforts, where specimen metadata are transcribed and uploaded onto an online database, such as Symbiota, a national biodiversity database funded by the NSF ADBC grant.

The nominal genus *Hesperia* contains 19 species and 52 subspecies, including the IUCN listed *H. dacotae, H. ottoe,* and *H. leonardus montana*[4], each with current populations reduced to marginalized patches[5]. The goals of my proposed GRFP project seek to utilize frozen tissues, museum specimens, and occurrence records to:

Goal (1)—Construct a phylogeny of Hesperia to better understand its evolutionary history and evaluate its historical biogeography. *Methods:* Restriction associated DNA sequencing (RADseq) will be conducted on museum specimens and frozen tissues on all species and subspecies of *Hesperia*. I propose to conduct this research in the Kawahara Lab at the University of Florida's McGuire Center (MGCL), which houses the largest collection of *Hesperia* in North America. Phylogenetic methods will largely follow (Wang et al.), using maximum likelihood and coalescent-based tree inference methods adapted for RAD loci allowing for a better understanding of the evolutionary history of the genus.

Goal (2)—Conduct population genetics analyses to understand population connectivity and genetic structure within *H. dacotae, H. ottoe,* and *H. leonardus montana.* *Hypothesis: H0:* There is no difference in population connectivity and genetic diversity throughout time and space. *HA:* Due to loss of suitable habitat and shrinking population sizes, population connectivity and genetic diversity have decreased over time and space. *Methods:* A minimum of 8 specimens from historic populations (population ranges that will be determined by historical records; see Goal 3) will be sequenced using RADseq[9]. The majority of the specimens will be obtained from the MGCL, which has hundreds of pinned specimens collected across multiple populations over time for each of the endangered species examined in this study. For current populations, permits will be obtained with the help of PIs A. Kawahara and J. Daniels at the MGCL, who have histories of working with rare and endangered butterflies, and A. Warren (MGCL Collections Manager), a skipper expert

ESSAY #39: "NSF GRFP—BUTTERFLIES" (CONTINUED)

familiar with the remaining populations. Following the methods outlined in Saarinen *et al.*[10] on the endangered skipper *O. poweshiek*, skippers will be non-lethally sampled by removing a leg and released. Samples will be RAD sequenced and analyzed to find population connectivity and genetic diversity between these populations over time and space utilizing the program STRUCTURE[11] following a recent study[12].

Goal (3)—Conduct ecological niche modeling to identify factors potentially linked to decline for *H. dacotae, H. ottoe,* and *H. leonardus montana.* Hypothesis: *H0:* Climatic, land-use, and agricultural covariates will have no effect on distribution over time and space. *HA:* Increasing extreme temperatures, decreasing suitable habitat coverage and connectivity, and increasing pesticide use will correlate with distribution over time and space. *Methods:* A comprehensive dataset revising the historic and current distribution of the three *Hesperia* species will be constructed, consisting of all available data from digitized natural history collections, citizen scientists, and federal and state agencies, as well as the 846 specimen records available for these species online on Symbiota. These data will be standardized, curated, and aggregated following the methods outlined in a previous paper that I co-authored, Belitz *et al.*[13], and used to identify individual populations. The coordinates of these populations will be imported into ArcGIS[14] and used to construct historic and current distribution maps of the endangered species. Conservation areas, determined by the newly constructed maps, will be identified and selected for ecological niche modeling. Climatic variables, land use variables, and agricultural variables will be evaluated using data readily available from online national databases. Models will be developed using maximum entropy modeling in Maxent[15].

Intellectual Merit: This study seeks to show the utility of museum specimens and digitized data to answer ecological and evolutionary questions about species that are endangered, and potentially rapidly declining. It will be among the first to utilize digitized data from Symbiota to conduct historical biogeographic analyses. I believe it will encourage future studies to utilize these digital data for studies of conservation concern, while promoting digitization of museum specimens. The ADBC LepNet project[16] is currently generating millions of Lepidoptera records, but only a few studies have been published utilizing these records[13].

All sequence data will be uploaded onto GenBank, greatly increasing the current available data for *Hesperia,* which currently has 139 entries (110 from one species, *H. comma*). The tree from Goal (1) will serve as a baseline for understanding species-level relationships and trait evolution. This study will gather data that may have direct and indirect applications for the conservation of endangered taxa (Goals 2 and 3). The aggregated dataset and historic distribution maps constructed in Goal (3) will not only be made openly accessible via Symbiota, they will also be used to evaluate variables that may have contributed to these species' decline and lead to more informed conservation practices.

different, because that takes away from your intellectual merit if they believe the project is impossible or that you don't really understand what you are talking about. I would also recommend submitting a little earlier than the deadline, because the computer system has had issues in the past with too many people trying to submit at the last minute on the deadline. I would also triple check your transcripts and make sure that they are the correct ones and that all of them are there since I talked to two people who were disqualified because of errors with their transcripts."

ESSAY #39: "NSF GRFP—BUTTERFLIES" (CONTINUED)

Broader Impacts: I will recruit undergraduates from the University of Florida (UF) to assist me in this research with techniques such as sequencing, specimen digitization, and curation of museum specimens and digital data. I will actively search for underrepresented groups in science including women, people with low income, and first-generation college students through programs like the UF's McNair program. Since data generated from citizen science activities will play an important role in understanding the biogeography of *Hesperia*, this study provides an opportunity to unite the public to help answer questions about well-loved species. Social media platforms will be used to disseminate information about this project and provide information on collecting useful data through apps like iNaturalist. Utilizing my skills to develop educational programs (see personal statement), I plan to work with the McGuire Center to create student-led teaching platforms to educate students about butterfly ecology, evolution, and conservation, centered around poorly studied groups like skippers. The program will allow students to become involved in citizen science, and train them how to use biodiversity-related apps to capture data that can inform this project and future studies.

References:

1. van Nieukerken *et al.* 2011. Zootaxa 3148;
2. Toussaint *et al.* 2018. BMC Evolutionary Biology 18:101;
3. Warren *et al.* 2009. Systematic Entomology 34;
4. Xerces Society Red List;
5. Swengel *et al.* 2011. J Insect Conserv 2011. 15;
6. Wahlberg *et al.* PLoS ONE 8(11): e80875;
7. Drummond *et al.* 2007. BMC Evol. Biol.;
8. Johns *et al.* 2018. Proc. R. Soc. B 285:20181047;
9. Pritchard *et al.* 2000. Genetics 155;
10. Saarinen *et al.* Insect Conserv 2016. 9;
11. Drummond *et al.* 2007. BMC Evol. Biol.;
12. Halbritter, D.A. *et al.* Ecol. Evol. In Review;
13. Belitz *et al.* Biodiversity Data Journal 6: e29081;
14. ESRI 2013. Version 10.2;
15. Phillips *et al.* 2006. Ecol. Model. 190;
16. Seltmann *et al.* 2017. Zootaxa 4247.

ESSAY #40: "CHILD AND ADOLESCENT CLINICAL PSYCHOLOGY"

Statement of Purpose, Martina Greene

Question: "What influences in children result in happy adults?"

In my experiences as a preprofessional psychological worker, I have adopted a working hypothesis that the majority of outpatient-treatable mental health problems stem from negative childhood experiences. These negative experiences are overwhelmingly traceable to influential adults in the patient's past, primarily parental figures and teachers.

When we were children, my father used to get my sister and me to stand in front of a mirror and say affirmations to ourselves. It didn't matter what we said, as long as it was positive. He did not make us stand in front of the mirror and say nice things to ourselves; he jumped around and coached us and encouraged us until we did this almost every morning as a matter of getting up. My family provided warmth, fair and consistent discipline, and a true feeling of secure, inclusive boundaries separating us (the family) from the greater society in which we lived.

Due to the juxtaposition of my own experiences and the experiences of others, I have long been quite interested in familial and educational influences on the development of children's adjustment. Although it has faced some public ridicule in the past, my own area of greatest interest is self-esteem: Where does it come from? How do we get it? How can we repair it after assaults against the factors that engender it?

I am particularly interested in resiliency and the development of self-esteem in late childhood, puberty, and adolescence. I have always been interested in children, and I have consistently and diligently prepared myself to become a specialist in child and adolescent clinical psychology. In addition to the details in my CV, I would like to address three major influences on my career direction:

(1) When I was at the University of Massachusetts–Amherst (UMass), I had the good fortune to work with Dr. M. Burke, dean of social sciences and founder and executive director of the Farm School. Dr. Burke is an inspiring professor, and he encouraged me to pursue my interest in the internal and external influences on socioemotional development. He accepted a proposal of mine to launch an experimental class at the Farm School to test teaching techniques. The program had the working title of "Testing Models of Self-Esteem Training in an Elementary Class of Girls and Boys: Toward Developing Applied Techniques for Teachers." I was the teacher, with free rein to develop and run the class.

(2) As a psychological worker with Boston Free Psychological Services, I was intake counselor for a very diverse and multicultural incoming patient population. In this position, I was the very first contact many self-referrals had with a mental health services organization. I got a feel for my clinical aptitude, and how I might enjoy clinical services. I was able to establish a quick rapport with patients, and

Clinical psychology programs are extremely competitive. Many are statistically much harder to get into than your average medical school. The programs look for psychology research and any kind of experience in a mental health clinical setting. Often an interim degree, such as a master's in developmental or child or counseling psychology, is the key. This candidate did everything right, and then wrote about it well.

Be sure to mention key professors by name.

ESSAY #40: "CHILD AND ADOLESCENT CLINICAL PSYCHOLOGY" (CONTINUED)

gain their trust and cooperation. I was lauded by the staff psychologists for my skills in triage and assessment, and my ability to get an accurate and complete psychological history from patients. My success with and enjoyment of this position was a major influence on my resolve to pursue clinical psychology concurrent with my interest in developmental psychology.

(3) While I have always respected the integrity of psychology as a science, I must credit Dr. M. Kowalski of the graduate program in psychology at Boston University (BU) for giving me a solid grounding in experimental methodology. Although I had a working knowledge of experimental methods, and I had certainly designed and executed a number of experiments in psychology, over the last two years I have developed a passion for correct methods. In my clinical career, I may not have to design many original research projects, but my increased understanding of methodology has influenced all my thinking about psychology and has especially improved my ability to critique the research I read in journals.

This is a good way to deal with a rough start to an academic career. Let the reader know that the grades that count are good, and explain your rationale.

Finally, I would like to address the issue of my academic career. As you have my transcripts, you can clearly see that I was not especially serious in my first few years as an undergraduate at UMass, and you can also see that I have improved dramatically. I have done quite well in my master's program here at BU, and I expect to continue or exceed this performance in your program.

This is an excellent example of reductionism.

My eventual goals are to divide my time between (a) clinical outpatient treatment of children and adolescent patients, (b) program development and consulting with schools and institutions on resiliency, specifically development of parental and educational practices that enhance it, and development of treatment programs that repair it, and (c) teaching at the university level on developmental and clinical psychology areas.

Predict your own success, as a graduate student and as a practicing professional.

I am confident of my ability to excel in your program academically, and to be an effective and valuable clinical psychologist both in practice and in consulting roles. I would like to think that I am the type of candidate that would be a good representative of your program.

ESSAY #41: "FROM ARRANGED MARRIAGE TO MOLECULAR BIOLOGY"

The Prompt: "Why do you wish to pursue this course of study and how does it relate to your ultimate career goals?"

Words such as "impossible" and "no" once signaled definite boundaries to me, but experiences over the last few years have drastically changed my view and action when such words are now directed at me. In Guyana, my native country, a good daughter does what she's told. For a young girl in much of the developing world, there is little choice. At eighteen, soon after high school, I was told that I would be married and school was therefore unnecessary; I was pressured into marriage at nineteen. Two years later, living in the United States, I decided it was time to pursue a college degree. My spouse declared that my place was in the home and that I was not allowed to attend college; the next day I walked into my local community college. For the first time, I stepped over a clear boundary and stepped into a world where I knew I belonged. Now, words such as "impossible" and "no" signal an opportunity to test boundaries and discover. In this new world at the University of Akron, it is difficult not to discover and become interested in polymers.

This essay gives an excellent example of mixing the personal into the academic. A little personal goes a long way, however. This is a profound story, but she doesn't belabor it. She gets on to the science pretty quickly. This is the right way to do it. Personal history, no matter how dramatic, is the spice, a bit of flavor, but the heart of the meal is the academics.

This interest prompted me to design an independent study, under the direction of Dr. C. M. Turner, to investigate the feasibility of biodegradable plastics as a current alternative to nonbiodegradable plastics and the financial and environmental cost of underutilization of the recycling process. Following this, I had the good fortune of being selected for the NSF-REU program at the Maurice Morton Institute of Polymer Science at the University of Akron. In this program, under the guidance of Dr. C. Pugh, I pursued research with the working title "Synthesis and Thermotropic Behavior of Polynorbornenes with Laterally Attached Mesogens." This project seeks to investigate methods for regulating and transforming mesophases exhibited by liquid crystalline polymers through self-organization and self-assembly upon the mixing of complementary monomers via electron-donor-acceptor interactions. Upon completion of the REU program I decided to continue to work on this project for my senior honors thesis. The synthesis of the monomers, as shown in the Scheme 1 below, has allowed me to gain significant experience in standard Schlenk and drybox techniques, nuclear magnetic resonance spectroscopy, differential scanning calorimetry, polarized optical microscopy, and gel permeation chromatography.

There may not be a study that proves this, but it is my theory that students who successfully mix the personal and the academic get into better programs than their grades and scores would predict.

You know what I love about this essay most of all? She never says one word about what happened to the husband.

ESSAY #41: "FROM ARRANGED MARRIAGE TO MOLECULAR BIOLOGY" (CONTINUED)

Scheme 1

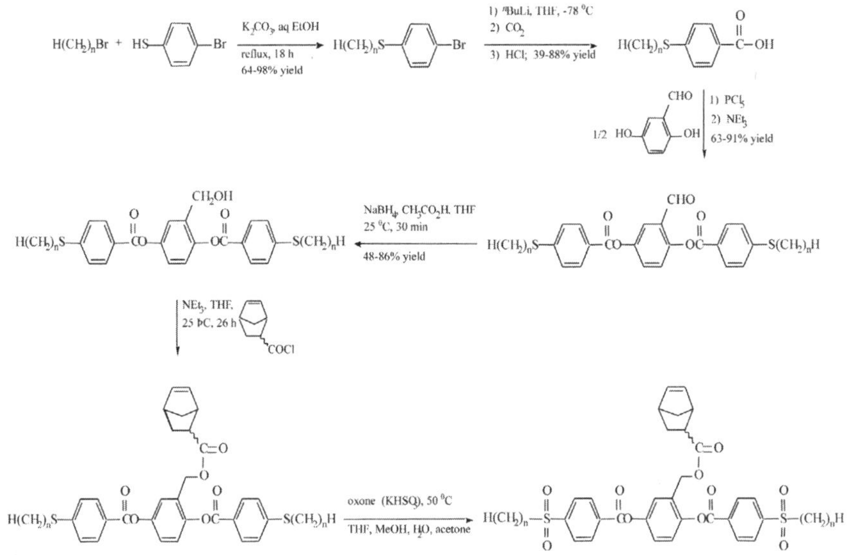

Through the REU program and the Ronald E. McNair Postbaccalaureate Achievement Program, programs designed to prepare students for graduate research opportunities, I have had many opportunities to attend academic meetings and present this data (see attached CV). My laboratory experience has also been enhanced through specialized training in infrared, fluorescence, and UV/VIS spectroscopy, gas chromatography/mass spectrometry, high-performance liquid chromatography, and atomic absorption.

Providing a laundry list of bench, lab, or technical skills is prudent. Don't assume they'll infer such skills from your projects.

For the last five years, I've worked as a research aide in the laboratory of Dr. D. Stinner conducting basic research into the availability of nutrients to crops from soil for the Ohio Food, Farm, Education, Research (OFFER) program, with the purpose to conduct research and education activities in support of Ohio's organic farming community. Under Dr. Stinner, I have gained experience in spectrophotometric analysis of nutrient content of soil extracts along with additional supporting information as to soil sample moisture, organic matter pools, combustion analysis, mass determination on a micro and macro scale, and nutrient lability. Other responsibilities include the training and supervision of graduate and undergraduate students in laboratory methods, quality control and assurance aspects, inventory management, and maintenance of laboratory solutions. I have also had the opportunity, with the guidance of Dr. L. Phelan, to design a method to analyze protein fraction content in

ESSAY #41: "FROM ARRANGED MARRIAGE TO MOLECULAR BIOLOGY" (CONTINUED)

grain using spectrophotometry and to further test samples for amino acid content utilizing GC/MS methods. This new process has subsequently been used by others within the department for such analysis.

With this combined research experience, I feel well prepared for graduate studies at the University of Oregon. Through these experiences, I've also realized that graduate education will be transformative and that my interests will develop and change as I engage in graduate classes. My experience so far has resulted in a deep interest in the concepts of self-assembly. I perceive a match in Dr. G. Richmond's research into the molecular processes occurring at water/phospholipid monolayer interface and the biological importance of these processes. I am also interested in Dr. K. Doxsee's research into phase- and shape-selective assembly of solid-state materials from small molecule precursors and developing a green chemistry undergraduate curriculum. I hope to have the opportunity to explore these interests at the University of Oregon.

Upon the completion of my graduate studies, in what I hope will be the minimum time, I hope to enter a career in academics and research with an emphasis on teaching. Serving as a teacher after graduating high school, I was fortunate to be selected by the chemistry teacher (my former teacher) to teach her General Certificate Examination Advanced level (GCE "A" level), a British examination covering the equivalent of the first two to three years of college in specific subject areas, when she was unable to do so. I felt honored to be the first teacher of my level to be selected to take complete control of a GCE "A" level chemistry class; historically teachers of my level taught only the third through fifth form (grades seven through ten). My life experiences have left me with a very strong desire to be not just a chemistry teacher, but to provide young students with the confidence and tools to wisely investigate, develop, and test the boundaries of their ideas in both science and life.

The interest this program gives to education, with the opportunities for students to intern at neighboring colleges, along with the outstanding faculty, assures me there is a match between what I hope to achieve and what the graduate chemistry program at the University of Oregon offers. In addition, I look forward to living in Oregon; its mild weather and amazing natural attractions will be additional and welcomed benefits.

Mentioning, briefly, that you are attracted to the locale of the targeted institution is a good idea, especially if it is far away.

You may think that once you get into medical school your career is set. Not so. Medical doctors must compete vigorously for residencies and fellowships. This essay was used as part of a successful application for a residency in otolaryngology, at *fifty-to-one odds*.

When professors or other mentors have encouraged you or commended your skills, be sure to mention them. Also, refer to supporting documentation submitted with your application.

Predict your own success. This is not bragging. It's confidence based on self-knowledge and an understanding of the challenges ahead.

ESSAY #42: "OTOLARYNGOLOGY"

Personal Statement for Residency in Otolaryngology

Otolaryngology attracted me for three main reasons. First, my father recently retired as director of the Boston Center for Hearing and Speech. Through his involvement in speech pathology and audiology, I've been exposed to some aspects of otolaryngology all my life. Second, I'm interested in the opportunity to practice with all ages of patients, from children to the elderly. Third, I am drawn by the combination of medical and surgical practice.

I've done very well in school, both as an undergraduate at MIT and as a medical student at [name withheld]. Last year I was awarded one of the two Lange Book awards for outstanding scholastic achievement. I also have significant undergraduate awards for scholarship (see CV for listings).

Research is an aspect of graduate medical training for which I have both an interest and a sound background. This summer I was a research assistant to Drs. S. McQuown and T. A. Cook in a study on the effects of liposuction on porcine fat cell populations. While at MIT, I learned well the investigative thinking of basic research, with experience in biochemistry, cell biology, and histology. During my last year, I completed a senior honors thesis involving the laboratory investigation of protein-folding mechanisms: "Deamidation of Glutamine and Asparagine Residues: An Approach to the Study of Protein Folding."

I find working with my hands quite satisfying. For the last seven years, I have supported myself in part by cleaning and repairing microscopes at colleges, universities, and research centers throughout the greater metropolitan area. During my surgical rotation at Good Samaritan Hospital, I was encouraged by two of the attending surgeons, who remarked that I showed surprising facility for surgery for one so early in a medical career (see letters of recommendation).

In addition to these technical and academic facilities, I am able to interact with and enjoy a great spectrum of people; this is one of my strongest personality traits. I am that doctor who knows the technicians' and orderlies' names, the names of their children, and where they went on vacation last year. I find this helps with team cohesion, but really this just comes naturally to me.

I believe I have the skills (academic, social, and manual) and the interest to excel in the field of otolaryngology. The time ahead of me will be exciting. I look forward to the discovery and the challenge of my chosen career.

ESSAY #43: "CARDIOLOGY"

Statement of Purpose, Cardiology Residency

I am currently completing my third-year internal medicine residency program at Presbyterian Hospital, where I have been exposed to their cardiology service. This of course includes experience with critically ill patients, and also includes a transplant service. We have referrals of patients with all types of chronic heart conditions, and we have addressed the moral and therapeutic problems associated with critical organ transplant cases.

Like essay #42, this is a residency essay. It helps to have a combination of outstanding academic preparation and clinical skill.

My first interest in cardiology results from my assessment that it is a "rational" subspecialty. I have always enjoyed the classical "hard" sciences such as physics and physiology because they make sense to me. These principles apply directly to cardiology. What appeals to me is the excitement of working in this area, with an opportunity to make rapid decisions according to specifiable formulae, with a critical impact on a patient's status. Needless to say, it is quite satisfying to see observable improvement as a result of one's actions.

My second interest in the subspecialty comes from my appreciation of the diversity of cases and treatments available. I have always been good with my hands, including success in trades work (carpentry and amateur auto mechanics). I feel I could deliver the reason, diagnostic sense, and mechanical finesse required to excel in the field. I would relish the opportunity to use such a collection of diverse skills in one disciplinary area.

Third, I have been particularly impressed by the versatility demonstrated by the cardiologists whom I have met to date. They were skillful not only in a broad variety of cardiac problems, but also in all their responsibilities as internists. The high degree of acumen and skill which I have witnessed in the cardiology staff suggests to me that a special type of person is attracted to this field and that their training must shape these individuals into highly skilled medical professionals.

It doesn't hurt to know the latest trend in your specialty and to be laudatory about the field's professionals.

Finally, I view cardiology as one of the more vital subspecialties (no pun intended). I feel that we are poised for a period of continuing rapid advancement in both diagnostic and therapeutic methods. So far I am particularly interested in invasive treatments, e.g., thrombolytic therapy, coronary angioplasty, and valvuloplasty. Whether or not invasive treatments continue their great advances, the field will continue to have a bright future, and will continue to be the preferred area for those of us who want to advance our knowledge and skills throughout our careers.

I complete my current residency in June. In the meantime, the Technical University Berlin has awarded me a stipend to perform clinical research on ischemic mitral insufficiency at the German Heart Center in West Berlin. I expect to have the opportunity to become involved in clinical drug trials as well. I strongly believe in the importance of research, not only to investigate specific problems and questions, but to become a more well-rounded professional.

ESSAY #43: "CARDIOLOGY" (CONTINUED)

This is the magic trilogy: practice, research, teach.

I previously had the opportunity to complete an elective at the German Heart Center. I have found that the exchange of experience with colleagues abroad demands that one reexamine one's experiences closely. Cross-cultural study of medicine remains a strong interest of mine.

My immediate goals are to complete a fellowship in an academically stimulating environment, to be able to participate in the ongoing development of the science of cardiology, and to gain experience in clinical management.

My medium-term goal is to combine clinical practice with research and to teach at a medical center affiliated with a medical school. I know from experience that the best way to learn and keep learning is to teach as well.

My long-term goal is to contribute directly to the advance of cardiology as a clinical science for the ultimate benefit and well-being of patients.

I appreciate your considering this application, and I hope this statement has helped you to make your decision about the fit between my background and this medical and academic specialty. I look forward to visiting your program and meeting all of you personally.

ESSAY #44: "DECISION SCIENCES"

Most people raise at least one eyebrow when they hear that I study mathematics, psychology, and philosophy, and hope to pursue a PhD in decision sciences. But the fact is, I've had a fascination with schemes, cheats, and ways to take advantage of systems for a long time. These interests have led to my passion for the interdisciplinary study of game theory, decision making, and moral philosophy; specifically, how people make decisions, how they *should* make decisions, and why the answers to these questions differ.

In my view, game theory studies what people in strategic situations do when their goals have already been explicitly decided. The study of decision making, on the other hand, illuminates how people do and should make choices between means given ambiguous ends. And finally, moral philosophy questions what our goals should be in the first place. This insight (or belief), together with my passion for the study of decision making and teaching in general, has led me to Carnegie Mellon University's PhD program in social and decision sciences.

In particular, the opportunity to use game theory to better understand real-world behavior, under the direction of Profs. R. Weber and J. Miller, is a thrilling prospect for me. I am particularly interested in studying how artificial adaptive agent models can accurately describe and predict real behavior and how they do not. I am also very excited by the possibility of taking behavioral economics with Prof. G. Loewenstein and human judgment with Prof. R. Dawes.

The core of my attraction to social and decision sciences at Carnegie Mellon University is my continuing fascination with strategic behavior and decision making within systems. Several experiences and courses have furthered this interest and are outlined below.

+ Last summer, I was selected to participate in the Research Experience for Undergraduates Program funded by the National Science Foundation. I worked with five other students under the direction of Prof. R. Muncaster at the University of Illinois at Urbana–Champaign. (Reference letter provided.) The overall topics were evolutionary game theory and social networks; specific topics included Markov chains, game space manifolds, and decision dynamics. Pursuing my interest in decision making and error, I produced an independent project studying the effects of anticipatory error on decision making in normal form games. I found that recognition of an opponent's chance of making mistakes can lead to new, stable equilibria that are not Nash equilibria of the original game. Upon the recommendation of Prof. Weber, I explored the relationship between my work and quantal response equilibria and have continued this project as my mathematics thesis entitled "Error-Awareness and Equilibria in Normal Form Games."
+ A short internship with a labor mediator for the State of California illuminated the importance of conscious and subconscious strategic social

It is my contention that most students customize too far down in their essays. Notice how this writer customizes near the top, so that readers know he wrote this essay just for them. This is clearly not another cut-and-paste essay, with a few faculty members mentioned at the bottom as an afterthought. This is the level and type of customization that gets students into elite programs.

ESSAY #44: "DECISION SCIENCES" (CONTINUED)

This is an outstanding demonstration of knowledge of the major players, contemporary and historical, in a targeted field. When you demonstrate that you know the theories and theorists, you demonstrate you are ready for graduate study.

behavior. Conducting "shuttle diplomacy" between union headquarters and a county human resources department, I gained a greater appreciation for the realities of decision making—from the limits of calculating ability to emotional, tactical "mistakes" and their unintended benefits. This experience strengthened my interest in negotiation and desire to pursue further research at the graduate level.

+ While studying at the London School of Economics (LSE) during my junior year abroad, I took a yearlong course in Evolution and Social Behavior, taught by Dr. C. Badcock. (Reference letter provided.) The topic that I found most interesting was the psychology of cooperation. In particular, Cosmides and Tooby's ideas of mental modules and cheat detection mechanisms continue to influence my interest in decision making within groups.

+ Another relevant course from my year at the LSE was Philosophy of Economics, which included the study of rationality and decision paradoxes. In particular, I was intrigued by Selton's three-level decision making of routine, imagination, and reasoning as an explanation of his Chain Store Paradox. Though he views this solution as a severe threat to game theory at large, I see it as turning the issue of common knowledge versus bounded rationality into its own game of incomplete information. That is, the level at which a decision is being made can be viewed as analogous to the hand that a poker player holds. Also integral to the course were theories of justice such as Brian Barry's justice as fairness versus justice as mutual advantage. I hope to further pursue such perceptions of justice in the context of strategic decisions.

+ Currently in my senior year at Swarthmore College, I am taking Thinking, Judgment, and Decision Making taught by Prof. B. Schwartz. (Reference letter provided.) What excites me most about the subject is the identification of systematic loopholes in human thought and discovering how they might be manipulated and remedied.

Based on these experiences and courses, I am especially excited about the prospect of pursuing further research in the Department of Social and Decision Sciences in the areas of artificial adaptive agent modeling, strategic error making, and the shortcomings and refinements of behavioral economic models.

My long-term professional goal is to obtain a challenging research and teaching position in the field of decision making and behavior. Though I may find this in a business school professorship, I also am passionate about excellence in undergraduate education. In this context, I would be equally excited by the prospect of teaching undergraduates in psychology, economics, or other disciplines relevant to the interdisciplinary study of game theory and decision making.

ESSAY #45: "AFRICAN KASHMIRI"

Letter of Interest—African American Studies

I was born in Arusha, Tanzania, on the slopes of Mt. Kilimanjaro. My father was a son of a Kashmiri immigrant. My grandfather came to Tanzania as a cheap laborer for the British colony. My mother is a daughter of a Segeju woman (Tanzania coastal indigenous group). As a child of these two great parents, I had an interesting childhood that continues to inform my personal and academic life. The union of my parents, my mother having been an "African," caused a split in my father's family. Furthermore, in school and public areas, my fellow Tanzanians called me a "Hindu," while I am an African and a Muslim. And the Indian Diaspora community derogatorily referred to us as "half castes." As a child, I could not grasp these racial and identity issues; it is only when I came to America that I seriously began analyzing and questioning my childhood experience. I have learned that the African American experience in North America is a heroic narrative that speaks of similar quests for identity, belonging, and ownership for the past five hundred years. This is one of the many reasons I want to pursue a graduate course in the African and African American Studies Department at Harvard. The African American experience, past and present, is a useful model in explaining a wide array of issues such as identity, politics, and ownership in other countries of the world. Harvard's African and African American Studies Department is an environment that can personally empower me to explain my social and historical bits and pieces through the study of the Black experience.

It is important to know the level of competition you are facing when applying to elite programs. This young student has more accomplishments than most of us could fit into a lifetime.

My life experience as a person belonging to either the African or Kashmiri side has offered me a unique perspective to life. Therefore, I am endowed with, or have developed through no particular effort of my own, the ability to look at issues in many different perspectives. I can be neutral (invoking neither African nor Kashmiri side), I can take a side (invoking African, Segeju, Kashmiri, or the Muslim side, etc.), and I can also employ the meshed perspective (invoking all the parts). The permutations of my perspectives are endless as they are continuously enriched through experiences and age. For example, I grew up with an exiled Black Panther community in Arusha, Tanzania, where I learned about American history and its people away from America and especially from an exiled American/highly politicized point of view. This ability of employing multiple perspectives on issues resembles the call in academic settings for a multidisciplinary approach. I am interested to join African and African American Studies at Harvard because it has a long tradition of scholarship and research on issues of culture and race that I am interested to explore. W. E. B. Du Bois, who was also of mixed ancestry such as mine and whose life reflects some of my own experiences, was educated at Harvard. Training at Harvard will equip me with tools that will transform my experiences and passion into practical and tangible outcomes such as research skills, networks, and resources.

Being a unique candidate always garners interest from reviewers. So many candidates seem all the same to admissions readers. But not this one.

ESSAY #45: "AFRICAN KASHMIRI" (CONTINUED)

Harvard has a lot to offer in raising my intellectual capacity as a critical scholar of African culture and experience through analytical training, research, and networking with like-minded scholars. While at Harvard, I would like to explore the evolution of a poetic performance called *Mashairi ya Kuimbana* (poetic form of criticism) practiced in the 1940s in Tanga, into a newer form known as *Mipasho,* practiced in commercial centers such as Dar es Salaam. Specifically, I would like to analyze the performance of two female artists,[1] who are contemporary exponents of this form in Tanzania. This exploration will also look at how Mipasho embodies social and political criticism. The research will analyze both the poetic texts and performance aspects of Mipasho to paint a coherent picture of this dynamic cultural form. Lastly, I would like to make a comparative analysis between Hip Hop's "dissing" and "beef" phenomena with Mipasho. I believe the faculty, peers, and resources at Harvard are best equipped to transform my interest into an exciting and rewarding research experience. While at Harvard, I would like to work with Prof. William Julius Wilson, who is an expert on youth culture, and politics of race. Working with Prof. Francis Irele, known and respected expert on postcolonialism and cultural renaissance, will guide my research with appropriate theoretical tools. Additionally, I would like to seek the guidance of Prof. Marla Fredrick; her expertise on religion, culture, and gender issues will be crucial in giving my research the appropriate academic nuances. A diverse and resourceful faculty body at the African and African American Studies Department will provide me the right place to shape and nurture my intellectual faculties. At Harvard, I expect to learn a lot from students and faculty members and at the same time, I hope to share some of my own experiences.

Note how he mentions specific professors he would like to work with, and shows that he has more than passing knowledge of their areas of expertise.

I have been fortunate to conduct research under the guidance of Dr. A. Julien, funded by the project on African Expressive Traditions Grant on Mashairi ya Kuimbana (mentioned above). The research entailed the audio-video recording of the poetic texts as recalled by the few remaining exponents of the form. In addition to the earlier research, which was well received by faculty and my fellow researcher, I conducted additional research on Mipasho, the contemporary form of poetic criticism practiced in urban centers of East Africa. Specifically, the research looked at the enduring relevancy of poetic criticism forms in airing grievances. This research was guided by Prof. Adesokan and generously funded by the Ronald E. McNair Scholars Program at Indiana University, Bloomington. The research was presented at numerous academic meetings and conferences (see attached CV for complete list).

It is not enough for me to be purely a scholar, with no direct impact on this world. I have put my background and interests into action when I cofounded Aang Serian, a global NGO that works on preservation of indigenous knowledge. Aang Serian is of diverse ethnic, gender, religious, and international composition and works in

1 Hadija Kopa and Nasma Khamis are thought to be bitter enemies.

ESSAY #45: "AFRICAN KASHMIRI" (CONTINUED)

mainly three areas of development: appropriate education, audio-video recording studio, and fair-trade initiatives. Aang Serian's education program, which currently runs a secondary school in Masailand, Tanzania, has created a unique and innovative educational model for the indigenous communities of Tanzania. This model was cited by UNEP as a model for Africa as it combines Tanzania's national syllabus with Aang Serian's indigenous knowledge curriculum. This educational model aims to address these communities' immediate needs, systematically record the indigenous knowledge, and instill confidence and identity among the indigenous youth. I intend to interest Harvard's faculty and student body to volunteer and conduct research in Tanzania, an engagement that will enrich and impact the lives of both parties, I am hoping.

Besides the preservation of indigenous knowledge through creation of an innovative model, I helped cofound a community recording studio (now a radio station[2] in Arusha, Tanzania) and a media center.[3] The objectives of the recording studio and the media center are to encourage Tanzanian youth to use media technology to voice, critique, store, and disseminate their cultural heritage and personal voices. The community recording studio, a space for underrepresented youths, has been an enormous success. Some of the members of our media and recording studio have attained international reputation such as the Xplastaz,[4] a music group that fuses Hip Hop with Swahili/Masai tribal chants. A graduate of our media center won a National Geographic grant to create a documentary on the disappearing rock paintings of central Tanzania. I had an opportunity to speak about my experiences and projects at Harvard last May and received positive feedback from students and faculty members. I have kept my connections with Harvard ever since working with the project on African Hip Hop as an advisor and contributor of audio-visual resources. These are some of the experiences and projects that I would like to continue.

Harvard's innovative teaching experience and research facilities offer me an unparalleled academic and personal opportunity. Attaining an education at Harvard will not only answer some of my fundamental personal questions but will offer me an opportunity to serve my people who have invested so much in me. In addition, I am looking forward to being in the Cambridge area to reunite with friends and colleagues. After my education, I intend to return to Tanzania to work as a professor, lecturer, consultant, and as a professional writer.

Thank you for your attention to this material, and I am deeply grateful for your consideration.

This candidate uses footnotes appropriately, which means sparingly and only to keep citations from disturbing the flow of the narrative.

2 Provided by generous assistance from Prometheus Radio Project at www.prometheusradio.org.
3 See www.asdrum.org for further details on the project.
4 www.xplastaz.com for further details on the music group.

The student who wrote this essay told me she thought she came across to the admissions counselors as ridiculous. She said she earned an interview with this essay, and she won over the committee with her sense of purpose and commitment to her goal. Once again, admissions counselors are drawn to people who they think will succeed whether they are admitted or not. This candidate certainly leaves that impression.

ESSAY #46: "THE RADIO LADY"

Statement of Purpose for Graduate School of Business

Radio has been my passion for as long as I can remember. I was one of those high school kids who sat by the radio waiting for the magic touch tones to dial in and win; my fascination with the medium was kindled.

My college radio station, WXX at [major university], actually let me on the air. I'd get up for my 3 a.m. shift to play the immortal Dead Kennedys to insomniacs in the greater metro area. An internship at a "real world" station substituted for my senior thesis, and launched me into professional radio.

In the seven-plus years that I've been out in the working world, my objective has not changed: I want to own my own radio station. Maybe a station group, even a network.

I often try to analyze what it is about this medium that excites me so much. The immediacy of it. The power to reach people, relay a message, get under people's skins. As a work environment, I adore the wacky people attracted to radio. The casual type of workplace. The fact that a station is a small business where creativity can flourish, and one person can make an impact. And as an institution, a radio station can and should be an integral part of its community. Its voice, its friend.

And despite all the predictions to the contrary, radio is still alive and well and thriving. Prices of stations remain sky-high. Radio is omnipresent. As an industry, there is a lot of action—more and more stations are becoming increasingly specialized—all-talk, all-sports, all-Elvis? Is satellite going to take over the world? Is free digital HD going to more than hold its own? Will a new administration change the joint ownership laws? What is the future of AM radio as young people grow up listening only to FM and EV car manufacturers are threatening to drop the band altogether? There are so many questions, and in my mind, a lot of opportunity for bold thinkers who have the knowledge to make their ideas into reality.

Recently I made a decisive move toward attaining my goal. I became an account executive for a major-market station. I knew that unless I could effectively sell radio, I'd never be able to successfully run a station. Sales is the traditional route to advancement in radio: good salespeople become sales managers who become general managers. I know that if I stick with it, I can rise to the top via this route.

The truth is, I've worked for a good number of general managers who rose through the ranks through the sales department and, frankly, I am not impressed.

This business requires more knowledge than one can acquire by simply climbing the sales ladder. I need to know accounting and finance. If I don't know how to put together a deal, who's going to bankroll my first acquisition? With an increasingly media-intensive market, how can I strategically position my station to garner its share of ad dollars? With all the diverse personalities and egos in a "showbiz" enterprise like a radio station, being a good people manager is essential, but so is

ESSAY #46: "THE RADIO LADY" (CONTINUED)

knowing how to utilize resources and how to streamline an organization. These are just a few of my goals for business school.

I am very impressed by Columbia's diverse offerings in all these areas. I will learn the entrepreneurial skills I need, while having the opportunity to interact with leaders and top students, with interests both similar to and diverse from my own. I hope to take advantage of some of the Graduate School of Journalism's offerings as well. And by staying in New York City, I hope to keep up with my valuable contacts, developed in my years already in this business.

ESSAY #47: "STRIP CLUB CULTURE"

This scholar designed her own undergraduate research project in an environment where field studies might seem daunting. Then she researched graduate programs well enough to identify a program with a bias toward students with undergraduate field studies experience. This is the epitome of a smart application to graduate school. Her interest is not simply admission, but admission to a program where she can excel and gain maximum benefit.

The bouncers at the strip club are beginning to recognize me. I am the woman who comes in with a notepad asking questions but is not interested in a job. I am intrigued by the small but significant population of dancers who use stripping as an economic means of supporting their higher education. They contradict stereotypes regarding both dancers and educated women. These dancers and their ever-increasing business- and professional-class clientele affirm the success of the upscaling campaign that the "Gentlemen's Club" industry has implemented over the past decade. These upscaled strip clubs play out socially relevant concepts such as power, gender, and class in an unusual arena that commodifies sexuality in an increasingly acceptable forum.

I find efforts to alleviate the stigma that has been traditionally associated with patronage and employment in these cultural meeting spaces to be engaging. Gentlemen's clubs are prominently featured in media, appearing in movies and serials with the most tenuous connection to plot development. They raise interesting historical questions regarding their forerunners in the sex industry (such as the burlesque theater) and regarding American culture as well. Ethnographic interview and historical research methods form the basis of my American civilizations honors thesis project (to be completed for presentation this spring).

My American civilizations major has provided me with a versatile background for intellectual inquiry. Since high school, American cultural history has been a substantial part of my intellectual life. My long-standing interest in this field led me to consider becoming a historian. However, I wanted a broad-based foundation in American culture for my undergraduate studies. Therefore, I chose a major with a multidisciplinary approach. My undergraduate training as an American culturalist has been in historical fields and in diverse subjects such as material culture, historical archaeology, anthropology, sociology, women's studies, and American literature.

The transition from American culturalist to American cultural historian became logical to me as I realized both the importance of concentrating on an established theoretical framework, and that many history programs have now embraced a palette of cultural studies. This allows me to have an intellectual home and disciplinary community, which is important for scholarly work beyond the doctoral research project. I will bring my American civilizations training to both the study of American cultural history and to a future career as a professor and researcher. The program that has sparked the most interest in me is the American cultural history concentration within the history program at Johns Hopkins University.

I am very impressed by the helpfulness and enthusiasm of the several professors who spoke with me regarding their own work and the work of other members of the department. Prof. R. Walters described his work and the work of several of his students in twentieth-century popular culture. Having a multidisciplinary background in American culture, I was delighted to learn that the department's approach

ESSAY #47: "STRIP CLUB CULTURE" (CONTINUED)

to courses of study is, as Prof. Walters phrased it, "driven by problems rather than by rigid fields." Prof. Walters also discussed with me the graduate history program's unique mentorship system.

I feel that it is important to develop one's academic career in an environment that has visible and accessible mentors. I greatly value independent research and independent thought—my undergraduate work and the structure of my major coursework attest to this. Nevertheless, I feel fortunate to have had close interactions with several professors—all of whom I would consider academic role models—who helped me to critically evaluate my ideas and my work. I believe that such relationships become even more essential in a doctoral program as one's chosen discipline becomes increasingly specific. My understanding of Johns Hopkins's graduate history program is that these relationships are not only encouraged but also fostered by the department.

Johns Hopkins's history program is known for its rigorous course of study and for its ready inclusion of graduate students into its intellectual community. I think that a strong society of peers is essential in developing one's academic career. All of the professors with whom I spoke described the departmental graduate seminars as engaging forums of intellectual exchange in which both students and faculty participate. Structurally, Johns Hopkins's history program seems to benefit from a close mentorship system and an interactive community of scholarship. I welcome such a learning environment.

Substantively and temporally, my interests in American history have generally led me to the industrial and postindustrial eras. I plan to study cultural history in general and women's history specifically. For these reasons, I particularly look forward to the opportunity to study with Profs. R. Walters and J. N. Brown for their work in twentieth-century topics of political and popular cultural history, respectively, and with Prof. T. Ditz, who discussed with me her work in women's and family history and in cultural history.

My undergraduate work in American civilizations has allowed me to explore my many interests in American culture. I look forward to defining my research and intellectual paths in a more rigorous historical framework. I hope that the committee views my credentials and my interests to be complementary with Johns Hopkins's resources, professors, and focus.

Feel free to quote professors, as long as you do it accurately. Note that the entire rest of the essay deals with the alignment of the targeted graduate program with this candidate's interests.

Note how specific this essay is to this specific, targeted school. The best essays give the impression that the entire essay was written only for this application. They are fully customized, from first to last word.

10

Letters of Recommendation

Your grades, your test scores, your essay, and your letters of recommendation make up the entire body of evidence upon which the admissions committee will base its decision. Each admissions officer will weigh these factors differently, but no matter how they view them, letters of recommendation are one of only four sources of information about you, and thus are vitally important.

Interestingly enough, the more competitive the program, the more the letters count in the final decision-making process. All the finalists for these programs will have outstanding grades, academic preparation, and test scores; the committee will decide based on the essay and letters of recommendation. The less competitive the program, the more likely it is that the committee will be able to make sufficient differentiation from quantitative measures such as grades and scores. In either case, if you are a borderline candidate, your essay and letters of recommendation become even more important. Even one well-thought-out and laudatory letter of recommendation can push you into the admit category, while a handful of lukewarm endorsements can leave you to languish on the wait list or be rejected.

Here are two letters of recommendation. They could be for the same person. Which of these letters do you want?

> *Cecily has asked me for a letter of recommendation and I am happy to provide it. She was in my "Biology Bench Lab Skills" course, and earned one of the few A's that I give in that course. In a lab with 60 students, she was one of only 6 students who earned an A, which places her in the top 10% of students. In this class, students learn a range of skills including preparation of cell and tissue cultures, preparation of slides for microscopy including use of dies and staining techniques, and photography techniques for light microscopy. They learn to isolate and analyze DNA, RNA, and proteins and to use PCR machines. They also observe demonstrations of electron microscopy. They are required to breed and maintain a population of drosophila, and to recreate classical experiments with them. The analytical techniques from the lab include biochemistry, chemistry, microbiology, molecular biology,*

and genetics, as well as general statistics. Cecily's performance in this lab would indicate that she is ready for study at the graduate level, with additional training in whatever specialized techniques would be needed, of course.

Did you learn much about Cecily?

Now look at this letter of recommendation, same Cecily:

In my lab course of 60 students, Cecily stood out right from the beginning. She was inquisitive, asking questions to dig deeper into the science behind the bench lab techniques we were instructing. Most students in this required course are interested in the "how," but Cecily always wanted to understand the "why." She often came early to help set up apparatus, and she was one of the few students who would stay late into the night to repeat protocols and procedures that had not succeeded in the scheduled lab periods. She helped other students become proficient in difficult bench techniques. Perhaps most amazing of all, she found two errors in a lab procedure that was designed by postdocs. The whole lab was failing in an experiment that should have worked easily, and she is the only one who found the two missing steps, alerted me to the problem, and led everyone to success. We have had many discussions about her vision of her future as a researcher. Her zeal for field and bench biology is quite genuine. I predict that she will be an asset to any research team, and go on to be an impressive scientist herself in whatever area that captures her focus.

How can a professor write this second version, when they have 60 students in a lab, semester after semester, all blending together over time? Easy. Cecily helped them remember. And you can help your recommenders remember your uniqueness, too.

There are several strategies for ensuring that your letters of recommendation are outstanding. Look again at the handout on page 40, Getting Fantastic Letters of Recommendation. The first and most obvious strategy is to approach your letter writers at the earliest possible moment. These are busy people; you must be considerate of their other time commitments. Be very clear about when you are going to apply, and get the recommender to agree to *your* deadline; let them know that you would appreciate it if they would post the letter as soon as possible.

Usually you will be asked to declare who your recommenders are on your online application, and the university then emails those recommenders log-in instructions and codes for uploading their letters. Each recommender will submit the letter either by filling in a window or submitting it as an attachment. They usually have to fill out a form, as well. Whenever a letter appears suspicious or unusual, admissions staff will verify that the sender is (a) who they claimed to be, and (b) did in fact write the specific letter in question. *If a recommender has a .edu email address, they should use that address for all communications about letters of recommendation.*

A warm, customized letter that mentions personal ties between the recommender and the targeted school is always better than a letter that is not customized at all. It is far better to have a letter from someone who knows your work well than to have a letter from a famous person who obviously does not know you well at all. Letters from coaches, religious leaders, and politicians may not have any effect, but there are always exceptions. For example, if you have lost all contact with your professors and many years have passed, you will have to get recommendations from people who know you recently. Sit down with them and explain your academic goals, what they could say that would indicate your seriousness, and how, if at all, your recent activities would support your return to studies. Bosses, peers from work, mentors, colleagues from volunteer experiences, and people who know you from your community can be your recommenders in this case. Better yet, however, is to take a couple of classes to show your academic interest, get some recent good grades, and ask those professors for recommendations.

It is your job to prompt your letter writers to actually write and submit the letters on time. How long does it take for faculty and, in some cases, your professional colleagues to write a letter of recommendation? Recommenders generally want two to six weeks to write a letter, and some want even more time. A letter due in a week is considered a rush job. You want to approach your recommenders early in the process. Use the portfolio method; that is, prepare a portfolio to help recommenders do their jobs. See the handout on page 236 for how to prepare that. This is the single most important page in this book. Read that memo and prepare your portfolio for recommenders!

Faculty need dates, accurate names of classes, copies of papers and labs you wrote (even if they just graded that paper a month ago). They need details of the tasks and intellectual contributions you made to projects. Do not just say you "worked on" or "assisted with" something. Those words are too vague. Dig into the details and differentiate between when you performed tasks and when you made more intellectual contributions. If you conceived of a project, that's very different from sitting at a bench and following protocols. Did you write those protocols? Did you capture, enter, analyze, and report data in tables that were adopted into the eventual publication? Did you train and supervise others? The same type of precision is required for nonfaculty recommenders, like a boss or colleague or someone who supervised you at an internship or service experience. Recommenders need those details to write a recommendation for you. The most detailed letters are the most cogent.

Your recommenders need to adopt *your* application deadlines. This is very, very important. If you don't sell your target application deadline to your recommenders, they will submit letters right before the published deadline, thus ruining all your prudent planning. "Dr. Wilson, I am going to have my application to Harvard completely ready by November 1st. The final deadline for this program is December 10th but, if you don't mind, could you submit the letter on or before November 1st?" If you are asking for this commitment several weeks before your adopted deadline, the answer is usually in the affirmative.

Your recommenders *do* want you to bug them. Recommenders tell me that they do not consider it good practice for you to ask for letters and then disappear. You need to gently remind them of their commitment, emphasizing in each interaction your agreed-to deadline. My counsel is to bug them at intervals that are half the distance to the deadline. If you ask for a letter in a month, check in with them two weeks before.

At two weeks, you should send a prompt: "Dr. Wilson, that letter for Harvard is due in two weeks, so it matches up with my application submission. I'm just checking in to make sure that's still going to work for you. Do let me know if you have any questions for me. I truly appreciate your agreeing to write this for me," and so on.

Half of two weeks is one week, so at one week out, you prompt her again: "Dr. Wilson, my letter for Harvard is due in one week. I'm just checking in to remind you. If you have any questions for me, don't hesitate to email or text me and I'll respond right away."

Half of a week is three or four days, so you do it again: "Dr. Wilson, the letter for Harvard is due on Thursday, three days from now. That will be November 1st, and as we discussed back in

September, that's when I'm going to have my application completed and submitted. I am truly grateful for your agreeing to write a letter for me and for submitting it by then," and so on.

After that, I would just follow them around: "Dr. Wilson, that letter of recommendation for Harvard is due today. I'll just stand over here in case you have any questions for me. Enjoy your lunch."

I'm joking but I'm not joking. You need to get your recommenders to agree to and observe *your* deadlines, not the deadlines from the programs. Obviously, if you are applying to ten programs, and they have ten different deadlines, and you have three or four recommenders, this requires a lot of precise communicating.

Many professors try to catch up on their work during long weekends and holidays, so it is a good idea to put a little extra pressure on them right before such breaks, but avoid asking for letters near the end of a semester when faculty are super busy writing and grading exams. Be sure to let a letter writer know if their letter is the last item you need—many schools will not review your application file until it is complete, so turning in your essay and application two months early is of little use if your last letter of recommendation arrives after the deadline.

It may be a good idea to have in mind at least one more recommender than the target school or program requires, as a backup plan. If you have to, ask the admissions coordinator how to swap out a recommender if one fails to deliver. Some candidates just plan on submitting one extra recommendation, just in case, although there is not always a way to submit an extra letter through the application portal. Again, ask the admissions representative. Programs do not become alarmed about one extra letter, but avoid any temptation to send an onslaught of meaningless endorsements. One admissions officer received some twenty letters in favor of one candidate, including one from his pediatrician. "You could tell from the letter," the admissions officer recalled, "that the pediatrician didn't have any better idea why he was writing that letter than we did." One extra letter is usually okay, and requesting one allows your application to be complete as soon as the minimum number is posted. Remember, admissions teams often will not look at an applicant portfolio before it is complete.

• • •

Handout for Faculty

Better Letters of Recommendation

1. Be sure you want to recommend this student.
   + Discuss the student's academic plans and preparation *before* agreeing to write a recommendation.
   + Help the student choose grad programs that match their interests, skill, and preparation.
   + Consider declining some to do a better job on others.
2. Get enough data to do your job. Ask for:
   + Transcripts and/or a list of classes taken in their major,
   + A graded work sample, such as a paper or lab,
   + Their resume or CV with a list of honors and awards,
   + Some idea of what the student would like you to focus on,
   + Letter and recommendation instructions and codes from the target grad school,
   + *The student's deadline, which may not be the same as the school's deadline.*
3. Laundry list basic skills; assume nothing.
   + E.g.: "__________ has command of coherent wave optics, Fourier optics, laser physics, lens design, optical metrology, optics of thin films, paraxial optics, physical optics, and related areas of physics."
   + Include anything you have to say about the student's understanding of research ethics and data handling, if pertinent to the program they're applying to.
4. Describe a particularly successful project.
   + Differentiate tasks the student completed from their intellectual contributions.
   + Find one or more "above and beyond" stories to focus on.
   + Can you frame the candidate as special, out of the ordinary?
   + Include if they were a proctor, TA, RA, tutor, or showed other forms of departmental service and maturity.
5. Get personal when appropriate.
   + Did they overcome adversity?
   + Did they face work, health, family, or other special challenges?
   + You can be a candidate's advocate on these issues, which is more sophisticated than having the student address them.
   + Also, do you enjoy having this student in your classes?

6. Be careful with criticism.

    + A little is okay, in fact, expected, especially if it is a story about skills development; letters with no criticism are not considered credible, *but* letters are overwhelming positive these days. Try using faint praise to convey any reservations, rather than any major, overt criticisms.

7. Close by predicting success.

    + "One of the most promising students I've worked with in recent years."
    + "Razor-sharp mind."
    + "Tremendous potential."
    + "More than adequately prepared."
    + "I am confident that __________ will be an outstanding graduate student and go on to make major contributions in the field through both research and teaching."

8. Love the student? Then take the time to customize.

    + Make every letter a customized effort, not a copy-and-paste project.
    + Mention your own connections to the target departments, when appropriate.
    + Be mindful of each department's approach to the discipline and their match to the student's skills.

Handout for Students

Letters of Recommendation

This is a relationship, not a transaction. I prefer a month's notice, and two weeks is a minimum. I have made exceptions in extraordinary cases (late decision or late discovery of a very attractive option).

I need a portfolio from you with the following contents:

1. A preliminary list of the graduate programs you are considering, and how you differentiate them. Most faculty recommend you apply to two safe schools, two reach schools, and two schools from the middle of the spectrum, more for law and medicine. If you are going to go through the trouble of applying to graduate school, please have a strategy to succeed at the process.
2. A printout of your transcripts.
3. Names of classes we had together, when the classes were, and any special interactions we had in class or out. Please don't assume I will remember.
4. Copies of two or three graded work projects that represent the quality of your work. These can be theses, papers, labs, or write-ups from my classes or others.
5. A rough draft or outline of your personal statement or statement of purpose. If you want help with this, see Donald Asher's *Graduate Admissions Essays* (the bestselling guide to the graduate admissions process).
6. A CV or resume for me, including student activities and volunteer and service experiences, etc. If you have a different CV or resume crafted for submission to graduate schools, I'd like to see that version also.
7. A brief list of what *you* think would be most important for a graduate program to know about you.
8. Clear instructions for submitting the letter. This is now usually handled by the universities you are applying to, but check and be sure. The less secretarial work I have to do, the more effort I can put into your letter itself.
9. *A very clear indication of when you need the letters submitted.* Otherwise, I will assume that anything ahead of the deadline is satisfactory.

After I submit your recommendations, I need two more things:

1. You need to share with me any communiqués from the graduate programs about secondary inquiries, admission offers, wait list notices, funding/support/fellowship/assistantship offers, telephone contacts, meet-and-greet events, and so on. This helps me be a better advisor.
2. I need to know where you decide to go!

These forms provided by Donald Asher from faculty examples. These forms can be modified and used by faculty and staff at any university. This line is all the permission you need.

• • •

You should select your letter writers carefully, using three criteria: Do they know you well enough to write about you in a detailed and persuasive manner? Will they say wonderful things about you? Are they reliable enough to write and post your recommendation in a timely manner? Most schools do not require that all your letter writers be professors; read and follow the school's requirements carefully.

Although it may be hard to resist, avoid those celebrity letter writers who offer letters of recommendation to all comers. For example, a certain politician who lives in San Francisco will write a letter for practically any nonincarcerated Democrat. Well, maybe it would be okay even if you were incarcerated. These letters work better the farther from San Francisco you are, but in California they are viewed with snickers. (For one thing, they are all virtually identical.) Every state has politicians like this, who write such letters on behalf of the sons and daughters of friends and benefactors.

Schools usually prefer that you have letters of recommendation written by employers and professors who have the most intimate knowledge of your work and study habits. A specific letter from your immediate supervisor will carry more weight than a vague letter from someone higher up in the organization who obviously does not know you very well.

Of course, you should select letter writers who will say the most wonderful things about you. Some professors are known for writing letters of recommendation that are timely, well wrought, and successful; you should ask around and discover who they are. Do not assume just because someone is friendly with you that they will write a good letter for you. A professor or supervisor who respects you, no matter how they feel about you personally, is probably the best bet.

Finally, keep in mind that the admissions committee will expect letters from certain key people. If you conducted a senior research project or wrote an honors thesis, the committee will expect a letter from your faculty advisor. If you reported directly to the president at your last company, an MBA admissions committee will expect a letter from that president. However, you may have a good reason to intentionally fail to solicit a letter from one of those people.

When you have your list of preferred writers, ask each of them to tell you honestly what they could say about you in a letter of recommendation. This can be tough, but it is far better to find out that a professor is not able to endorse your candidacy than it is to have your targeted school find this out before you. Sometimes you can negotiate with professors; for example, you might get them to agree not to mention your habit of turning in papers late, and to keep the focus of the letter on the quality of your writing and scholarship. If you feel that someone is less than thrilled to write a letter of recommendation for you, select someone else. A reluctant and tepid "endorsement" can be the kiss of death. And you never, ever, want to get a letter like this next one. It was sent to an acquaintance of mine, a dean of graduate student enrollment at an elite university:

David asked that I write a letter of recommendation for him. I advised him he would be better off to seek a letter from someone else. He insisted. This is the letter.

Sincerely,
Prof. U. Gottalisten

For better or worse, most letters are not customized or are barely customized. The most effective letters are fully customized. So, if you are applying to elite programs, beg for customization. When you show your recommenders your list of schools, provide it as an annotated list; that is, write a full paragraph or more about each program, how it is different, which faculty are attractive, and why and how that matches up with your skills and preparation.

Should you waive your rights?

Letters of recommendation used to be secret testimony. Now, however, you have the right to review every item in your educational files—thanks to the Family Educational Rights and Privacy Act (FERPA), commonly known as the Buckley Amendment. Because this student right made some professors nervous, and because some graduate schools believed that nervous professors may be less than honest and forthcoming, graduate schools have invented a waiver for those rights. On almost every application extant today, you have the opportunity to sign away your rights, or to retain them, and therein lies a dilemma: Should you, or shouldn't you?

The answer is simple. You should waive your rights. First of all, you should do your best to select recommenders you can trust. You should sit down with them and ask, point blank, "What will you be able to say about me in a letter of recommendation?" Even the best letters may include some little criticism; listen for the overall tone. Is this a strong endorsement you're discussing, or not?

Second, it is always the prerogative of the professor to share the letter with you—*many professors will.* This is the best of all possible worlds. Of course, some professors, as a matter of personal policy, will not ever share the contents of letters with applicants. Personally, I would think twice about using a recommender who refuses to even discuss with you what will be in the letter.

Third, graduate programs discount the recommendations—even when they are strongly laudatory—when the student retains the right to review the file. *Some will not even distribute the letters to the committee* if the student does not waive their rights to review the contents. This is patently unfair, as some faculty acknowledge. One professor wrote this in response to one of my surveys on faculty attitudes about letters of recommendation: "If there is integrity in the process, professors should have the backbone to state their opinions and back them up with evidence." To paraphrase Dr. Johnson, secrecy is the first resort of scoundrels. Nevertheless, your goal is to be admitted to a challenging program. If your laudatory letters could be discounted because you choose to retain your rights, this is a concern.

I think you should waive your rights. I have seen some very strong students refuse to waive their rights. I have interviewed students who failed to get into programs because of mean and spiteful comments by professors in their letters of recommendation. It's your decision. Make it thoughtfully.

Should you use a credentials service?

Credentials services are often available from national trade groups (AAMC, for example), national vendors, college and university career centers, and sometimes from individual departments, such as education. For such a service, you have "To Whom It May Concern" letters written by your recommenders, and they are uploaded into a confidential folio. The service then directly sends the letters to graduate schools, or, in some fields, potential employers, on a demand basis.

Although these services are an efficient system, you should avoid them when you can. You may be applying to dental school and a doctoral program in physical anthropology at the same time, and the same letter of recommendation for both targets will not serve your best interests. As we covered above, beg your recommenders to customize for each school. Ask them to mention any colleagues they may know at the targeted institutions, or to relate your skills specifically to what they know of the targeted program. If a professor is too busy to write individual letters for all the schools you are applying to, ask if they would customize for your top three choices, and then revert to a boilerplate version for the remainder.

Once you have verified that the letter was sent to the graduate program, be sure to send a prompt and sincere thank-you card to the author. As one doctoral student wrote me, "You'll find that you use your recommenders again and again, and they'll be more inclined to help you next time if you really appreciate it this time." It is customary to provide a modest gift to professors for writing a set of letters for you. Do not give them something too expensive, no little blue boxes from Tiffany's, but something to acknowledge their effort on your behalf. If you are broke, weave them a friendship bracelet.

Note that you are expected to provide a summary of your outcomes to faculty recommenders at the end of the season. It is considered rude not to do this. This is a table with your list of schools and what happened at each one, and it can look like this:

> *Dr. Wilson, my season is over, and I chose Vanderbilt. I really enjoyed the visit and their program aligns with my plans. No funding for the first two years, but then full funding for completing the doctorate. Thank you so much for your help! Here's my report:*

University of Illinois–Urbana Champagne	Master's	Admitted with no funding.
University of Connecticut	PhD	Admitted with full funding, stipend is $XX,000 for research assistantship.
University of Texas	PhD	Admitted with full funding, stipend of $XX,000. They couldn't tell me what my assignment was going to be, but either RA or TA.
Vanderbilt	Master's with bridge to doctorate	Admitted with no funding, but after the master's they said "everyone gets funded" for PhD phase.
Harvard	PhD	Rejected.
University of Wilsonville, NC	PhD	Oddly, they never admitted me or rejected me, and I sent several emails and never got any response at all. Weird.

Content

An effective letter will address the candidate's intellectual capacity, work habits, social skills, and particular academic preparation. These statements need a frame of reference, so some letter authors will rank students in a greater context, such as "I find Ms. Ashton's academic performance to fall consistently in the top 10 percent of students I have ever instructed," or "Mr. Herzel is a solid student, certainly ranking in the top half of students at St. John's, but you have to take this ranking in the context that the overwhelming majority of St. John's students obtain an advanced degree within a few years of graduation, most of them from the top programs in the nation."

Some letters will describe specific academic accomplishments that illustrate the student's abilities. Such letters are usually compelling because the reader can personally judge the performance described. (This is also a particularly apt style of letter to request if you have had a spotty career. Ask your professor or employer to focus the entire letter on your most successful project.)

Authors often cite challenges the student has overcome or unusual aspects of the student's background. In order to remain believable and to demonstrate objectivity, letters of recommendation almost always contain some modicum of criticism or warn of some weakness. So, if you review your own letters and discover moderate criticism, do not despair. In an outstanding letter, of course, the weakness will be a strength in disguise, just as in the essays; for example: "If Johanna has any fault, it is that she spends too much time on her extracurricular activities. However, as you can see, her academic performance remains excellent."

One admissions reader told me that he is particularly impressed when a professor cites a student's contributions to her undergraduate department or school. On a similar note, one highly successful candidate told me, "The trick is to look like a rising star, somebody who is going on to do wonderful things whether you attend their school or not. Remember, in the long run *they* want to be associated with *you*." Graduate schools are seeking people who will contribute to their programs as outstanding students, who will enhance the reputation of the program by the success of their careers, and who will later on return to be involved as benefactors. A good letter of recommendation will definitely predict a bright future for the candidate, as a scholar and later as a professional with a career. This is often an effective way to close a letter of recommendation.

As you read the sample letters of recommendation in this chapter, look for these components: credentials of the writer; depth of knowledge of the candidate as a person and a scholar; testimony as to the candidate's intellectual capacity, work habits, and preparedness for graduate studies; some small fault to demonstrate the writer's objectivity; and predictions of the candidate's future career contributions.

LETTER #1: "CONSOLIDATED LETTER"

Attn: Selection Committee

Marsdon-Stein Medical Fellowship for Women

The Marsdon Family Foundation

Chicago, Illinois

Dear Selection Committee:

This is a letter of introduction for Ms. Meredith Archer of Lake City, Iowa, who is making application for the Marsdon-Stein Medical Fellowship for Women. Ms. Archer graduated summa cum laude from [school withheld] two years ago, receiving a bachelor of arts degree in anthropology with a minor in psychology. Ms. Archer completed an honors thesis, Age and Gender Differences in Delivery of Medical Services in Afghanistan under the Taliban. *She is a member of Phi Beta Kappa and Lambda Alpha, the anthropology honors society. Ms. Archer has been accepted into the fall entering medical school class at three universities, all of which meet the criteria for the Marsdon Fellowship.*

It is indeed a pleasure for me to write this letter. Meredith is one of the most engaging, intelligent, and talented students that I have encountered in my fifteen-plus years in higher education. Her curiosity and quest for excellence, coupled with her joie de vivre and infectious nature, make her an extraordinary student and a charismatic personality. I remember when she first came to my office to tell me that she thought that she had begun to consider medicine as her professional goal. This was three summers ago. The only premedical requirement that she had fulfilled was calculus. In her senior year, she took introductory chemistry, and following graduation she enrolled at the University of Iowa, where she completed the premedical requirements with a 3.89 cumulative GPA. When she took the MCAT exam last April she received a score of 34. She will shine as a medical student and walk away with prizes like the Frieman Prize she won for excellence in writing the spring of her freshman undergraduate year here.

This letter is an example of a consolidated letter of recommendation, a style sometimes used by medical school advising committees. This is a particularly rich example, showing the student as a real human being, with a personality and a unique set of experiences. Note the honest depictions of the student's academic limitations as well as her assets. This student's advisors went to a great deal of trouble to assemble this letter, and that effort alone supports the student's endeavor. Needless to say, this letter won the fellowship.

I am certainly not the only person at [school withheld] who has been impacted by this impressive young woman. I was particularly struck by the words of her introductory chemistry professor. Meredith made one of her few B's in Prof. T. Blair's section. (And it is worth noting that she did make an A in the first semester of introductory chemistry.) Prof. Blair writes, "She is a unique student and person. Although she is not the most clever student I have met in eighteen years of teaching, she is among the top in commitment, creativity, curiosity, energy, and love-of-life. During help sessions, she persisted (through the groans of classmates) until she understood. Often it was clear that the object of her question was not relevant to the upcoming exam (hence the groans), but that didn't stifle her. She loves to understand. I find it interesting that she made an effort to become acquainted. I was one of the few faculty who gave her a grade of B. That didn't bother her as much as her impatience with herself to learn basic chemistry. She could see its relevance, but sometimes had problems with quantitative thinking. As you study her record, you will see that her quantitative background as a student was—at the time—not as strong as it would have been had she started her studies in basic science."

Meredith took advantage of the study-abroad program while she was an undergraduate here. We offer the opportunity to participate in a special program at the University of Paris (Sorbonne). Meredith studied there in the spring of her junior year. Dr. Q. Dupree in the department of anthropology at the Sorbonne was her advisor. Dr. Dupree writes, "In terms of the combination of energy, enthusiasm, and intelligence, Meredith has been one of the more exceptional students I have come across in years, and she is most suitable for medical training. In addition to being a rigorous student, extremely hard-working and diligent, she also has a strong humanistic side, is very compassionate and generous with her peers. She possesses the most important qualities required of a physician: she is wise, responsible, and empathetic; these traits, combined with her resourcefulness and industriousness, will prove a tremendous asset in her chosen field."

Meredith took abnormal psychology as part of her psychology minor and was taught by Prof. W. Andrews. Prof. Andrews was so impressed by her abilities as a student that he invited her to join a senior seminar devoted to developing in-depth psychiatric roles. He writes of her work: "What Ms. Archer had to do was master both the theoretical as well as the clinical literature about both of her assigned syndromes . . . [and] master how these particular patients would express their psychopathology in cognitive psychological tests. . . . [This] requires of the student the capacity to know herself very well, to not be frightened by another person's psychopathology, and yet to be able to put themselves into a particular patient's mind-set and to develop the subtle nuance of behavior as well as the cognitive styles reflective of the particular role assigned. Ms. Archer was so successful in playing one role (that of a borderline personality disorder who was also an incest victim), that I made a special training video to use in future years. Her performance of this role, and her profound understanding of both the theoretical and the clinical literature, really represented high-level graduate work."

Meredith, as you might expect, was involved in a number of extracurricular activities. She was an active member of a social sorority and a member of the All University Choir. Her sophomore year she played the role of Emily in Thornton Wilder's Our Town *at the university's Circle Theatre. Following that role, she was nominated to compete in an acting competition of soliloquies held at Carnegie Mellon University. When she was at home in the summers, I know that she participated in a soup kitchen. Also, in the summers, she was a food server thirty hours a week to earn money to help defray college expenses. Being the adventuresome soul that she is, when she studied in Paris, she joined a parachute club and "dropped in" around the countryside.*

Since she has been a student at [school withheld], Meredith has made a significant volunteer commitment to a free health clinic. The executive director, Laura Collins, writes, "Volunteering here requires some unique traits above and beyond the professional skills expected of most volunteers. We found that Meredith had no trouble negotiating the sometimes intimidating first few sessions here. Though she has been with us only five months, she has demonstrated a wonderful 'can-do' attitude, though not overbearing in any way. Meredith is industrious, resourceful, and determined to complete any task assigned to her. In addition, she seems to possess the innate compassion and sensitivity so sorely needed in modern caregivers."

Meredith has also worked as a nurse extender at City Hospital, emptying bedpans, giving baths, changing linens, etc. This young woman is no prima donna; I can assure you that she did all these things with grace and good cheer.

What else can I say? Meredith is one of the jewels that we all treasure: the curious and dedicated student; the effective and committed volunteer; and the warm, sensitive, and empathetic person whose enthusiasm for life is enviable. Clearly, this remarkable young woman will be a leader in her class and leave her imprint wherever she goes. She will most certainly be an excellent caregiver, as illustrated by her commitment to volunteer work and her well-thought-out choice to pursue the role of physician. It is, indeed, with great pleasure that I recommend Meredith to you with effusive enthusiasm and the utmost confidence. I envy the people who will have the pleasure of her company in the classroom, in the lab, in the clinics; they can look forward to four very rewarding years indeed. Her patients can look forward to an intelligent and caring physician who will always give the very best of herself and her knowledge.

Please give every consideration to this most remarkable young woman as you review her application for the Marsdon-Stein Fellowship.

LETTER #2: "LETTER FROM THE PRESIDENT OF THE COMPANY FOR GRADUATE SCHOOL OF BUSINESS"

Dear Admissions Committee:

I am pleased to write this letter of recommendation for Shane Whittington to attend graduate school in business. I have close daily experience with Shane's work habits and contributions to this company, and I can only report that I rank him in the top 5 percent of businesspeople I have ever had the pleasure to know.

His analytical abilities are first rate. In addition to his research and reporting work, he has designed several metrics that are now in use throughout the company. Even more important, and perhaps harder to define, he always understands the reasoning or the goal behind any analysis that he performs. This is a rare and refreshing trait.

His interpersonal skills are one of his most outstanding traits. Everybody who knows him thinks

Note how this letter covers the candidate's analytical skills, interpersonal aptitude, and mental acuity in general. The letter was from the president of a finance company and was on company stationery. The details of the candidate's career are covered in his resume and his application essay, so this letter is free to focus on the president's impressions of the candidate.

favorably of him, and I know I can trust him to represent the company to our shareholders and business associates. He is enthusiastic and optimistic in his dealings with investors, and this has been of benefit to the company. Shane's duties have included several opportunities for direct sales, and it is clear that he could have a highly successful career in this area should he choose to do so.

In short, when I give an assignment to Shane, I know it will be done right, on time, and in excess of my specifications. If he has any fault, it is adding enhancements to assignments, doing more than what was asked. In summary, he is a tremendous asset to management, and will surely rise rapidly in any organization in which he is employed.

LETTER #3: "LETTER FROM PROFESSOR FOR GRADUATE SCHOOL OF ENGLISH"

Attn: Prof. Sarah M. Hardesty

Chair, English Language and Literature

St. Lawson University

Dear Dr. Hardesty:

It is a great pleasure for me to recommend Ms. Celeste Wallace for admission, and fellowship support, to graduate school in English. I first encountered her in a large lecture course I was teaching three years ago. Within days, Ms. Wallace had distinguished herself as an extraordinary student—one who could ask the most penetrating questions about the assigned reading and expound her ideas with effortless extemporaneous elegance. I soon found that in a class of 150 students, I was beginning to carry on a dialogue with just one—much to the fascination of her classmates. Not surprisingly, Celeste's written work proved to be of the same caliber as her conversation; she received a grade of A+ for the semester, and even that seemed inadequate to evaluate her accomplishment. I give very few class grades of A+. In most years I give none.

Since then, I have stayed in touch with Ms. Wallace and have helped to steer her toward courses and experiences worthy of her gifts. I have read four of her subsequently written papers, and have noted in them a deepening and broadening of theoretical concerns. With her boundless curiosity and energy, her wit, her good humor, and her blazing intelligence, she has all the makings of a first-rate critic and college teacher. I would rank her among the top few undergraduates I have ever taught in thirty-three years at Michigan. As I understand it you do not require applicants to state a focus in the discipline, and Ms. Wallace has not specified any. I can vouch for her strengths in contemporary novel and contemporary literary criticism, and I believe her writing sample will impress.

This letter is short, sweet, and overwhelmingly effective. I read three letters recommending this student, and each was unequivocal and unreserved in its praise. This student does not appear to have any faults, so none is mentioned. Note how the author describes the candidate's performance in a specific class so clearly that the reader is able to think to herself, "I want a special student like that."

LETTER #4: "LETTER FROM DEAN OF SCHOOL OF DENTISTRY FOR RESIDENCY IN ORTHODONTICS"

To Whom It May Concern:

It is my pleasure to write a letter of recommendation on behalf of Akira Tokuyoshi in his pursuit of postdoctoral education in the field of orthodontics. I can state unequivocally that his academic and clinical skills have placed him among the top students in his class. His polite manner, his concern for his studies and his patients, and his emotional maturity are well known and respected among his peers and the faculty and staff.

His academic credentials alone qualify him for postdoctoral study and advanced training, but I can recommend this student enthusiastically for other reasons as well. He has complemented his academic schedule with leadership activities in many extracurricular areas, and he has enhanced the reputation and the image of [major university] Dental School as much as a student can.

Akira was selected student editor of the [major university] Dental School's journal, the Dental Explorer. *As such, he has worked closely with many faculty and students to put together the annual issue, which will be released soon, and which has already been highly praised by the faculty reviewers.*

Akira has served (by invitation) as a preceptor in the [major university] Dental School's Summer Enrichment Program. There he taught dental morphology and head and neck anatomy to incoming dental students. Also, he has volunteered as a tutor for the preclinical laboratory classes every year since his arrival. In these capacities, his professors have rated him very highly on both communication skills and technical knowledge. His concern for his fellow students is admirable, and a credit to himself and the success of our program.

Akira's natural ability to work with and motivate others has helped him hold several offices. He is currently president of our campus chapter of Delta Sigma Delta, the international dental fraternity, and he is vice president and senior editor of our Student Research Group, an IADR affiliate to promote primary research in dental science.

Akira has also participated in research with distinguished members of our faculty and has participated in several presentations and table clinics at scientific meetings. I understand that somehow he finds time to play sports as well.

In summary, Akira distinguishes himself as an individual who exhibits an organized, scientific approach to work and an ability to plan, organize, and implement projects of varying complexity. He is a team player, who with a high degree of motivation, innovation, and initiative, can accomplish his goals.

I know him to be a most personable and sincere young man, well liked and respected by those who work with him. I enthusiastically recommend this individual as an outstanding future orthodontist, and I predict he will have a bright future.

This letter is for a postdoctoral residency in orthodontics. The letter is warm and personal, and clearly demonstrates how a student's contributions to his own school enhance his desirability as a graduate or postgraduate candidate. It is clear that this candidate provided the author of the letter with a complete list of his accomplishments and activities.

LETTER #5: "LETTER FROM FORMER EMPLOYER FOR FELLOWSHIP AWARD"

Dear Members of the Committee:

I worked with Maureen D. Klusmann, an applicant for the ULI Land Use and Development Fellowship, for five years while she was employed by the East Bay Regional Park District. As a program analyst in the Land Acquisition Department, she was invaluable in a wide variety of acquisition and land planning projects. The issues that Maureen dealt with were involved, sensitive, and difficult. She proved time and again that she was capable of handling complex land use and development issues, often in the face of opposition. Many acquisitions involved developers, planners from several local governments, and a variety of community groups; she worked well with each. She was always well informed, prepared, and insightful on the range of interests represented.

I consider among Maureen's strengths her genuine enthusiasm for the subject of land use planning and development, her ability to analyze the subject at hand and cut through the mire to the essence of the situation, her attention to the necessary details (including the numbers), and her intelligence. She was an outstanding employee.

Maureen D. Klusmann is an excellent choice for this fellowship; she has my highest recommendation.

Fellowships and scholarships often require letters of recommendation in addition to an essay and an application. This letter cites the author's intimate knowledge of the candidate's background, then praises her strengths in all areas necessary for success in the field in question. In addition, the author is a well-known figure to the members of the fellowship awards committee. This letter, combined with a persuasive application and a cogent essay, is worth thousands of dollars.

LETTER #6: "RECOMMENDATION FROM PROFESSIONAL ACQUAINTANCE"

Admissions Committee

The Accelerated Premedical Studies Program

University of New England

Biddeford, Maine

Re: Matthew M. Moffett

Dear Members of the Committee:

As a writer specializing in careers and education, I interview and write about academic and business leaders on a regular basis for the Wall Street Journal. *I originally learned of Matthew Moffett over ten years ago through a mutual acquaintance, who told me Matt was an engineer who had never gone to college. I was fascinated to hear about this rather unusual career path and called Matt to interview him for an article. I found him delightful and unique, and since then have written about him in several articles and mentioned him and his accomplishments in two of my books. I think Matthew Moffett's story is an inspiration to others, and I have told it many times.*

Over the years, I've watched Matt's development rather closely out of professional curiosity. I do not know of another person even remotely like him. Matt is really a throwback to Renaissance ideals. Who could imagine that in this day and age someone would teach himself the math, programming, and physics required to be an engineer? Who could imagine that in this day and age someone with a technical orientation would also be able to win over the management of not one but a continuing series of Fortune 500 employers? We live in a credentials-driven society, and Matthew Moffett has repeatedly used his mind as his most powerful and impressive credential. I hesitate not one bit to say that Matthew Moffett could teach himself any subject and master any profession. There is no other person I know about whom I would say this.

I've come to know Matt rather well. He met his wife at a gathering at my house, and I've served as an informal career counselor for him since we first met. I know how and why he's made each move he's made, career-wise, for the last ten years. He's given me blanket permission to share with you what I know of him. Matt has been searching for integration and purpose, and a way to use his mind in helping service to others. For some at his stage in life, entering premedical studies with the goal of pursuing a health care career would be imprudent. But I know that Matthew Moffett will continue to surprise us. This is a young man of seemingly unbounded potential, and any way you can assist him in his quest will be returned many times over to us all.

Please call me if you would like me to elucidate further on any point.

Most graduate schools will expect letters from professors or employers who have had direct supervisory experience over you. However, Letters 6, 7, and 8 explore some other options for recommenders, including a professional acquaintance, a colleague, and a pertinent character reference.

LETTER #7: "RECOMMENDATION FROM FORMER COLLEAGUE"

Dear Admissions Committee:

David Arthur has asked me to write this letter of recommendation for him for the Executive MBA program at Stanford, and for the Faculty Committee Merit Scholarship, and I am honored to do so.

As I have known David Arthur for almost ten years, both professionally and personally, I feel qualified to comment on his abilities. I was his office manager when we were running Crash Marketing, a small business consulting firm, and we have remained in close contact ever since.

In fact, Mr. Arthur is the most valuable mentor I have ever had. I graduated magna cum laude from UCLA Anderson with an MBA, and have gone on to become a top-ranked business analyst in Taiwan, but I credit Mr. Arthur with the most important parts of my business education. He has the best business mind I have ever encountered, and I work daily with business leaders of global enterprises. Without his valuable mentorship in "the human element," I could never have achieved my goals in the corporate world.

In addition to his intelligence and insight, he is a very efficient person. I've seen him write a book on small business marketing in six weeks while running a very demanding business daily. He leads by example and was good at motivating others beyond their normal abilities. It was a very exciting company to work in while I was a business student.

Finally, I must say something about David Arthur's congeniality. People respond well to Mr. Arthur. People walked into his office and within ten minutes they were willing to tell him everything about themselves and their businesses. Launching a company can be a stressful time in people's lives, and they always seemed to trust Mr. Arthur. They were always happy with our plans and programs, because they were happy with the experience of dealing with

When you own the company, or you cannot find your former bosses, or they would say awful things about you, letters from colleagues, clients, or customers may be your only option. If you solicit a colleague or customer letter, choose someone who will say wonderful things about you and say them well. Such letters need to be substantive, as this one is, or they will be discounted. Note how this recommender lays out her credentials for the reader, which lend credence to the recommendation.

Mr. Arthur. Clients enthusiastically recommended our company to their colleagues. At the same time, I think it was the parade of different people who came into the office every day that excited Mr. Arthur the most about the company. People like him because he likes them, whatever their gender, race, politics, income level, or personal style. He is very much at home in an international, multicultural environment. And although he focused on serving an entrepreneurial and high-tech clientele, he was just as successful working with tradesmen who wanted to start their own companies, or the founders of family businesses—if they came to our office, and they frequently did. He has an uncanny ability to establish rapport with anyone.

In closing, Mr. Arthur is one of those rare individuals who seemingly can do anything he sets out to do. He is certainly the type of person who would be a credit to a quality graduate business program. I recommend him without reservation. He will make an outstanding addition to your alumni.

Should you need any additional information, please contact me. Perhaps email is best due to the time difference between Taiwan and California.

LETTER #8: "CHARACTER WITNESS LETTER FOR MEDICAL SCHOOL"

Dear Members of the Committee:

I am pleased to recommend to you Aaron [last name withheld]. It is my opinion that Aaron will make an uncommonly good medical doctor, and that he has demonstrated character traits that will ensure this. Since I have known him well over ten years, I hope my letter will have weight of consideration commensurate with that length of time.

My organization, International Organization for Sephardic Rescue (IOSR), is dedicated to rescuing Sephardic Jews from oppressive regimes, mostly in the Middle East. We brought Aaron [last name withheld] to New York City from Iran ten years ago. He was a child of eleven years when he emigrated, leaving his parents behind. It was thought at the time that they would complete some business matters and follow their son, but in fact they were detained for several years.

During this time, from when he was eleven until he was thirteen, Aaron lived under the benevolent protection of IOSR. He lived in a dormitory situation, and in the homes of some of our more dedicated members. He was always a delight to us all, and his personal strength and courage were a testament to human potential. I say this not out of appreciation for his ability to carry on without his own parents, and in spite of his deep and ongoing concern for them, but because of his ability to excel and thrive in these adverse conditions.

Being of a young age, he mastered the English language and went on to study at the Talmudical Seminary here in New York, a very rigorous Orthodox Jewish high school with a national reputation. There he excelled in a program of science, religion, and classical liberal arts (just for the record, all subjects except Hebrew language studies are taught in English). He was the valedictorian of his class, and he of course graduated with honors.

Then at just the moment when some students would have gone on to a carefree college experi-

Professors and employers are the preferred authors of letters of recommendation, but sometimes someone with a long-term personal knowledge of you can be quite persuasive. This example is a "character witness" letter. Admissions committees will not be impressed if all your letters of recommendation are of this type; however, one may be effective when submitted in addition to a full set of letters from those who know your work and study capacities. If your character witness cannot add compelling weight to your application, it may be a good idea to forgo such a letter altogether. Note how this letter is full of factual evidence for the committee's consideration.

ence, Aaron's parents finally arrived from Iran. I know of his dedication and his daily assistance to them. He smoothed the path for these new immigrants who were without the language and social skills he had learned so well. At the same time, he was highly active in youth programs for IOSR, rising to the position of director of youth programs, including our summer program involving hundreds of students.

So you see how I have watched this young man grow and develop, and I know the tremendous focus he has upon his studies and his service to mankind. It is my firm belief that his maturity, initiative, and self-reliance could only lead to success in medical school, and that his strength of character could only lead to an outstanding contribution to humanity as a medical doctor.

I highly recommend Aaron to your school. It is my unconditional belief that he will become an ethical, compassionate, and extremely competent physician.

INDEX

Q

R

ABOUT THE AUTHOR

DR. DONALD ASHER is a veteran career and higher-education consultant, and one of the nation's foremost authorities on the graduate admissions process. He is a featured speaker at more than 100 colleges and universities from coast to coast every year and has spoken internationally on careers, higher education, and globalism in Ireland, Germany, India, China, Hong Kong, South Korea, Morocco, Mexico, and Canada. He has been a contributing writer to the MSN homepage and *The Wall Street Journal*'s CareerJournal.com and CollegeJournal.com. He divides his time between northern Nevada and San Francisco.

ALSO BY DR. DONALD ASHER

Who Gets Promoted, Who Doesn't, and Why, Second Edition

12 Things You'd Better Do If You Want to Get Ahead

How to Get Any Job

Life Launch and Re-Launch for Everyone Under 30 (or How to Avoid Living in Your Parents' Basement)

Cracking the Hidden Job Market

How to Find Opportunity in Any Economy

Available from Ten Speed Press wherever books are sold.

www.tenspeed.com